AF345293

The Journal of the Polynesian Society

THE JOURNAL

OF THE

POLYNESIAN SOCIETY

CONTAINING

THE TRANSACTIONS AND PROCEEDINGS
OF THE SOCIETY

VOL. XXVIII.

1919.

New Plymouth, N.Z.:
PRINTED FOR THE SOCIETY BY THOMAS AVERY, DEVON STREET.

1919.

No. 112.—December, 1919.

VOL. XXVIII.—1919.

ANNUAL MEETING OF THE SOCIETY,
For the Year Ending 31st December, 1918.

THE Meeting took place on the 29th January, 1919, at the Hempton Room, where the Society's Library is installed. There were several members present, the President being in the chair.

The minutes of the last annual meeting were read and confirmed, and then the Annual Report of the Council and the year's accounts, which were passed and ordered to be printed in the March number of the ' Journal.' They will be found below.

In accordance with the rules, the President retired and two members of the Council also, the latter by ballot. Mr. S. Percy Smith was re-elected President, and Messrs. M. Fraser and W. W. Smith re-elected to the Council.

A vote of thanks was passed to Mr. W. D. Webster for auditing the accounts, and he consented to act in the same capacity this ensuing year. Also a vote of thanks was accorded Mr. W. H. Skinner for preparing the Index to last year's volume.

The following new members were then elected :—

Hubert E. Vaile, Queen Street, Auckland.

The Adalbert College, Western Reserve University, Cleveland, Ohio, U.S.A.

A discussion took place on a paragraph in the annual report referring to the reading of papers before the Society, and the question was finally referred to the Council.

A resolution was passed expressing the opinion of the members present as to the desirability of the appointment of a Curator of the New Borough Museum, New Plymouth, which was ordered to be conveyed to His Worship the Mayor.

ANNUAL REPORT OF THE COUNCIL,
For the Year Ending 31st December, 1918

THE Council of the Society has pleasure in presenting to the Annual Meeting its Twenty-sixth Report, showing in brief form the activities of the Society during the past twelve months.

The most noticeable feature of the past year has been the removal of the headquarters into the commodious apartments of the Hempton room where our library and office have been installed, and which was opened by His Worship the Mayor, as referred to in our last annual report. The additional accommodation thus provided by the generosity of a lady of New Plymouth, has allowed · of our library being for the first time arranged in a form where access to the books has become easy, just as in other libraries ; whilst the comfort in working by the officers of the Society has been greatly appreciated. The books

SILAS WRIGHT DUNNING
BEQUEST
UNIVERSITY OF MICHIGAN
GENERAL LIBRARY

that have accumulated by exchange and gift during the past twenty-seven years now occupy 240 feet of shelving, with wall space for at least three times as much. Arrangements have been made for opening the library to the public on Monday and Saturday afternoons, and on Wednesday evenings for the purpose of reference or study, and for the issue of books to members, an officer of the Society being in attendance at these times. We should be glad to welcome more visitors to the library for purposes of study, for though our collection naturally consists mostly of works on ethnology, the liberality of our exchanges provides us with works on most of the sciences; our American exchanges are particularly liberal in this respect.

The rules passed by the first meeting of the Society in 1892, defined our objects as follows : "The Society is formed to promote the study of the anthropology, ethnology, philology, history and antiquities of the Polynesian races by the publication of an official journal to be called 'The Journal of the Polynesian Society,' and by the collection of books, manuscripts, photographs, relics, and other illustrations." We think that these objects have been fairly well carried out as exemplified in the 27 volumes of our journal, which contain original matter that would otherwise, but for our Society, have been lost for ever to the world and the future students of the race. Naturally the great problem that presents itself for solution is the origin of our Pacific Island peoples. The mystery surrounding this question has had for very many people a great fascination. The tendency of all observation so far is to carry the ancestors of the people back to Indonesia, and this view is supported by all lines of study. Beyond that, the matter is in some doubt, though some of us hold strong opinions about it and see in the early Aryan migrants into India the ancestors of the Polynesians. Towards the final solution of the question we may fairly claim to have helped to lay the foundations, by the original matter preserved in our journal. But much yet remains to be done. For instance, no reasonable hypothesis has as yet been formulated accounting for the Easter Island statues, some light upon which may, however, be thrown by the publication of Mrs. Scoresby Routledge's forthcoming work, the results of a year's sojourn on that island.

Our Rules, in defining the functions of the Society, do not provide for the reading and discussion of papers by members at meetings to be held for the purpose, as is the custom in similar societies. But there is no reason why this course should not be adopted if members wish it. Such discussions often bring out points that are not alluded to in the papers read, and thus are beneficial. Were this course adopted, aided by occasional lectures—not necessarily on strict ethnological lines—it might tend to popularise the work of the Society, and if the public generally were invited to attend, the result would furnish people with something to think about in addition to their daily round of duties.

Our membership was slightly increased during the year, and on December 31st the roll was as follows:—

Patrons	.. 3
Honorary Members	.. 12
Corresponding Members	.. 13
Ordinary Members	.. 158
Total	.. 186

During the year three members resigned and four died—Mr. W. Kerr, S.M., who was a member of our council for several years; Dr. H. Colley March, an original member, and a well-known writer on ethnology; Mr. A. H. Turnbull, of Wellington, well-known in connection with his celebrated library of works relating to New

Zealand; and Mr. J. H. Wilson, judge of the Native Land Court, who succumbed to the influenza epidemic. We have also reason to fear that another promising member was killed in France, but as yet have no certain information. The number of members who joined the Society at its formation in 1892 are now reduced to 17. We exchange publications with 44 societies, universities, Government departments, etc., and receive in exchange more than an equivalent from some of them.

There is a considerable demand for sets of our publications from various parts of the world, which we are no longer able to meet so far as some of the earlier volumes of our "Journal" are concerned, as they are out of print. If satisfactory arrangements can be made these ought to be reprinted; it would pay the Society in the long run to do so. Furthermore, our library is increasing so fast that immediate expansion of the shelving accommodation has become necessary.

On December 31st there were 27 members in arrear for one year, nine for two years, and four for three years. These latter will have to be struck off the roll in accordance with our rules.

It will be seen from the treasurer's statement that financially we are in a good position, as there is a balance in hand of £45. Our correspondence with all parts of the world increases, for the Society is getting known far and wide, so that we are frequently applied to for information on Polynesian ethnological subjects.

POLYNESIAN SOCIETY.

BALANCE SHEET FOR THE YEAR ENDING 31st DECEMBER, 1918.

RECEIPTS.	£	s.	d.	EXPENDITURE.	£	s.	d.
Balance from last year	31	10	0	Thomas Avery, Printing and Publishing Journal—			
Members' Subscriptions and Sales of Journal	161	17	4	No. 4 of Vol. XXVI.	28	10	0
				No. 1 of Vol. XXVII.	32	17	6
				No. 2 of Vol. XXVII.	28	15	0
				No. 3 of Vol. XXVII.	36	0	0
				„ Stationery	1	12	0
				Dawson's Ltd., Lithographers	4	13	7
				Sash and Door Co., fittings	2	5	6
				Alliance Insurance Co.—Premium on Library (£500)	1	6	8
				Custodian to 31st December (8 months)	3	6	8
				Postage	8	3	10
				Bank charge	0	10	0
				Balance at Bank of New South Wales	45	7	1
	£193	**7**	**4**		**£193**	**7**	**4**

CAPITAL ACCOUNT.

	£	s.	d.		£	s.	d.
To Balance 1st January, 1918	189	14	11	By Furniture Account (withdrawn)	49	0	0
„ Donation	1	0	0	„ Balance at New Plymouth Savings Bank—			
„ Interest	7	3	8	1st January, 1919	148	18	7
	£197	**18**	**7**		**£197**	**18**	**7**

Examined and found correct—
WILLIAM D. WEBSTER, Hon. Auditor.

W. L. NEWMAN, Hon. Treasurer,
New Plymouth, 24th January, 1919.

VOL. XXVIII.—1919.

MEMBERS OF THE POLYNESIAN SOCIETY

As from 1st January, 1919.

———

The sign * before a name indicates an original member or founder.
As this list will be published annually, the Secretaries would be obliged if members will
supply any omission, or notify change of address.

———

PATRONS:

The Right Hon. Baron Plunket, K.C.M.G., K.C.V.O., ex-Governor of New Zealand, Old Connaught. Bray, County Wicklow, Ireland.

The Right Hon. Baron Islington, K.C.M.G., D.S.O., ex-Governor of New Zealand, Government Offices, Downing Street, London.

His Excellency The Right Hon. The Earl of Liverpool, M.V.O., G.C.M.G., Governor General of New Zealand.

HONORARY MEMBERS.

Rev. R. H. Codrington, D.D., Chichester, England.

Rev. Prof. A. H. Sayce, M.A., Queen's College, Oxford, England

Right Hon. Sir J. G. Ward, Bart., K.C.M.G., P.C., LL.D., M.P., Wellington

H. G. Seth-Smith, M.A., c/o W. T. Williams, 7, St. Helens Place, Bishopsgate Street, London, E.C.

Prof. Sir W. Baldwin Spencer, M.A., C.M.G., F.R.S., The University, Melbourne

*Edward Tregear, I.S.O., Wellington

Dr. A. Haddon, M.A., D.Sc., F.R.S., 3, Cranmer Road, Cambridge, England

Churchill, W., B.A., F.R.A.I., Yale Club, 30, West Forty-fourth Street, New York

Sir J. G. Fraser, D.C.L., LL.D., Litt. D., Brick Court, Middle Temple, London, E.C.

*Elsdon Best, Dominion Museum, Wellington

Chas. M. Woodford, C.M.G., The Grinstead, Partridge Green, Sussex, England

S. H. Ray, M.A., F.R.A.I., 218, Balfour Road, Ilford, Sussex, England

CORRESPONDING MEMBERS:

Rev. T. G. Hammond, Putaruru, Auckland

Major J. T. Large, Masonic Institute, H. M. Arcade, Auckland.

Hare Hongi, 3, Stirling Street, Wellington

Tati Salmon, Papeete, Tahiti

Tunui-a-rangi, Major H. P., Carterton

Whatahoro, H. T., Putiki, Whanganui

Christian, F. W., Otaki

The Rev. C. E. Fox, San Cristoval; viâ Ugi, Solomon Islands

Skinner, H. D., B.A., D.C.M., Hocken Library, Dunedin

Rev. Père Hervé Audran, Fakahiva, Tuamotu, Tahiti

M. Julien, His Excellency, Governor of French Oceania, Tahiti

A. Leverd, Papeete, Tahiti

ORDINARY MEMBERS:

1894   Aldred, W. A., Bank of New Zealand, Wellington
1899   Atkinson, W. E., Whanganui
1916   Avery, Thos., New Plymouth
1918   Adalbert College, Western Reserve University, Cleveland Ohio, U. S. A.

1892   *Birch, W. J. Thoresby, Marton
1892   *Barron, A., Macdonald Terrace, Wellington
1894   Bamford, E., Arney Road, Auckland
1896   British and Foreign Bible Society, 146, Queen Victoria Street, London, E.C.
1898   Buchanan, Sir W. C., Tupurupuru, Masterton
1902   Boston City Library, Boston, Mass., U.S.A.
1907   Buick, T. Lindsay, F. R. Hist.S., Press Association, Wellington
1917   Brown, Prof. J. MacMillan, M.A., LL.D., Holmbank, Cashmere Hills,
           Christchurch
1909   Bullard, G. H., Chief Surveyor, New Plymouth
1910   Burnet, J. H., Virginian Homestead, St. John's Hill, Whanganui
1910   Burgess, C. H., New Plymouth
1911   Bird, W. W., Inspector Native Schools, Napier
1913   Buddle, R., H. M. S. " Northampton," c/o General Post Office, London
1914   Brooking, W. F., Powderham Street, New Plymouth
1914   Beattie, Herries, P. O. Box 40, Gore
1916   Bottrell, C. G., High School, New Plymouth
1918   Beyers, H. Otley, Professor Department of Anthropology, University of the
           Philippines, Manilla
1918   Brown, A. Radcliffe, Nukualofa, Tonga Island

1892   *Chapman, The Hon. F. R., Wellington
1892   Chambers, W. K., Fujiya, Mount Smart, Penrose, Auckland
1893   Carter, H. C., 475, West 143rd Street, N.Y.
1894   Chapman, M., Wellington
1896   Cooper, The Hon. Theo., Wellington
1900   Cooke, J. P., c/o Alexander and Baldwin, Honolulu
1903   Chatterton, Rev. F. W., Te Rau, Gisborne
1903   Cole, Ven. Archdeacon R. H., D.C.L., Parnell, Auckland
1908   Coughlan, W. N., Omaio, Opotiki
1908   Carnegie Public Library, Dunedin
1908   Carnegie Public Library, New Plymouth
1910   Cook R., New Plymouth
1917   Cowley, Matt, P. O. Box 72, Auckland
1918   Chambers, Bernard, Te Mata, Havelock North
1918   Corney, Geo., Devon Street, New Plymouth
1918   Crooke, Alfred, S.M., Devon Street, New Plymouth

1892   *Denniston, The Hon. Sir J. E., Christchurch
1902   Dulan & Co., 38, Soho Square, London
1902   Drummond, Jas., " Lyttelton Times " Office, Christchurch
1903   Dixon, Roland B., Ph.D., Harvard University, Cambridge, Mass., U.S.A.
1910   Downes, T. W., P. O. Box 119, Whanganui
1911   Drew, C. H., New Plymouth
1917   Dominion Museum, Wellington
1918   Davidson, J. C., Motunui, Waitara

1892 *Emerson, J. S., 802, Spencer Street, Honolulu, Hawaiian Islands
1894 Ewen, C. A., Commercial Union Insurance Co., Wellington
1918 Etheridge, Robt. Director, Australian Museum, Sydney

1896 Fletcher, Rev. H. J., Taupo
1900 Forbes, E. J., 5, Hamilton Street, Sydney, N. S. W.
1901 Firth, John F., Survey Office, Nelson
1902 Fraser, M., New Plymouth
1902 Fisher, T. W., Tikitiki Road, Te Mapara, Te Kuiti
1903 Fowlds, Hon. G., Auckland
1906 Field Museum of Natural History, The, Chicago, U.S.A.
1912 Fisher, Mrs. Lillian S., 560, Hancock Street, Brooklyn, New York, U.S.A.
1912 Fisher, F. Owen, c/o Credit Lyonaise, Biarritz, B.P., France
1913 Fildes, H., Box 740, Chief Post Office, Wellington

1892 *Gudgeon, Lieut.-Col. W. E., C.M.G., 39, King's Parade, Devonport,
        Auckland
1902 Gill, W. H. Marunouchi, Tokio, Japan
1902 Graham, Geo., c/o Commercial Union, P.O. Box 166, Auckland
1910 Godding, Fred W., U.S. Consul General, Guayaquil, Ecuador

1898 Hastie, Miss J. A., 11, Ashburn Place, Cromwell Road, London
1908 Hallen, Dr. A. H. Clevedon, Auckland
1909 Holdsworth, John, Swarthmoor, Havelock, Hawkes Bay
1910 Hawkes Bay Philosophical Society, P.O. Box 166, Napier
1910 Hocken, Mrs. T. M., Hocken Library, Dunedin
1910 Home, Dr. George, New Plymouth
1911 Heimbrod, G., F.R.A.I., Lautoka, Fiji
1911 Henniger, Julius, Motuihi Island, Auckland
1917 Hocken Library, Dunedin
1918 Hodgson, N.V., c/o Norman Potts, Opotiki
1918 Harvie, Rev. G. F., The Vicarage. Vivian Street, New Plymouth
1918 Hart, Henry H., 3751, Clay Street, San Francisco

1907 Institute, The Auckland, Museum, Auckland
1907 Institute, The Otago, Dunedin

1892 *Johnson, H. Dunbar, Judge N.L.C., 151, Newton Road, Auckland
1918 Johnston, E. G., Education Board Office, New Plymouth

1902 Kelly, Thomas, New Plymouth
1910 King, Newton, Brooklands, New Plymouth

1894 Lambert, H. A. Belmont, Tayforth, Whanganui
1911 Lysnar, W. D., Gisborne
1913 List, T. C., New Plymouth
1913 Lysons, E. W. M., New Plymouth
1916 Leatham, H. B., M.R.C.S., L.R.C.P., Lond., New Plymouth
1917 Ledingham. T. J., "Montecute," St. Kilda, Melbourne
1917 List, C. S., Rata Street, Inglewood
1918 Laughton, Rev. J. G., Ruatahuna, viâ Rotorua

1892 *Marshall, W. S., Maungaraupi, Rata
1892 *Major, C. E., 22, Empire Buildings, Swanson Street, Auckland

ORDINARY MEMBERS:

1894   Aldred, W. A., Bank of New Zealand, Wellington
1899   Atkinson, W. E., Whanganui
1916   Avery, Thos., New Plymouth
1918   Adalbert College, Western Reserve University, Cleveland Ohio, U. S. A.

1892   *Birch, W. J. Thoresby, Marton
1892   *Barron, A., Macdonald Terrace, Wellington
1894   Bamford, E., Arney Road, Auckland
1896   British and Foreign Bible Society, 146, Queen Victoria Street, London, E.C.
1898   Buchanan, Sir W. C., Tupurupuru, Masterton
1902   Boston City Library, Boston, Mass., U.S.A.
1907   Buick, T. Lindsay, F. R. Hist.S., Press Association, Wellington
1917   Brown, Prof. J. MacMillan, M.A., LL.D., Holmbank, Cashmere Hills,
          Christchurch
1909   Bullard, G. H., Chief Surveyor, New Plymouth
1910   Burnet, J. H., Virginian Homestead, St. John's Hill, Whanganui
1910   Burgess, C. H., New Plymouth
1911   Bird, W. W., Inspector Native Schools, Napier
1913   Buddle, R., H. M. S. " Northampton," c/o General Post Office, London
1914   Brooking, W. F., Powderham Street, New Plymouth
1914   Beattie, Herries, P. O. Box 40, Gore
1916   Bottrell, C. G., High School, New Plymouth
1918   Beyers, H. Otley, Professor Department of Anthropology, University of the
          Philippines, Manilla
1918   Brown, A. Radcliffe, Nukualofa, Tonga Island

1892   *Chapman, The Hon. F. R., Wellington
1892   Chambers, W. K., Fujiya, Mount Smart, Penrose, Auckland
1893   Carter, H. C., 475, West 143rd Street, N.Y.
1894   Chapman, M., Wellington
1896   Cooper, The Hon. Theo., Wellington
1900   Cooke, J. P., c/o Alexander and Baldwin, Honolulu
1903   Chatterton, Rev. F. W., Te Rau, Gisborne
1903   Cole, Ven. Archdeacon R. H., D.C.L., Parnell, Auckland
1908   Coughlan, W. N., Omaio, Opotiki
1908   Carnegie Public Library, Dunedin
1908   Carnegie Public Library, New Plymouth
1910   Cock R., New Plymouth
1917   Cowley, Matt, P. O. Box 72, Auckland
1918   Chambers, Bernard, Te Mata, Havelock North
1918   Corney, Geo., Devon Street, New Plymouth
1918   Crooke, Alfred, S.M., Devon Street, New Plymouth

1892   *Denniston, The Hon. Sir J. E., Christchurch
1902   Dulau & Co., 38, Soho Square, London
1902   Drummond, Jas., " Lyttelton Times " Office, Christchurch
1903   Dixon, Roland B., Ph.D., Harvard University, Cambridge, Mass , U.S.A.
1910   Downes, T. W., P. O. Box 119, Whanganui
1911   Drew, C. H., New Plymouth
1917   Dominion Museum, Wellington
1918   Davidson, J. C., Motunui, Waitara

1911 Vibaud, Rev. J. M., Hiruharama, Whanganui
1919 Vaile, Hubert E., Queen Street, Auckland

1892 *Williams, Archdeacon H. W., Gisborne
1894 Wilson, A., Hangatiki, Auckland
1896 Williams, F. W., Napier
1896 Wilcox, Hon. G. A., Kauai, Hawaiian Islands
1898 Whitney, James L., Public Library, Dartmouth, Boston, U.S.A.
1902 Webster, W. D., New Plymouth
1903 Walker, Ernest A., M.D., New Plymouth
1910 Wilson, Sir J. G., Bulls
1912 Westervelt, Rev. W. D., Honolulu, Hawaiian Islands
1914 Waller, Captain W., Moturoa, New Plymouth
1915 Williams, H. B., Turihaua, Gisborne
1915 Wilson, Thos., Captain, New Plymouth
1916 Welsh, R. D., Hawera
1916 White, Percy J. H., New Plymouth
1917 Wheeler, W. J., Inspecting Surveyor, Gisborne
1917 Wilkinson, C. A., M.P., Eltham
1918 Wallace, D. B., Masonic Club, H.M. Arcade, Auckland
1918 Western, T. D., Puketapu, Bell Block, New Plymouth
1918 Wilson, Kenneth, M.A., 92, Rangitikei Street, Palmerston North

1892 *Young, J. L., c/o Henderson and Macfarlane, Auckland

PRESIDENTS—Past and Present:

1892-1894—H. G. Seth-Smith, M.A.
1895-1896—Right Rev. W. L. Williams, M.A., D.D.
1896-1898—The Rev. W. T. Habens, B.A.
1901-1903—E. Tregear, I.S.O., etc.
1904-1919—S. Percy Smith, F.R.G.S.

LIST OF EXCHANGES.

THE following is the List of Societies, etc., etc., to which the JOURNAL is sent, and from most of which we receive exchanges :—

Anthropologie, Société d', 15 Rue Ecole de Medicin, Paris
Anthropologia, Societa, Museo Nazionale di Anthropologia, Via Gino Capponi, Florence, Italy
Anthropologie, Ecole d', 15 Rue Ecole de Medicin, Paris
Australasian Association for the Advancement of Science, 5 Elizabeth Street, Sydney
American Oriental Society, 245, Bishop Street, Newhaven, Conn., U.S.A.
American Philosophical Society, Philadelphia, U.S.A.
American Museum of Natural History, Washington
Asiatic Society of Bengal, 1, Park Street, Calcutta
Anthropological Department, University of The Philippines, Manilla.

Bataviaasch Genootschap, Batavia, Java
Bureau of American Ethnology, Smithsonian Institute, Washington
Bernice Pauahi Bishop Museum, Honolulu, H. I.

Canadian Institute, Ottawa, Canada
Canadian Department of Mines, Ottawa, Canada

Dominion Museum, Wellington

Ethnological Survey, Manilla, Philippine Islands

Fijian Society, The, Suva, Fiji Islands

General Assembly Library, Wellington (two copies)
Géographic, Société de, de Paris, Boulevard St. Germain, 184, Paris
Geographical Society, The American, Broadway, at 156th Street, New York

High Commissioner of New Zealand, 13, Victoria Street, Westminster, London
Historical Society, Honolulu, Hawaiian Islands

Institute, The New Zealand, Wellington

Japan Society, 20, Hanover Square, London, W.

Kongl, Vitterhets Historie, och Antiqvitets, Akademen, Stockholm, Sweden
Koninklijk Instituut, 14, Van Galenstratt, The Hague, Holland

Na Mata, Editor, Suva, Fiji
National Museum Library, Washington, U.S.A.

Peabody Museum of Archæology, Harvard University, Cambridge, U.S.A.
Philippines, Bureau of Science, Manilla

Queensland Museum, Brisbane, Queensland

Royal Geographical Society, Kensington Gore, London, S. W.
Royal Geographical Society of Australasia, Brisbane
Royal Geographical Society of Australasia, c/o G. Collingridge, Waronga,
    N.S.W.
Royal Geographical Society of Australasia, 70 Queen Street, Melbourne
Royal Society, Burlington House, London
Royal Anthropological Institute of Great Britain, The, 50, Great Russell Street,
    London, W.C.
Royal Society of New South Wales, 5, Elizabeth Street, Sydney
Royal Colonial Institute, The, Northumberland Avenue, London
Royal Geographical Society of Australasia, Adelaide

Smithsonian Institute, Washington
Société Neuchateloise de Geographie, Switzerland
Société d'Etudes Oceanienne, Tahiti Island

Tokyo Imperial University, Tokyo, Japan

University of California, Library Exchange Department, Berkeley, California
University Museum, 33d and Spence Streets, Pennsylvania, U.S.A.

POLYNESIAN SOCIETY.

BALANCE SHEET FOR THE YEAR ENDING 31st DECEMBER, 1918.

RECEIPTS.	£ s. d.	EXPENDITURE.	£ s. d.
Balance from last year	31 10 0	Thomas Avery, Printing and Publishing Journal—	
Members' Subscriptions and Sales of Journal	161 17 4	No. 4 of Vol. XXVI.	28 10 0
		No. 1 of Vol. XXVII.	32 17 6
		No. 2 of Vol. XXVII.	28 15 0
		No. 3 of Vol. XXVII.	36 0 0
		,, Stationery	1 12 0
		Dawson's Ltd., Lithographers	4 13 7
		Sash and Door Co., fittings	2 5 0
		Alliance Insurance Co.—Premium on Library (£500) ..	1 6 8
		Custodian to 31st December (8 months) ..	3 6 8
		Postage	8 3 10
		Bank charge	0 10 0
		Balance at Bank of New South Wales	45 7 1
	£193 7 4		£193 7 4

CAPITAL ACCOUNT.

	£ s. d.		£ s. d.
To Balance 1st January, 1918	189 14 11	By Furniture Account (withdrawn)	49 0 0
,, Donation	1 0 0	,, Balance at New Plymouth Savings Bank—	
,, Interest	7 3 8	1st January, 1919 ..	148 18 7
	£197 18 7		£197 18 7

Examined and found correct—
    WILLIAM D. WEBSTER, Hon. Auditor.

W. L. NEWMAN, Hon. Treasurer,
    New Plymouth, 24th January, 1919.

VOL. XXVIII.—1919.

MEMBERS OF THE POLYNESIAN SOCIETY

As from 1st January, 1919.

The sign * before a name indicates an original member or founder.
As this list will be published annually, the Secretaries would be obliged if members will
supply any omission, or notify change of address.

PATRONS:

The Right Hon. Baron Plunket, K.C.M.G., K.C.V.O., ex-Governor of New Zealand, Old Connaught, Bray, County Wicklow, Ireland.

The Right Hon. Baron Islington, K.C.M.G., D.S.O., ex-Governor of New Zealand, Government Offices, Downing Street, London.

His Excellency The Right Hon. The Earl of Liverpool, M.V.O., G.C.M.G., Governor General of New Zealand.

HONORARY MEMBERS.

Rev. R. H. Codrington, D.D., Chichester, England.

Rev. Prof. A. H. Sayce, M.A., Queen's College, Oxford, England

Right Hon. Sir J. G. Ward, Bart., K.C.M.G., P.C., LL.D., M.P., Wellington

H. G. Seth-Smith, M.A., c/o W. T. Williams, 7, St. Helens Place, Bishopsgate Street, London, E.C.

Prof. Sir W. Baldwin Spencer, M.A., C.M.G., F.R.S., The University, Melbourne

*Edward Tregear, I.S.O., Wellington

Dr. A. Haddon, M.A.. D.Sc., F.R.S., 3, Cranmer Road, Cambridge, England

Churchill, W., B.A., F.R.A.I., Yale Club, 30, West Forty-fourth Street, New York

Sir J. G. Fraser, D.C.L.. LL.D., Litt. D., Brick Court, Middle Temple, London, E.C.

*Elsdon Best, Dominion Museum, Wellington

Chas. M. Woodford, C.M.G., The Grinstead, Partridge Green, Sussex, England

S. H. Ray, M.A., F.R.A.I., 218, Balfour Road, Ilford, Sussex, England

CORRESPONDING MEMBERS:

Rev. T. G. Hammond, Putaruru, Auckland

Major J. T. Large, Masonic Institute, H. M. Arcade, Auckland.

Hare Hongi, 3, Stirling Street, Wellington

Tati Salmon, Papeete, Tahiti

Tunui-a-rangi, Major H. P., Carterton

Whatahoro, H. T., Putiki, Whanganui

Christian, F. W., Otaki

The Rev. C. E. Fox, Sau Cristoval; viâ Ugi, Solomon Islands

Skinner, H. D., B.A., D.C.M., Hocken Library, Dunedin

Rev. Père Hervé Audran, Fakahiva, Tuamotu, Tahiti

M. Julien, His Excellency, Governor of French Oceania, Tahiti

A. Leverd, Papeete, Tahiti

ORDINARY MEMBERS:

1894   Aldred, W. A., Bank of New Zealand, Wellington
1899   Atkinson, W. E., Whanganui
1916   Avery, Thos., New Plymouth
1918   Adalbert College, Western Reserve University, Cleveland Ohio, U. S. A.

1892   *Birch, W. J. Thoresby, Marton
1892   *Barron, A., Macdonald Terrace, Wellington
1894   Bamford, E., Arney Road, Auckland
1896   British and Foreign Bible Society, 146, Queen Victoria Street, London, E.C.
1898   Buchanan, Sir W. C., Tupurupuru, Masterton
1902   Boston City Library, Boston, Mass., U.S.A.
1907   Buick, T. Lindsay, F. R. Hist.S., Press Association, Wellington
1917   Brown, Prof. J. MacMillan, M.A., LL.D., Holmbank, Cashmere Hills,
         Christchurch
1909   Bullard, G. H., Chief Surveyor, New Plymouth
1910   Burnet, J. H., Virginian Homestead, St. John's Hill, Whanganui
1910   Burgess, C. H., New Plymouth
1911   Bird, W. W., Inspector Native Schools, Napier
1913   Buddle, R., H. M. S. "Northampton," c o General Post Office, London
1914   Brooking, W. F., Powderham Street, New Plymouth
1914   Beattie, Herries, P. O. Box 40, Gore
1916   Bottrell, C. G., High School, New Plymouth
1918   Beyers, H. Otley, Professor Department of Anthropology, University of the
         Philippines, Manilla
1918   Brown, A. Radcliffe, Nukualofa, Tonga Island

1892   *Chapman, The Hon. F. R., Wellington
1892   Chambers, W. K., Fujiya, Mount Smart, Penrose, Auckland
1893   Carter, H. C., 475, West 143rd Street, N.Y.
1894   Chapman, M., Wellington
1896   Cooper, The Hon. Theo., Wellington
1900   Cooke, J. P., c/o Alexander and Baldwin, Honolulu
1903   Chatterton, Rev. F. W., Te Rau, Gisborne
1903   Cole, Ven. Archdeacon R. H., D.C.L., Parnell, Auckland
1908   Coughlan, W. N., Omaio, Opotiki
1908   Carnegie Public Library, Dunedin
1908   Carnegie Public Library, New Plymouth
1910   Cock R., New Plymouth
1917   Cowley, Matt, P. O. Box 72, Auckland
1918   Chambers, Bernard, Te Mata, Havelock North
1918   Corney, Geo., Devon Street, New Plymouth
1918   Crooke, Alfred, S.M., Devon Street, New Plymouth

1892   *Denniston, The Hon. Sir J. E., Christchurch
1902   Dulau & Co., 38, Soho Square, London
1902   Drummond, Jas., "Lyttelton Times" Office, Christchurch
1903   Dixon, Roland B., Ph.D., Harvard University, Cambridge, Mass., U.S.A.
1910   Downes, T. W., P. O. Box 119, Whanganui
1911   Drew, C. H., New Plymouth
1917   Dominion Museum, Wellington
1918   Davidson, J. C., Motunui, Waitara

1892 *Emerson, J. S., 802, Spencer Street, Honolulu, Hawaiian Islands
1894 Ewen, C. A., Commercial Union Insurance Co., Wellington
1918 Etheridge, Robt. Director, Australian Museum, Sydney

1896 Fletcher, Rev. H. J., Taupo
1900 Forbes, E. J., 5, Hamilton Street, Sydney, N. S. W.
1901 Firth, John F., Survey Office, Nelson
1902 Fraser, M., New Plymouth
1902 Fisher, T. W., Tikitiki Road, Te Mapara, Te Kuiti
1903 Fowlds, Hon. G., Auckland
1906 Field Museum of Natural History, The, Chicago, U.S.A.
1912 Fisher, Mrs. Lillian S., 560, Hancock Street, Brooklyn, New York, U.S.A.
1912 Fisher, F. Owen, c/o Credit Lyonaise, Biarritz, B.P., France
1913 Fildes, H., Box 740, Chief Post Office, Wellington

1892 *Gudgeon, Lieut.-Col. W. E., C.M.G., 39, King's Parade, Devonport, Auckland
1902 Gill, W. H. Marunouchi, Tokio, Japan
1902 Graham, Geo., c/o Commercial Union, P.O. Box 166, Auckland
1910 Godding, Fred W., U.S. Consul General, Guayaquil, Ecuador

1898 Hastie, Miss J. A., 11, Ashburn Place, Cromwell Road, London
1908 Hallen, Dr. A. H. Clevedon, Auckland
1909 Holdsworth, John, Swarthmoor, Havelock, Hawkes Bay
1910 Hawkes Bay Philosophical Society, P.O. Box 166, Napier
1910 Hocken, Mrs. T. M., Hocken Library, Dunedin
1910 Home, Dr. George, New Plymouth
1911 Heimbrod, G., F.R.A.I., Lautoka, Fiji
1911 Henniger, Julius, Motuihi Island, Auckland
1917 Hocken Library, Dunedin
1918 Hodgson, N.V., c/o Norman Potts, Opotiki
1918 Harvie, Rev. G. F., The Vicarage. Vivian Street, New Plymouth
1918 Hart, Henry H., 3751, Clay Street, San Francisco

1907 Institute, The Auckland, Museum, Auckland
1907 Institute, The Otago, Dunedin

1892 *Johnson, H. Dunbar, Judge N.L.C., 151, Newton Road, Auckland
1918 Johnston, E. G., Education Board Office, New Plymouth

1902 Kelly, Thomas, New Plymouth
1910 King, Newton, Brooklands, New Plymouth

1894 Lambert, H. A. Belmont, Tayforth, Whanganui
1911 Lysnar, W. D., Gisborne
1913 List, T. C., New Plymouth
1913 Lysons, E. W. M., New Plymouth
1916 Leatham, H. B., M.R.C.S., L.R.C.P., Lond., New Plymouth
1917 Ledingham. T. J., "Montecute," St. Kilda, Melbourne
1917 List, C. S., Rata Street, Inglewood
1918 Laughton, Rev. J. G., Ruatahuna, viâ Rotorua

1892 *Marshall, W. S., Maungaraupi, Rata
1892 *Major, C. E., 22, Empire Buildings, Swanson Street, Auckland

1897 Marshall, J. W., Tututotara, Marton
1897 Marshall, H. H., Motu-kowhai, Marton
1907 Minister for Internal Affairs, The Hon., Wellington
1912 Marsden, J. W., Isel, Stoke, Nelson
1915 Mahoney, B. G., c/o C. Mahoney, Esq., Ruatoki, Taneatua
1916 Mitchell, Library, The, Sydney
1917 Marshall, P., M.A., D.Sc., F.G.S., Collegiate School, Whanganui
1918 McDonell, A. F., Queen Street, Auckland
1918 Morris, G. N., Resident Commissioner, Niuē Island
1918 Missionary Research Library, 25 Maddison Avenue, New York

1895 Ngata, A. T., M.A., M.P., Parliamentary Buildings, Wellington
1900 Newman, W. L., New Plymouth
1902 New York Public Library, Astor Buildings, New York
1906 Newman, Dr. A. K., Hobson Street, Wellington

1894 Partington, J. Edge, F.R.G.S., Wyngates, Burke's Road, Beaconsfield,
         England.
1907 Public Library, Auckland
1907 Public Library, Wellington
1907 Public Library, Sydney, N.S.W.
1907 Philosophical Institute, The, Christchurch
1907 Postmaster General, The Hon. The, Wellington
1913 Potts, Norman, Opotiki
1914 Parliamentary Library, (the Commonwealth), Melbourne
1917 Patuki, J., Topi, M.L.C., Ruapuke Island, Invercargill
1917 Platts, F. W., Resident Commissioner, Rarotonga Island

1892 *Roy, R. B., Taita, Wellington
1903 Roy, J. B., New Plymouth
1918 Rylands, John, Library Deansgate, Manchester University, England
1918 Rockel, R. H., M.A., Gover Street, New Plymouth

1892 *Smith, W. W., F.E.S., Pukekura Park, New Plymouth
1892 *Smith, F. S., Blenheim
1892 *Smith, M. C., Survey Department, Wellington
1892 *Smith, S. Percy, F.R.G.S., New Plymouth
1892 *Stout, Hon. Sir R., K.C.M.G., Chief Justice, Wellington
1892 *Skinner, W. H., Chief Surveyor, Christchurch
1896 Smith, Hon. W. O., Honolulu, Hawaiian Islands
1904 Smith, H., Guthrie, Tutira, via Napier
1904 Samuel, The Hon. Oliver, M.L.C., New Plymouth
1905 Schultz, Dr. Erich von, late Imperial Chief Justice, Samoa, Motuihi Island,
         Auckland
1907 Secretary of Education, Wellington
1910 Savage, S., Rarotonga Island
1915 Smith, Alex., c o W. W. Smith, New Plymouth
1916 Shalfoon, G., Opotiki

1913 Tribe, F. C., Vogeltown, New Plymouth
1915 Thomson, Dr. Allan, M.A., D.Sc., F.G.S., A.O.S.M., Museum, Wellington
1916 Te Anga, Hone Tukere, N.L. Court Office, Whanganui
1917 Tarr, W., Government Printing Office, Nukualofa, Tonga Islands
1918 Trimble, Harold, Inglewood

1911 Vibaud, Rev. J. M., Hiruharama, Whanganui
1919 Vaile, Hubert E., Queen Street, Auckland

1892 *Williams, Archdeacon H. W., Gisborne
1894 Wilson, A., Hangatiki, Auckland
1896 Williams, F. W., Napier
1896 Wilcox, Hon. G. A., Kauai, Hawaiian Islands
1898 Whitney, James L., Public Library, Dartmouth, Boston, U.S.A.
1902 Webster, W. D., New Plymouth
1903 Walker, Ernest A., M.D., New Plymouth
1910 Wilson, Sir J. G., Bulls
1912 Westervelt, Rev. W. D., Honolulu, Hawaiian Islands
1914 Waller, Captain W., Moturoa, New Plymouth
1915 Williams, H. B., Turihaua, Gisborne
1915 Wilson, Thos., Captain, New Plymouth
1916 Welsh, R. D., Hawera
1916 White, Percy J. H., New Plymouth
1917 Wheeler, W. J., Inspecting Surveyor, Gisborne
1917 Wilkinson, C. A., M.P., Eltham
1918 Wallace, D. B., Masonic Club, H.M. Arcade, Auckland
1918 Western, T. D., Puketapu, Bell Block, New Plymouth
1918 Wilson, Kenneth, M.A., 92, Rangitikei Street, Palmerston North

1892 *Young, J. L., c/o Henderson and Macfarlane, Auckland

PRESIDENTS—Past and Present:

1892-1894—H. G. Seth-Smith, M.A.
1895-1896—Right Rev. W. L. Williams, M.A., D.D.
1896-1898—The Rev. W. T. Habens, B.A.
1901-1903—E. Tregear, I.S.O., etc.
1904-1919—S. Percy Smith, F.R.G.S.

LIST OF EXCHANGES.

THE following is the List of Societies, etc., etc., to which the JOURNAL is sent, and from most of which we receive exchanges:—

Anthropologie, Société d', 15 Rue Ecole de Medicin, Paris
Anthropologia, Societa, Museo Nazionale di Anthropologia, Via Gino Capponi, Florence, Italy
Anthropologie, Ecole d', 15 Rue Ecole de Medicin, Paris
Australasian Association for the Advancement of Science, 5 Elizabeth Street, Sydney
American Oriental Society, 245, Bishop Street, Newhaven, Conn., U.S.A.
American Philosophical Society, Philadelphia, U.S.A.
American Museum of Natural History, Washington
Asiatic Society of Bengal, 1, Park Street, Calcutta
Anthropological Department, University of The Philippines, Manilla.

Bataviaasch Genootschap, Batavia, Java
Bureau of American Ethnology, Smithsonian Institute, Washington
Bernice Pauahi Bishop Museum, Honolulu, H. I.

Canadian Institute, Ottawa, Canada
Canadian Department of Mines, Ottawa, Canada

Dominion Museum, Wellington

Ethnological Survey, Manilla, Philippine Islands

Fijian Society, The, Suva, Fiji Islands

General Assembly Library, Wellington (two copies)
Géographic, Société de, de Paris, Boulevard St. Germain, 184, Paris
Geographical Society, The American, Broadway, at 156th Street, New York

High Commissioner of New Zealand, 13, Victoria Street, Westminster, London
Historical Society, Honolulu, Hawaiian Islands

Institute, The New Zealand, Wellington

Japan Society, 20, Hanover Square, London, W.

Kongl, Vitterhets Historie, och Antiqvitets, Akademen, Stockholm, Sweden
Koninklijk Instituut, 14, Van Galenstratt, The Hague, Holland

Na Mata, Editor, Suva, Fiji
National Museum Library, Washington, U S A.

Peabody Museum of Archæology, Harvard University, Cambridge, U.S.A.
Philippines, Bureau of Science, Manilla

Queensland Museum, Brisbane, Queensland

Royal Geographical Society, Kensington Gore, London, S. W.
Royal Geographical Society of Australasia, Brisbane
Royal Geographical Society of Australasia, c/o G. Collingridge, Waronga, N.S.W.
Royal Geographical Society of Australasia, 70 Queen Street, Melbourne
Royal Society, Burlington House, London
Royal Anthropological Institute of Great Britain, The, 50, Great Russell Street, London, W.C.
Royal Society of New South Wales, 5, Elizabeth Street, Sydney
Royal Colonial Institute, The, Northumberland Avenue, London
Royal Geographical Society of Australasia, Adelaide

Smithsonian Institute, Washington
Société Neuchateloise de Geographie, Switzerland
Société d'Etudes Oceanienne, Tahiti Island

Tokyo Imperial University, Tokyo, Japan

University of California, Library Exchange Department, Berkeley, California
University Museum, 33d and Spence Streets, Pennsylvania, U.S.A.

BOOKS, Etc., RECEIVED IN EXCHANGE,
GIFT OR OTHERWISE, IN 1918.

From Java—
    Bataviaasch Genootschap.
From England—
    Royal Colonial Institute
    John Rylands Library, Manchester
    Royal Geographical Society
    Royal Anthropological Institute
From The Philippine Islands—
    The Philippine Bureau of Science
From America—
    Smithsonian Institution
    American Geographical Society
    American Philosophical Society
    United States National Museum
    American Oriental Society
    University of Pennsylvania
    University of California
    American Bureau of Anthropology
    Carnegie Institution, Washington
From Switzerland—
    Société Neuchateloise de Géographie
From Fiji—
    The Editor, ' Na Mata '
    The Fijian Society
From Australia—
    The Australian Museum
    The Commonwealth Government
    Royal Geographical Society, South Australia branch
    Public Library, Victoria .
From Hawaiian Islands—
    Pauahi Bishop's Museum
    Hawaiian Agricultural Experiment Station
From France—
    Société d'Anthropology de Paris
    Société de Géographie
    Ecole d'Anthropologie de Paris
From Holland—
    Koninklijk Instituut
From New Zealand—
    The New Zealand Institute
From Italy—
    Societa Italiana D'Anthropologia
From Tahiti—
    Société d'Etudes Oceanininue de Tahiti
From Ed. Tregear, The Rev. Père H. Audran, Elsdon Best, W. W. Smith, Capt.
    W. Waller, W. Churchill, W. M. Borge, B. Glanvill Corney, and S.
    Percy Smith
From W. L. Newman and S. Percy Smith   Admiralty and other Charts.

THE LAND OF TARA

AND THEY WHO SETTLED IT.

THE STORY OF THE OCCUPATION OF TE WHANGA-NUI-A-TARA
(THE GREAT HARBOUR OF TARA) OR PORT NICHOLSON,
BY THE MAORI.

By ELSDON BEST.

PART VI.

(Continued from page 177, Vol. XXVII.)

MAORI OCCUPATION OF WELLINGTON DISTRICT.
NOTES ON SOME ARCHÆOLOGICAL REMAINS, CONTRIBUTED BY
H. N. McLEOD.

Orongorongo. Remains of native occupation in former times are to be seen at this place, and a number of stone adzes have been found here. One seen by the writer was nine inches long and three wide.

Pencarrow Head. Indistinct traces of native occupation have been noted on the hill near the lighthouse.

Point Arthur. Signs of old time occupation seen here.

Rona Bay. In this and adjacent bays a number of stone implements have been found.

Day's Bay. On the ridge to the north may be seen the remains of a fortified position, as evidenced by levelled hut sites, an earthwork defence, and butts of *totara* posts.

York Bay. Signs of native occupation on hill and beach have been here seen.

Lowry Bay. The headlands or hills to north and south show signs of occupation, while old ovens have been seen on the flat near the beach. A shell midden of the talus type is seen by the side of the road as one proceeds to Waiwhetu.

Nga Uranga. Years ago signs of occupation were seen on the hill whereon the fort is situated, above the former position of the Wharepouri cenotaph.

Kaiwharawhara. Signs of occupation were seen here in past years, apart from the Ngati-Awa hamlet occupied when the first European settlers arrived. These last native dwellers here had potato gardens on the range above the village.

Thorndon. We have already seen that a number of small Ngati-Awa hamlets were settled along bluff and beach from Pa-kuao to Kumutoto, but apparently this part was not much occupied in pre-Ngati-Awa days. A few signs of occupation were seen by early settlers, but some of these might be the result of Ngati-Awa occupation.

Point Jerningham. Omaru-kai-kuru. The tokens of former occupation seen here were hut sites and a shell midden. Of the former some traces still remain.

Evans Bay shores. On a fair slope above the steep bluff about ten chains north of the U.S.S. Coy. Laundry are some fairly distinct narrow terraced formations that are probably old hut sites.

On the ridge extending downward from Mt. Victoria to Te Akau-tangi, the bluff above the lower end of Wellington Road, signs of occupation were visible in several places. One of these was the knoll above Arawa Road, another east of Rata Road; others on the spurs on each side of the gully near Kilbirnie Reserve. The bluff immediately overlooking the Reserve showed until lately a number of small artificial terrace formations, hut sites of the men of yore. In the sixties could be seen signs of old time occupation above high-water mark on the shores of the little bay, now reclaimed, extending from the tram waiting shed southward. Hut sites also appear to be traceable on Te Ranga-a-Hiwi, at Aka-tarewa, and on the spur running down toward the hospital.

On an old plan of Port Nicholson district, issued by the N.Z. Company, the words "coal has been found here" adorns the foreshore at Wellington Road. That coal has not been rediscovered yet.

The small stream from Moxham Avenue that runs into Evans Bay near Wellington Road is marked Good Water on Captain Herd's chart of 1826. A stone adze was found here.

Miramar Bay. The little cove just below the old Crawford homestead. Here, on the slope above high-water mark, as also on the northern extremity of Rabbit Hill, which thrusts Shag Point out into Evans Bay, are, or were, shell middens, ovens and hut sites showing that this was a favoured place of residence in olden days. In the hollow on Bridge Street was the Miramar Lagoon, on which a pleasure boat was kept for some years. In its former bed were found two stone adzes, and also human remains. Excavations along Bridge Street have clearly shown that, at some time in the past, Rabbit Hill, over which Tirangi Road passes, was an island.

Rongotai. The ridge extending from the block cutting near Miramar wharf southward. At several places along this ridge shell middens and levelled hut sites tell of former occupation (see map). At the southernmost knoll ovens and human remains were found in addition to shell middens and hut sites. The next knoll northward also shows signs of occupation, while between the two knolls is a singularly level area, which may have been occupied, or may have served as a plaza, or a cultivation ground. The site of the old Crawford homestead is also said to have shown signs of former occupation.

Maupuia. This old stockaded village, already mentioned, covered about two acres at and near the deep cutting through the above ridge. About a dozen butts of the old *totara* posts of the stockade have been found in late years; in the forties they were plainly visible. One dug up in 1906 was 4½ feet in girth, and is now in the Newtown Museum. Two stone adzes were found here, one of which was of greenstone; also a grinding stone, with human and other remains. Food storage pits were also in evidence. On the border of Burnham Water, below Maupuia, the skull of a *moa* was found.

The Rongotai ridge was occupied long generations ago by the Ngati-Hinepare clan. The famous Nepia Pohuhu, of Wairarapa, a man learned in the ancient lore of his people, was a member of this clan. Further along this ridge, toward Mt. Crawford, several places show signs of native occupation. Shell middens were formerly visible at Shelly Bay, and at several other places at the base of the ridge.

Burnham Water. Rotokura or Pārā Lagoon. Drained by the late J. C. Crawford in 1847-49 by means of a tunnel piercing the ridge, thus allowing the lagoon waters to flow into Evans Bay. On the northern border of this lagoon a greenstone adze was found, and other stone adzes at Rima Street and Ira Street ·East, also the tusk of some sea creature at Park Road. At the junction of Devonshire Road and Princes Street a rib bone 15 inches long was found 20 feet below the surface. Evidences of old occupation were noted at George Street and May Street, and some other places; also on the hill top at Old Farm Road and Kings Road, and the cave at its base. Our early settlers found patches of bush in the gullies at the northern end of the lagoon, and those clumps of bush were occasionally frequented by pigeons and *kākā*.

Point Halswell. A number of hut sites, represented by small terraced formations, have been located on the spur extending upward from this point. Indistinct remains are, or were, seen at what is thought to be the site of the old time stockaded village of Matakikaipoinga. A few chains westward of this place, on a jutting spur north of Shelly Bay are a number of hut sites; old ovens are also in evidence.

Owing perhaps to the rocky nature of the ground we see nowhere in this district any considerable terrace formations such as are seen in many other places. No long continuous terraces are here seen, but merely linchets of small area, often only large enough to accommodate one or two huts; occasionally one may be seen fifty feet in length; few are longer.

Kau-whakaarawaru is said to have been a village in Kau Bay, immediately east of Point Halswell. Shell middens show that the place has been occupied.

Te Mahanga. Talus middens are in evidence here, shell and oven refuse. Small terraced hut sites were at one time visible on the hills above, where, in excavating operations for the modern fort, the butts of some *totara* posts are said to have been unearthed. In the waters below a *taniwha* or water monster is said to have abode in days of yore.

Between Te Mahanga and Te Karaka or Karaka Bay is the place we call Searching Bay, where many signs of native occupation have been seen, including such refuse of bones of man, fish and birds, including *moa* bones, together with shells and oven stones. On the slopes above .terraced sites were noted, as also on the crest of the ridge between Crawford and Fortification Roads. Hard by a grinding stone was found.

Karaka Bay or Te Karaka. Here over a considerable area are signs of occupation ; evidently this was a favoured place of residence. Large quantities of shell and oven stones on and below the surface, and a number of implements of the neolithic Maori have been recovered here, such as stone adzes and chisels, bone combs and tattooing implements. Here also was found a fine piece of greenstone 5¼ lbs. in weight, in a partially ground condition ; apparently it was intended to fashion a *mere* therefrom.

At the entrance to a cave near the wharf were found human bones and a stone chisel. At the point just south of Karaka Bay and north of Worser Bay, which Rangiwhaia Te Puni maintained is the true location of the name Taipakupaku, terraced hut sites are seen on the ridge. Here also a human skeleton was disinterred, by the side of which a stone adze was found. See "Transactions of the New Zealand Institute," Vol. XXXII., p. 271. Other human remains have been found here, as also some stone adzes, bone needles and other objects. South of the point eight human skeletons were unearthed during some excavation work.

Kakariki in Worser Bay. The small flat-topped spur point here has been a fortified hamlet in the past, as shown by levelled top, terraced sides and fosse whereby it was cut off from the ridge. Hard by were found two human skeletons, also a very fine stone weapon (*patu*) of the *mere* type, which is preserved in the Board Room of the Wellington Harbour Board. On the north side many scattered and broken human bones have been found.

The famed fortified village of Te Whetu-kairangi is said to have been situated about the site of the State School on the ridge above the Bay. At the base of the bluff, near the spring Te Puna a Tara, or Te Puno a Timirau, have been seen signs of old-time occupation.

Across Seatoun Heights Road from the School is a knoll which carries marks of human occupation, as also does the spur south of it.

Seatoun. On this sandy flat, and near the hill numbers of old implements have been found, some of which are in the local Christie Collection in Newtown Museum. Among the discoveries may be cited adzes, stone flake knives, fish-hooks, pendants, needles or awls, spear points, bone toggles, a fine *moa* bone *ripi pana*, cloak pins, as also a cut human jaw bone, other human bones, and *moa* bones. Several implements were found in a deep rock cleft. There has been much native occupation of this flat in past times.

On the highest part of the ridge above the flat, as also half-way up, hut sites have been noted, as also on the spur terminating at Ira Street and Broadway junction. Above Church Street are terracings. At the quarry, below the Church Street level, a cave was opened up which at some time in the past had been both accessible and occupied. Herein was found the biggest collection of *moa* bones found on the peninsula, with bones of other birds and of seals, as also human bones. The *moa* bones are preserved by the Miramar Borough Council.

A number of middens were formerly in evidence on Seatoun Flat. Remains of human skeletons, scattered skulls, etc., have been found here, also a fine greenstone ear pendant. Old native ovens were seen on the slope near the tunnel, and on the ridge above are signs of occupation for some distance in the form of terracings and small levelled areas, evidently hut sites. Other such traces are seen on the hill west of the signal stations. It is now impossible to tell which of these occupied places were open settlements, and which were defended by stockades, save that some of the places occupied on fairly steep slopes could not have been defensible positions.

Oruaiti. Fort Dorset now occupies the site of Oruaiti *pa*, one of the old stockaded villages of past centuries. Prior to being interfered with the ridges showed many levelled hut sites, sufficient to accommodate about fifty huts. A number of water-worn boulders scattered about were probably used as blocks on which to pound fern root, and for other purposes. Butts of posts, one of which is in the Newtown Museum, were found here, as also stone flakes and other tokens of former occupation. Some information concerning this place, and other matters pertaining to Hataitai are contained in the works of Jas. Mackay and Canon Stack. At one time Oruaiti is said to have been occupied by the Rangitane folk.

Paewhenua. In the bay below the Signal Station signs of occupation have been noted in the form of shell heaps and human remains. The tooth of a sperm whale, partly cut through, and half a stone *mere*, bored by marine creatures, were found on the beach. At one time a considerable number of *karaka* trees grew along this coast, but many have disappeared and others are dying, as at Te Rimurapa. The finest tree of this species in the district in the sixties was that which stood at Nga Uranga.

The raised beaches along this coast line are plainly discernible, and form an interesting study. The pieces of flint found on the beach in this vicinity have apparently been brought hither in late times in some unknown manner, otherwise flint flakes would assuredly be much more numerous at places formerly occupied by natives.

Tarakena. The three points which form the southern portion of the peninsula bear marks of former occupation. The termination of the eastern spur shows a considerable number of terraced hut sites, much weathered. The western spur is but little marked; the middle one bears the plainest group of hut sites to be seen in the neighbourhood. Butts of stockade posts, shells and oven stones are seen here. In the mouth of the gully below, the original Pilot Station is the best preserved midden of the district. Here many implements have been found by Mr. H. M. Christie, the writer, and other seekers, such as stone adzes, chisels, pounders and grinding stones, stone cutters, flake knives, bone spear points, also pendants, and carving implements and fish hooks, with teeth and bones of dogs, birds and fish. Mr. Green here found a fine greenstone chisel, and also a curious carving in soapstone, the design being that of a human figure reclining on the back of some creature, presumably a whale. Students of Maori myths will recognise the meaning of the design. A somewhat similar figure is said to have been found in the South Island.

The following remarks on the site of the old *pa* on the hill on the western side of this little bay are from one who made a close examination of it :—This is the best preserved of the old *pas* of Miramar. The upper part of the position, overlooking the beach, has been scarped ; on the northern slope a part of the scarp, about five to six feet in height, is still extant, also another piece on the eastern slope ; the other two sides being precipitous. There are six small residential sites, artificial terraces, at the upper part of the position, and seven more on the eastern slope to the bluff head, the largest of which is about 19 yards long and 3 to 4 yards wide. The remains of the scarp on the northern side still shows signs of having had a ditch or small fosse at its base. The terraces of the upper part would accommodate about twelve small huts. At the western extremity of the *pa* summit, above a small saddle in the spur, the butt of a half decayed *totara* post, 10 inches in diameter, is still in position. It may be one of the original stockade posts. Another near the bluff head is probably modern, of the Pilot Station days. It is probable that the folk who lived hard by the midden in the mouth of the gulch below, were the inhabitants of this *pa*, which served as a refuge when enemies appeared.

Palmer Head. This point is on the eastern side of the gulch of Tarakena, and the high bluff-browed hill shows a number of hut sites, now much eroded, but still recognisable. On the eastern side of the extremity of the spur is a ditch-like depression that may be an old entrance way from the beach below. If this place was ever defended by stockades, then the lines of defence would include the first knoll on the ridge so as to take advantage of the depression or saddle just beyond it. Hut sites also seem to be in evidence further up the spur. Up the gully from Tarakena runs an old road made in early days to give access to the Pilot Station.

Proceeding along the beach westward of Tarakena we come to the stone quarry, near which some *moa* bones were found below the road level.

On the crest of the hill at Hau-te-taka, the eastern headland of Lyall Bay, have been found many fragments of *moa* egg shell, as also on the sandy area on the lower levels. Old ovens have been seen on the summit of the headland, which is pretty sure to have been occupied in former times, for it is just such a position as appealed to the neolithic Maori. Erosion and drift sands have, however, concealed all evidence of such occupation, save the *umu* or oven. In the first, second and third gullies east of this hill a number of interesting finds have been made, including shell middens, implements, human, whale and *tuatara* bones, with fragments of *moa* egg-shell, and probably the gizzard stones of that creature. Large whale bones have been seen as much as 140 feet above high-water mark on the sandy slope of the second gully; others on the sands between the two first gullies. When exposed these bones soon crumbled away. Further on toward the Golf Links, at the base of Green Spur, the long spur trending down from the Orongo Ridge, are tokens of former occupation in the form of ordinary village refuse, stone and shell.

Lyall Bay. The name of Hue-te-para assigned by Crawford to the foreshore and sandy beach is not recognised by any Ngati-Awa or Wairarapa natives who were questioned twenty-five years ago, nor is the name Tapu-te-rangi known to them. Some interesting middens were formerly in evidence on the isthmus, and one still exists about ten chains south of Rongotai Terrace. On the eastern side portions of charred *moa* bones and pieces of egg-shell have been found a few chains from the beach. *Moa* and human bones have been found on the sands in past years. Mr. W. Capper has found numerous implements, a carved piece of whale's bone, twelve inches long, at the foot of Moa Hill, as the headland hill above Hua-te-taka is sometimes called; also a *moa* skull and toe bones near the quarry, *moa* bones and shell fragments at Māranui and the east side gullies, as also some stone adzes, one of which is greenstone. Most of these objects went to England. Mr. Bourke found a piece of carved wood, probably belonging to a canoe on the isthmus. Mr. A. Hamilton found a well-worked piece of greenstone, *moa* egg-shell fragments, and jaw bones of *tuatara* near the site of Māranui School. Sand out stones of curiously symmetrical form have been found in numbers on the isthmus, and the raised beaches of this area are an interesting feature of the place. Many stone knives of flake form have been found in common greywacke, a few flint specimens, and some obsidian knives.

Te Ranga-a-Hiwi. We have seen that this is the Maori name of the range extending from Pt. Jerningham to the coast between Lyall and Island Bays, and on which are the three peaks known as Mt. Victoria, Mt. Alfred and Mt. Albert. Some traces of former occupation on this range we have already noted ; a few more remain to be mentioned. On the slope north-east of Newtown Park, and on a spur above Māranui School, such signs are seen. On Queens Drive, south-east of the school, a village has existed in the past. Along the old beach levels at the hill bases in Lyall, Haughton and Island Bays have been seen old ovens and other tokens of native occupation. On the spur above the Corporation stone quarry, western side of Lyall Bay, a number of small terraced hut sites formerly existed, but many have been destroyed. A stockaded village has undoubtedly existed on this hill, as shown by the remains of a defensive trench at the upper end of the spur, where it juts out from the hillside. It is a similar position to the one on the bluff north of Days Bay.

Haewai or Haughton Bay. Here we see that no suitable sites were available near the beach, but signs of occupation were formerly observed by the streamlet at the head of the bay. On the hills above, however, a number of old hut sites are still in evidence. On the western slope of the ridge that separates Lyall Bay from Haughton Bay, near the point known as Te Rae-kaihau, are a number of small terraces on a small spur offshoot above Haughton Bay. On the steep slopes on the western side of the bay similar sites are seen. In all cases these terraced hut sites would be wider when occupied than they are now, owing to several causes.

Island Bay. Prior to European settlement traces of native occupation were discernible all round the bay, on the flat and the hills on both sides; it appears to have been a favoured place of residence. A number of stone implements have been found here, some of which are in Mr. Beckett's collection. Old ovens and midden refuse of shell, bone and stone, including human bones have also been seen in the past. Small terraced hut sites are seen at Uruhau, the high hill on the eastern side of the flat, on the hillock above Liffey Street, and on the central one ; at Milne Terrace and on the hill at High Street. The terraced knoll above Cliff House may have been surrounded by a stockade. The island also retains impressions of man's handiwork, both on the central butte or hillock, and below it, where the piled up stones possibly surrounded huts with sunken floors. On the eastern side of the Tawatawa range, further north, a spur jutting out from Vogeltown may also have been occupied. Part of a broken *patu* (a short stone weapon) found on the island is probably a relic of some old time fight.

Owhiro. This has been another much favoured place of residence, and two middens were in evidence until lately. Here a number of stone implements have been found, including the smallest and most interesting greenstone graver known. As late as 1915 a number of interesting relics have been found here, many stone knives and flakes bearing the mark of percussion, worked bones, and an *autoru* or ochre muller, etc. A village site, with its debris is on the hill on the eastern side of the Owhiro road, with its midden below. On the western side a talus midden shows that the spur above was occupied. The flat on the western side of the road, north of the bridge, has probably been cultivated, as food storage pits are, or were, in evidence near the creek.

Sinclair Head. On the eastern side of the point a midden was formerly visible, though now obliterated by debris from the hillside. On the hill above the point are much weathered hut sites.

Waikomaru pa. This small position showed, as late as 1911, post butts, hut sites and shell refuse. The hamlet must have been a very small one.

Karori Stream. At the mouth of this stream a village has stood in the past, and signs of occupation are seen in other places in the vicinity. A considerable amount of village debris is still observable, and a number of old implements have been found here. The Opuawe hamlet, far up stream, was occupied in European times, as shown by the peach trees growing there many years ago.

Waiariki. This place was occupied for some time after the arrival of Europeans. The small hill by the stream side was possibly defended by a stockade in pre-Ngati-Awa times.

Oterongo. Here many signs of occupation are still seen on the shores of the bay and on the banks of the stream. A number of implements have been found here. At other places on the coast small middens betoken native occupation.

Ohau. The shores of the bay carry signs of much occupation in the form of middens, ovens, etc. The tableland of Te Rama-a-paku has also been occupied.

Te Ika a Maru. This place shows the only old fortified position in the district which is entirely surrounded by earthwork defences, which consist of rampart and fosse. On the central spur facing the bay this position measures some 80 yards. The fosse still shows a depth of 4½ feet, and the rampart a height of 4 feet, though erosion has played sad havoc. Pits, some post holes, and waterworn boulders are the only other tokens of former occupation. On the hill to the west of the station homestead other signs of native occupation are seen.

Owharia. Bay. On the point at the western side of the bay is a well preserved *pa*, name unknown. The earthwork defences of wall and ditch across the base of the point were in good preservation 25 years ago, and are still in fair condition. Butts of stockade posts were seen here, and shell refuge is in evidence all round the bay, where a number of places have been occupied in past times. Signs of occupation have also been noted above the beach south of the bay, towards Te Ika-a-Maru.

With the exception of the little Ngati-Awa hamlet in a clearing at Opuawe, it will be seen that all the native settlements were on or near the coast. With the exception of the Miramar Peninsula, the Ranga-a-Hiwi ridge, and a smaller area at Te Aro, the whole of the main peninsula was forest covered in the old Maori days. Most of the native settlements were on the outer coast line, either just above high-water mark or on the hills overlooking the beach. There was little occupation of the western side of the Wellington Harbour, apparently, in pre-Ngati-Awa days, but more on the eastern side, and as far as Hutt River. This manner of occupation would be owing largely to the fact that a great part of the food supplies of the people must have been obtained from the ocean. This district can never have supported any large population, such as did the fertile lands of Taranaki, Turanga, Whakatane, the Auckland isthmus, Taiamai, Oruru, and some other areas. It was not a suitable place for the cultivation of the sweet potato, which could never have been an important part of the food supply. A certain quantity of food stuffs, principally birds, would be obtained from the forest, but the procuring of these supplies necessitated nothing more than temporary camps in the bush; there were no permanent hamlets within the forest. The aim of the people was to preserve the forest, not to destroy it.

In the Dominion Museum are preserved some old native implements found in this district, including the following objects :—

Stone adze found in (old) Government House grounds.
Stone adze found on site of the museum.
Stone adze found at Pipitea.
Stone weapon (*patu onewa*) found at Island Bay.
Stone adze found at Lowry Bay.
Stone flake implements from Miramar and Owhiro.
Stone hammers from Owhiro.
Shell trumpet (*Septa rubicundum*) from Somes Island.
Bone fish-hooks, barbs, shell teeth (pendants). Miramar.

Stone fibre beater from Pauatahanui.

Stone adzes, etc., from Titahi.

In the local collection made by Mr. H. M. Christie, and now in the Newtown Museum, are some interesting relics of neolithic times, including stone adzes, chisels, sinkers, and borers or drill points, also flakes of flint, obsidian, &c.; bone fish-hooks, barbs, awls, needles, spear points, cloak pins, &c. Human bones and shell teeth (the latter used as pendants) are also included. The piece of obsidian marked ' tomahawk ' can never have been employed as such a tool, however. The rude hand-made iron axes or adzes are a very interesting relic of early European trade, as also are the locks of flintlock muskets.

Mr. Beckett's collection of old atifacts found in this district is probably the best ever made in this area.

*   *   *   *

In any examination· of the sites of native settlements in the vicinity of Wellington, the observer is impressed by two facts, the very few signs of hamlets having been fortified, and the situation of a number in places that could not possibly have been defended. The evidence before us seems to show that the people of this district were never so much harassed by the raiders as were those of many other places. One of the principal causes would be that occupants of this area were, in most cases, nearly related to those of the Wairarapa district, hence most of their quarrels were with Muaupoko of the Otaki district, and other tribes to the north of them. Hamlets situated in the mouths of narrow gullies, such as existed at Tarakena, or on slopes such as Owhiro, would be indefensible, yet the middens at such places call for prolonged occupation. Doubtless the men of yore lived much of their time at such places, as they also did at Porirua, but, on the approach of enemies, retired to stockaded positions, or took refuge in the forest. Presumably stockade defences were employed owing to the rocky nature of the land which, in most places suitable for hill forts, did not lend itself to the formation of ramparts and fosses by means of wooden implements, hence the uninteresting aspect of old village sites here in comparison with those of other districts. The positions where even a single line of earth-work defence was employed, are but few, and consist of one at Days Bay, one each at Kakariki, Tarakena, Waitaha and Owhariu, while Te Ika-a-Maru is the best specimen.

It is interesting to note that Cook, who anchored off Palmer Head, makes no remark as to seeing any native *pa* or open village, as he seems to have done whenever he saw any. If either the hills at Tarakena had then been occupied at that time he could not fail to have seen the huts and stockades.

*   *   *   *

The story of the settlement of this district, as preserved by native historians and given above, is one of much interest. In no other case have we gained so clear a description of the settlement of a district, and the definite statement made as to Miramar being at that time an island much enhance the interest of the narrative. The details of construction of stockade defences and of the manipulation of weapons, as explained by Whatonga, are the most illuminating notes on those subjects ever collected, and the various illustrations given of old customs and beliefs throw considerable light on the mode of life of the Maori.

Like all Maori narratives, however, the story has certain unsatisfactory aspects and inconsistencies. If we accept all statements made in the above story we must believe that about six generations of the Toi family were alive and flourishing at one and the same time. This is a common weakness of native traditions. As to Whatonga being still alive when the "Takitimu" canoe arrived on these shores; this cannot be accepted. Again we scarcely believe that, prior to the death of Tara, the band of 200 immigrants had so increased in numbers as to occupy five fortified villages, and be able to raise so forminable a body of fighting men. This leads to other matters of questionable aspect, for the Muaupoko tribe is said in tradition to have originated a long time after the time of Tara. Perhaps the most interesting question of all is this one of early inhabitants of these southern parts of the island. During the exploration and settlement of the district there is no word of any people occupying the more southern parts of the island, including the Napier district, yet our party under Tara and Tautoki deem it necessary to construct fortified villages, and prepare to defend them. Against whom were these local villages so fortified ? Any enemies to be feared in the time of Whatonga must have been of the Mouriuri or Maioriori aborigines, and there is no evidence to show that these folks occupied any area in the southern part of the island. They occupied Taranaki, we are told, and the Mamoe clan of that people settled in the Napier district apparently after the arrival of Toi on these shores.

There is another point of much interest that may be alluded to and that is the fact that we have collected no tradition as to the first Maori settlers having seen the *moa* in this district. Remains of those creatures have been found at both Wellington and Porirua, and in some cases such discoveries seemed to show that the *moa* had formed part of the food supply of residents of this district at some time in the past. For instance bones and fragments of egg-shell have been found near old ovens. Mr. Chapman found *moa* bones at Paremata said to show marks of some cutting instrument. Mr. Beckett found a bone near Sinclair Head bearing similar marks. At the same time these nicked bones are no actual proof of Maori knowledge of the great bird in this district. The marks may possibly been made in late times, or at least long since the birds disappeared. Certain old settlers have remarked that *moa* bones were seen on hills and in gullies west of Owhiro in former years, when the bush was burned off, but that they soon disappeared. After the destruction of the forest on steep slopes the surface began to fritter away, and the creeks to remove great amounts of debris. The late Mr. Travers found a *moa* leg bone on a hill above the Hutt Road, beyond Nga Uranga. Other bones have been found at Miramar, Porirua, Pae-kakariki and Wairarapa.

A vast amount of nonsense has been written concerning the hapless *moa*. It has been accused of strolling about Gollan's Valley in 1842, and thereby annoying certain veracious sawyers. See "Transactions of New Zealand Institute," Vol. XXVI.; a paper by H. C. Field. A still worse case was that in which a stalwart *moa*, 16 feet high, so far forgot its proper place as to perambulate the Rangitikei district in 1870. When a journal of this nature publishes such childish fables, it is time for modest folk to retire.

We are told in native tradition that, when the party of Toi reached the Bay of Plenty, the *moa* was seen inland of Maketu, and, after much trouble, one was trapped by Rua-kapanga, hence the saying, " *Te Manu nui a Rua-kapanga*" (The great bird of Rua-kapanga.) Thus we might well expect to hear that others were seen in this district when Whatonga and his sons arrived here, more especially as we are led to believe that this district was uninhabited at that time. But local tradition, so far as it has been preserved, is silent as to the lost bird. The old men who have passed away may have known something about it, and we must remember that the traditions that have been recorded are but a very small part of what was known when Europeans first arrived here.

EARLY VESSELS TO PORT NICHOLSON.

Native tradition speaks of two vessels as having entered this harbour early in last century, of which we appear to have no record. In 1878 Karauria Pahura stated that, prior to the time when Ngati-Ira were ejected from these lands, a whale ship entered the harbour and anchored off Te Korokoro, where a native village existed in those days, the principal house of which was called Te Putawarorangi. The vessel lay there for at least several days and took in water and fuel, and the captain gave the natives two spotted pigs. He cohabited with a native woman named Raumata-nui, whom he wished to take away with him, but to this the people objected. This incident is mentioned in song. The vessel had come from a place called Tiakitene (Jackson), hence a child born at Te Korokoro about that time was named Tiakitene. "In after days we learned that Poihakene (Port Jackson) was the proper name of that place."

Native tradition also mentions a ship, commanded by one Rongotute, that is said to have been wrecked at Palliser Bay prior to the Nga-Puhi incursion described above, i.e., prior to 1820.

Te Whaiti, of Whātārangi, in Palliser Bay, states that a vessel was wrecked in that Bay early in the last century, and that he has a bell obtained from the wreck. This bell carries an inscription which, he has been told, is in French.

Local natives of Ngati-Awa told the writer many years ago that Amuketi, the name by which Capt. Kent, an early coastal trader, was known to the Maori, entered Port Nicholson in enry days, a considerable time before European settlers arrived here. We have already noted a place at Seatoun named after him. This seafarer entered Hokianga in 1820, was wrecked near Ruapuke, Foveaux Strait, in 1824, and took Earle and Shand to Hokianga in 1827.

Local natives also remembered the visit of Capt. Herd to this port in 1826. This is the first visit of Europeans to this harbour that has been fixed beyond doubt, as will be seen by a reference to the late Mr. McNab's "Murihiku," 1907 edition, pp. 364-376. Herd's chart of the harbour is an excellent one, and shows about 130 soundings. Burnham Water, the small lagoon near the old Crawford homestead, and Otari peak are shown on it. He it was who named the port Nicholson's Harbour or Port Nicholson.

When, during his third voyage, Captain Cook left Queen Charlotte Sound in 1777, he took with him two natives, one of whom he calls Taweiharooa. (? Te Waiharua.) This native told him that a ship "had put into a port on the north west coast of Teerawitte, but a very few years before I arrived in the Sound in the Endeavour, which the New Zealanders distinguish by calling it Tupia's ship. At first I thought he might have been mistaken as to the time and place; and that the ship in question might be either Monsieur Surville's, who is said to have touched upon the north-east coast of Eaheinomauwe the same year I was there in the Endeavour; or else Monsieur Marion du Fresne's, who was in the Bay of Islands, on the same coast, a few years after. But he assured us that he was not mistaken, either as to the time or as to the place of this ship's arrival, and that it was well known to everybody about Queen Charlotte's Sound and Teerawitte. He said that the Captain of her, during his stay here, cohabited with a woman of the country, and that she had a son by him still living, and about the age of Kokoa, who, though not born then, seemed to be equally well acquainted with the story. . . . .

I regretted much that we did not hear of this ship while we were in the Sound, as, by means of Omai (Cook's Tahitian interpreter), we might have had full and correct information about her from eye witnesses. For Taweiharooa's account was only from what he had been told, and therefore liable to many mistakes. I have not the least doubt, however, that his testimony may so far be depended upon as to induce us to believe that a ship really had been at Teerawitte prior to my arrival in the Endeavour, as it corresponds with what I had formerly heard. For in the latter end of 1773, the second time I visited New Zealand, during my late voyage, when we were continually making enquiries about the Adventure, after our separation, some of the natives informed us of a ship having been in a port on the coast of Teerawitte. But, at the time, we thought we must have misunderstood them, and took no notice of the intelligence. . . . Taweiharooa told us their country was indebted to her people for the present of an animal, which they left behind them, but as he had not seen it himself no sort of judgment could be formed, from his description, of what kind it was."

If this native story contained any truth, the pre-Cook ship must have laid in Port Nicholson, Porirua, or under Kapiti; she would find shelter at no other place. The N.W. coast of Tarawhiti would seem to imply one of the latter places!

Years ago the remains of an old wreck were uncovered at Lyall's Bay. In the " Proceedings of the New Zealand Institute " for 1892 occurs the following paragraph pertaining to the meeting of October 26th:—"The chairman drew attention to some pieces of pottery and copper nails, etc., found by Mr. Capper at Lyall's Bay, near the wreck. The pottery was carbonaceous, and it was generally thought that the nails were of French make."

Subsequent to the visit of Capt. Herd in 1826, the next vessel to enter the harbour, whose visit we are sure of, was the schooner " Joseph Weller " of Sydney, in 1835.

*   *   *   *

THE COMING OF THE WHITE MAN.

When European settlers arrived here in 1839-40, they were well received by the natives, and very little trouble arose between the two peoples, when we consider the many causes for friction that inevitably arise when two races so dissimilar in customs, beliefs, prejudices and modes of thought are commingled. The Rangatahi clan, that gave some trouble at the Hutt, was not of Ngati-Awa, though related to Ngati-'Tama.

The cause of this attitude on the part of the local natives lay in their position at the time. Many of their fighting men were away at the Chathams, their Kahungunu neighbours eastward were hostile, and Ngati-Toa of Porirua were but doubtful friends; hence the Children of Awa were situated between the devil and the deep sea. That is why they welcomed the advent of an alien people, who not only proposed to settle here, but also brought with them many highly desirable products—muskets, tomahawks, blankets, etc., not to speak of jews harps, sealing wax and red nightcaps!

When Te Rangi-haeata sought allies among the Kahungunu clans to assist in sacking Wellington and wiping out the *pakeha*, the answer he received was:—"If the white men are expelled, where am I to obtain red blankets?" (*Kei hea he tahurangi moku.*)

. In a speech made by Tamati Wāka Nene at the Kohimarama Conference in 1860, he said to the assembled natives:—"*E nga tangata o Whanganui, o Wairarapa, o Poneke, o Ahuriri! kia atawhai koutou ki te pakeha. Ki te kino koutou, maku e ki atu ki a koutou—e kore taku wahine e matau ki te whatu kakahu, koia ahau i mea ai ma te pakeha e whatu he kakahu moku.*" (O people of Whanganui, of Wairarapa, of Wellington, of Napier, be kind to the Europeans. Should you treat them badly, let me say to you—my wife does not know how to weave garments, hence I have decided that Europeans shall weave garments for me.)

*   *   *   *

And now we must say farewell to the Land of Tara and they who settled it. The bones of the old pioneers of these lands have long since mouldered into dust, the few descendants of the old neolithic ocean rovers dwell in the vale of Wairarapa, beyond the rugged ranges of the red sun. That sun shines as of yore upon the restless waters of the Great Harbour of Tara, but not upon the homes of the Sons of Tara, the offspring of Toi, who dared the pathless wastes of Hine-moana. For their picturesque stockaded villages have passed away for ever, the fair green forests they loved have been torn from the breast of the old Earth Mother, whilst the riven and tortured land supports an alien and intrusive folk. The descendants of Tara, the explorer, and of Ira, the Heart Eater, are unknown in the land, their culture of the stone adze has passed away for all time, nought remains of long centuries of neolithic occupation save grass grown village sites and middens, a few rude implements and place names.

In the days that lie behind, the Maori had traversed the great water-ways of the Pacific, and made known many lands and far scattered islets. He explored the rolling realm of Tahora-nui-atea, the far spread plaza of Hine-moana, the playground of the Wind Children, who come forth from the four quarters to gambol in the vast open spaces of the Ocean Maid. In his primitive outrigger he had sighted all the isles of the sunlit sea, and made his landfall under alien stars; he had tied far spread lands together with the wake of his carvel-built craft, and carried his ancient tongue from Hawaii to Aotearoa, from Rapanui to the Carolines. He traversed his rolling water-ways with fine skill and sublime confidence to reach these lands of the far south, and spent long centuries in settling them. He brought with him his rude neolithic arts as the first wave of human culture, and practised them after the manner of his kind and according to his lights. As to what plane he may have attained we know not, for the advent of

Europeans called a halt in his progress and shattered the stone age
fabric of many centuries. The gulf that yawned before him, traversed
by us in doubt and ignorance and much suffering for countless years,
was too wide for him to cross in the span of a man's life. The fleeting
years leave him of the stone adze stranded on the shores of the river
of progress; across the hurrying waters we greet the last camp fires
of the Maori pioneers.

*   *   *   *

Of all the scenes familiar to the men of yore in the Land of Tara
nought remains unchanged save the contour of the great hills and the
rippling waters of the Great Harbour of Tara. No more are seen the
hamlets that girt the Red Lake round, the cultivations that fringed the
Awa a Taia, the paddling of many canoes to the fishing grounds. No
longer are the fortresses of Motu-kairangi crowded with fierce fighting
men as of old, ready, at the sign of the signal fires on the Ranga-a-
Hiwi, to grasp spear and club in defence of their homes. Never again
shall the chieftain's war canoe swing across the waters of Tawhiti-nui,
and never more shall the hills of the Land of Tara re-echo the roaring
chorus of the war song.

And the Children of Awa, where are they? Of a verity are their
numbers few in the land. Of all those stalwart, war-seasoned migrants
who welcomed our fathers, none are left. Anon you may see a brown
skinned descendant on your streets, a lone figure from the age of the
neolithic, a descendant of the sea kings who ranged a great ocean when
our forbears were hugging coastlines, a lone figure gazed at curiously
by passers by. He is not of us, nor of our time; in the words of a
survivor of the days of the levelled spear—" *Me te mea he wairua tangata
e haere ana* "—Like a human spirit moving abroad !

Wherefore have we rescued from oblivian these few fragments of
the long past history of the Land of Tara, even that the few survivors
from that past may say :—

> " And from their scholars let us learn
> Our own forgotten lore."

THE FATHERLAND OF THE POLYNESIANS.

ARYAN* AND POLYNESIAN POINTS OF CONTACT.
No. 4.

By S. Percy Smith.

As time passes, more and more notes accumulate on the subject of "Aryan and Polynesian points of contact," and in what follows some further information on the subject is supplied in continuation of papers printed in the "Journal of the Polynesian Society," Vols. XIX., XX. It is believed by the writer that further research into this question by one who has sufficient enthusiasm, and above all an extensive knowledge of Polynesian myths, traditions, legends, folk-lore, and customs, and the same of the Aryan Hindus, would lead to very great results. But it means years of study, and access to the Sanskrit literature, which, it is believed, is as yet not obtainable in this country. Dr. Newman has made a start in this direction by the publication of his "Who are the Maoris?" in which he has collected much useful information relating to India in connection with Polynesian matters. But our old friend will, it is hoped, excuse us when we say he has made some mistakes due to the want of a more complete knowledge of Polynesian traditions, etc.

It is probable that in what follows some of the apparent identification mentioned may appear to the reader to be fanciful; but they are the result of an honest attempt to place the source of these old Maori traditions in their true bearing. Mr. Ed. Tregear in his many papers on the language, and some other points, ought to be consulted in this connection.

H. T. Pio's MSS., Vol. XII., p. 44 (for which the Society is indebted to Mr. Elsdon Best), referring to the peaceful nature of the people of New Zealand prior to the advent of Toroa and his party in the "Matatua" canoe, in the fourteenth century, says, "That is the descent from Toi-te-huatahi (which he quoted); it is the descent of the Ngati-Awa tribe, and the original people of Aotearoa, or New

* The word Aryan is here used strictly for the people that invaded India from 1500 to 1000 B.C.; the ancestors of the Hindus.

Zealand (i.e., Toi's descendants), they owned Aotearoa, nor did they practise evil, and hence the saying of Tuoi when the canoes (of the fleet of the fourteenth century) arrived in Aotearoa, and the crews commenced to kill Ngati-Tuoi; this was his word, '*Ahaha! riri noa! Ahaha! patu noa! He aha te take o tenei mahi e mahi mai nei nga tangata o Hawaiki? Kore rawa e mohiotia ana e nga tangata o Aotearoa.*' (Aha! Anger and killing without reason! What is the cause of the deeds of these men of Hawaiki? The people of New Zealand do not at all understand such proceedings.) The origin of the evil doings is from the people of Mataora, of Hawaiki-nui. All evils and all good originated in the times of (the gods) Tāne, Tangaroa, Tu, Tawhiri-matea and Haumia. The evils commenced at the *whainga* (or consecration) of their house (or temple) named Te Tatau-o-Rangiriri, and the place where they lived and where the house stood was Au-roroa. It was here that everything in the world originated. The chief cause of the evil was the destruction of the 'vital essence' (*patunga i te hau*) of the above gods; that was the cause of all evil in the world. Let me explain the *hau* of Tāne and the others; it was their *mana* (power, authority, prestige).* Tāne's enemy was Tangaroa, and Tu was the enemy of both Tāne, Tangaroa and Tawhiri-matea, and hence these evils came into the world. Those who escaped (or were not subjects of the above evils, or perhaps survived them) were the 'Heketanga-Rangi' and the 'Hapu-oneone' who continue to practise good works in the world. It is said (of them) that (the arranging of) peace-making, great and small quarrels, differences between brethren" (were due to their teaching, or were their principles).

Such was the teaching of old H. T. Pio, who had been taught in his childhood in the Maori College, and there are some things in it that differ from the usual traditional lore of the Maoris. First we have three names of the original Fatherland, two of which are (I think) found nowhere else. Hawaiki-nui, or Hawaiki-the-great, is a name known to all tribes, and from other accounts implies a continent. Mataora and Au-roroa are not such wide spread names. In one place old Pio says, "The first home of the people of Aotearoa (New Zealand) was Au-roroa, then Mataora, then Hawaiki-nui, then Aotearoa." It is a question if any light can be thrown on the geographical position of these places through the meanings of the words.

Au-roroa: While there are quite a number of meanings to *au* in Maori, there is only one that might be used in a topographical sense; and that is as a 'current,' in which case the name means 'a long current.' This is a very unlikely name to be given to a country, and

---

* In another place Pio says that the *hau* was the *kura* for which the gods strove, and *kura* means "knowledge" of a sacred character. This agrees with the account in "Memoirs Polynesian Society," Vol. III.

au-roroa does not seem to belong to the class of words usually associated with currents, such as *au-kume, au-rona, au-whiro,* etc.   It might be suggested, perhaps, that it is an equivalent of Taheke-roa (which means a long rapid), but in the sense in which this latter name is used, namely as the "current of death" leading on to Rarohenga or Hades, it can scarcely be a proper name for a country. One is therefore inclined to think that the Maori meaning of *au* must be abandoned for that of the Hawaiian given below.

We will try to follow the word *au* back along one of the known lines of migration of the Maori people, i.e., viâ Rarotonga, Tahiti, and Hawaii.   In Rarotonga *au* means "the government," i.e., of a people and country by a ruling chief.   In Tahiti it has the same meaning as in Maori, while *hau* is "the government," "a reign."   In Hawaii it means "time," "a reign," "one's life," "a season," and (besides others) "a territory," usually where food will grow.

This last seems the only meaning likely to be used in a topographical sense.   It is suggested, seeing that one of the Maori migrations dwelt for a time in Hawaii, that *au* as a word for "territory" was in use there (and long before), and has since gone out of use with the Maoris during the 600 or more years since the two peoples have ceased to have communication with one another. Hence it is thought Au-roroa may be translated as the "(very) long country."

Next as to Mataora; the second stage of migration according to H. T. Pio.   This word in Maori means "alive," "in health," and in Rarotongan means "pleasure," "pleasant," "happiness," and one is inclined to translate the word as "land of happiness," and consequently of plenty and safety.   H. T. Pio himself says that the name was given after the wars referred to later on, and that it expresses the feeling of safety, peace and plenty, on the cessation of those wars.

As to Hawaiki-nui, it is well-known that this is the general name of the fatherland of all Polynesians, and is identical with Atia and Irihia. It has been suggested that the first part of the name "Hawa," in Hawaiki, is derived from Sindh-hava, a name for the northern parts of India, whilst another of the ancient Maori names of the fatherland, Irihia, has been suggested as the equivalent of Vrihia, a name for India, or of some part of it.

The question is of interest as to whether these names can be located as an indication of the original home, or fatherland, of the Polynesians. No doubt the following attempt to do so will not be considered as a proof; but absolute proof is almost impossible, and there are so many things that point to India as their fatherland, that any evidence in support of that theory ought to be acceptable.

It is now acknowledged that the Polynesians belong to the Caucasian family of the human race, as do the Aryan people of India. It is known that the mythology of the former (the Polynesians) has many affinities to the mythology of the Aryans, and they have, or had, very many customs in common. If the Polynesians belong to the Aryan people, they must have separated off from them in very early times, before the rigid caste system of the latter people came to predominance, which was after their occupation of the whole of the Panjab, and also after the Aryans came into contact with the dark Bharata* people of Dravidian origin who were the original inhabitants of India. This contact took place in the country now known as the Panjab, or north-west India, in the early days of the irruption into India; and if the Polynesians formed part of that migration, it were better to use the name of Proto-Aryan for them, as indicating the contact of the first advance of the Aryans into India from their fatherland called Eran, which—it is suggested—is the equivalent of the name of a very ancient country known to the Polynesians under the various forms of Herangi, Erangi, Holani, and Harani, according to the part of Polynesia from whence each name originates, as recorded in their traditions.

The brief history of the Aryan migration into India is as follows†:— The dates of the migration into India are variously given as from 1500 to 1000 B.C., when they crossed the mountains by the Kyber and other passes into the Panjab, from Eran (or, as it is sometimes called, Iran), and gradually spread eastward to the upper waters of the Ganges. During the occupation of the Panjab the tribes —for they appear to have had a tribal organisation at that time—came into conflict with the Bharatas or Dasus, or original inhabitants, and fierce fighting took place. Many battles were fought, ending in a gradual amalgamation, to a certain extent, between the two peoples. These original inhabitants are described in the various Sanskrit works of the Aryans, as a very dark, or black people, and were much despised and abhorred by the fair "Heaven born" Aryans. The eastern part of northern India, which was occupied by the Aryans after some centuries dating from their first arrival in the Panjab, is described as a richer and pleasanter and more wooded country than that of their first settlement. This country was much coveted by, and was eventually conquered by the Aryans, and in the course of many centuries the people spread down the Ganges to its mouth, and all over northern India to the Vindhya mountains that partially cut the Indian peninsula in two, the south of the mountains being to this day occupied by the Dravidian (Bharata) people. It was during the occupation of the Panjab that the priestly craft gained

---

* It is from this Bharata people that comes the oldest name for India. viz., Bharata-vasha. See Hewitts' "Myth Making Age," p. 281.

† See "Vedic India," by Ragusin; "The Original Inhabitants of India," by Oppert; "The Myth Making Age," by Hewitt, and other works of the same author; "Sanskrit Literature," by Prof. Macdonnell; "Brief History of the Indian People," by Sir W. W. Hunter.

great ascendancy, and then the rigid caste system of India was instituted.

The suggested explanation of H. T. Pio's story is this: Au-roroa (the long territory) stands for the western Panjab with its plains and great rivers, where the gods—offspring of Heaven, Rangi (the Aryan Dyaus*) and the Earth, Papa (called Prithivi with the Aryans, having the same meaning as Papa, broad, extended)—were created. It was here the "Heketanga-rangi," or "descendants of heaven," of H. T. Pio, a term which the Aryans apply to themselves, came into collision with the original people, the Bharatas or Dasas, which are perhaps represented by the "Hapu-oneone" of H. T. Pio, meaning "the tribe of the soil," or in other words the original inhabitants. The wars that then took place may be represented in Maori traditions by the wars of the gods, known under the general name of "Te Paerangi," in which the names of twenty-one battles have been recorded in Maori history. (See "Memoirs Polynesian Society", Vol. III., p. 134.) This epoch may be descriptive of the "Wars of the ten Kings" of Aryan history. Although the Maori traditions say this series of wars was between the gods, and that "they fought as gods," it is perhaps easier for people of the 20th century to consider this strife as between human beings, and that the record of it has become glorified in process of time, and in the form of myth to represent gods instead of men.

In the series of battles "of the gods"—"Te Paerangi"—referred to above, the principal enemy of the side that eventually conquered (led by Tāne, often said to be a god of light) was Whiro, who after his defeat became the chief god of Hades. Whiro is often called Whiro-te-tupua, Whiro-the-demon, Whiro-the-uncanny, Whiro-the-evil-doer, in which *tupua* has many other meanings, as "strange," "gifted with unusual powers," "evil," etc. Whiro has become the god of thieves and evil doers; the dark night of the moon is called Whiro also. He is the great rebel of the Polynesian Myths.

It would seem probable that this name, Whiro-te-tupua, might appropriately be applied to the powers opposing the Aryans in their struggle against the original Dasas or Bharata aborigines of the Panjab. *Tupua* is just such a name as would be (and has been) applied to an uncanny dark race. In the language of myth, Whiro is the enemy of the "children of light"; in other words the opponent of the immigrant Aryan people.

As to the Hapu-oneone, H. T. Pio states that both this people and the Heketangi-rangi were peace lovers, and a genealogy is on record

---

* The name Dyaus, for the Heaven-father, in later times obtained another name Varuna ("the all covering heavens"). Now in the Ngata-Awa dialect of Maori, Wa-runa means the "space above." Probably this similarity of names is quite accidental.

from the former to the present day, numbering 35 generations. This latter record is of no very great value, for it probably is based on the same footing as so many genealogies with the name of Rangi, the sky-father, at the head of them, and which only means that the names following the descent acknowledged Rangi, as the progenetor of all mankind. But the supposed peaceful character of the Hapu-oneone militates against their representing the Bharatas—and there we must leave it.

The next stage in H. T. Pio's migrating movement was Mataora, which we have seen a few pages back is possibly translateable as " the land of happiness and plenty," which, it is suggested, may represent the richer country to the east of the Panjab, so much coveted by, and afterwards conquered by the Aryans, as referred to above. It has been suggested that Mataora is represented by the ancient Indian state of Mathura, which is on the Jumna river (a principal branch of the Ganges), and now called Muttra, and where the Kuru branch of the Aryans lived. It is in the country " coveted by " the Aryans. But we do not know enough of the legitimate letter changes between Sanskrit and Polynesian to say if the one name may represent the other. There is perhaps more justification in supposing that Mataora as a descriptive name represents the richer lands of the country east of the Panjab, watered by the many branches of the upper Ganges.

It is perhaps possible that the ascendancy of the priesthood among the Aryans when caste was introduced, is represented by the prominence given to the priests in the Rarotongan recitation of the classes of people who attended the great meetings for public purposes under the rule of Tu-te-rangi-marama in Atia, the fatherland, as described in "History and Traditions of Rarotonga," Part V., which ruler was the builder of the temple called " Te Koro-tuatini "; and, we may say, was a king in Atia, the name by which the fatherland is known to the Rarotongans. This man was afterwards deified as a god.

With regard to the dark or black people the Aryan records speak of—the Bharatas or Dasas, or original inhabitants of India—it is possible they are referred to in the history of the original expulsion or migration of the Polynesians from the fatherland, one description of which is to be found in "Memoirs Polynesian Society," Vol. IV., p. 9. There are five tribes or different kinds of men mentioned, two of whom were "lanky, thin people, whilst the three others were a black people, one kind was very black : they were not brown like the Maoris." It is said above that the Aryan migration into the Panjab abhorred and despised the black aborigines. This disgust at black people (Negroes) was quite characteristic of the Maoris sixty to seventy years ago.

It is suggested above that if the Polynesians are a branch of the

Aryan people, they must have separated from them before the rigid caste system became so pronounced; and it is quite clear also that the separation took place before Buddhism developed in India (fifth century B.C.) for there is no trace of it in Polynesia. Ragusin says, the caste system came to prominence about the end of the Vedic age, which Macdonnell fixes at about 200 B.C.; and as the Polynesian pedigrees leading back to the time of the exodus from (as I suppose) India, and from which we calculate dates, fixes that date at 475 B.C. (see "Memoirs Polynesian Society," Vol. IV., p. 12) the Polynesians knew neither of the caste system nor of Buddhism.

It is clear from the Indian records that the Aryan people gradually moved down the course of the Ganges to the sea, and this movement according to General Forlong's tables, took place in about 600 B.C. He also notes, "Time of great disturbances in India 500 to 400 B.C." If, as has been suggested above, the Polynesians were the forerunners of this migration (or Proto-Aryans), and they migrated down the Ganges in 600 B.C., they would not have been affected by the caste system, or by Buddhism, which were at first northern Indian institutions.

A tradition of the Maoris, told to the writer many years ago by the most learned man of the South Island then living, was to the effect that Hawaiki-nui was a *tuawhenua*, a mainland, not an island, that the southern part was mostly plains, with a high ridge of mountains to the north, always snow-clad, and through which country ran the river Tohinga, associated with the deluge. This is not a bad description in general terms of that part of India, and the river Tohinga (which means the Maori form of baptism) is possibly the Ganges, a sacred river of the Hindus.

The story about the deluge, however, is an instance of the transference of an occurrence localized in another place, of which we have such numerous examples. Although the story of the flood is well-known and fully described in Aryan records, it is believed by scholars to have been introduced from Mesopotamia, where great floods in the Euphrates and Tigris gave rise to the story, and formed the basis of the Biblical account. The Noah of the latter account is the Manu of the Aryan story, which word in Maori means "to float," possibly an accidental similarity.

The Proto-Aryans formed, on their occupation of the lower Ganges, the people quoted by Logan (the Indonesian Ethnologist) as the "Gangetic Race," from whom he traces the Polynesians and some of the most ancient peoples of Indonesia.

There is a Maori tradition to the effect that all fish come from a spring called Rangiriri,* and Dr. Newman in his book† says, there is such a place-name on the Hugli branch of the Ganges above Calcutta. There is always some foundation for similar stories, and it is suggested that this "spring" is where the tidal flow ceased on the Hugli, and where salt-water fish were first seen by the Polynesians. In Nobin Chandra Das's "Ancient Geography of Asia," his map of India shows, that in Aryan times, the sea flowed up to where the Mandar hills come near the Ganges, or some 200 miles inland of the present coast line, forming a great bay now filled up by the delta of the Ganges. At the head of this bay he marks a country or district called Vanga. Now Whanga is the Maori name for a bay. Is this similarity of name purely accidental? and could the Rangiriri "spring" be situated at the head of this ancient bay? It will be noticed in the notes from H. T. Pio, *ante*, he mentions a building named Tatau-o-Rangiriri.

But there is another and possible explanation of this "spring" from which fish originate at Rangiriri. Hewitt in "The Ruling Races of Prehistoric Times," p. 220, says, "It was from the belief in the life-giving waters as the author of life that the cult of the prophet fish god arose. This . . . . was first developed in India where the conception was naturally engendered by the annual recurrence of the apparent miracle of the birth of fish from the life-giving rain. For it is there that water-tanks formed by excavations, or by throwing dams across the hollows between hills or rising grounds, are, though dried up every year by the heat of the dry season, found to be swarming with fish as soon as they are filled by the rains.‡ These fish . . . . proved by actual experiment, have been hibernating during the dry season. . . ."

The above is just such an occurrence as would give rise to the Maori story. And what does Rangiriri mean? It is the "angry sky," descriptive, it is suggested, of the storms and downpour of rain that mark the inception of the monsoon season in India.

There is one (and one only I think) Maori tradition to the effect that a man named Kahukura introduced the knowledge of the *kumara* (sweet potato) to the Maoris. It is said in this tradition that he brought it to New Zealand. This, however, is another instance of the shifting of locality, as so often occurs. It is suggested that this

---

* A place of this name is recorded in the tradition of the Mangareva Islanders, but not apparently connected with fish.

† "Who are the Maoris?"

‡ These south-west winds, that bring the Monsoon rains, are called *martu* in Sanskrit; and *mātū* is the Samoan for a northerly gale, perhaps derived from the Sanskrit, but the direction altered because the Samoans came from the north.

Kahukura is the same man who is mentioned on page 12, "Memoirs Polynesian Society," Vol. IV., and he flourished, according to the Rarotonga genealogies (on which Kahukura is also mentioned), in the middle of the fifth century B.C., that is, when these people were living (as I hold) in the valley of the Ganges, and it was in the same generation that the early exodus from there took place to the east, to Tawhiti-roa, and other places on the way to the Pacific. Dr. Newman (loc. cit., p. 267) mentions that in Bengal the tuber is called *kumar*, and that it grows wild in Orissa, the country lying to the south-west of the mouth of the Ganges. It is suggested that it was the above named Kahukura who got the tuber from Orissa, and introduced it to the knowledge of his compatriots when they were living in the Ganges valley. (See also what Dr. Newman says on this subject in the work quoted.)

Just here it will be well to introduce the Maori account of the origin of the *kumara*, which is a true myth, but which has underlying it in all probability an historical basis, couched in the language of myth. We quote from the same H. T. Pio's MS., Vol, XII., p. 109. He says, "The *kumara* were the offspring of the star that takes its flight (low down) on the side of the ocean; it is named Whanui (alpha Lyrae or Vega). It was his younger brother Rongo-Maui that introduced the *kumara* to this world. The "basket" in which he placed those children was his own body. On his arrival he cohabited with Tinaku (or Pani-tinaku); she was his wife. When she became pregnant, that man said to her, "You must go to the waters of Mona-riki and give birth there," at the same time teaching her the appropriate *karakia*. She did so and repeated the *karakia* as follows:—

E Pani! E Pani-tinaku e!	O Pani! Pani-of-the-seed-tubers
Ki te wai opeope ai	In the water bring them forth
Ka heke i tua, ka heke i waho	Let them descend behind, outside
Me kowai? me ko Pani	Like whom? like Pani
Ka heke i taku aro	Descended from my front

Then were born her children named Nehu-tai, Patea, Waiha, Pio-matatu, Pou-aro-rangi, Toroa-mahoe, Anu-rangi, and Nehu-tai-aka-kura (names of varieties of *kumara*). Such were the *kumara* offspring, which those ancients appointed for the sustenance of their descendants of this world. On their birth Rongo-Maui said. "Now (let us) institute the (ceremonial) ovens, *imu-tapu, imu-kirihau, imu-potaka, imu-maharoa, imu-kohukohu*. (He then describes the uses to which these *imu*, as he calls them, or *umu*, the common name, which were for special classes of priests and people at various ceremonies.) All of these things originated at Mata-ora in Hawaiki-nui, and when Hoake and Taukata came from Tahiti to New Zealand (a well-known story) they introduced this knowledge to New Zealand" (somewhere about the twelfth century).

From the foregoing myth we learn that the *kumara* tuber was originally the offspring of the star Vega, or Whanui, the position of which is about 38° north of the equator, and consequently does not rise high in the sky in New Zealand. From Pio's home in the Bay of Plenty it would be seen "at the side of the ocean" as he says. It is clear from its low elevation that the star myth did not originate in this southern hemisphere. The importance of the star Vega is due to the fact that in very ancient times this star was the *whetu o te tau*, the "year star," marking the commencement of the new year among the northern people, afterwards superseded by Matariki, the Pleiades, which group was used by the Polynesians to denote the commencement of the new year down to the nineteenth century A.D. And, it is suggested, it was due to the importance given to Vega as the "year star" denoting the time for preparing the ground for the *kumara* crop, that it is said to be the parent of the tuber. Who Rongo-Maui was, we have nothing to indicate, except to suggest that this may be another name for Rongo-marae-roa (Rongo-of-the-wide-spread-courts, or fields), the god of agriculture. He married Pani-tinaku, who was the real mother of the *kumara*. Now, in the various Sanskrit works of the Aryans, we find that Pani was the name given to the original inhabitants of India, as expressive of their "hard dealings in trade and their acquisitiveness," and there is a very pretty story illustrating this feature, quoted by Ragusin (loc. cit., p. 257), taken from the sacred books of the Aryans, the Rig-Veda, X., 108, though that story has nothing to do with the transfer of agricultural products. If the *kumara* was growing wild, or cultivated, in Orissa, as stated by Dr. Newman, in the country of the Bharata aboriginies, it is suggested that the Aryans (and Polynesians) derived the *kumara* from these people nick-named Pani. H. T. Pio says the "birth" (? exchange) took place in Mata-ora, which has been suggested as the parts of India lying east of the Panjab.

Kahukura is associated with the *kumara*, as will be seen in the following part of one of the *karakias*, or invocations, used in planting this tuber, everything to do with which was considered as of a sacred nature:—

Tenei te whangai	This is the offering.
Ka whangai na	That is here offered.
Ko te whangai o wai?	'Tis the offering for whom?
Ko te whangai o Rongo-mai	'Tis the offering of Rongo-mai
Ko te whangai o wai?	'Tis the offering for whom?
Ko te whangai o Kahukura	'Tis the offering of Kahukura
Ko te whangai o wai?	'Tis the offering for whom?
Ko te whangai o Uenuku	'Tis the offering of Uenuku
&c. &c.	&c. &c. &c.

This was the commencement of the ceremonies, when the priest offered the *marere*, or propitiatory tuber to the powers above. Rongo-mai is probably the same as Rongo-Mani before mentioned, god of agriculture (though Rongo-mai is usually said to be a meteor in which form that god appears), and Uenuku is another name for the rainbow, thus are these two names (Kahukura and Uenuku) and the *kumara* connected with the rainbow in some manner we have not yet got at.

It is perhaps only natural that a people like the Polynesians (a branch, as suggested, of the Aryans) should, on first becoming acquainted with (to them) a new and valuable food, ascribe its origin to some super-human source, and connect the discovery with the star guiding the preparations for planting, and stars are often referred to as deceased ancestors, meaning probably deified ones. The introduction of the breadfruit to the knowledge of the Polynesians has a somewhat similar mythical story connected with it.

The Turehu, or fair, or white people, mentioned in the traditional history relating to the times just preceding the exodus of the Polynesians from the fatherland—a date fixed by their genealogical tables—are difficult to account for. In modern times the Maoris have come to look on the Turehu, or Patu-pai-a-rehe, as fairies inhabiting parts of New Zealand. This localization is characteristic of very many legends, all the world over; and the fact that the Niuē Islanders have some of the same stories about the Turehu as the Maoris, proves at once that this localization of an ancient legend has taken place. This is the description of the Patu-pai-a-rehe as given to the late Sir Geo. Grey by the Waikato people : "The fairies are a numerous people, merry, cheerful and always singing, like crickets. Their appearance is that of human beings, nearly resembling an European ; their hair being very fair, and so is their skin. They are very different from the Maoris, they do not resemble them." * It is said of them that their music, as they played their flutes, was very pleasing. Although called fairies by Europeans it is obvious the Maori tradition considered them as a people, not exactly like themselves, but still human—indeed much the same as they considered white people when they first came in contact with them.

The Maori tradition is that their ancestors learnt the art of making fishing-nets from the Turehu people. Obviously this indicates that there was a time when the Polynesian ancestors did not know much of salt-water fishing—very naturally so, if our supposition is right that they sprung from the inland Aryans ; and the race they learnt the art from must have been a sea-faring people. The Maori

* In a note to be found under the Maori text, Sir G. Grey adds, " Upon the 27th October, 1853, Te Wherowhero (head chief of Waikato, afterwards the first Maori king) described the fairies as a white race, elegantly clothed in garments quite unknown to the natives, and as delighting in music."

tradition states that a man named Kahukura first learnt this art from
the Turehu, and it is suggested that he is identical with the Kahukura who introduced the *kumara* to the knowledge of his people. If
so, this would be some time in the fifth century B.C., when Kahukura
flourished.

Kahukura is also a name for the rainbow, and when this appears
as a double one, the upper bow is said to be a male, the lower a
female.

But the question arises, what white, or fair race, this could be ?
The Aryan records mention more than one fair race, and Mr. Hewitt[*]
seems to consider that branch of the Aryans (or perhaps one of the
northern races, it is not clear which) called Chamar, connected with
the Yadu Turvasu (who lived on the banks of the Indus) to be an
early migration of fair people into India. He says (p. 217) . . . .
"connects them with the very ancient immigrant race of India, the
beardless Charmars . . . . . p. 219 . . . . . in Chuttisgurh, where I knew
them best, by their fair skins and the beauty of their women."
Another fair people was the Pāndyas or Pandavas. The same author
says of them (p. 40), "The Pāndyas or fair (*pandu*) men . . . . Their
father star, Canopus, controls the tides in Hindu astronomy by
drinking up the waters of the ocean . . . . ." which quotation also
illustrates a Maori belief, to the effect that a monster named Parata
causes the tides by the inhalation and exhalation of his breath—
identical with the Pāndyas' belief. It was these Pāndya people who
held the state of Madura, which (says Sir W. W. Hunter, loc. cit.,
p. 127) was founded in the fourth century B.C. So far as can be made
out these Pāndya people are not Aryans, but rather a northern people
living among the Dravidians of the south of India, along the coasts,
Madura being not far from the south extremity of India (Cape
Comorin). These people apparently were the earliest navigators and
traders of the Indian seas, obtaining the timbers for their craft from
the west coast of India, where the forests formerly came down to the
waters edge. It is these Pāndyas or Pandavas, the *pandu*, fair people,
that possibly are those from whom the Polynesians learnt the art
of making fishing nets and, no doubt, the art of sea-faring, which in
the end they so developed as to carry them all over the Pacific. It
may possibly turn out that in the word *pandu*, we have the first part
of the name Patu-pai-a-rehe, a word to which we can otherwise give
no meaning, though *patu*, in Niuē Island means a chief, with more
probability derived from *whatu*, also meaning a chief.

There is also another possible, though not perhaps probable, white
race, that might be that of Maori tradition, that frequented the
southern shores of India in very ancient times. In "Journal Royal

----

[*] "The Myth Making Age," p. 215 ff.

Anthropological Institute," Vol. XLVIII., p. 176, H. J. Fleure and L. Winstanley say, ". . . we may note that the Milesians (Gaels) are said to have visited Taparobane (Ceylon), India, Asia, etc." This appears to have been long before Christ, and if these Gaels reached Taprobane, a port in the Straits dividing Ceylon from India, they might easily have come in contact with our Proto-Aryans. Our authors do not indicate how the Gaels reached that part of the world.

Mention of the monster Parata above, reminds one of the belief of an old friend, long since dead, who had deeply studied Maori traditions, to the effect that the "Waha-o-te-Parata," said to be a maelstrom in the ocean, is situated near the mouth of the Persian Gulf, where he had noticed the turbulence of the currents in former times. It is this "mouth-of-the-Parata" that is supposed to influence the tides, as does Canopus who drinks up the water according to the Pandava belief. One naturally wonders whether the Maori name Parata is associated with Bharata, the name of the original Dravidian people of India, and of the country.

Such a large number of notes have accumulated on the subject of "Aryan and Polynesian points of contact," that they must be deferred to another occasion.

TRADITIONS OF AND NOTES ON THE PAUMOTU (OR TUAMOTU) ISLANDS.

Collected by the Rev. Père Hervé Audran, of Fakahiva, Paumotu Islands.

TRANSLATED FROM THE FRENCH BY R. H. ROCKEL, M. A.

PART IV.

A GLORIOUS EPISODE IN THE LIFE OF MOEAVA.

[In the following legend Père Audran furnishes us with some of the adventures of the Paumotu chief Moeava. It is interesting to note that the Rarotongan Traditions bear witness to the existence of this man, and from them we are able to deduce an approximate date at which he flourished. First, we may note that Moeava's canoe named "Murihenua," is known to the Rarotongan's under the variant "Muri-enua," which formed part of the fleet of the chief Naea which "came from Avaiki (Hawaii) to Iva (Marquesas) and from Iva to Tahiti and thence to Rarotonga. This was before the time of Tangiia and Karika." (See "Hawaiki," 3rd Edition, page 274.) The period of Tangiia and Karika of Rarotonga has been fixed tentatively as the middle of the 13th century.

Next we have in the following paper a reference to Hono'ura—or as the Rarotongan call him Ouokura—whom, we may infer from the text, lived before or at the time of Moeava, and this will agree with the Rarotongan genealogies, for Onokura lived five generations before Tangiia, mentioned above.

In the Rarotongan account of Onokura, which describes his voyage from Tahiti by way of Takaau and Te Pukamaru to the Marquesas, we find that at the latter island he came across Te Ika-Moeava who is probably the hero of the following Paumotu account. Onokura found at Te Pukamaru a Marquesan chief named Ngarue with whom some fighting occurred, ending in a peace-making, and then the latter accompanied Onokura to the Marquesas. During the fighting the high chief Tangiia-ariki of Tahiti was killed, and in revenge Onokura, with his magic sling, sent a stone with such force that Ngarue's canoe was smashed. In one of the thirty-nine songs that illustrate Onokura's adventures, we find Te Ika-moeava referred to as Moeava, which seems to identify the former with the Paumotu hero. The song is a long one, but this is the reference referred to :—

> Tangi ua maira i te pāŭ mei tai e—
> Rai ka tari ki o Rongo, ka tari ki o Rongo,
> Nga kai a Moeava, kia katoatoa rei iri . . . . .
>
> The drums are sounding from seaward,
> Prepare a great offering to (the god) Rongo,
> Take all the food of Moeava as offerings . . . . .

If we are right in identifying these two individuals, it follows that the period of Moeava is about the year 1125 A.D.—EDITOR.*]

A REMARKABLE COMBAT BETWEEN MOEAVA AND PATIRA
AT MAKEMO.

A BOLD and brilliant action, which had Makemo Island for its scene, spread the renown of Moeava throughout the whole of Eastern Polynesia. The memory of this action is deeply graven in the minds of the natives, who still speak of it with pride, and make it their boast.

Moeava, as is well-known, sailing in his "Murihenua,"[1] made constant journeys throughout the Tuamotu Group, traversing the islands in all directions. One day, while sailing off Kaukura, he happened to meet another traveller, who was a stranger to him. According to the custom in such circumstances, the two challenged each other. Moeava asked the new comer into these parts: "*O vai to ia vaka i taku tara nei?*" (What is that boat which is lying thus beside me?)

In a loud and sonorous voice the stranger replied: "It is Patira whom you see."

Patira was a famous *kaito*, a warrior cast in the same mould as Moeava. His fame no longer required to be made; as it represented him as one of the greatest champions of the isles beyond Tahiti. According to tradition, he had sprung from the great host of Marama. ("*No roto mai oia i te tini raki o Marama.*") The ancient and famous territory of Marama was, it seems, in the Cook Islands or in the islands to the leeward, if not still further off. Between Tahiti and Ra'iatea is "*Te miti o Marama*" (the sea of Marama). In the South Island of New Zealand (Te Wai Pounamu) on the east coast between Okarito and Orepuke is a district bearing the name of Marama. May not this *tini* spring from here? † Patira, who sprang from it, was a valiant warrior of collossal stature. The story goes that, with one of his ordinary steps, he strode easily from island to island, and that he could, without a boat, go the round of all the different islands of our archipelagoes, at his own sweet will.

Prompted by curiosity Moeava proceeded with his questions: "Where are you going?" he asked Patira. The latter replied enigmatically, "*Te tere ana vau i te kwrikuri o te huraro.*" (I am

---

* Readers must remember that the Paumotu dialect always has the letter "n" before the "g," thus, "the tribe of the Goio" must be read "the tribe of the Ngoio."—EDITOR.

† We do not think this likely. It is much more probable that Patira came from "the sea of Marama," i.e., Ra'iatea, etc., or from the island Whiti-marama, said to have sunk out of sight at the present time, and which tradition says was to the east of Tahiti.—EDITOR.

following up the pleasant scent of a "*huraro*," by which I am attracted.) By this figure he meant to typify Huarei.

"Where is this *huraro*?" inquired Moeava.

"It is at Te Pukamaruia," answered Patira carelessly, without even suspecting that by all these words he was rousing the feelings of his interlocutor.

Thereupon Moeava retorted drily, "This *huraro tuiragapua* belongs to me. It is already the property of Moeava."

On one of his previous voyages he had been betrothed to Huarei. Patira, on his part, had heard that Huarei was a fair and peerless maiden. Her fame had spread even to Marama. But he wished to satisfy himself by personal experience, and for that reason was going to pay her a visit.

With one stride Patira was alongside the "Murihenua," almost touching her. Thereupon Moeava, already greatly excited, cried out as loudly as he could: "Off . . . Keep off, or else you will have to do with the point of my Puanea!" Puanea was the name of his famous spear.[2] At this threat Patira drew off. But in spite of this justified warning of Moeava, Patira none the less continued on his way to Napuka. On his arrival at this island he managed to obtain an interview with Huarei. She was in very deed a fair and beauteous maiden. If ever there was a Polynesian beauty, she was one. Assuredly she had not her equal in all the surrounding isles. Her beauteous eyes were clear as crystal, her figure was tall and slender. Patira was completely charmed, and so, without more ado, he came straight to the point. At the end of his interview with her, in order to give her a convincing and tangible proof of his love, he stroked her cheek. Then addressing her he said, "Remain here at home in Te Pukamaruia; I am going away to look after my possessions, and in good time I shall return to Te Pukamaruia and marry you." So saying he departed homewards, utterly scorning the words which Moeava had spoken to him off Kaukura: "*E huraro tuiragapua Huarei na Moeava.*"

From this time on Huarei was the cause of their mutual bitterness, and a little later the cause of the tragic meeting at Makemo. Huarei had been betrothed to Moeava from her earliest childhood, and the bethrothal ceremony had taken place on Moeava's first voyage to Te Pukamaruia. If, therefore, she did not belong exclusively to Moeava, at least he had rights with respect to her, which Patira had not. Now, the latter, as we have seen, utterly ignored these.

The "Marihenua" continued, as usual, to furrow the seas of our archipelago, going to the right and to the left, venturing into such powerful currents as the Te Koihagaiti, Te Koihaganui, Te Maratuhakonokono, Te Marapoto, Te Mararoa, etc. Thus he reached almost the middle of the famous current Te Moemoe, situated in the narrow channel (*te gure*), which separates Napuka from Te Poto. While in this situation Moeava suddenly heard the plaintive cry of a bird. He immediately cried out, "*O vai ra teie i papaki i te tara o Murihenua?*" (What is it that is thus splashing against the side of the "Murihenua"?)

It was a small Rupe,[3] a kind of pigeon, which was making itself heard near the "Murihenua." As it flew away it repeated over and over again, "*O vau teie o Rupe i fano.*" (It is I, the Rupe, who am thus flying about). "I am the Rupe who bathes in the waters of Te Fanomaruia, on my island of Te Pukamaruia." Moeava on looking up saw that it was indeed a Rupe. Its cry revealed the beautiful voice of a maiden. He was perhaps mistaken about it. Moeava addressing it said, "*E Rupe e! e huraro tuiraga pua koe na Moeava.*" The gentle pigeon uttered its plaintive cry once or twice, then swiftly fleeing in a trice reached Te Pukamaruia, which was visible on the horizon. Upon this significant omen Moeava said to himself, "I shall go and see my little flower that is unfolding herself at Te Pukamaruia." Just at that moment the breeze sprang up, the sails of the "Murihenua" filled, and, in a short time, Moeava had the happiness of landing on the island he desired so much. Before landing and going to meet his beloved betrothed, Moeava composed the following *pehe* (or song) for the occasion :—

Ko vau ra ki to moe E aha e Rupe ! i fano mai Teie te Moemoe rihi e ?	It is I who am in this place. Why then hast thou, Rupe, had to fly thitherward over this terrible current of Moemoe ?

Ko vau ra, etc.

Natira (? Katira) te moe !
E aha ko vau ra ki Te Pukamaruia
    Kahopu, kapahakeo
E aha ko vau ra ki te vahine
    nui tapairu, Huarei
    te rihi ro mai i.
	Why am I at Te Pukamaruia ? 'Tis love ; 'tis the meeting. Why am I here, if 'tis not to see this charming Huarei, who this day is mine for good and all ?

E aha koti hoki manu iti te ipo tagi mai teie te kuriri tagi mai ra Ko vau ra ki Matiti maru, e ! Ko vau ra ki Matiti maru, e ! Kahopu, kapahake.	What dear birdling, Means thy plaintive song ? This is the *kuriri* which makes its voice heard. 'Tis I, the man of Matiti maru, Objects of my love and my desire.
E aha ko vau ra ki te toa uui, Moeava, te rihi ro atu u ; E aha koti hoki mapu iti to ipo tagi mai Teie te kuriri tagi mai o rau e ei ai i i e.	'Tis I Moeava, the great warrior, Who have just given up myself wholly. What is there then, dear little friend, To make thy calls understood ? 'Tis the *kuriri* that raises its voice.

Such was the *pehe* sung by Moeava before going on to embrace
his beloved Huarei, who dwelt hard by the *marae* of Ragihoa. With
her consent previously gained Moeava married her. The bride was a
direct descendant of Maruia, the first queen of Napuka. Consequently
she was herself, it is said, queen of Te Pukamaruia, Te Poto-nui and
Mahina-te-Tahora. Soon she gave birth to a beautiful little boy,
whom his father called Kehauri. While giving him this name
Moeava addressed to him the following words : " *O tei toe ia'u nei na
oe ia e amu, e ia pau roa.*" "All that I shall have left you will devour,
you will finish."

Kehauri was endowed with a fresh, ruddy complexion, which
earned for him the nickname of "O-ura-noa" (the ever burning).
From his birth up to early manhood he scarcely ever left his father's
side. As soon as his son had fully attained his manhood, Moeava
armed him in knightly fashion with a strong and beautiful spear
named "Pakekerua-ki-te-rangi." It was this famous spear which
dealt the death-blow to the numerous host of Muta, and to the others
who accompanied him. Thus did it avenge the death of Tagihia and
his brothers.

Now, Patira at the time previously arranged, put his plan into
execution, and came to seek Huarei at Te Pukamaruia. Several
years after their marriage Moeava had taken his wife back to this
island, and had left her there with her relatives during one of his
voyages round the group. Patira therefore found Huarei all alone.
In vain did she remonstrate and use every means to dissuade him
from his intention to carry her off. Amongst other words she said :
"Is it possible that you do not know the *toa* (valiant and powerful)
Moeava ?" Patira pretended not to know him. "No," said he, " I
do not know him." "What!" said Huarei greatly puzzled, "You
do not know Moeava, the hero, the champion of Vahitu,[4] of the tribe
of the Goio-Tuarehu, who hovers with swift flight in the clouds of the
North ?" Patira persisted all the more, constantly repeating, "No,
I do not know him, but what I do know is that I myself am champion
in Marama, in the tribe of Tokorega." So saying he seized Huarei
in his arms, by force, and carried her across the seas.

At that time Moeava was also on the high seas, and by a happy
chance one day saw Patira crossing at a single stride the channel
separating Napuka from Katiu, and holding in his grip the
unfortunate and beloved Huarei more dead than alive. Immediately
the blood rushed to his head, and he was seized by a frenzy of rage.
To glut his vengeance Moeava then and there challenged Patira to
single combat. "*E ho atu ta taua tamaki i Makemo i te tahua e roa.*"
(Come, let us settle our quarrel at Makemo-roa-hua.) The wrath of
Moeava knew no bounds, while Patira was quite willing to accept the

challenge. It was therefore arranged that the encounter should take place on a fixed date in Makemo, at a place named Te Pohue.[5] As a matter of fact, there was in this spot an arena eminently suitable for jousts and challenges of this kind. The two antagonists were almost equal in strength and skill, while they both enjoyed great renown in their respective islands. At the time appointed, true to their engagement, they arrived at the place of combat. In spite of Patira's rapid means of travel, his antagonist, however, reached the island several days before him. As Moeava was sailing along keeping a sharp lookout on the channel between Katiu and Makemo, he suddenly saw Patira plant one foot on Te Pana. The former was just then in the place called Raumati, while the other foot of the latter was still in the sea of Gatika. On seeing his foe Moeava immediately seized his magic belt, "Manava-apoapo," and put it on. Without delay he tore from the ground a kind of liana, correctly known by the name of *pohue*, plaited it into a solid cord and made a sling of it. Into this sling he placed a hard, smooth stone called, "Amiomio-i-te-ragi," [6] brought in olden times from Tahiti, according to tradition, by Hono-ura, who left it at Te Poto on the death of Toarere, a Marquesan *toa*, whom he had conquered.

Moeava, sling ready in hand, stood erect on the islet of Raumati, scanning with well-skilled eye the horizon from North to South to detect the arrival of his foe Patira. Suddenly he saw a foot planted on Ororia. Then Moeava, in order not to neglect his good custom raised his war-song.

It is a prayer to the god Tu.

<table>
<tr><td>

Ka hohora i tai eki te heiva
E Tu e, e rorei o,
E Tu e, rorogoi ai te matai
  Ka hohora i tai eki te heiva
  E Tu e, e rorei o,
  E Tu e, rorogoi ai te matai.
    rau e—i—ai—i—i—e.

</td><td>

O Tu, come to the combat on the lagoon's marge. 'Tis calm, oh Tu, dead calm. Oh Tu, brave Tu, come and be present at the combat on the lagoon's marge. 'Tis calm, oh Tu, dead calm.

</td></tr>
<tr><td>

Ka hohora i tai eki te heiva
E Tu e, rorei o,
E Tu e, e rorogoi ai te matai
  kia hume. kia hume Moeava-
  Tukirima noho i ta ora e e;
  E Tu e; e roroi o;
E Tu e, rorogoi ai te matai kia
  heke mai ru; kia heke mai
  ruga e tupuna ra ko
Tapakia; E Tu e, e rorei o
E Tu e rorogoi ai te matai rau
  e—i—ai—i—i—e.

</td><td>

Come to the combat, Oh Tu, on the lagoon's marge. 'Tis calm, oh Tu, dead calm. Come protect and save from death Moeava. Oh Tu, calm reigns, dead calm. Come, call on my ancestor Tapakia. 'Tis calm, oh Tu, dead calm.

</td></tr>
</table>

No sooner had Moeava finished his *pehe* than he saw Patira bringing up his other leg. " Now," said he to himself, " is the time." He adjusted the stone in the sling, swung it backwards and forwards with ever increasing rapidity, and finally whirled it round his head as vigorously as possible. After manoeuvring thus for several minutes, he discharged the stone with remarkable accuracy.

Patira was struck fair in the forehead and killed on the spot. The stone after having struck Patira rebounded to Rehega, on the edge of the lagoon. The result was therefore fatal to Patira, and Moeava as conqueror was covered with glory from this fight, which has remained famous in the annals of the archipelago. A huge crowd of Paumotuans had gathered to be present at the combat, being anxious to learn the issue of a contest in which feeling ran so high. By a skilful and well calculated turn of his arm Moeava had overthrown with the first blow his gigantic and terrible adversary, who fell face downwards, stretched out at full length. While his head extended beyond the outer reef, to the north of the island in the direction of Taonga (Tautau), his feet remained bathed in the calm waters of the lagoon. The stone which dealt the fatal blow to Patira is still to be seen to-day at about a metre's depth, covered with a young growth of coral, in the clear water of the lagoon off Makemo.

At the fall of Patira there went up from the excited crowd of onlookers a mighty shout of joy, accompanied by endless cries of " Huro " and frantic applause. Moeava immediately rushed to his victim, and, spear in hand, ran along the full length of his body from foot to head, as though he were crossing a bridge, and with his mighty Puanea he cut off his head. With one hand he seized the head of Patira by the hair, and with the other he released his beloved Huarei from the grip of his vanquished foe. Both these he carried to the interior of the island, where he at once prepared the oven for his enemy. Patira's head he gave to Kehauri. Thus having satisfied his vengeance, he returned to Takapua in a happy frame of mind, taking with him his wife and son. He had never yet been parted from the latter.

It is clear, and there is not a shadow of doubt about the matter, that Huarei was the true and only cause of the strange combat between Moeava and Patira, the combat in which the latter was slain.

On the other hand the death of Patira was soon avenged by his fellow-countrymen, the numerous tribes from Marama, and especially that of Muta. They made an inroad upon Takaroa, and, not finding Moeava there, avenged themselves on his nephews, who had become his adopted sons.

Moeava, in turn, was not slow to exact vengeance for the deaths of Tagihia, Parepare and Rogotama, by capturing at Punaruku (Makemo) the host of Muta. It was certainly not jealousy on the part of Kehauri about the turtle's head, that caused the tragic death of Tagihia-ariki, and of his two brothers, as some have thought. As a matter of fact, Kahauri had no intercourse, still less any consanguinity, with these tribes from Marama. On the side of his father Moeava he was from Vahitu, of the tribe of Goio-Tuarehu, who originally came from Takapua and Haoroagai, and on his mother's side he belonged to the tribe of Gati-Hopu (Napuka).

Later on, after the conversion of the natives to Christianity, and after they had gained a knowledge of the Bible, they did not fail to compare the strange combat between Moeava and Patira with that between David and Goliath. There is indeed a striking resemblance between the two.

NOTES.

1. The following is a brief description of this canoe :—
    The outrigger was called Oheohe
    The bow " kiato " was called Hotutaihenuku
    The stern " kiato " was called Paratito
    The steering paddle was called Taripo
    The mast was called Tiriatofa
    The sail was called Kukuti ki te ragi
    The forward thwart was called Kifakatakuariki
    The aft thwart was called Tearokaharia
    The end of the mast was called Kifaretataha
    The extreme end of the sail was called Kitaiomere
    The " tatakoto " (boom of sail) was called Tiriakoukou
    The extreme end of the " tatakoto " was called Fani
    The forward cabin was called Te piha tuanaki

2. The spear in Polynesian lands is the emblem of worth and courage. The spear of Parepare was called Te Arovaru, and that of Rogotama, Terefa.

3. I am informed that this bird was at one time found at Te Poto. To-day it is found nowhere except at Makatea ; elsewhere it is unknown in the Tuamotu Group.

4. Vahitu, of which Tufaruia was king, is the ancient name of the second group lying to the West of the Tuamotu. It comprised the following nine islands : Aho, Manihi, Takaroa, Takapoto, Tikei, Taiaro, Aratika, Kauehu, Raruka.

5. Tahua was the name of this region of the island, and its king was Manumea. The *marae* was called Te Utuga, the lagoon in this place Waihunu, and the *tahora*, o Taganini ia.

6. According to Piritua, the present chief of Makemo, the name of this stone was " *Pohatu taka i marama*."

7. Tu was one of the gods of Moeava. But his chief divinity was the god Tagigorigo. For Tu see Mangarevan-French Dictionary, p. 111, under Tu, and also this " Journal," Vol. XXVII., p. 124.

THE SAN CRISTOVAL *HEO.*

By the Rev. C. E. Fox of San Cristoval.

THOUGH the island of San Cristoval is not large—about eighty miles long and twenty miles broad—and has now only a population of about 8000, a great many methods of disposal of the dead are found on it. More than twenty different methods are known to me, but some of these differ little from one another. Burial on the *heo* is only one of these.

The following sketch of the *heo* at Ubuna is by a native, and I have not seen this particular one.

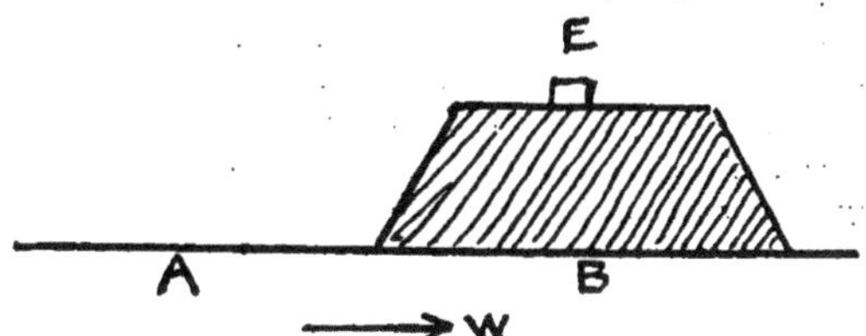

(a) *Hera,* an open space ; usually the name for the village burial place, also for the open square of the village.

(b) *Heo,* of earth and stones.

(c) *Hau suru,* a stone receptacle for the bones of the dead, made of five large stones, forming the four sides and top.

The *heo* (of which there are many score) are not usually large, the largest being perhaps twenty feet high and thirty feet square. Two large ones were lately levelled at Wango, and the bones, of which there were a great number, removed. All these bones showed burial in the horizontal extended position.

The *heo* sometimes belonged to particular families of chiefs, and so far as I know at present only people of the chief's clan were buried on them. A hollow was made on the top of the *heo,* and in this hollow a platform, on which the dead man was laid, bound up in pandanus mats. The corpse was then taken at frequent intervals to running water ; it was carried pick-a-back by a man called "the keeper of the dead "; when he reached the stream he crouched down, with the dead man still on his shoulder, and water was poured over the corpse from the stream, after which it was carried back to the *heo*. " The keeper of the dead " had a very unpleasant time and usually could not eat for some days, and did not speak until then. His head was protected by a native bag. In some parts, however, water was brought to the *heo* and there poured over the corpse, till the flesh came away, when the bones were buried on the *heo*, or put in the *hau suru* (all the *heo* did not possess a *hau suru*). Over the platform on the *heo* a roof of sago palm thatch was made.

The *heo* are found all over the western part of the island from Wango on the north coast round to Makira Harbour on the south coast. They are usually of earth, flanked with stones, and the ones I have seen are more or less rounded, with flat tops, oblong in shape, but hardly suggesting a pyramid, as the sketch does.

It seems to me that the *masitawa* of Haununu on the south coast (to the east of the district where the *heo* are found) throw light on the *heo*. The *masitawa* (a word that in neighbouring parts means boat harbour) are the burial places of that part—circular cleared spaces. Common people are buried round the circumference, facing outwards, lying horizontally. Chiefs are buried in the centre of the *masitawa*, usually at least facing east (a very unusual position in other parts of the island). A hollow is made about thirty or forty feet long and twenty feet broad and in this a house is built, rather different, however, from an ordinary native house, as two poles are fixed crosswise at each end x—x, a ridge pole placed on top, and sloping sides and ends of sago palm added, like a sago palm tent. An opening is left, so that the jawbone of the chief may be taken when the body on the platform, within the house, decays. The whole is then covered over with earth, and large stones placed along the sides. After a time the whole falls in making a broad, low mound, only a few inches high, flanked by stones, and such are the only *masitawa* I have yet seen, in each of which only one chief was buried; but if, as I am told is the case, a number of chiefs are buried in succession in the same *masitawa*, one would expect a mound similar to the western *heo* to be the result.

The *masitawa* themselves seem to be modifications of the burial places inland, which are circular cleared spaces, of about the same size; but in these a sacred tree is found in the centre instead of the chief's mound, and the dead are buried fairly deep, in a sitting position, securely tied, in concentric circles facing the sacred tree, which is called " the village of the dead."

The *heo* of the western district differ from the *masitawa* mounds, in that they are always at the west end of the *hera*, which is not circular like the *masitawa*, but oblong.

The chief other methods of disposal of the dead, on San Cristoval, are : (1) burial in the sea in either upright or sitting position, (2) cremation, (3) laying out in extended position in large bowls or on platforms till the flesh decays, (4) embalming in canoes called "the canoe of the sky," (5) laying out on crags and pinnacles of rocks along the coast, in extended position, (6) partial burial up to waist in upright position.   But there are many modifications of these different methods.

The note on the *heo* and *masitawa* must be considered as preliminary only, as I have not yet sufficiently examined them.

TRADITIONS AND LEGENDS.

COLLECTED FROM THE NATIVES OF MURIHIKU.
(SOUTHLAND, NEW ZEALAND.)

By H. BEATTIE.

PART IX.

Continued from Volume XXVII., page 137.

IN gathering the material for these articles the Collector has secured a large number of notes which, while meagre in themselves, are yet worthy of record both because of their intrinsic value and because they may put historians on the track of further information.

These notes are herewith presented.

FIRST FIRES.

In an old exercise book (of which the first page had most unfortunately been torn out and lost) on page 2, there were the following two notes :—" *Na Pou i whakaka te ahi ki Tawhiti-nui, ko Pou-tama-nui te kauati ;* " and " *Na Tura i whaka (? whakaka) te ahi ki Tawhiti-nui-a-Rua ; ko Mata-aitu te kauati ; ko Tauira-o-hua te tamaiti a Tura.*"

These notes signify that Pou was the man who first lit a fire in the land called Tawhiti-nui, and that the name of his firestick was Poutamanui; and that Tura was the first man who lit a fire in the land called Tawhiti-nui-a-Rua, his firestick being named Mata-aitu, and his son was Tauira-o-Hua.

Mr. S. Percy Smith supplies the following :—" Pou is supposed to have been carried away to Tahiti by a big *taniwha*, and a bird brought him back. The Tawhiti-nui mentioned is probably the island of Borneo while Tawhiti-nui-a-Rua is Tahiti Island. Rua after whom it is named lived there—he is known traditionally to the present Tahitians."

The collector asked Tare te Maiharoa regarding the islands known to the Maoris and who lit the first fires on them, but he replied he had never memorised the list. The first page of the manuscript book, which had been lost, had contained a list of the islands and the first

men to build hearths on them. There was not room to write all on
the one page so two entries had been placed at the top of the second
page. This page has been preserved; the other went astray many
years ago and no one can now recite the list. This is the tragedy of
this information not having been collected thirty or forty years ago.
(My informant added he did not know the name of Pou's canoe, but
Tura went from one land to the other on a rainbow, whose particular
name he forgot.*)

AN ANCIENT KARAKIA

The following is a very ancient *karakia*, but the collector has no
particulars of its origin or use :—

> Mo Raki
> Kia Tuhaha
> Kia Tumoremore
> Kia Tu Tahaka
> Kia Tu Koauanake
> Ko Te Kapua
> Ko Te Mihaia

CREATION OF MAN.

One or two of the Waitaha genealogies, copied by the collector,
were prefaced by the following remarks—"A genealogical account
of the descendants of Tāne who created man from the earth. Tiki
was the first, and the second created by the same process was Io, a
female, whom Tāne gave as a wife to Tiki, and they 'poured out'
mankind and filled the earth."

One of my informants said :—"Tāne, the god, at the beginning
of the world, married Hine-ti-tama and had two sons named Tahu-
kumea and Tahu-whakairo. When these two died Tāne went to
another land and there he created mankind, Tiki being the first man,
and Io the first woman. Tāne altogether had seven wives of whom
six bore issue. From the third wife, named Hotupapa, there is a
very long *whakapapa* which comes down to the Kati-Mamoe tribe,
but I cannot repeat it. From the fifth wife of Raki (? Tane) the
descent comes down to Matiti and the Waitaha tribe. The men of
knowledge among the Maoris forty or fifty years ago could have
recited all those things but they are now forgotten."

A CELEBRATED AXE.

In a notebook written by Wi Pokuku in 1880, occurs the following
karakia accompanied by a short account concerning the axe used by the

---

* Tura is a well-known ancestor of the Maoris and flourished in the time of
Whiro, or twenty-six generations ago. Apparently he lived in either Ra'iatea or
Porapora Islands of the Society Group.—EDITOR.

famous Rata to fell the tree for his canoe.   The name of the axe was
' Aumapu,' and its *karakia* was :—

E amo te toki e aku tauka
E wa (? waha) ki te tumu o te rakau e,
E aku tauka ko 'Aumapu ' ma te toki
E uru taku loki e uru ki tokerau
E aka taku toki e aka ki te uru o te ra
E tua taku toki e tua ki te uru o te tonga
E tere taku toki e tere ki te ua o te raki
   Tere taku toki e, tere taku toki
   Tere taku toki e, tere taku toki
Uruuru atu taku toki ki te tua o te ra
   Tere taku toki e, tere taku toki
   Tere taku toki e, tere taku toki.

*Koia nei te karakia o taua toki, o ' Aumapu,' kia mohio ka takata ko
te toki nana a ' Takitimu' i tarai ko ' Aumapu,' i a Rata tena toki e
takoto ana, na Kahue i tuku mai ki a Rata.   Ko Rata ki te tapahi i taua
rakau nei, te ra kei te whawhai a Ruru, mahara ki to te moana takata.
Ka mate a Ruru ka whakarauoratia e Rata a Ruru, no muri mai ka
haere a Rata ki te kimi rakau hei waka mo ona kai kaki i te mate o tona
hakoro, o Wahieroa.*

Notes.—Rata according to the tables in "Memoirs of the Polynesian Society," Volume IV., lived 39 generations ago. (See page
234—the table facing page 120 is numbered eight too many right
through, and makes Tamatea 30 generations ago instead of 22).   He
(Rata) was the contemporary of Kupe and Ngahue.   When
Rata wished to fell a tree to make a canoe to go in search of the
people of Matuku who had killed his father, Wahieroa, he went to
Ngahue (or Kahue) and asked for an axe.   Ngahue broke a slab of
stone and made three axes—one for himself named ' Kapakitua,' one
for Kupe named ' Tauira-a-pa,' and one for Rata called ' Te-papa-
ariari.'   Rata sharpened his axehead, put a handle on it, and named
it 'Aumapu.'   (White's "Ancient History of the Maori," Vol. 1, p.
74, gives this name as ' Mapu-naiere.')   With this axe Rata went into
the forest to cut a tree—one of the most frequently told incidents in
Maori history.

RATA AND RURU.

In all the many versions of the story of Rata the collector has
never noticed the name of Ruru, except in the fragmentary account
given by Wi Pokuku just recorded.

Asking after Ruru, the collector was told that Ruru was the king
of the small bush birds, even as Totara is king of the forest trees.   In
the days of Rata the bush birds fought the sea birds, and were defeated
and fled into the bush.   Rata saved the life of their king Ruru, and

in return for this kindness the latter helped Rata to get a canoe.
Twice the tree that Rata had cut during the day was erected during
the night by the small birds and the leaves of the forest. He watched
the third night and saw this done. Ruru appeared and told him the
reason the tree he had cut had been re-erected was because he had said
no *karakia* prior to his work. Ruru taught him the *karakia* to say and
told him to go home. In the morning he returned to find the bush
birds, under Ruru, had hollowed out a fine canoe for him. He named
the canoe 'Tarai-po' because it had been chipped out in one night.
This canoe was afterwards re-named 'Taki-timu' (in memory of the
stump of the tree from which it was cut), and voyaged about a good
deal. With the aid of Te-Tini-o-te-para-rakau people, Rata
accomplished his revenge on the Matuku people for the murder of his
father.

(Note.—The 'Taki-timu' canoe mentioned is evidently not the
famous one of the same name which came to New Zealand. The name
of the canoe of Rata was also given to the collector as 'Niwaru.'
Another old man said, "Tinitini-o-te-pararakau are now the evil
spirits of the trees, and if you do not *karakia* to them will hinder your
tree-felling. They sometimes appeared as birds, and in this form they
helped Rata.")

[The story of Rata and the Ruru is well-known to the Rarotongans, and will
appear in great detail when the series of Rarotongan traditions are printed in
our pages. The scene of the story is laid in the Samoa Islands. A brief
account of Rata's adventures appeared in "Journal Polynesian Society,"
Vol. XXI., p. 61.—EDITOR.]

A CATALOGUE OF FIGHTS.

The collector came across two lists of fights compiled from
Kai-tahu and Kati-mamoe sources, and herewith presents the names
with such brief details as he could gather:—

1. **Te Kiore-mauhope,** fought in North Island. No details
available.

2. **Rauwhata** (North Island). Here Tu-kake-mauka and Te
Whatu-kaipapai were killed. They died without issue. They were
the sons of Tu-maikuku, by his wife Irakukuru, and were grandsons of
Hikaororoa and Urupa.

3. **Whata-roa** at Turaka (Poverty Bay). Rakatoatoa and
Manumai the only chiefs of the defeated side who got away, escaped
in the smoke. This fight is also known sometimes as Kai-whakaware.

4. **Te Kai-whakatari,** at Poverty Bay, is said to have been
fought over a dog. Kurawhaia an ancestor of Tu-te-kawa was killed
there.

5. **Te Kakihaua** fought in North Island. No details.

6. **Hikaororoa** fought in North Island. No details.

7. **Marukore** fought in North Island.   No details.

8. **Te Piki-tu-roa.**   Here Marukore was to be cooked, but his youngest brother Roko-pae-kawa put on Marukore's *piki* (plume), and took his place for the oven.   The plume stuck out of the oven (a bad omen) and the body did not cook properly so was cast away.   Hence the name Piki-tu-roa (long-standing plume).

9. **Te Kaihuka** (North Island).   Pito and Raukawa were killed here.

10. **Hukete.**   Here Huirapa and Te Maraeroa (brothers) were killed.   They were *tapapataka* (lying down) when killed.

11. **Tapapanui** (also called Tapapa-ruahine).   The Maori text is translated by Mr. S. Percy Smith as: " The deaths of Huirapa and Te Maraeroa were avenged by their younger brother Tahumata, and hence came the tribe Te-aitaka-o-Riti to this island in order that they might incorporate with Te-aitaka-o-Tapuiti and Waitaha tribes to save themselves (from extermination ?), but Waitaha would not consent; then turned on them and avenged (the deaths) in this island."

12. **Waipapa.**   Here Kai-Tahu beat Kati-Mamoe.   It is in Marlborough.   The Kati-Mamoe were caught unawares carrying loads of fern-root on their backs and were vanquished.

13. **Te-ika-a-Whaturoa.**   " Up Kaikoura way."   No details.

14. **Huriwai.**   Here Tuhuku the Kati-Kuri chief was killed by the Kati-Mamoe who won—it was a canoe fight.

15. **Pauariki** (also Pouariki).   The Kai-Tahu chief Tahu-tutua was killed here.

16. **Puhirau.**   Rakaimomona, a Kati-Mamoe chief and father of Tukiauau, was sitting with his back to the sun, sunning himself outside the Opokihi *pa*, when Manawa, a Kai-Tahu chief, from an adjacent cliff threw a spear, which killed him.

17. **Opokihi.**   Here Rakai-tauheke killed Popoia and Tarere, while Maru killed Te Puehu and Te Aweawe.   Rakai-tauheke was a man of gigantic strength and killed his *purua* (pair) with one blow of his *kauri* (a black stone weapon held like a *mere*).   The weapon not only killed the two victims but stuck in the *karaka* tree behind where it is said its embedded head can still be seen.   The Opokihi *pa* contained Kati-Kina, Rakitane and Kati-Mamoe people and fell before the invaders.

18. **Peketa.**   Kai-Tahu beat Kati-Mamoe.

19. **Te Pari-whakatau.**   Manawa was killed by Tukiauau, and honors were even.   The account briefly says " *te otika o te riri* " (the end of the war).   It is in the Kaikoura district.

20. **Teihoka** fought near Colac Bay.   Kati-Mamoe administered a decisive drubbing to Kai-Tahu and saved their tribal identity.

21. **Taupiri** was a *pa* on the northern side of the Hokanui Hills,

and was evacuated by the Kati-Mamoe before a Kai-Tahu *taua*. Some people were killed here at a later date.

22. Tarahau-kapiti (also known as Wai-taramea) was fought on the Five Rivers Plain. One old man said: "Kaweriri grabbed an old Kati-Mamoe chief Te Kairere, and also the latter's nephew Tu-te-makohu. He killed the uncle, but the nephew killed him. The heart of Te Kairere was roasted and eaten." Another said that though Te Kairere was killed he was doubtful if Kaweriri personally killed him, and although some of the hearts of the slain were eaten, he never heard that Te Kairere's was. The Kai-Tahu won the fight, but disheartened by the death of so many of their band (including Kaweriri their leader) they returned to Canterbury, and Tu-te-makohu dwelt peacefully at Otaupiri until his death.

23. Otauaki was fought in Westland. There were a few words in Maori against this name, and Mr. S. Percy Smith writes:—"This note is interesting as it gives the name of one whom we may call ' the warden of the marches.' The translation is: Tauaki gave birth to Hauaki who was the great chief of Patea. He was the ' shield ' against Poutini (i.e., the West Coast Maoris)." A further note, partially undecipherable, says that 'Te-aitaku-a-Riti' and 'Te-aitaka-a-Tapu-iti' had something to do with the fight. The collector was told that the people known as Patea were a combination of Rapu-wai and Kati-Mamoe. They were attacked by Kati-Mamoe from another part, led by Takai-waho, and were defeated, Hauaki being killed.

24. Hunoa. This was in the time of the Kaihuaka troubles on Banks Peninsula, but the collector has no details.

25. Kai-huaka ("eat relatives") is the name of a feud which occurred between sections of the Kai-Tahu tribe shortly before the White people came to Canterbury. The collector was told the name originated through the starving people in a *pa* eating each other's children, and again he was informed that in the fighting a number who were killed had their heads cut off, and the bodies were eaten by relatives unawares.

26. Kai-whareatua is said to be the name of a southern foray against the North Islanders in Te Rauparaha's time.

27. Taua-iti is the name of a raid made by the Kai-Tahu and Kati-Mamoe against the Kati-Toa in Marlborough.

28. Tau-whare-kura was a fight between Manuhune and Takapo in the lake district at a hill called Mt. Grey by the Europeans. Kati-Kuri built a fortification there, but the collector has no further details.

29. Oteihoka was a fairly recent fight in Canterbury. A section of a tribe known as Ohapuku was chased by a composite brigade of

Waitaha, Kati-Mamoe and Kai-Tahu descent to Te-Umu-kaha, and satisfaction obtained at the Harakeke-tau-toru *pa* there.

30. **Taiari.**   Here Tu-takahi-kura was killed by Tu-te-makohu.

31. **Ohinekete** on the Otago Peninsula, was where the Kai-Tahu chief Tane-whaka-toro-tika was killed by Te Maui, a Kati-Mamoe chief.

32. **Ohou** was a fight at the lake of that name. The notes briefly say, "Te Kaimutu was killed by Te Rakitauhopu," but the collector was told:—"Pohowera, a Kati-Mamoe chief, was killed by two Kai-Tahu chiefs Te Kaimutu and Tawhiriruru. Pohowera's son Te Rahitauhope (my informant was positive this name finished with an *e* not *u*) killed these two chiefs at Ohou in revenge. Then another *taua* went up there and Te Rakitauhope was killed by Kaunia."

33. **Katiki.**   "Te Matauira a famous Kai-Tahu chief was killed at Katiki (now known as Kartigi). He was told to say *karakia* before entering the *pa*. The war was caused by Taoka killing someone up North. Te Matauira was killed as follows: A man was running round a *whare*, and another man threw a spear over the house, and it landed on Te Matauira. Other killings followed this."

Notes.—This list of fights known in Southern history is not in chronological order by any means, and is very incomplete as the collector could name off-hand half-a-dozen fights that are not mentioned, and that were more important than many on the list. It is valuable, however, as it records several names that are new to the collector, and about which little appears to be known.

The collector has further notes to the effect that Hapai-ki-waho was killed at Rakaia by Tu-manihi and Tu-te-kaehe (?), and that his death was avenged by Hikatutae and Te Ariki (?), and that further fighting took place at Arowhenua where Taka-ahi and Hāpī were killed, but his notes require corroboration and extention. A further note states that the natives at Te Muka built a fortification at Wai-a-te-ruati when Te Rauparaha took Kaiapohia, but the collector has no further details of it. This was the last of the memoranda jotted down in the Maori notebooks and copied by the collector, but he has details of fights not mentioned in the list and not hitherto recorded and these will be given later.

MULTUM IN PARVO.

The collector has a large selection of miscellaneous jottings, a number of which he will give here with the hope that they may put those engaged in research work on the track of fresh information on some of these points:—

Pipiwharauroa.   This bird, "the shining cuckoo," is called Te-manu-a-Māui in Murihiku, because its song repeats some of the words sung by Māui when in the form of a bird on the handle of his father's *ko* (spade).

Te-Tau-a-Tarawhata was a canoe belonging to Waitai when the Kati-Kuri invaded the South Island. Waitai came down to Otago in this canoe, which was afterwards dashed to pieces at the foot of the lofty cliff now known as Te-tau-a-Tarawhata. The railway line north of Port Chalmers passes round this cliff.

Te-tatau-o-te-whare-o-Māui (the door of the house of Māui) is the Murihiku name for the insect known as Daddy-long-legs. The name has something to do with the story of Māui, but the collector could not ascertain what.

Uruuru-whenua. At the head of the Rakaia River near Mt. Somers is a sacred *tawai* (beech) tree standing by itself. It was used as an *uruuru-whenua*, and was reverently approached by the people who laid offerings of food and other things before it.

Papapuni. According to tradition Tukete, a chief at Rakiura (Stewart Island) was prodigiously fat. It is said he suffered from *papapuni*, a stoppage of the bowels that permitted nothing to pass through him. He was killed at the fall of the *pa* at Putatara.

Kauheke. Some of the men of old wore the *kauheke* or chaplets of ribbonwood. Chaplets were made of *toatoa* or celery-top pine. The wearing of this ornamentation was a *tohu rakatira* (a sign of chieftainship).

Te kai. In the south food was sometimes eaten only once a day, but as a general rule there were two meals a day, the morning one being called *kai-mo-te-ata*, and the afternoon one *kai-mo-te-ahi*.

Piopiotahi is the Maori name of Milford Sound. It is said it was called after a canoe which came from Hawaiki. Kahotea was the captain, and Tangiwai one of the crew, and these two names are now applied to different kinds of greenstone.

Herekopare is an island off Stewart Island. When the Waitaha first visited this locality they landed on the island, a chieftainess named Mahihi stepping ashore first. Prior to doing so she bound her hair-fillet, and the island out of courtesy to her was named "Te-hereka-o-te-kopare-o-Mahihi," now abbreviated into Herekopare. It is said there is on the island a hill with a mound on it which perpetuates the shape of her head and it is called Te Tihi ("the summit" or top).

Tamatea was the captain of 'Takitimu' and lived at Tarahaukapiti at the foot of Mt. Takitimu for a time. This was a *pa-kakari* of Waitaha. The *rua* (pit) was there where his people got the *karehu* (soot) for the *moko* (tattooing). "Te whakatakaka o te karehu o Tamatea" is a proverbial saying.

Tono te kararere [*sic*] was to send word by a messenger. Sometimes when not convenient to send anyone and the wind was in the right direction a quantity of dry toe-grass would be scraped and flattened into a hoop and let go to be carried by the wind to the other village. Such was the statement made to the collector.

Te Mu and Te Weka are two old names given to the pakeha. Matiaha Tiramorehu mentions them in his *Waiata* in the " forties."

Ruatapu is well-known in the south. The name of the canoe of which he drew the plug was 'Tu-te-pewha-raki,' and his club was named 'Kahutia-te-raki.' There is an extremely lengthy song about this affair. Extra big waves round the Murihiku coasts are. still called ' Ruatapu ' in memory of him.*

Kokopu is the New Zealand trout. There is a proverbial saying, " *Ko te kakopu te kai a Māui,*" but what originated it the collector cannot say.

Harakeke, the flax, was put to many uses, but probably none more novel than signalling. My informant said big white mats were made of it, and when visitors were leaving a *kaika*, or village, these mats would be spread out on a hill-side facing the next village to let people there know of and to expect the travellers. My informant cited the case of the *kaikas* at Tuturau and Hokanui, which had a regular system of this method of signalling.

Waiariki, or Waitapu, is said to have been the Maori name for the hot springs at Haumer. The Maoris went there for *matekohi* and other troubles, and it is said there was a special pool for those under *tapu*.

Matachu caused a great flood, said one of my informants, which nearly covered the South Island. It was before Rakai-hautu's time, and it had the effect of thinning out the Moas, which had been too numerous before then. It decimated them almost to the point of extinction.

Te-ahi-a-Ue is a name applied to lignite burning in the ground. Fires of this kind last many years, and have occurred at Te Muka, Waihao Downs, Pomahaka and elsewhere. The first fire of this sort was ignited by a man named Ue many centuries ago.

The Kumara was brought to New Zealand by the canoe ' Arai-te-uru,' which arrived at Whitiaka-te-ra (east coast of North Island), and landed some of its cargo. A storm arose, and it ran to Matakaea (Otago), where it was wrecked and its cargo turned into boulders, but the *kumaras* were not all lost as the Kahui-Roko people at Whitiaka-te-ra made good use of the ones landed there.

---

* Rather in memory of ' Te tai o Ruatapu,' a well-known flood (due probably to a hurricane) that took place in Rarotonga not long before the fleet sailed for New Zealand in about 1350, and of which Ruatapu gave warning.—EDITOR.

Whetu. Among the southern names for stars are two which the collector has not seen recorded by White, Tregear and others, and these are the constillations Kahuiwhetu and Whakarepu-karehu.

The collector still has an accumulation of material relative to southern history and folk-lore which has never been in print, and some of this will be given in the next instalment.

(To be continued.)

THE SCIENCE CONGRESS, CHRISTCHURCH, NEW ZEALAND.

(Communicated.)

———

THE Science Congress, which was opened at Christchurch in the first week of February, marks a new departure in the history of science in New Zealand; a departure which it is hoped will have considerable results as far as ethnology is concerned. The congress affords an opportunity which has never existed before of periodical meetings and discussions at intervals of two years. It is hoped that at future Congresses anthropology may be constituted into a separate section; at the Christchurch Congress it was included in Section D, General. Archdeacon Herbert Williams, M.A., was elected chairman of the section.

The only papers relating to Polynesian ethnology were those of Mr. H. D. Skinner on the material culture of the Moriors, and of Archdeacon Williams on the Moriori language.

In the former paper traditions preserved by Alexander Shand were quoted as showing that some, at any rate, of the Moriori ancestors came to the Chathams more than seven centuries ago from a land there was no difficulty in recognising as New Zealand. As the Chathams produced no trees large enough for canoes to be made from them, the Moriori claim to isolation might safely be allowed. The special interest of Moriori material culture lay in the light it threw on the history of Maori material culture and art. In the writer's opinion New Zealand, in pre-European times, was divided into two culture-regions whose boundaries coincided in a general way with those of the two islands. Between these two regions was a broad intermediate area where the two cultures blended. This division into two areas was based solely on the evidence of material culture and art, but it was believed that a considerable amount of evidence in support might in future be drawn from the study of Maori dialects, and perhaps from anthropometric investigations. Moriori material culture might be looked on as a fragment of the Southern Culture of New Zealand. In one or two respects—for example, the peculiar wash-through boat— it had developed features of the parent culture until, to a superficial view, they appeared entirely new. But even these could be traced to a New Zealand source, while in very many classes of manufactured article it was not possible to distinguish the Chatham Island article from that made in Otago. This was conclusive evidence that seven centuries ago, when the Morioris left New Zealand, the Southern Culture of New Zealand had developed most of the features it presented at the beginning of the nineteenth century; in other words, that the difference between the culture-regions in New Zealand was ancient. It seemed probable that future investigations would indicate a relationship between the Northern Culture and that of the Western Pacific, especially of the Solomons and the islands and coasts north-west of them. The Southern Culture seemed to find its nearest relationship in the material culture of Easter Island. It seemed probable that that culture had been obliterated in intermediate islands by later ethnic waves and by the influence of intercommunication.

Archdeacon Williams briefly sketched Moriori traditional history. Our knowledge of the language was due almost entirely to the late Alexander Shand, who published a series of papers in the "Journal of the Polynesian Society," and later compiled a vocabulary which it was hoped might shortly be published. A study of these materials revealed the fact that the language differed in grammar and vocabulary very greatly from the Maori language. Words were altered materially in form, and differed in meaning from their Maori cognates, while about ten per cent. were derived from roots no longer preserved in Maori. These foreign words exhibited relationships with the languages of the Marquesas, Tahiti, Samoa, Hawaii, Tikopia, Easter Island, Mangareva, Tonga, Uvea, Futuna and Rarotonga, the likeness being closest in the case of the Marquesas, and diminishing in that order. These divergences from Maori were the more important when it was remembered that the Moriori people had been under Maori dominance for over thirty years when Mr. Shand began his investigations. As it was the language was further removed from Maori than the dialects of Rarotonga, Tahiti, Uvea, Niue, and could not be designated, as formerly, as a mere sub-dialect of Maori. It could not, however, be claimed that the language afforded reliable positive indications of the original home of the Moriori, though it was remarkable that his investigation and that of Mr. Skinner, conducted independently, by different methods, and on wholly different material, should both point towards Eastern Polynesia.

NOTES AND QUERIES.

The Teaching of Ethnology.

Mr. H. D. Skinner, B.A., D.C.M., has been appointed lecturer in Ethnology at the University of Otago, and assistant curator of the University Museum. During the session of 1919, au introductory series of lectures will be delivered by Dr. W. B. Benham, F.R.S., Dr. Benson, Mr. Skinner, and Dr. Dunlop. In the following session the syllabus for the Diploma in Anthropology will be put into operation. The Senate of the University of New Zealand has decided to institute a Diploma of Anthropology, and has asked the Otago committee to report on the syllabus.

PROCEEDINGS.

POLYNESIAN SOCIETY.

The Council met on the 26th March at the Hempton Rooms, when current business was conducted, including correspondence.

New Members:—

Mrs. Edith Nairn, Oteka, Havelock North.
Miss Olive Nairn, Oteka, Havelock North.
Charles Davis Lightband, New Plymouth.
Richard Ormsby, P.O. Box 99, Te Kuiti.
Charles Arthur Budge, Stratford.

The following papers have been received:

Fakahina Island, Paumotu. By Rev. H. Audran.
History and Traditions of Rarotonga, part VI.
The Period of Hiro and Hono'ura. By A. Leverd.
The Fatherland of the Polynesians.
Rangi-hua-moa. By G. Graham.
The Science Congress, Christchurch.

The death of Mr. J. P. Cooke, of Honolulu, one of our members, was reported.

Enquiries were ordered to be made in England as to whether some early volumes of the "Journal" could be reproduced by the Anastatic process.

HISTORY AND TRADITIONS OF RAROTONGA.

BY TE ARIKI-TARA-ARE.

PART IV.

(Continued from Volume XXVII., page 198.)

[EVERYONE who has studied the "Rarotongan Traditions" in their relation to those of the New Zealand Maori, must acknowledge the close connection between these two branches of the Polynesian race, a connection which is further emphasized by their having ancestors in common, as has been shown more than once in the pages of this "Journal."

And yet it is somewhat surprising that the grand old epic of the New Zealand Maoris relating the birth of the gods as the offspring of the Sky-father (Rangi) and the Earth-mother (Papa), does not seem to have held the same important place in the beliefs of the Rarotongans. This is somewhat difficult to account for, as it is now fairly well established that many of the New Zealand Maoris and Rarotongans formed part of the second and probably largest migration into the Pacific from Indonesia, and which for convenience we use the Samoan term "Tonga-fiti." to distinguish it from the earliest migration (Samoan, Tongan, and some others), and from the third, which, so far as can at present be ascertained, was of much later date, and, while including the East Coast of New Zealand Maoris, it also assisted in peopling the Hawaiian Islands and Tahiti, before its members came on to New Zealand in the fourteenth century.

This is a question that might well occupy the attention of the younger generation of Polynesian scholars now gradually coming to the fore, but it means a vast amount of study. There can be little doubt that the belief in the origin of all living things originating from the Sky-father and Earth-mother, was the primary belief of the Aryan-speaking people of India, dating probably from times antecedent to their migration into India, that is, in the times of the Proto-Aryans, so called—for which see *inter alia*, Ragozin's "Vedic India," p. 136, and Dr. A. K. Newman's "Who are the Maoris?" p. 161, "Myth, Ritual and Religion," by A. Lang, and many other works.

The question is too large a one to be dealt with here; but what follows may help to throw some light on it. In the 194 pages of closely written MSS. obtained in Rarotonga in 1897, being the teachings of Te Ariki-tara-are (said by Dr. Wyatt Gill to be the last of the high-priests of Rarotonga), the tradition given below is the only thing that approaches the Rangi and Papa story of the New Zealand Maoris, and as compared with the full detail in the records of the latter people, expressed in the teaching of the Maori College (see our "Memoirs," Vol. III.), it will be acknowledged to be a greatly attenuated account.

First of all we note that the Maori name of the Sky-father (Rangi) is not used with the Rarotongans. Te Tumu appears to represent Rangi, whilst the Earth-mother is Papa in both accounts. Among the many meanings of *tumu* in Rarotonga, is that of "the stem," "the foundation," whilst in Maori combination (*tumuaki*) it means "the crown of the head," "the chief," and as *tumu-rae* a supreme chief or king. We may translate the word as "the original being," and is, in that sense, a god like Rangi. Papa (the Earth-mother) means "broad," "flat," as does Prithivi, the Sanskrit name of the Earth-mother. The Hawaiian name for the first man was Kumu-honua, in which *Kumu* is their form of *tumu—honua* being the Maori *whenua*, land. In this we have the same idea of "original," or "stem" as in Rarotongan.

The Maori idea of the earth is that of a woman lying flat on her back with her head to the east.

It will be noticed that the Rarotongan Te Tumu is looked on as an *ariki* or chief—not as a god—and that the three eldest offspring of Te Tumu and Papa are quite unknown to the Maori account of the creation of the gods. From Mr. Savage's note their names are seen to be emblematical terms for the accompaniments of child-birth. Te Uira (M, *te uira*) means lightning; Te Aa (M, *Te Awha*) means a tempest; Te Kinakina (same in M) means a full belly. After the birth of these three come three of the well-known gods, Tane, Tu, and Tangaroa, common to the whole race.

The next name (Te Nga-taito-ariki) is very peculiar in that it includes in it both the singular (*te*) and plural (*nga*). I do not remember a similar case in any dialect of the Polynesian language; and suggest that Nga-Taito-ariki was the name of a tribe or people, rather than that of one person—like Nga-Puhi of the Maoris.

We are next told that certain priests of old, who appear to have flourished prior to the creation of man, searched the earth, and by "knocking" on the earth discovered man. This account seems somewhat to be the Rarotongan rendering of the Maori account of the search of the gods for the female, eventuating in one being formed of earth, who, by the god Tane, became the progenitor of mankind.

From Te Nga-taito-ariki, the genealogy decends down to Tangiia-nui, the great ancestor of the Rarotongans who flourished in the thirteenth century, 69 generations from the first named. But the account of him will be found in a separate part to follow.

A reference was made a few lines back to the belief of the Proto-Aryans in the origin of mankind from the Sky-father (Dyaus) and the Earth-mother (Prithivī). In Z. A. Ragozin's "Vedic India," p. 166, we find this belief fully referred to, and he says, "Numerous are the passages in which 'community of race'—kindred—is claimed with gods for men, explicitly, though in a general way : thus the verse, 'We have in common with you, O gods ! the quality of brothers in the mother's bosom," is fully explained by this other: 'Heaven (Dyaus) is my father, who bore me ; my mother is this wide earth (Prithivī).'"

Maori scholars will recognise in the last quotation a close approximation to a well-known form of Maori address. It was not etiquette among the Maoris to ask a stranger's name directly, but the following is the usual and polite way of ascertaining it. The one asks the other, "*Na wai taua ?*" (By whom are we two ?) The reply is, "*E ! Na Rangi raua ko Papa taua !*" (We two are descended from the Sky-father and the Earth-mother !) The first then says, "*Nau mai toku tuakana (or taina) ! Kowai to taua tupuna ?* (Welcome my elder (or younger) brother ! who was our common ancestor ?) And from the answer to this the relationship becomes known. It will be seen that this is almost the exact equivalent of the quotation from the Rig Vida, or most ancient traditions of the Indian-Aryan people.

The following is the original and the translation thereof from which the above notes have been made, the latter having been kindly supplied by Mr. S. Savage, of Rarotonga. It must be understood that this Part IV. is the commencement of the history of Tangiia-nui, hence the leading paragraph.]

A HISTORY OF TANGIIA-NUI.

TRANSLATED BY S. SAVAGE.

248. Tangiia, it is said, was a son of Pou-vananga-roa-ki-Iva, a son of Tupa and Oa-ariki, a son of Te Arutanga-nuku, a son of Te Maru-ariki, a son of Te Nga-taito, and a son of Te Tumu (i.e., he descended from those ancestors). (There was) a land named Avaiki-te-varinga-nui. Au *ariki* (thereof) named Te Tumu, took as his wife Papa, and by her begat their three eldest children, namely, Te Uira, Te Aa, and Te Kinakina (see note for explanation), and

afterwards came forth Rongo and Tane and Ruanuku and Tu and Tangaroa; these were the godly sons.

Then Te Nga-taito-ariki begat Atea, and Te Tupua-nui-o-Avaiki and Te Pupu and Ka'ukura, these were the *ariki* sons, the progenerators of all *ariki* lines. (This should read: Then were begotten Te Nga-taito-ariki and Te Tupua-nui-o-Avaiki and Te Pupu and Ka'ukura; these etc.)

249. Now concerning those who opened up Papa (that is to say those who discovered the secrets contained within Papa the Earth-mother) they were named Rua-kana-kui, Rukana-kura, Ruakana-era and Rua-kana-taunga, six all told; their parent was Te Veka-o-te-po, alias Tongaiti, alias Tumu-ngao. They were the ones who opened up Papa. The following is the method or manner by which they did it, as was taught to us :—They came through the land called Avaiki-te-varovaro, otherwise called Raro-pu-enua, and, behold, they heard mumurings below (within the earth). They listened, and from the sounds they heard came to the conclusion that the murmuring sounds came from a great number (of people). They said one to the other, " Whence come those sounds?" Then said Rua-taunga, "I know, those murmurings come from within Papa." " We shall see." Then some said, "O! those people are great!" Another said, " What shall we do so that we may see?" Then one exclaimed, "Go slowly. Now let us move along slowly and pat the surface of Papa above and below, in the front and behind, inland and seaward, and thus we may discover all." After they had searched all about (that is all over Papa (the earth)) they then commenced to knock on the earth, and made a great noise in doing so, and peered here and there intently until they came to a certain spot or place, and, behold, they saw from whence the sounds came. Hence they knew that they would eventually discover all the secrets contained within Papa.

250. They then recited in thunderous voice as follows :—

The Papa (earth) is growing up (asuming shape)
'Tis the Papa of Avaiki—
The Papa will stand up
It will grow—and night is born.
Then day is born—
Now it is heaving up—
Now it is subsiding—
Now we see Arii and Toro
'Tis growing thick—
'Tis growing solid
etc.

251. They looked, and, behold, what they did appeared to their minds to be good, and therefore they continued :—

O Papa (the earth) O ! the Papa will grow up
The earth will arrive at maturity
    ,,   ,,   ,,   become ripe
    ,,   ,,   ,,   grow in height
    ,,   ,,   ,,   bud and flourish
    ,,   ,,   ,,   bear leaves
    ,,   ,,   ,,   become upright
There will be many (people) in the east
    ,,   ,,   ,,   ,,   ,, west
    ,,   ,,   ,,   ,,   ,, south
    ,,   ,,   ,,   ,,   ,, north

252. The above were the proceedings of the company of priests towards Papa (the earth) by which they became priests, and everything that should concern the descendants of Te Tumu and Papa became known to them and justified their titles of priests (*taunga*).

[Explanatory note *re* portion of paragraph 248, which says: "And by her begat their three eldest children, namely, Te Uira, Te Aa, and Te Kinakina."

More-taunga-o-te-tini tells me that the meaning of this is as follows, which I give in his own words :—

"It is language that was used by the priests in reciting the ancient legends to the people, but it really meant a description of a woman giving birth to a child. Te Uira was the shooting pains experienced. Te Aa was the pressing by the woman with her hands to her back and sides when the labour pains were severe and the delivery of the child was about to take place. Te Kinakina was the breaking forth of the fluid prior to the birth of the infant, and then were born Rongo, Tane, etc.," but he says these are only a few of the children mentioned, there were many others.

Tangiia-nui—of whose history the above is the introductory part— was also a great high-priest. He taught in the Are-Vananga all the knowledge he obtained during his sojourn in Avaiki. His name as great high-priest was Te-ariki-tai-vananga-tara-keu-ki-te-rangi.

More-taunga-o-te-tini (Tamuera Terei) is a direct descendant of Ruakaua-kura, one of the priests named in paragraph 249, on his father's side.—S.S.]

E TUATUA NO TANGIIA-NUI.*

248.   E tamaiti a Tangiia-nui na Pou-vananga-roa-ki-Iva, e tamaiti na Tupa-ma-oa-ariki; e tamaiti na Te Ara-tanga-nuku; e tamaiti na Te Maru-ariki; e tamaiti na Te Nga-taito-ariki; e tamaiti na Te Tumu.

E enua ko Avaiki-te-varinga-nui; e ariki ko Te Tumu. Te Tumu ko noo i tana vaine—i a Papa; kua anau akera ana puke tamariki, tama mua tokotoru, ko Te Uira, ko Te Aa, ko Te Kinakina.

Kua mama mai i muri i reira ko Rongo, ko Tane, ko Rua-nuku, ko Tu, ko Tangaroa.   Ko te angai aitu ïa.

Kua anau maira ko Te Nga-taito-ariki, ko Atea, ko Te Tupua-nui-o-Avaiki, ko Te Pupū, ko Kau-kura.   Ko te angai ariki ïa.

NO TE ARONGA I KANAIA I TE PAPA.

249.   Ko Rua-kana-kui, e Rua-kana-tea, ko Rua-kana-kura, ko Rua-kana-uri, ko Rua-kana-ero, ko Rua-taunga. Tokoono ratou; ko Te Veka-o-te-po to ratou metua—ko Tonga-iti rai; koia a Tumu-ngaro. No ratou te papa i kana. Teia te tu e kite ei tatou e, na ratou i kana. Kua aere maira ra ratou, na roto i te kainga ra ko Avaiki-te-varovaro—koia a Raro-pu-enua. E ina! e mūmū teia i raro. Kua akarongo aere ua-o-rai ratou; "Teea ua teia mū?" Kua tuatua a Rua-taunga, "E, tei roto i a Papa!"   Kua na-ko-maira tetai aronga e, "O! e aronga tangata maata tena!" Kua na-ko-mai tetai, "Ka akapeea tatou e kite ei?"   Kua manono maira e tokotai, na-ko-maira, "Eia, ka aere ana tatou, ka pakipaki aere ana i o Papa nei, i arunga, i araro, i a mua, i a muri, i a uta, i a tai, kia kite tatou."   E oti akera ta ratou aaro aereanga i te Papa, kua topapa ratou i te papa i te paūūanga, e te maro, e te akeakeanga; kia tae ra ratou ki tetai ngai, kua kitea, te tangi paūū ua ra i tetai ngai.   Kua manako iora ratou e ka rauka.

250.   Kua rau-vanangananga iora ratou, ratou ua-o-rai, na-ko-akera :—

> Ka oi te Papa—
> Ko te papa ki Avaiki,
> Ko te Papa ka tu ki runga,
> Ka tupu, ka tumu te po,
> Ka tumu te ao,
> Ka eaau ki runga,
> Ka eaau ki raro,
> Ko Ari, ko Toro,
> Ka pararau-are,
> Ka patapata-tue,
> Ka matoru.

* Expressed in the Rarotonga dialect.

251. Kua akara iora ratou, e iua! kua tau meitaki ta ratou akonoanga; kua na-ko-akera ki te Papa :—

> E Papa e ! ka tupu te Papa,
> Ka metua te Papa,
> Ka pakari te Papa,
> Ka rito te Papa,
> Ka roa te Papa,
> Ka kao te Papa,
> Ka rau te Papa,
> Ka tia te Papa,
> Ka tini ki te itinga,
> Ka tiui ki te opunga,
> Ka tini ki Apatonga,
> Ka tiui ki Apatokerau.

252. Ko te au angaanga teia a te aronga taunga i rave i a Papa, i taka ai ratou e, e aronga taunga, ko te au mea te ka tupu i te uanga o TeTumu e Papa, i kitea puia ai ratou e, e taunga.

PART V.

DESCRIPTION OF THE FATHERLAND AND HISTORY OF THE TAMARUA FAMILY.

TRANSLATED BY S. PERCY SMITH.

[THE following, whilst professing to be the history of the Tamarua family of Rarotonga, whose residence is at Nga-Tangiia, on the east coast of the island, really gives the most detail concerning the Fatherland of the Polynesians to be found anywhere in the traditions of the people.

It is a strange story altogether, and describes how the gods assembled together with the chiefs and people to celebrate important functions. It was in this land of Atia-te-varinga-nui, that the Sky-father, Te Tumu, and the Earth-mother, Papa, created the gods and mankind (see part IV. hereof), and to this country in the west the spirits of the dead departed to their final home, in the same manner as the New Zealand Maori says his spirits of the dead went to the Fatherland, Hawaiki-nui, or Irihia (which latter name Mr. Elsdon Best suggests, with great probability, to be the same as Vrihia, an ancient name for India, or some part of that country).

In the book " Hawaiki," it was suggested that the name Atia-te-varinga might be translated " Atia-the-be-riced," from *vari*, a common name for rice in India and Indonesia ; and that meaning may still hold good; but other meanings of *varinga* have since come to our knowledge. In "Myths and Songs," Dr. W. Wyatt Gill, deriving his information from Mangaia Island, lying to the east of Rarotonga, says that *vari* means "the beginning"; and in Rarotonga itself *varinga* means "the very beginning," or "ancient." Either of these two latter names might be correct as implying the most ancient land the people were traditionally acquainted with. That is, if *vari* and *varinga* are not derivative words from *vari* (rice), to which the meaning "ancient" has been affixed in later times, in the same manner that the word *vavao* with the Samoans now means "ancient," though it probably was the name of one of the oldest countries that people were acquainted with, and which is retained in the traditions of other branches as that of an island. Dr. A. K. Newman traces *varinga* to the *waringa* or *waringin* tree, the sacred *Ficus religiosa* of India.*

The high-chief Tu-te-rangi-marama, who may be looked on as a king, is the great ancestor of the Rarotongans; and the building he erected called Koro-tuatini, was the place of assembly of gods and men in the Fatherland. The word means the "place of many enclosures," and being twelve fathoms high could scarcely be built of anything but stone—it was no doubt a temple; and the New Zealand Maoris, who have the same name, say it was identical with Te Whare-kura, the first and original house of learning at (or identical with) Te Hono-i-wairua, where the spirits of the dead gathered from the four quarters of the earth before departing, either to the supreme god Io in the twelfth heaven, or to Whiro, the evil spirit in Raro-henga—which we usually term Hades, though it was a very different place to the common acceptation of the meaning of that word.

The history says, "It was also in this land that originated the wars that caused them to spread to all the islands," which statement agrees exactly with the New Zealand Maori account of the cause of the exodus from the Fatherland.

At the fourteenth generation, or 350 years after the great chief Tu-te-rangi-marama, we come to Te Kura-a-moo, "who departed for the east and dwelt there" on account of troubles about some fishing matters. This appears to represent the New Zealand Maori account of the wars that originated through fishing rights in Tawhiti-roa, which has been tentatively identified with Sumatra, and from other legends these ancestors of Tamarua probably went on to Java, which is one of their Avaikis, while one of the New Zealand Maori branches went to Tawhiti-nui, tentatively identified with Borneo.

Sixteen generations (or 400 years or 750 years from Tu-te-rangi-marama) after Kura-a-moo, we come to Tamarua-metua of Avaiki

---

* "Who is the Maori?" p. 222.

(Java or Sumatra), and the statement is made that in his time "all Avaiki was broken up and scattered in small parties." This is a most important statement, for it seems to indicate—without stating the cause—the date at which this particular migration (the Tongafiti) became scattered and left Indonesia for the Pacific Islands, or perhaps moved on to some other parts of Indonesia, such as the Celebes, etc., and then commenced the exploration of the Pacific, whether at once, or after a more or less prolonged further stay in Indonesia, we have no means at present of determining.

For the use of future students it may be stated here how the date of this exodus from Avaiki (Java or Sumatra) is fixed. A reference to our "Memoirs," Vol. IV., p. 12, in the note at bottom of page, it is shown how the period of Tu-te-rangi-marama was determined by the mean of four descents from him to the year 1900, and the date B.C. 475 arrived at. Taking the two descents mentioned previously in this paper (350 and 400), we get 750 years, which deducted from B.C. 475, gives the year A.D. 225 for this "scattering of Avaiki."

The table given below in the original Rarotongan, from which these notes are compiled, does not agree at all with the four other Rarotongan tables which correspond in themselves very fairly, and are therefore used in preference to the table of descent given below. This latter table has always seemed to the writer to be open to question; firstly because it differs so wildly from all other known genealogies in length, and secondly because of the introduction of so many geographical names as those of ancestors—in this latter feature it is like the long Marquesan tables. It will be observed therein that there are fifteen Avaikis mentioned, and the question arises whether these are not really names of some of the Indonesian Islands, rather than ancestors' names?

In paragraph 525, we come across the celebrated navigator Ui-te-rangiora, whose name, however, does not enter into the genealogical tables of the Tamarua family; but it is to be found in the table at the end of the book "Hawaiki," and there he is shown to be living fifty generations back from the year 1900. He was certainly one of the principal explorers and navigators of the race. For some account of his voyages see "Hawaiki," p. 167 (third edition), and our "Memoirs," Vol. IV., p. 37, where the discrepancy of dates between Maori and Rarotongan accounts of this celebrated sailor are pointed out. According to the latter people he flourished about A.D. 650.

It is upon such traditions as these that the whole of the chronology of the Polynesian race rests, and it is to be remarked that we shall in all probability never get anything better. The songs included in the original text below it is impossible to translate as a whole without the aid of the Rarotongans themselves, and it is doubtful if they can do so at this time.]

THE TAMARUA FAMILY OF RAROTONGA.

[Translation.]

515. This is the history of Tamarua-te-Aia and Tamarua-te-akaariki and their families; their ancestors, etc.

He (the first named) was a descendant of Tamarua-mau-o-matatia, of Pouara, also of Tamarua-orometua, also of Tamarua-puangi, also of Tamarua-miti-rima, also of Tamarua-pai, also of Tu-te-rangi-marama, and also of Te Tumu.

The (original) land (in which the latter lived) was Atia-te-varinga, and here was born Te Tupua, son of Te Tumu :—

> Te Tumu
> Te Tupua-o-Avaiki
> Tu-te-rangi-marama.

This man, Tu-te-rangi-marama, was the High Chief of Atia-te-varinga (the most ancient land known to the Rarotongans, and identical with Hawaiki-nui and Irihia of the New Zealand Maoris), and he arranged for the construction of a most glorious sacred place (a building), and surrounded it with a great enclosure, very high, twelve fathoms in height; very spacious and of great width. It contained many beautiful things. It was a place where the spirits of mankind and of the gods assembled, as also those of the High Chiefs. It was called "The Koro-tuatini" of Tu-te-rangi-marama; and then he appointed a guardian for the place, named Io-tini. (The Maoris know of this name Koro-tuatini as a name for some temple in the "Fatherland" where the spirits of gods and men foregathered, but which is more generally called "Te Hono-i-wairua.")

516. We shall see from what follows that that place was a gathering place of human spirits. The mother of Tau-toro—the son of Varo-kura—whose name was Varo-tea, when she died her spirit went to the place of Tu-te-rangi-marama, to the "Koro-tuatini." We also see it in that the spirit of Kuikui-tatau also went to that "Koro," and because it was an assembling place of all the spirits of men. It was the gathering place also of gods and the High Chiefs, because there originated the many wonderful things (such as customs, ritual, etc.) at Atia-te-varinga. We know it also through Tiki, who also went to that "Koro"; and through Ngaro-ariki-te-tara, who was carried there by Koura and Tiaka after the bathing in the dammed-up water of the sisters of Ngata-ariki, and they two handed her over to the Peneneki (water sprites)* who took her to Avaiki-atia. She had seen that Avaiki-atia.

* Peneneki, according to Major Large, are water-sprites. But it is possible this name is synonymous with the New Zealand Turehu, Patu-paiarehe, or Parehe, usually said to be fairies. They are light-coloured, and from the description of them evidently a light-coloured race known to the Polynesians in the Fatherland. For the adventures of Ngaro-ariki-te-tara see Part III. of this history.

517. But the principal and most delightful things at Atia-te-variuga were the "Takurnas" (feasts, ceremonies, songs and dances) that were instituted by Tu-te-rangi-marama to animate (inspirit, glorify) his country; such as the Pu (trumpet), the Pau (a drum), the Kaara (a drum), the Eva-tipa, the Eiva-puapua-aki, the Eiva-tataumaa, the Peu, the Eva-tapara, the Eva-tea, the Ura, the Akaao, the Karioi, and all the *akaaka-puauau* (? certain kinds of dances) at Avaiki.

518. There was also the "Takarua-tapu" (the sacred ceremonies connected with the annual feasts of first fruits), when there came the company of the gods to the assembly altogether at Avaiki—Rongo and his company, Tane, Ruanuku, Tu, Tangaroa, Tongaiti, and Tu-tavake, with their separate attendants. There also came the High Chiefs, with their attendants, at the command of Tu-te-rangi-marama of Avaiki. There came Te Nga-taito-ariki, Atea, Kaukura, Te Pupu, Te Uira, Te Aa, Rua-te-atonga, whose was the first part of the Takarua—named "Iikaa." This was the origin of all the (succeeding) commands of old at Avaiki-atiu.

519 There were (assembled) there also the female gods: Taa-kura and her attendants; and Ari, Tupua-nui, Te Rangi-putai-ua; Te Pao-o-te-rangi, and the daughter of Rua-te-atonga—Te Kura-akaipo—and their respective attendants.

520. There were also the Pereneki (water sprites),* very numerous, whose country was Te Rangi-topa-rere, whence they originated.

Tu-te-rangi-marama, Te Tumu, and their attendants were also there. They were the (people who inaugerated) the institution of the "Takarua" at Avaiki.

That was the land of splendid head-dresses of all the Chiefs, and it was from that land of *matea* (? gorgeous plumes) that (these customs) spread to all the islands. It was also in this land that originated the wars that caused them to spread to all the islands.

It was in this land that lived Te Tumu and Papa, and there also were born their sons and daughter.

521. It was here that assembled the company of priests: Rua-kana-kiri, Rua-kana-tea, Rua-kana-kura, Rua-kana-ero, Rua-kana-uri, Rua-taunga, and their attendants. It was the assembly of all to the one ceremony in that land, and it was they who selected the Chief, and they who set him up and annointed him; that is, *akaparapara.* †

(These things were done) to search out the correct procedure in the land, to search for means of safety and welfare for men, slaves, and

---

* See above—probably a mistake for Peneneki.

† These names commencing with Rua, are probably represented in Maori by the names (also beginning with Rua) recorded by John White in "Ancient History of the Maori," Vol. I., p. 3, but there said to be sisters of Tinirau—surely a mistranslation, judging by the meanings of the names.

children.   Such were the kind of men in that land; and it was these
same people that spread over this great ocean.

522. There was born to Te Tupua

Tu-te-rangi-marama

|

Rua-i-te-karii

|

Te Ake-kura

|

Te Ake

|

Moo-uri

|

Moo-tea

|

Te-tini-i-Avaiki

|

Kura-a-moo

|

Tau-tonu

|

Amou-aitu

|

Te Ariki-ivi-roa

|

Kake-tua-ariki

|

Tua-ariki

|

Te Ariki-oki-tini

|

Te Kura-a-moo

Te Kura-a-moo departed for the east, and dwelt there, on account
of trouble that grew up between him and his sisters: it was on account
of a basket of fish-hooks which one of the sisters trod into the mud.

523.   He remained in these parts, and there was born to him :—

Te Moo-take-kura

(and then follows the names of 79 descendants (see the original) down
to :—)

Tamarua-o-Avaiki

|

Tamarua-nui

|

Tamarua-paipai

|

Tamarua-tukinga

|

Tamarua-taunga

|

Tamarua-oki-rua

|

Tamarua-te-aranga

|

Tamarua-pai

He (the latter) lived in the times of Tangiia, and whom he joined
(in the many voyages made by the latter, as the principal navigator).

His home was at Papa-uriri and at Ati-maono (on the south coast of Tahiti) and also at Pape-ate (on the north coast of Tahiti). At Mo'orea is a channel (? in the reef), cut by Tamarua-pai, named Utu-kura.

524. (Then follows 18 generations down to Tamarua-orometua, who in 1897 was between 90 and 100 years old when I saw him at his home near Nga-tangiia, Rarotonga.)

525. In the times of Tamarua-metua of Avaiki all Avaiki was broken up and scattered in small parties; everyone had become possessed of canoes. One canoe was that of Ui-te-rangiora, and it was this one that enabled all Avaiki to scatter to different islands. In that same division (scattering) three of them joined, Tamarua, Te Aia, and Tai-vananga, and this was their (final) separation from (living in) a single land, Avaiki (or Atia-te-varinga), and they spread to every land from there. They (the three) embarked on the canoe of Ui-te-rangiora, and they it was who navigated that canoe to all the islands of the world. There was not any place they did not visit; and hence they became very expert sailors. When their vessel became rotten they renewed it, and when repaired they returned with their canoes to conquer Te Ravaki; and when that was accomplished they went on to Rangi-ura and Mata-te-ra and subdued those islands; at the latter place they killed the chief named Te Ango-noo-rangi, whose name was (afterwards) given to a *tapora* (? mat) at the *marae* by Tamarua. They also went to Nukare and subdued that land and all other islands, as follows:— *

The greater part (of the names) remain (unwritten); it was not possible to write them all. Those are the names of the islands that they visited.

526. The following are the names of the lands in which they permanently dwelt in this ocean: Avaiki-raro, i.e., Kuporu (Upolu) and Avaiki-ki-runga, i.e., Taiti and Iva (Tahiti and Marquesas); and they also went as far as Avaiki-tautau, i.e., New Zealand. Tamarua dwelt at Avaiki-raro, i.e., Samoa, but Avaiki was the principal name. He dwelt at Avaiki (Savaii), and Amoa was the name of his district, where he had a fish-pond named "Te Puapua-a-tiare." The fish in it were the *kanae*, that came in numbers in the proper season, from Viti (Fiji). It was (? first) brought there from that land by Tamarua-te-ikumea, who had two sides (i.e. natures); one side was human, the other a fish. When he brought the fish he led them into the fish-pond by a channel from the sea; a very small channel, probably like a ditch. By this channel the fish went to the pond, which was very large. Now, the men who had to watch it, went to the narrow place and there watched until the channel was full to the sides, and then

---

* See list of islands in the original.

they stopped up the channel in the narrow part near the sea, enclosed it closely, and then they stood on the banks and snared them, placing them in heaps, and carried them off. If the heaps (*au*) were not ? consumed (the rest) were thrown away.

Tamarua brought the name of that fish-pond with him to Rarotonga, hence "Nga-te-tiare."

527. (Sometimes) Tamarua dwelt at Taiti (Tahiti), at Pape-uriri and Atimaono. Te Aia and Tu-vananga lived at Pape-ete. At Moorea is the channel cut out by Pai (? Tamarua-pai). (After living) at Tahiti (for a time) he would go to Avaiki-raro and stay there, (sometimes) to Antaria and stay there, and (even) to Atia-te-varinga. And so it was from generation to generation down to the time that Tangiia settled in Rarotonga, when these long voyages ended, even to the present time.

528. In the times of Avaiki-te-paipai (? Tamarua-paipai) there grew up disputes at Avaiki-raro between Naea and his younger brothers. The origin of the quarrel was a spring of water; one spring was set aside by the *ariki* for himself, not to be used by the younger brothers. A second cause was in connection with the division of the food as arranged by the *ariki*, Naea, for himself; it was the younger brothers' business to arrange the distribution, the *ariki's* share and theirs. The *kikomua* (? fore-quarters) of the pigs and the *kikomua* (? best parts) of all foods were for the *ariki* alone, while the *kikomuri* (? hind-quarters) and the (? inferior) parts of all foods were for the brethren. The younger brothers considered that they should take it turn and turn about, but the *ariki* would by no means consent to this. So the brethren seized the chief; and thus commenced a new war in Avaiki, and its inhabitants were scattered far and wide. Naea fled to Avaiki-runga (usually means Tahiti and these parts, but here the Sage includes the Hawaiian Islands in that expression), that is, Vaii (ancient Tahitian and Maori name for Hawaii, i.e., Vaihi and Waihi) and Tangaungau (now called Lanai) at Vaii, and which are called "Avaiki-nui-o-Naea," and after he was driven out by the younger brethren. Avaiki belonged to Naea.

529. The names of those younger brothers were Tu-oteote, Karae-mura, Tu-natu, Kakao-tu, Kakao-rere, Uki, Pana, Pato and Ara-iti.

(Then follow several songs).

533. There were three men all of one family; Te Angai-aroa, was their father, Ati-aroko was the elder, Ati-aroa the younger, and Ati-kavera the youngest of all. They named the districts in which they lived (in Rarotonga) after themselves: that is, Aroko, Aroa, and Kavera. That man Te Angai-aroa was Tamarua (? which) and his children.

NO TAMARUA.

515. E tuatua no Tamarua-te-Aia-Pitimani, ma Tamarua-te-akaariki i to raua anauanga.

E tamaiti na Tamarua-mau-o-matatia i Pouara. E tamaiti na Tamarua-orometua i Aroko. E tamaiti na Tamarua-puangi; e tamaiti na Tamarua-miti-rima; e tamaiti na Tamarua-pāi; e tamaiti na Tu-te-rangi-marama, tamaiti a Te Tumu.

E enua ko Atia-te-varinga; e kua anau ta Te Tumu ko Te Tupua :—

130. Te Tumu.
        Te Tupua-o-Avaiki.
128. Tu-te-rangi-marama.

Ko Tu-te-rangi-marama, koia te ariki o Atia-te-varinga; kua akataka aia i tetai ngai-tapu kakā, e kua akapini ki te koro maata e te teitei, okotai-ngauru ma rua te teitei. E koro atea maata, e te pararau-are, e ngai akakiia ki te au meitaki tini; e ngai uipaanga no te vaerua tangata, e uipaanga no te au atua ravarai ma te au tupuranga ariki ravarai. Ko te "Koro-tuatini" i o Tu-te-rangi-marama taua kainga ra; e kua tuku aia i te tangata ki roto ei tiaki, ko Io-tini tona ingoa.

516. Teia te mea i kitea e, e uipaanga vaerua tangata: Ko te metua vaine o Tau-toru te tama a Varo-kura; Varo-tea taua metua vaine ra; ka mate ei taua vaine ra, kua aere te vaerua ki o Tu-te-rangi-marama, ki roto i taua "Koro-tuatini" ra. Kua kitea katoaia ki te vaerua o Kuikui-tatau, kua aere rai ki roto i taua "Koro" ra. No te mea e ngai uipaanga no te au vaerua tangata purotu taua "Koro" ra. Kua uipa ïa te au atua e te au ariki ki reira; no te mea ko te ngai ïa i akatupuia'i te au ravenga katakata tini, ko Atia-te-varinga. Kua kitea ki a Tiki; kua tae katoa aia ki roto i taua "Koro" ra. Kua kitea ki a Ngaro-ariki-te-tara, ka apaiia mai ei e Koura ma Tiaka i te paianga i te vai pa o nga tuaine o Ngata-ariki, tukuia atura e raua ki nga Peneneki, apaiia atura e nga Peneneki ki Avaiki-atia. Kua kite aia i taua Avaiki-atia ra.

517. Teia te angaanga maata e te mataora i Atia-te-varinga, ko te takurua i akatupuia'i e Tu-te-rangi-marama ei akaau i tona enua; ko te pu, ko te pau, ko te kaara, ko te eva-tipa, ko te eiva-puapua-aki, ko te eiva-tutau-mau, ko te pen, ko te eva-tapara, ko te eva-tea, ko te ura, ko te akaao, ko te karioi, ko te au mea akaaka-puauan ïa i Avaiki.

518. Ko te takurua tapu, koia te tere a te au atua ravarai i te uipaanga ki Avaiki i te ngai okotai; ko Rongo ma tana tere; ko Tane ma tana tere; ko Rua-nuku ma tana tere; ko Tu ma tana tere; ko Tangaroa ma tana tere; ko Tonga-iti ma tana tere; ko Tu-tavake ma tana tere:

No te au ariki i to ratou uipaanga ki te takurua i Avaiki, i a o

Tu-te-rangi-marama i te akonoanga i teianei takurua.   Ko Te Nga-
taito-ariki ma tona pae; ko Atea ma tona pae; ko Kau-kura ma tona
 pae; ko Te Pupu ma tona pae; ko Te Uira ma tona pae; ko Te Aa
ma tona pae; ko Rua-te-atonga ma tona pae; nana te takurua
mua—ko te Ii-kaa; ko te akakapuaanga teia i te au akonoanga, i
taito, i Avaiki-atia.

519.   No te au atua-vaine; ko Taa-kura ma tana tere; ko Ari
ma tana tere; ko Tupua-nui ma tana tere; ko Te Rangi-putai-ua ma
tana tere; ko Te Pao-o-te-rangi ma tana tere; ko te tamaine a
Rua-te-atonga—ko Te Kura-akaipo—ma tana tere.

520.   Ko te tere a Te Pereneke, manotini ratou; ko Te Rangi-
topa-rere to ratou motia, ko te varinga ia.

Ko Tu-te-rangi-marama ma tana tere; ko te tera i a Te Tumu.
Ko te au akonoanga teia no Avaiki.

Ko te enua pare-au tikai teia no te au ariki ravarai, no teianei enua
matoa aere mai ei ki te pa enua katoatoa. E tupu rai i roto, i roto i tana
enua nei rai te tamaki i rato aere ei ki te pa enua katoatou.

Ko te Te Tumu e Papa, ko raua ana tei noo ki runga i taua kainga
ra, ka anau ei ta raua tamariki tamaroa e te tamaine.

521.   Ko te kau taunga i ta ratou tere: Ko Rua-kana-kiri, ma tona
pae; ko Rua-kana-tea ma tona pae; ko Rua-kana-kura ma tona pae;
ko Rua-kana-ero ma tona pae. Ko Rua-kana-uri ma tona pae; ko
Rua-taunga ma tona pae. Ko te nipaanga teia ki te akonoanga okotai,
ki roto i taua enua ra; e na ratou i iki te ariki, na ratou rai e kimi te
ariki e, i ururenga i te ariki—koia rai te akaparapara.

Ko te kimi i te tika ki runga i te enua, ko te kimi i te ora e ora ai
te tangata, te unga, ma te potiki. Ko nga pae taugata teia ki roto i
taua enua ra. E ko nga pae tangata rai teia i rato aere mai ei ki
teia moana maata nei.

522.   Anau ta Te Tupua, ko Tu-te-rangi-marama.   128.

```
                        |________________________|
                        |
               Moo-kura
               Rua-i-te karii
          125  Te Ake-kura
               Te Ake
               Moo-uri
               Moo-tea
               Io-tini-i-Avaiki
          120  Kura-a-moo
               Tau-tonu
               Amau-aitu
               Te Ariki-ivi-roa
               Kake-tua-ariki
          115  Tua-ariki
               Te Ariki-oki-tini
          113  Te Kura-o-moo
```

Kua aere a Te Kura-o-moo ki te itinga o te rā, kua noo atu aia ki reira, no te pekapeka i tupu ia ratou ma nga tuaine; e kete matau te ara, e taomi e tetai tuaine ki raro i te vari.

523. Kua noo atura aia ki reira; kua anau ta Kura-o-moo:—

112	Te Moo-take-knra		Te Angai-tura
	Avaiki-ia-atea		Te Angai-rao-ta
110	Tu-veka-o-moo	65	Te Angai-tiritiri
	Te Tupua-me-neke		Te Angai-enua
	Te Tupunga-aitu		Te Angai-ki-ura
	Te Pai-tua-tini .		Te Angai-ariki-ki-Atia
	Avaiki-tia-inga		Te Angai-ki-tau
105	Atia-a-mata	60	Te Angai-moneka
	Te Tupua-nui		Te Angai-kl-Iti
	Te Tupua-iti		Te Angal-mauta
	Te Tupua-raunga		Te Angai-tuma
100	Kau-tupua		Mau-o-tai
99	Te Einga-a-mata-o-Avaiki		Mau-o-penea
	Tamarua-a-papa	55	Mau-o-kapura
	Tamarua-akaau-takurua		Mau-o-kianga
	Tamarua-metua-o-Avaiki		Mau-o-rangi-topa-rere
95	Te Avaiki-po		Mau-o-to
	Po-atanga-o-Moo		Mau-o-tere
	Vainga-atua-ki-Avaiki		Mau-o-uru-o-kura
	Te Uinga-ki-Avaiki	50	Mau-o-rere-taua
	Avaiki-tai		Mau-o-te-nere
90	Avaiki-na-oti		Mau-o-te-ringi
	Avaiki-miri-reka		Mau-o-te-niro
	Avaiki-te-maora		Mau-o-te-angai
	Avaiki-tupa-ero	45	Mau-o-te-riko
	Avaiki-raita		Mau-o-te-eaau
85	Avaiki-a-ora		Te Itonga
	Avaiki-po-ta		Te Akerua
	Avaiki-ka–rona		Nae-tu-kura
	Avaiki-mea-a-reka	40	Nae-iki-aitu
	Avaiki-kokoia		Tua-ariki
80	Avaiki-ka-kite		Taki-varu
	Avaiki-noe-aa		Te Pu-rara
	Avaiki-toro-uka		Avaiki-maine
	Te Angai-ariki	35	Tu-te-iku-mea
	Te Angai-atua		Tu-mai-oni
75	Te Angai-aro		Tamarua-o-Avaiki
	Te Angai-taunga		Tamarua-nui
	Te Angai-o-te-pereneki		Tamarua-paipai
	Te Angai-mua	30	Tamarua-tukinga
	Te Angai-ki-roto		Tamarua-taunga
70	Te Angai-ki-vao		Tamarua-oki-rua
	Te Angai-ki-a-tiki		Tamarua-te-aranga
	Te Angai-tapu	26	Tamarua-pai (ko teia to
			Tangiia tuatau ia)

Kua piri aia i reira ki a Tangiia; kua noo aia ki Pape-uriri e Ati-maono e noo atu ki Pape-ete. Tei Morea te ava tarai a Tamarua-pai, ko Utu-kura te ingoa.

524. Anau ta Tamarua-pai :—

Tamarua-keu
Tamarua-viri-tai
Tamarua-nui-rai
Tamarua-tei-vao
Tamarua-te-ariki, e-raka
Tamarua-atero
Tamarua-tauraki
Tamarua-tairi-i-te-rangi
Tamarua-miti-rima
Tamarua-te-angai
Tamarua-une
Tamarua-pei-kuru
Tamarua-puangi

3 Te Mato	1 Tamarua-akua	2 Te Tauna-a-toka*	3 Te Mato
Putanga-i-mate-kia-ruki	Tamarua-tu-kaka	Io-tako	
Tumu-rakau	Tamarua-kui-nau	Tamarua-aere-marie	
Te Ua-takiri	Tamarua-tavake	1 Tamarua-kaki-ta 2 Tua-ariki	
Tamarua-orometua†	Tamarua-mau-o-matatia		
Tamarua-te-aia-Piti-mana	Tamarua-te-akaariki		
	Tamarua-te-ruaroa		

525. I to Tamarua-metua o Avaiki tuatau, kua pueu rikiriki a Avaiki; kua rauka to pāi no Avaiki katoatoa. Ko te pāi no Ui-te-rangiora, ko te pāi ïa i pueu rikiriki ei a Avaiki ki te pa enua katoatoa; i taua pueu rikiriki-ke-anga ra, kua kapiti ratou tokotoru; ko Tamarua, ko Te Aia, ko Tai-vananga, ko to ratou topanga ïa ki vao me roto i te enua akotai, ko Atia-te-varinga, me te Avaiki katoatoa ki vao; e kia rato aere te tangata ki te pa-enua ravarai. Kua kake ratou ki runga i te pāi o Ui-te-rangiora; ki a ratou te akaaere i taua pāi ra ki te pa-enua katoa o te ao nei. Kare e ngai toe i te aere e ratou, e riro ratou ei aronga kite maata i te akatere pāi. E kia pe taua pāi ra, ei reira ratou e anga aere ei i to ratou pāi. Kia oti, aere ra to ratou au pāi, e reira ratou e oki aere ei e ta aere ratou ki Te Ravaki. Kua ta i tei reira enua ki Rangi-raro, kua ta i tei reira enua ki Mata-te-ra, kua ta i tei reira enua; kua ta i te ariki, i a Te Ango-noo-te-rangi, kua riro mai taua ariki ra ei ingoa tapora na Tamarua i mua i te marae. Kua aere ki Nu-kare kua ta; kua pera rai ki te pa-enua katoatoa :—

* Te Tama-a-toka i Vai-i-kura.

† Tamarua-orometua was living at Nga-Tangiia, Rarotonga, in 1897, and then between 90 and 100 years old.

Ki Nu-kare „ Nu-takoto „ Nu-taara „ Nu-mare „ Nu-pango „ Nu-iti „ Nu-tana „ Nu-ame	} Probably the New Hebridies and Loyalty Islands

Ki Iti-nui „ Iti-rai „ Iti-anaunau „ Iti-takai-kere „ Piti „ Pa-pua	} The Fiji and Lau Groups.

Ki Vaiï	...	... Hawaii	
„ Tavaï	...	... Tauai, now Kauai	} Hawaiian Islands.
„ Ngangai	...	... Lanai	
„ Maro-ai	...	... ? Oahu	

Ki Tonga-nui „ Tonga-ake „ Tonga-piri-tia „ Tonga-manga „ Tonga-raro	} The Tonga Group.

Ki Avaiki-raro	...	This name covers Samoa and the Fiji Group.
„ Nu-taata		
„ Ma-reva		
„ Piä		
„ Uea	...	Horne Island
„ Raro-ata		
„ Amama		
„ Tuna	...	Futuna
„ Rangi-arara		
„ Rotu-ma	...	Wallis Island.

Ki Vavau	...	Northern Isle of Tonga Group.
„ Niva-pou	...	Great Hope Island
„ Atu-apai	...	Haabai, of Tonga Group
„ Tangi-te-pu		
„ Rara		
„ Avaiki	...	Savai'i of Samoa Group
„ Kuporu	...	Upolu „ „
„ Te Tuira	...	Tutuila „ „
„ Manuka	...	Manu'a „ „
„ Tokerau	...	Union Group
„ Uru-pukapuka-nui	...	? Palmerston Island
„ Uru-pukapuka-iti		

Ki Enua-kura
  ,, Iva-nui
  ,, Iva-rai
  ,, Iva-te-pukenga   }   The Marquesas Group
  ,, Te Kirikiri
  ,, Te Rauao
  ,, Te Mae-a-tupa
  ,, Rau-maika-nui
  ,, Rau-maika-iti
  ,, Ngana
  ,, Te Pau-motu kotoatoa   ...   "The whole of the Paumotu Group"
  ,, Akaau ...   .   Fakahau Island

Ki Taiti   ...   Tahiti
  ,, Morea   ...   Morea or Aimeo
  ,, Rangi-atea ...   Ra'i-atea   }   The Society
  ,, Uaine   ...   Huahine   and
  ,, Taanga   ...   Taha'a   Tahiti Groups
  ,, Porapora ...   Porapora

Ki Rurutu   {   The Austral Group
  ,, Pa-pau
  ,, Rima-tara, " Ka ti-
     pia ki Rima-tara,
     ka tipia ki Rauta-
     mea, e ra tonga
     koia e ki Mauke."

Ki Mauke
  ,, Motea-aro
  ,, Atiu   }   The Cook
  ,, Auau   ...   Old name of Mangaia Island   Group
  ,, Raro-tonga, oki atu
     ki runga ki

Ki Rapa-nui   ...   Easter Island
  ,, Rapa-iti   ...   Rapa, or Oparo Island
  ,, Teni-te-ia
  ,, Pa-pua

Ki Au-te-ria-nui
  ,, Au-te-ria-iti
  ,, Kateta-nui
  ,, Kateta-iti
  ,, Panipani-maata-
     one-okotai

Te vai atu rai te maata, kare rava i ope te tataia; ko te au pa-enua toia i aereia e ratou.

526. Teia o ratou enua noo tamou i teia moana nei, ko Avaiki-raro, koia a Kuporu, e Avaiki ki runga, ko Taiti, ko Iva; e aere ua ratou ki Avaiki-tautau—koia "Nu-tirani." Kua noo a Tamarua ki Avaiki-raro—koia a Amoa; ko Avaiki te ingoa maata; kua noo aia i Amoa, tona tapere, ko "Te puapua-a-tiare" te ingoa o tana roto-ika; e kanae te ika: ka tere mai ki roto, kia tae ki te tuatau, no Viti mai taua ika ra, e ika tikina ki taua enua ra, ko Tamarua-te-ikumea te tangata i taoia mai ei taua ika ra. E rua tu o taua tangata ra, e tangata tetai pae, e ika tetai pae. Kua taoi maira aia i taua ika ra, e tae maira ki Avaiki kua arataki aia no roto i te ava i tai, e ava oiti ua me te avaava ua nei paa te tu. Ka na reira taua ika ma i te aerenga ki uta i te roto; e roto maata taua roto ra, ina ra, ko nga tangata i te akara, ka aere ïa ratou ki tai i te ngai oiti i te nia i taua avaava ra, ka akara ua rai ratou e ma te ki takiri ua te roto e pari ki te pae; te arai ratou i tai i taua oiti ra, te koro ra, e piri tikai e, ei reira roa'i e tutuia e te tangata, kia taei aere, ma te aū aere, ka tauta ua. E kare e rauka i te au, akaruke atu. Kua taoi mai aia—a Tamarua—i te ingoa o taua roto-ika ra ki Rarotonga nei—koia a " Nga te Tiare."

527. Kua noo a Tamarua ki Taiti; ko Pape-uriri e Ati-maono to ratou nooanga. Ko Te Aia e Tai-vananga ka noo ki Papa-ete. Tei Morea te ava tarai a Pai, (Tamarua-pai?) Ka noo ki Taiti ka aere ki Avaiki-raro ka noo ki reira; ka aere ki Au-taria ka noo i reira; ka aere ki Atia-te-varinga. Ka pera ua ra i tera uki, i tera uki e tae ua mai ki te tuatau e aere mai ei a Tangiia ki Raro-tonga nei, ko te mutunga mai nei ïa, e teia noa'i.

528. I te tuatau no Avaiki-te-paipai (? ko Tamarua-paipai ïa paa ?) kua tuputupu te pekapeka i Avaiki-raro, ko Naea e nga teina. Tera te tumu i te pekapeka i a ratou, ko te puna-vai; okotai ua puna rai i akatakaia e te ariki nona anake, nuraka o te ai teina. Tera te rua; ko te tuanga kai i akonoia e te ariki, e Naea nana, tei i a ratou katoa oki, tei te ai teina, te akaaereanga i te tuā i te kai i te koutu-ariki, e rua ua vaenga i te tuanga i te kai, ko ta te ariki, ko ta ratou. Ko te kiko-mua i te puaka ma te kiko-mua o te au kai ravarai na te ariki anake ïa. Ko te kiko-miri i te puaka e te kiko-miri o te au kai ravarai na ratou ïa. Ko te manako o te au teina, takitai i runga, takitai i raro. Kare roa te ariki i tuku mai ki ta te au teina; opukia io ei e te aronga teina; akatupuia te tamaki ou i a Avaiki, ko Avaiki ïa, e te pueu-rikiriki ke ra. Te oro ra a Naea ki Avaiki runga—koia a Vaii. Ko Tanganngau i Va'u (?) ra, i tuatua mai ei e, " Avaiki-nui-o-Naea," e nga teina, e nga teina oriori marie; no Naea rai a Avaiki.

529. Tera te ingoa o taua ai teina aue kai ra: Ko Tu-oteote, ko Karae-mura, ko Tiori, ko Tu-natu, ko Kakao-tu, ko Kakao-rere, ko Uki, ko Pana, ko Pato, ko Ara-iti.

530.   E AKATARA NO TAMARUA-TAIRI-TE-RANGI

1.   E ! e toro, e turou turou, e aitu,
     E tupuranga taua i Avaiki,
     Ka riri ngana, ka toto vero o tera,
     E karere tei aere mai nei,
     Ko Marere, ko Rua-a-toa,
     Maroto i te ranga rau, no Are-munamuna
     I te rapitoanga ara a Tangiia
     Taku ariki e, ko mei Avarua ra,
     E oo ka tupu ana.

2.   E ! e toro e, i tupu i Avarua
     Te tupuranga ariki, te ariki tapu aite
     Me roto i te kaponga a Rangi-o-Atea
     No Arai-te-tonga, te pu i te tamaki,
     I aaia ai te raui tangata o Tangiia
     Me runga me Anga-ta-kura,
     E iki mataiapo tei vao ariki o Tangiia,
     Ko Tairi anake te karakia atu,
     Ki nga atua, kia tapu roa ra,
     E oo ka roa, rire e.

3.   Tena ka ui, ka ui, ka ui au ana, ra toro e,
     Te ui Akimere e toru e,
     Ko Toa oki, ko Pare ko Tea,
     Urua ae e taku tama
     Tera tupuranga toa mei taito
     Kaore e korero, ko Tairi anake.
     Te toa rongo nui o Tangiia
     E uira, e rapa, e aruru i te rangi.
     Te karonga tamaki a Tairi
     Naringa, e taku tama !
     E takiri tu i te aerenga,
     E iku, e poroaki ei kinei koe,
     Ka ano au ra e.

4.   Tena te rongo, te rongo i te matangi,
     Matangi, matangi i au ana ra toro e,
     'Te rongo i te matangi toru e.
     Ko te rangi pua noa te ae ki rauka
     Ko Papa, ko Ei-tara, ko 'Tautu-tapuae,
     Mokora ; ko te toa i aere i te uru o te kare,
     Ko Tairi anake te toa rongo nui o Tangiia
     E uira, e rapa, e aruru i te rangi
     Te karonga tamaki a Tairi
     Naringa, e taku tama !
     E takiri tu i te aerenga,
     E iku, e poroaki ei kinei koe
     Ka ano au ra e, oo ka roa rire e.

5.   Tena oatu, oatu ra te rongo, o te rongo,
     Te rongo i au ana ra toro e,
     Oatu ra te rongo ki Make-vero, toru e,

Ki Arai-te-tonga, ki tana tamaine—
Ki a Tea-aruru-o-te-rangi
Kua euuminmi noa a Te Ii-o-te-ra-tunuku,
E tama e ! e tei ea Tairi ka ngaro oi nei,
Kua riro ake nei ki te ngaki kainga
Akairi matakeinanga no Makea,
Auraka e vaiio i Arai-te-tonga .
Ka amutia a miringao,
Ko Tairi anake te toa rongo nui o Tangiia,
E uira, e rapa, e aruru i te rangi,
Te karonga tamaki a Tairi,
Naringa, e taku tama !
E tukiri tu i te aerenga
E iki, e poroaki, ei kinei koe.
Ka ano au ra e—e—

6.   Tena ka ranga, tuetuea tei ipo ua
Ai a Kamaua e au ana ra toro e,
Kua karo tapere te tamaki a Tairi,
Tei uta te rotopu te ngaru rapa,
I tua te koko ki Ati-ua
Kua koi Tairi i te rau-papa-a-toa
Ei apaipai, ei kare puapuaaki ki Iti-kau,
Ko Tairi anake te toa rongo uui o Tangiia,
E uira, e rapa, e aruru i te rangi,
Te karonga tamaki a Tairi
Nariuga, e taku tama !
E takiri tu i te aerenga
E iku, e poroaki ei kunei koe,
Ka ano au ra e—e—

7.   Tena, teia, teia te mea kino, ka kinokino,
Ka kino i au ana, ra toro e,
Teia te mea kino e,
E ekai taeake na raua io
Ei kau te nio, te ki pepeke,
Ko nga tapere e toru,
Tukua ki Ro-riki-ina-ve ma Tokerau,
Nga pokoinui e rua i tangaruu ia
A Akaoa ma Are-renga
I rauka mai oi, akairi ake oi,
Ki Arai-te-tonga, ki te vaka e nui,
Koia Taki-tumu,
Ko Tairi anake te toa rongo nui o Tangiia
E uira, e rapa, e aruru i te rangi,
Te karonga tamaki a Tairi,
Naringa, e taku tama !
E takiri tu i te aerenga,
E iku, e poroaki, ei kunei koe,
Ka ano au ra e—

8.   Tena ka moe, ka moe, ka moe i au ana ra toro e,
Ka moe te angai no Ngati-Tangiia
Tei mua, motia ei Iti-kanapa,
Te vairanga ko te rotopu nei,
Ei tara tamaki te vairanga,
Oatu tei miri, motia ei rau-tiutiu,
Kua rere te toa rango nui ko Tairi,
Ki runga ki Tara-rau, tu eru atu ei,
Akareki atu ki Vai-moko,
Tukua ki Tuaunga, e tama e Tairi !
Akapou to oro ki runga Maunga-roa,
Akaruke atu oi,
Ko Tairi anake te toa rongo nui o Tangiia
E uira, e rapa, e arura i te rangi,
Te karonga tamaki a Tairi,
Naringa, e taku tama !
E takiri tu i te aerenga,
E iku, e poroaki ei kunei koe
Ka ano au ra e, e oo ka roa rire e.

[Tera atu te au pee te vai nei, kare e tataia i kunei ; ko

" Te pee i te akatara o Tamarua-tairi-te-rangi."
" E pee no Tamarua-koroia," nona te tuatua ra,
' E aa i oro ana Takinuku ' ; i mate ki te tamaki.]

533.   Ko te au ingoa teia no te anau a Tamarua, me te mua e tae
ua atu ki te ope :—

Ko Te Ei-tuputupu Tamarua
    ,, Tamarua-Te-Aia-Pitimana-Te Ariki-na-vao
    ,, Putiki-aumea-ki-atu-Tamarua
    ,, Tamatea-Iakopa-Atapa-Tamarua,
    ,, Te Ua-takiri-arapaki-te-Ariki-maro-Tamarua.
    ,, Noia-tooa-tauira-aki-Te Angai-Tamarua.

THE LAND OF TARA
AND THEY WHO SETTLED IT.

THE STORY OF THE OCCUPATION OF TE WHANGA-NUI-A-TARA
(THE GREAT HARBOUR OF TARA) OR PORT NICHOLSON,
BY THE MAORI.

By ELSDON BEST.

PART VII.

(Continued from page 17, Vol. XXVIII.)

THE MAORI TEXT.

IT has been considered advisable to preserve in print the Maori Text on which is based most of the story of "The Land of Tara." Although this text will interest but few of our members, it is nevertheless advisable in the interests of historical and philological research that the original should be printed for fear of accidents to the MS. volumes in which it is contained.

The original volumes are in possession of Te Whatahoro (the Scribe of our "Memoirs," Vols. III. and IV.), but copies are in private hands, and from these latter the text now printed below has been taken. The matter itself is the result of some years' work by the Scribe, who wrote it out to the dictation of the old priest of the Whare-wānanga, Te Matorohanga, who had been taught in his youth in that Maori college the ancient lore of his tribe. As the whole is expressed in the purest Maori language as spoken by the people prior to the advent of the European, it may serve to counteract the tendency to a bastard style of Maori now becoming prevalent in the writings of the present generation.

TE WHANGA-NUI-A-TARA.

Ka haere mai a Ngai-Tara, ka noho ki Motu-kairangi
me era atu wahi.

NA, i te whitu o Maehe i te tau 1867, i a matau i Kete-pakaru, ka mea mai a Te Waitere, a Kereopa, ki a Moihi Te Matorohanga :—
" E koro ! Korero ra ki a matau ko wai nana i noho mai nga tahataha tai nei, timata mai i Heretaunga nei haere mai nei ki Wairarapa nei."

Ka mea atu a Moihi Te Matorohanga:—"E ta ma! Kua hoha au i te korerotanga i nga korero tauawhi a nga tangata pupuri o te wananga ki a koutou, he kotikoti rahi no koutou i aku korero ina korero au."

Ka mea atu a Kereopa:—"E ta! Ko tou papa ano, ko Te Ura-o-te-rangi, e whakararuraru ana i au korero."

Ka mea mai a Te Matorohanga:—"E pai ana hei korero noa ake ma tatau. Me timata mai e au te whakatakitaki mai ki a koutou i Turanga-nui-a-Rua, i te rawhiti roa."

I te wa i wehe mai ai a Whatonga i a Toi-te-huatahi i Whakatane, ka mea a Whatonga ki te tipuna, ki a Toi:—"Hei konei noho ai i to kainga, kia haere ake au ki te whakatakitaki haere i o mokopuna ki nga wahi o te whenua nei e watea ana i te noho a te tangata, tirotiro haere ai he taunga iho mo te remu ki raro, a maku e hoki mai ki te toro mai i a koe i konei."

Ka mea atu a Toi:—"Haere i te taha rawhiti o te motu nei, kei te watea te whenua, ka kite taunga koe hei te taha moana e koe te taunga tangata, kia rua ai nga rourou, ko to te moana, ko to uta, hei matua mo te pani me te wahine, me nga tamariki. Haere, ko to matua iwi waiho kia tuwhera ana, hei ara kuia, hei ara mo nga tamariki."

Ka whakaae atu a Whatonga ki a Toi mo āna tohutohu mai ki a ia.

Ka haere mai a Whatonga me ona tamariki, me tona ope, e tata ana ki te rua rau tane me nga wahine, haunga nga tamariki. Ka tae mai a Whatonga ki Ohiwa, tae mai ki Huiarua, ka mahia tona kainga ki reira. Ka roa e noho ana i Huiarua, ka neke mai ki tetahi wahi ano noho ai; ka mahia tona whare, a ka oti, he wheki nga pakitara me te tuarongo, ko te whatitoka he rakau. Ka kawaia taua whare ko Tapere-nui-o-Whatonga te ingoa, ka mutu.

Ka roa e noho ana, ka neke mai a Whatonga me ona tamariki, me tona ope katoa, noho rawa mai ko Maraetaha. Kaore a reira i tau ki a ia, ka neke mai i Maraetaha tau rawa mai ko Nukutaurua. Ka roa e noho ana i kona, katahi a Whatonga ka korero ki a Tara raua ko Tautoki (Enei tamariki na Hotu-waipara, wahine a Whatonga, nana a Tara, i moe ra i a Umu-roimata, nana a Wakanui, a Tiwhana-a-rangi. Na Reretua, wahine tuarua a Whatonga, nana a Tautoki-ihunui-a-Whatonga, na Tautoki a Rangitane-nui. Ko te tuahine o Tautoki ko Rere-ki-taiari. Kati i konei)—ka mea atu ra a Whatonga ki a Tara, ki a Tautoki:—"E ta ma! Haere ki te mataki i te whenua e takoto nei. Kia mama he hoa mo korua, waiho ake nga wahine kia pepeke ai korua. Kei te rongo korua ki nga kupu mai a to korua tipuna i poroporoaki mai ra ki a tatau." Ka mea atu a Tara:—"Ae, e marama ana au ki ona kupu katoa."

Ka whiriwhiria te ope a Tara me tona taina, e toru tekau topu
taua ope a raua. Ka haere mai, tae mai ki Te Wairoa, haere tonu,
tae rawa atu ki Heretaunga, ka noho i reira mataki haere ai. Ka
haere mai, tae mai ki Rangi-whakaoma, haere tonu mai, ka tae mai
ki Okorewa, kaore i tau; ka haere, ka tae ki Para-ngarehu, katahi ka
titiro. Ka mea atu a Tara ki te taina ' Ka tau tenei wahi.' Ka tae
ki Porirua, ka haere tonu, ka tae ki Rangi-tikei ka ahu ma roto i te
awa, ka tae ki Patea, ka maro ki Tongariro, tae atu ki Taupo. Haere
tonu atu ma uta, ka tae ki Titi-o-kura, ka tapatu ki Mohaka, ka ahu
ki Te Wairoa, ka tae ki Nukutaurua. Ko Taka-raroa te kainga i
noho ai a Whatonga me ona tamariki, me ona mokopuna, me ona
tangata.

Ka tae atu a Tara ma me tona ope, ka nui te koa mai o Whatonga
kua tae mai ona tamariki. E tata ana ki te tau e ngaro ana taua ope
a Tara raua ko te taina. Katahi ka korerotia e Tara me te taina, me
ta raua ope katoa te ahua o te takoto o te whenua, te ahua o nga
awa nunui e puta ana ki roto ki nga moana wai tai, ki nga moana
wai maori. Me te ahua o nga moana e uru ana te wai tai, me nga
moana e uru te wai maori, ara moana wai maori tuturu. Me te
ahua o te takoto o nga maunga, me te ahua o nga ngahere, me te ahua
o nga mania. Pau katoa te korero i te ahua o nga taha moana me te
ahua o te takoto o te whenua o nga tahataha moana, pau katoa te
whakamarama.

Ka ui atu a Whatonga ki a Tara :—"Ki ta korua titiro kei
tewhea wahi te matua o te tanga* e ora ai?"

Ka mea atu a Tara me Tautoki:—"Kei te pongaihu tonu o te
motu nei, kei reira nga motu e rua i rongo ra tatau i tapaia e Kupe
ki nga ingoa o ana tamahine, ki a Matiu, ki a Makaro, Na, ko te
motu nui rawa kei te pu o te tonga, kei te puau o nga rerenga e rua
ki waho ki tahora nui a Hine-moana; engari ma te uma tangata tenei
e noho. Engari nga motu ririki e rua, ma te waka anake e whakataetae. Ahua pai te motu ki te taha mauru, tera e tipu te ora o te
kopu; ko te motu i te taha rawhiti (Ward Island) he horehore, he
kopuru te one."

Ka ui ano a Whatonga :—"E pewhea ana te motu rahi e ki na
koe mo te kumara?"

Ka mea atu a Tara:—"He pai te oneone, he onematua, he
tairanga te ahua o nga akaaka, ehara i te mahora, he one rere te
wai."

Ka mea atu a Whatonga :—"He one maroke ma te tau hauwai
e tipu ai te kai."

Ka mea atu a Tara:—"Ae, etahi wahi ahua maru ana, e pai
ana."

---

* Possibly in error for tangata.

Ka mea a Whatonga :—" Tena, he hohonu te wahaapu o nga awa na ki ta korua titiro, me ka timu te tai ? "

Ka mea atu a Tara :—" Tetahi, te wahaapu o te taha mai ki te rawhiti. Ko te ngutuawa ki te taha mauru he pae onepu, kei te pae moana o te taha moana tutuki rawa ki te moana o te tuawhenua. Ki taku whakaaro ake tera pea e whakaikeike te ngutuawa."

Ka ui ano a Whatonga :—" Kaore he ranga kowhatu o waho ? " Ka mea a Tara:—" Kaore, kei nga ripa rawa nga kowhatu e whakaika ana."

Ka mea ano a Tara :—" He tata mai tera motu ki te titiro atu, tera pea e po tahi ki te moana ka u atu ki uta ki te whakaaro ake."

Ka mea ano a Tara :—" Ko te moana o te taha mauru (Porirua) he wai tai, he moana pai, he moana ruru i te hau. Na nga pae hiwi i wahi te hau ki ta matau titiro; he onematua te one. He pai te ngutuawa o taua moana, engari he uaua ki te noho takitahi, ma te umauma tangata anake e noho. Kotahi te motu kei waho o te ngutuawa e takoto mai ana; tera pea e tae te waka ki te hoe atu i te atatu kia poutumaro te ra ka eke ai, ki te whakaaro. He motu pai tera ki te titiro atu, he marū, he papa tiraha, he kainga hau te ahua, engari e pai ana hei matua mo te wahine me nga tamariki. Na, te moana wai maori (Wairarapa lake) o te taha rawhiti o te pae maunga, he tahora nga tahataha, he moana kai ki te whakaaro ake, he repo nga tahataha, e heke ana nga awaawa o te pae maunga. He pae maunga kei te taha mauru, kei te taha rawhiti; he ahua papaku nga pae hiwi o te taha rawhiti. Ko te taha mauru he pae maunga ranga kowhatu, one takataka, one parahuhu, he tohetea te one, he tauranga puaheiri, e hara i te huka matua. Ko taua pae maunga he pokohiwi no te motu nei e takoto tonu mai ana, a tae mai ki te moana kei te taha mauru o tatau e noho atu nei. E heke ana nga awaawa o nga pae maunga e rua, o te taha mauru, o te taha rawhiti, ki roto. Ko te awa whakaheke o te moana nei kaore i rahi, e heke ana ki te taha marangai ki ta matau titiro. Kotahi rawa te motu paku nei e tau mai ana i waho i te taha rawhiti. He one punga nga tapa o taua moana, ma te umauma tangata ano e noho tenei wahi e taea ai. Pera hoki ra te moana i korero ake ra au i te pongaihu o te motu nei, taha rawhiti o te pae maunga ra, ma te umauma tangata e noho. He uaua te whakamatua ki te titiro noa atu, engari he pai te oneone, he one kai, he one paraumu, he one matua, he one pakirikiri etahi wahi; he pai nga mania, he tuwhera.

" Na, kotahi o nga moana ina tonu e tuwhera mai ra, he moana pai ano tera, he moana wai tai, e rere ana mai nga awa o te tuawhenua ki roto, engari he umauma tangata ano māna e whakatau ki te noho a reira. Kati, kua taunaha au i te moana wai tai o te pongaihu o te motu nei, ko reira he okiokinga mo tatau."

Ka mea a Whatonga :—"E pai ana. Kaua hei haohao nui te
noho a koutou i te whenua i haere na koutou. Ka pa kua ururuatia
te noho a te tangata e haohao nui ai te whakanro noho i te whenua;
ko tenei, whakatatanga ta koutou haere ki te whakanoho i te moana
o te pongaihu o te motu nei, te moana wai tai, te moana wai maori."

Ka whakaae nga tamariki, katahi ka whakatika te ope o
Whatonga ratau ko ona tamariki. Ko etahi o ona tangata i waiho e
ia ki Nukutaurua noho ai, hei tiaki i taua wahi ; e noho tahora noa
iho ana te noho a te tangata.

Ka haere a Whatonga, a Tara, a Tautoki, me era atu, nga tane,
nga wahine, me a ratau tamariki ano. Ka tae ki Heretaunga, ka
mihi a Whatonga ki te takoto pai o te whenua. Ka tae ki Rangi-
whakaoma, ka mea ia kia u o ratau waka ki reira noho ai, kia ta te
ngenge o nga tangata. Ko Akaaka-nui te wa i heke mai ai te ope o
Whatonga kawe mai i ona tamariki ki Poneke nei, tae atu ki
Wairarapa nei.

Ka noho ra i Rangi-whakaoma ra, a ka roa, ka pae he kai ma
ratau, he ika, he aruhe, ka haere ano te ope o Whatonga, ka tae ki
Okorewa. Ka haere tetahi o nga waka ki uta o te moana o
Wairarapa mataki haere ai, ka mutu, ka hoki mai ; ka haere ano te
ope nei, ka tae ki Poneke, ka u nga waka ki te motu e kiia ra ko
Matiu, ka noho i reira. Ka tahuri ki te mahi whare, he mea tiki nga
rakau i uta, me nga rau whare. Ka oti nga whare, ka tahuri ki te
mahi papa whakatipuranga kai kumara, korau, hei kao. Ka oti enei
mahi katoa, pae rawa te kai ki roto i nga rua, ara te kumara, ko te
korau he mea mahi ki runga i te whata karaho.

Ko te whare i mahia ki reira mo ona hunaonga, ka oti te mahi, ka
kawaia aua whare e toru, ko Haere-moana tetahi, ko Aotearoa tetahi,
ko Te Pu-o-te-tonga tetahi. Enei whare he whakanoho, ara he tino
whare, engari he hopara makaurangi te whakairo o aua whare e toru.
Ko aua ingoa mo to ratau haerenga mai i te moana i Hawaiki ki te
kimi haere mai i a Toi, a Haere-moana. Ko te motu i noho ai ratau,
i mahue atu ai Hawaiki, te kainga tuturu ; a Aotearoa, ara, na Kupe
tera ingoa i tapa Aotearoa, mo te haerenga mai i te moana, kaore i
kite whenua, a tae mai ana ki tenei motu, koia a Aotearoa. Na, ko
Te Pu-o-te-tonga, ko tenei ingoa mo te mahuetanga o ona tamariki, o
Tara, o Tautoki, me to raua tuahine, a Rere-ki-taiari, me ona
mokopuna, ki te pito rawa ki te tonga o tenei motu noho ai, hei
whakamaharatanga mo te wahi i a ia.

Ka kotahi te ngahuru e noho tahi ana a Whatonga me tona
whanau, me ona mokopuna, a Tuhoto-ariki, a Turia, a Hine-one, a
Rangitane-nui, me etahi atu o ratau, me te iwi hoki i wehea mai hei
awhina i ona tamariki. Kotahi rau topu nga tane, nga wahine, ka
wehea e Whatonga, kotahi rau takitahi ki a Tara, kotahi rau takitahi
ki a Tautoki-ihunui-a-Whatonga. Ko te tuahine o Tautoki, ko

Rere-ki-taiari, i mauria e Whatonga ki Nukutaurua hei tiaki i a ia. I tena wa kua kaumatuatia a Whatonga, kua mokopuna tuarua.

I muri o te otinga o enei whare, ka haere a Whatonga me Tara me etahi tangata hoe waka kia kite i Te Mana o Kupe. Ka tae ki Matakitaki, ka hoe atu ki Kapiti, a ka hoki mai, ka tae mai ano ki Matiu noho ai. Ka haere ki te mataki i nga ngutuawa o te moana, me te motu nui o waenganui o aua awa e rua; ka hoki mai ki Matiu.

Ka tae ki te Ihonui, ka ki atu a Whatonga ki ona tamariki tane me o raua iwi e rua ra:—"I muri i a au ka hoki nei kaore a konei e tau hei kainga tuturu. Waiho tenei kainga mo nga wahine me nga tamariki; haere nga tane ki roto i te motu wawahi rakau ai, kume-kume aka, hei mahi whare, hei mahi pa. Me mahi te pa tuwatawata ki te wahi i poua ra e au taku pou, kia pau taua wahi ki roto i te tuwatawata. Kia tu te pa, ko te puna wai hoki kia tata e koutou; me whakaara ano te tuawata (?) ara haerenga ki te wai, pekerangi ra a waho, koi tutakina e te taua whakaeke, kia taea ai he wai. Ko nga whata kai hei runga i te tihi o te puke ra. Ka hanga i te tuwatawata ki te wahi i poupoua haeretia ra e tatau, kia rahi tonu. Kia kotahi tonu te waha ngutu o te ara nui, ka tuwatawata ai te ara nui, ka hanga ai nga puhara, kia rua ki te tomokanga, kia rua ki te urunga ki roto i te marae nui o te pa, kia toru nga puhara mo tetahi taha, mo tetahi taha. Me take nunui katoa nga take, kia rua wana hei whakauru i waenganui o nga take, kia kore ai e taea e te taua.

Ko nga wahi manuka, rarauhe, hurupi, me tahutahu katoa ki te ahi i nga tau katoa e kitea atu ai kua ururuatia, koi mauria mai e te taua hei whakapuru i te take o te tuwatawata ka tahu ai ki te ahi, koinei te take e peratia ai e koutou nga wahi ururua.

Kia toru nga tuwatawata, kia kotahi te tuwatawata matahao, kia kotahi te tuwatawata pekerangi, ka tae ai ki te tuwatawata matua, ko to roto rawa tena o nga tuwatawata."

Ka mea atu ia i penei ai tana tohutohu kia noho pai ai nga kaumatua, me nga wahine, me nga tamariki.

Ka mea ano a Whatonga:—"Na, kia mahara, he pa koraha tenei no koutou, he pa mate i te kai kore, ko te rakau tena ma te taua, he whakaawhi kia mate ai i te kai, ka horo te pa. Me hanga e koutou he whare tatara ma koutou. Kia maha tonu ki nga pakitara tuarongo o o koutou whare tu ai, hei whatanga ika, hei pukaitanga kao kumara, korau, hei karaho punga pipi, kuku, paua maroke ma koutou. Mo te puta rawa ake he taua, e tu ana te poutaka o te kai, o te aruhe, o te karaka, o te tawa, te ora o to koutou tipuna, o Toi-kai-rakau,* e kiia nei ko Toi-kai-rakau."

* ? Toi-te-huatahi.

Ka mea ano a Whatonga :—" Nga papa māra e tata mai ana ki te
pa nei, e pai ana, ka moe hoki nga tangata ki roto i te pa nei. Engari
nga māra i matara atu ki tawhiti, me hanga rawa he pakokori tiaki
paenga māra.   Erua ona take o tenei tu pa, he tiaki i nga papa mara
kai, he whakaaraara i te pa tuwatawata, ka mohiotia he taua ka
huaki te taua."

Ka mea ano a Whatonga ki ona tamariki :—" Me wehe te pa
tuwatawata o tetahi o korua ki te puke i te taha katau o te ngutuawa
i te taha rawhiti ra; kia penei ano te mahi o te pa.   Engari ko nga
tino kaupapa mahinga kai hei te motu nui i kiia ake ra.   Ko nga
whare tatara kia pera ano me taku i korero ra te ahua o te mahi, o te
tu hoki.   I peratia ai kia titiro ai te taua whakaeke kaore he whata,
he pataka takotoranga kai, ka mohio e kore e roa e awhi ana kua
mate tenei pa i te kai kore, ka noho tonu ki te awhi i te pa.   Na, ka
mohio koutou ka roa e awhi ana, ma te mate kai e tute kia haere.
Mehemea e taea e koutou te whakaeke i tetahi wahi ke noa atu, e
kore e roa ka hinga tena taua, kua mate hoki ratau i te kai kore.
Koia te take i waiho ai nga kai i roto i te whare tatara.   I penei ai
au ki a korua kia waiho ai tetahi o o korua pa hei whakahauora i
tetahi, ka paaha te taua ki tetahi o o korua pa, ma tetahi e tiki
mai e whakauru, a ka pera hoki ki tetahi."

Ka mea ano a Whatonga :—" Na, tetahi mahi ma korua, me
haere ki te titiro i tetahi wahi pai e kore e kitea e te tangata haere,
era e uaua te kimi a te tangata, ka mahi he kainga ki reira.   Ka
kawe he kai takoto roa ki reira, he ika maroke, he kete aruhe paka,
he paua maroke, he tahā huahua, he karaka tao maroke, he kete tawa
tao whakamaroke.   Ka kiia tena tu kainga he kainga punanga, kia
kore ai e kitea.   Hei te po anake e tahu ai te ahi kai, kauaka i te
awatea, koi kitea te auahi e koiri ana.   Tenei punanga mo nga pa
horo; ka whakamau ki reira nga morehu noho ai, a mo te rongo
ranei he taua kei te haere mai, e whakahoro ana nga wahine, nga
kaumatua, nga tamariki ki reira noho ai.   Kia watea te pa tu tahora
mo te toa anake, kia mataratara te tu a te tangata, kia kore ai he
raruraru ki nga koroua, ki nga wahine, ki nga tamariki.   Ki te oti i a
koutou enei tohutohu aku, e kore koutou e rarua i te taua."

Ka mea atu a Tautoki ki a Whatonga :—" He pai rawa a runga i
nga moutere nei mo nga kaumatua me nga wahine me nga tamariki
hei nohoanga."

Ka mea atu a Whatonga :—" Kaore, ko te he o tena ka mohio te
taua kei reira nga koroua, nga wahine me nga tamariki, ka waiho te
nuinga o te taua kia awhi ana i te pa, ka tikina aua moutere ka
hurihia e te taua."

Ka mutu nga tohutohu mo te ahua o te mahi pa, me nga punanga,
me nga pakokori, me nga whare tatara, ka mea a Whatonga :—" E
toru nga rakau hei ako ma koutou, he tokotoko, he rakau poto, he

taiaha, he pouwhenua, kotahi tonu enei e rua. Kaua hei noho noa iho
ki te ako i te hapai o enei rakau. Ko te tino tohu mau mo enei rakau
kei nga timu o te tangata; ka kite koe e oi ana nga timu pakihiwi,
kua mea ia ki te patu i a koe. Ko tetahi o nga tohu, me titiro e koe
ki nga konui o te waewae whangai kaua te waewae tarewa, hei te
waewae whangai anake koe titiro ai, hei te timu hapai o
te rakau. Mehemea e rua nga ringa e pupuri ana i te tokotoko, i te taiaha, i te pouwhenua ranei, me titiro koe ko tewhea te
ringa taki o te rakau. E rua hoki ringa o te tangata matau, he katau
tetahi, he maui tetahi; kia pera ano tau hapai i tau. Ki te whiti ia
ki te maui, me whiti ano e koe ki te maui hoki tau, a ki te whiti ki
te ringa katau, me whiti ano tau ki te ringa katau tau rakau mau ai,
me te u ano o mata ki tona timu, ki tona konui ranei. Kaua enei
tohutohu e taka i a koe, kia kite ai koe i te patu mou.

Na, mo te rakau poto kaore he tikanga. Mehemea ki te mau koe
i tau ki to ringa katau, pai noa atu; a ki te mau mai ia i tana ki tona
ringa maui, pai noa atu—he rakau poto hoki tena. E rite ana tena ki
to ringa tonu ake nei. Na, ki te whakapiri korua ko to hoariri, kia
taka o waewae, kaua hei tu, whakataka ana ia kia hangai tona aroaro
ki to kaokao, whakataka ana hoki koe kia hangai tonu to aroaro ki
tona aroaro. Engari kia tere tonu to whakapiri ki to hoariri, ka
whangai e koe kia wawe ia te turapa. Kaua e tukua te mata o to
rakau kia tarewa ki waho, waiho tonu i mua i to waewae whangai te
mata o te tokotoko, o te taiaha, o te pouwhenua ranei. Ma te mata e
whakaoho, ma te rapa e patu mehemea he taiaha, he pouwhenua
ranei. Mehemea he tokotoko, kia tata tonu te mata o to tokotoko ki
to waewae whangai, taki ki tetahi kinga a waha. Ko te patu poto,
hei raro te rapa o to rakau poto, tetahi hapai tera. Ko tetahi hapai,
waiho kia tarewa ana to ringa i waho, kia wawe ia te whawhaia mai
ki te tuku mai i tana patu ki roto i a koe. Ka kite koe kua tuku mai
tona patu ki roto i a koe, me tuku ma to ringa maui e poka to karo,
kia watea ai to ringa i te patu ki te whiu i te patu, kia hoki rawa ake
te ringa i tona patu kua pa ia i to patu. Te wahi tere e mate ai te
tangata ko te pu o te taringa, he rahirahi te angaanga o kona, e kore
e hoki te tuarua o te patu; kaua te tinana, a ki te pai te watea o te
ringa hapai rakau, topea e koe i te ringa, hei raro iho i te timu o te
pakihiwi tope ai, engari kia tarewa te ringa ki runga ka tope ai."

Ka mea a Whatonga :—" Mo te whakaputa ki waho o te pa ki te
hoariri, kia tere te puta o nga toa, kia tokorua te rerenga kotahi,
pena tonu a muri mai, a muri mai. Ko nga toa ki mua kaua hei
puta ka tu mai i waho, oma rawa ki te wahi watea, waiho ma te toa
e whai, kia watea ai te waha ngutu ka tahi. Nga take o te pera kia
whai ai nga toa ki te mataika mana hei takiri i tona ingoa toa; ka
watea a muri i nga toa. Mehemea e kapi ana a waho o te ngutu,

kokiritia tonutia ki waenganui tonu o te matua, engari kia inaki tonu
te rere o nga toa hapai rakau ki mua. E kore tena ope e tu i a
koutou, ahakoa pewhea te nui o te ope taua."

Ka mea ano a Whatonga ki ona tamariki:—"Mehemea he ope
taua tau, tukuna kia tekau nga tangata kakama te waewae ki mua,
kia ahua matara atu ka tuku atu ai i nga (kaikape). Mehemea
kotahi tekau nga toa hapai rakau, kia tokorima e tuku i muri tata
tonu mai o nga tangata waewae, ara kia ahua matara atu ano. Ki
te whakaeke nga toa o tera taua, kia tata tonu mai ki nga tekau
tuatahi ka manukawhaki ai e to tangata waewae. Ki te huri mai te
aroaro o te itekau tangata tuatahi, kia ata haere atu te tokorima toa
taua, me te karanga atu—'Tahuri! Tahuri!' hei whakatau noa, e
kore e tahuri atu. Me tuku mai ki muri o te tokorima toa taua taua
tekau, ka tahuri atu hei whare mo nga toa tokorima ra. Na, ko nga
toa taua e rima i wehea ra mo muri me noho i muri tata tonu o te
tekau tangata waewae ra. Ki te pena te whakahaere, e kore e taea.
Ko te tino matua ki muri mai aki atu ai; kia kaha te whakatitiko
haere."

Koia tenei nga tohutohu a Whatonga ki a Tara raua ko tona
taina ko Tautoki-ihunui-a-Whatonga. Ka mutu nga tohutohu, ka
akona e Whatonga te karakia mata rakau, me te karakia hoa i te
tapuwae whai i te tangata. Ka mutu ena mahi a Whatonga, ka ki
atu a Whatonga:—"Ko te mauri o te tino pa kawea e korua ki te
taha ki raro o te paepae o te turuma o te pa, ki reira takoto ai. Hei
te kowhatu huka-a-tai, hei te kowhatu onewa ranei, kaua etahi atu
kowhatu: ka whakanoho ai ko Tuhinapo, ko Tunui-o-te-ika, kati
kia rua, koia na nga atua noho paepae whakaheke o mua iho; ko
Maru tetahi atua pera. Enei atua hei tiaki i te pa, hei whakaatu kei
te haere mai te taua, hei whakaatu i te tohu mate o te taua, o te pa
ranei."

I muri o enei tohutohu ka mea a Whatonga mana e haere, mana
e hoki mai ki te toro mai i a ratau. "Kia ngaro to koutou tipuna ki
te hopara nui a Papa-tuanuku, hei reira whakanekeneke mai ai i o
korua taina me te iwi ki tenei taha o Te Wairoa whakanoho haere
mai ai, a ma koutou hoki e whakanoho haere ake tenei pito o te tai
rawhiti o te motu nei. Ki te tae mai he heke i muri i a koutou tukua
atu ki te taha hauauru noho ai, kia mau a Te Mana o Kupe, o Kapiti,
i a koutou, hei okiokinga koroua, wahine, tamariki ma koutou i nga
wa e haere ai koutou i te ope taua. Kaua nga motu nei e waiho hei
okiokinga koroua, wahine, tamariki ranei, koi wehewehe i nga toa
taua hapai rakau. (Mo Matiu, mo Makaro enei kupu a te kaumatua
ra). Engari kia kaha te whakangau i nga tangata kakama te waewae
te hapai rakau, kia waitaka ai te whakaputa rakau i te aroaro tangata
ke."

Ka hoki a Whatonga i konei.

I muri i a Whatonga, i te marama o Putoki-nui-o-tau, ka timata te whanau te auga ki te whakaepa rakau, aka-tokai, mo nga whare, mo te pa hoki i poua haeretia ra e to ratau papa, e Whatonga.

Ka patai i konei a Kereopa:—"E Moi! He aha te tau o nga mahi e korero na koe, kia marama ai tatau ki nga tau o te nohoanga haeretanga mai o te motu nei tae mai ki naianei?"

Ka mea a Moihi :—"Kaore he tauhere o nga tau i te iwi Maori penei me ta te Pakeha nei. Ka mutu ano nga mea i marama ko nga marama me nga ra, me te raumati, me te hotoke."

Ka mea ano a Te Matorohahga :—"Me hoki ano taku korero ki a Tara raua ko te taina me o raua iwi. Ka mahi rakau ; ko etahi ki te mokihi rakau, ko etahi ki te tuku rakau ki raro; ko etahi ki te tuporoporo, ko etahi ki te wawahi, ko etahi ki te tarai tātā, ko etahi ki te amoamo ki te taha o te awa e kiia nei ko Heretaunga, katahi ka mokihi ai ki rawahi o Te Whanga nui a Tara.

Engari kia marama ano, i te wa i a Whatonga i wehe mai ra i tona tipuna i a Toi, kaore ano a Ohiwa i tapaia, a Hinarua. a Turanga, a Maraetaha, a Nukutaurua, tae mai nei ki Te Whanga nui a Tara, a Porirua, a Kapiti, engari a Matiu, a Makaro, a Te Mana o Kupe; kua tapaia era wahi e Kupe ratau ko oua tamariki; nga wahi i noho ai, i haere ai ratau, i whai ingoa. Na Katorangi, he mokopuna tuatoru na Kupe raua ko Hine-te-aparangi taua tangata e ki ana, na tona tipuna i korero ki a ia nga ingoa o nga wahi i tapaia haeretia e ratau ko oua tamariki, o te motu nei.

Kati, ka whakaarahia te pa nui touu, ara te pa tuwatawata, ka oti, ka mahia nga whare o roto. E rua nga tino whare whakanoho, ko Raukawa tetahi, he ingoa na ratau mo te moana i waenganui o tenei motu, o tera motu; ko tenei whare no Tautoki. Ko tetahi o nga whare whakanoho ko Whare-rangi, he whakamahara mo te wahi i tu ai a Wharekura i Te Hono-i-wairua, i Uru. Ka tapaia te ingoa o te puna wai ko Te Puna o Tinirau. Tera ingoa o ratau mo te hanga e hu na te pakake i te moana, koia na Te Puna a Tinirau. Ka tapaia e ratau te ingoa o te pa ko Te Whetu-kairangi. Ko te take o tera ingoa kaore e kite tangata o etahi iwi ke, ka noho moke noa iho ratau, ko nga whetu anake o te rangi nga mea hei matakitaki ma ratau i ia po, i ia po. koia a Te Whetu-kai-rangi.

Ka oti te pa nei katahi a Te Umu-roimata ka ki atu ki a Tara :— "Ko te moana nei me waiho te ingoa ko koe." Ka whakaae atu a Tara, koia Te Whanga nui a Tara.

Ka mea atu a Te Umu-roimata ki a Tara :—"Me whakaara he pa kia toru ki tera taha ki te tuawhenua hei mataki taua haere mai, ope haere mai ranei, o nga iwi o tawhiti, kia owhiti ai koe a Te Whetu-kairangi. Kia tu era pa hei whakaruru i Te Whetu-kairangi. Koi tihaehaetia matau o te tangata i te ra e whiti ana."

Ka whakaae a Tara kia mahia aua pa e toru. Ka mahia a Uruhau ki te pito ki te tonga, ka oti tena. Ko Te Maioha te whare nui i roto; ehara i te whare whakanoho tenei whare.

Ka whakaarahia ko Te Aka-tarewa, he pa ano, kei te taha tonga o Matairangi (Mt. Victoria) te tunga o tenei pa. Ko te whare o roto ko Moe-ahuru, e hara i te whare whakanoho. Ka oti tenei pa ka whakaarahia ki te matamata o taua taukahiwi e hangai atu ana ki te marangai. Ka ara tena pa ka tapaia te ingoa ko Te Wai-hirere; te take o tera ingoa mo te mate makutanga o nga wahine me nga tane i tetahi marangai nui, tu ana te wai i runga i taua kurae i te nui o te ua, he mea kari ki te awa-kari, katahi ka rere te wai ki te moana; ka tapaia he ingoa mo taua pa ko Te Wai-hirere. Ko te whare o roto ko Waipuna, he ingoa no te wai o taua pa, he puna kari te wai, ka waiho hei ingoa mo te whare.

Na, ko te wahi uaua o ta ratau mahi ko te mahinga mai i nga rakau. Ko te roroa o nga pou matua o Te Whetu-kairangi me te pa o Tautoki, a Para-ngarehu, i te rae o te taha rawhiti ra te tunga o Para-ngarehu, he pa nui hoki tera, engari kaore i rite ki a Te Whetu-kairangi te nui. Kati, ko te roroa o nga pou matua e toru whanganga te roroa; ko nga wana e rua whanganga. Kotahi te hau ki te whenua o nga pou matua me nga wana. Ko nga huapae o te pa e wha, he mea hohou ki te aka-tokai katoa. Ko nga pou take o te pa e rima whanganga te roroa; ko te nunui o ana pou, o te take kotahi, kotahi whanganga. Ko nga pou matua kotahi te hau te matotoru, haunga nga wana whakauru penei ano me nga wana pa o naianei engari ko te roa e rua whanganga me te hau. Ko te hohonu ki roto i te oneone e kotahi te hau. Na, ka kite mai koutou i te nui o te mahi me te taimaha o aua rakau, me te whakaterenga atu i te wahi i mahia ai tae atu ki tera taha o Te Whanga nui a Tara, mo aua pa, tae atu ki nga pa pakupaku, me o ratau whare ano. Ko te kainga punanga nohoanga mo nga wahine me nga koroua me nga tamariki, me ka horo i nga pa tahuri, i nga parekura ranei, ka kawea ki Takapau-rangi kei te kauru o Wainui-o-mata, he moana kei te taha rawhiti o Te Whanga-nui-a-Tara, kei uta atu o te pa o Para-ngarehu te pahī punanga.

Na, he maha nga papa mahinga kai; ko Kirikiri-tatangi kei te taha rawhiti o Te Whetu-kairangi. Ko Maraenui kei te taha mai ano ki Te Au a Tane nei. Ko Huriwhenua ko te wahi e kiia ra ko Te Aro tae noa mai ki raro iho o Tawatawa i te taha mauru marangai. Ko te wahi i waiho ra hei papa takaro ra ko Hauwai tera maara. Ko te wahi e kiia ra ko Watiwhaama (Watt's Farm, Newtown), taua tawhanga ra puta atu i te taha mauru o Uruhau ra, ko Pae-kawakawa tera wahi, he papa kumara na Hine-kiri. He wahine rangatira tenei, he uri na Tara, he tuahine no Wakanui; ko Hine-kiri to mua, ko Wakanui to muri, ko Tiwhana-a-rangi to muri iho; na Hine-akau anake ratau, wahine ariki a Tara, he mokopuna a Hine-akau ua Whata.

Ko tera pa ko Te Wai-hirere no Te Rangi-kai-kore, he tama tenei na Tuhoto-ariki, tuakana o Turia; he tangata rangatira tenei, pai, manaaki tangata ia. I mau mai tetahi wahine me ana tamariki tokotoru, no Mua-upoko, i te taua a Ngati-Rangi. Ka tae mai ki Uruhau; i a Pakau taua pa a Uruhau, ka tukuna taua wahine e Whirikai, rangatira o Ngati-Rangi, ki a Pakau, hei utu mo te kete mangā me te kete aruhe i haere ai ratau i te taua ki a Mua-upoko i te matenga i Pukehou; he pa tera kei te rawhiti o Otaki, a Pukehou. I mau mai taua wahine i reira, me ona tamariki, ka mauria oratia mai hei utu mo aua kai. I reira a Te Rangi-kai-kore e noho ana i te wa i tae mai ai a Ngati-Rangi. Ka tukua taua wahine me ona tamariki ki a Pakau, ka mutu, ka whakatika a Pakau, ka mea mai ki a Te Rangi-kai-kore:—"Kia rua ki a koe hei kinaki kumara mau, kia rua ki au hei kinaki kai ma taku tamahine ma Whakapiriuha."

Ka mea atu a Te Rangi-kai-kore ki a Pakau raua ko Whirikai:— "E tama! Kia toru rawa matenga mo te tangata? Ko te pa horo, a ko te tukutuku hei utu kai ma korua, a ko te ki hoki kia patua hei tamiwaha ma korua? E hara tenei i te whakaaro tika na korua."

Katahi ia ka karanga atu ki taua wahine, ki a Hinerau:—"E hine! Whakatika ki runga, hoake tatau ko o tamariki ki roto i Te Whetu-kairangi, ki te okiokinga o te tangata."

Ka mauria taua wahine me ana tamariki tokotoru; ka tae ki reira, ka ki atu a Wakanui:—"E ta! Te Rangi-kai-kore, haere, kawea te wahine ra me ona tamariki ki Pukehou, ki to ratau na kainga noho ai. Ka tika tau, kia toru rawa matenga mo te tangata i te ra tahi; ka ora ano ra, kia ora, kaua e whakamokaikaitia te tangata."

Koia au i ki ai he tangata rangatira pai a Te Rangi-kai-kore.

*　　*　　*　　*

TE TAUA A MUA-UPOKO KI TE WHANGA NUI A TARA;
KA PAAHA KI TE WHETU-KAIRANGI.

Na, taua pakanga a Ngati-Rangi nei kei te take i haere ai a Te Kopara, rangatira o Mua-upoko, ki Patea ki te amio i a Rauru, i a Ngati-Ruanui hei ngaki i te mate o Mua-upoko i Te Pukehou, i mate ai te rangatira o taua pa. Ka haere mai nei a Tamatea-kopiri, a Kakataia, nga rangatira tenei o taua ope taua a Te Kopara.

Kaore te taua nei i tika atu ki roto o te awa o Heretaunga ki Te Hau-karetu, ki Pa-whakataka, ki Purihoro, ki nga wahi i noho ai a Ngati-Rangi. Ka tika ke mai taua taua ki Hataitai, ki Uruhau, ki Te Aka-tarewa, ki Te Wai-hirere, kia tahuri enei pa, kia taea ai e ratau a Te Whetu-kairangi, te tino pa ariki o te motu nei o Motu-kairangi. Na Hine-kiri tenei ingoa i tapa, he kianga atu na Tara ki a Te Umu-roimata: "Wai ra he ingoa mo to tatau nei motu e noho nei tatau?" Ka mea atu a Te Umu-roimato, "He iti hoki a Te Whetu-kairangi?"

Ka mea a Tara:—"E, no te pa ano ra tena ingoa." Ka karanga atu a Hine-kiri:—"Waiho he ingoa ko Motu-kairangi.

Ka whakaaetia e nga matua me te iwi ko Motu-kairangi. Te take i whakaaetia ai taua ingoa, kaore rawa he wahi ahua raorao, mania he haereerenga atu ki te haereere; tiro tonu ake i te po ko nga whetu, ko te marama, i te awatea ko te ra, ko nga kapua e tere ana i te rangi; ko te moana i tahi taha, i tahi taha. Koia i kiia ai ko Motu-kairangi taua motu; ko Whetu-kairangi te pa.

Kei te taha mauru mai, kei reira tetahi roto hawai nei, he roto tuna whakamokai, he mea mau mai i roto i Te Awa-kairangi, ara i Heretaunga awa. Ko tenei ingoa ko Heretaunga no te taenga mai o Ranginui me tona ope ki te toro mai i a Tara raua ko te taina ko Tautoki, ka noho, titiro ake he hiwi tahi taha, tahi taha, he ngahere-here. Katahi ka mea:—"Aue! Taukuri ra! Ki te kainga o nga tangata nei; ko Heretaunga rawa pea to korua kainga kia whakamo-mori korua ki te noho i konei."

Ka mea atu a Tautoki:—"E ta! Hei aha te kete tuwhera, kaore ki te kete ruru tau ana te mauri."

Aua kupu a Ranginui mo te pai o Heretaunga, mo te marama, hei tawhiti ano te ope e haere mai ana ka kitea atu, kaore e ngaro. Ko Te Whanga nui a Tara he kino, he hiwi, he ngaherehere anake. Me ohorere te kitenga i te ope haere mai o tawhiti. Na, ko ta Tautoki e ki ana ia he pai rawa atu a Te Whanga nui a Tara i Here-taunga, ora te tangata i te ope taua whakaeke, he ora i te kai moana, ka rahi te kai mahi a te ringa, e ora i te kai moana, i te manu o te ngaherehere, koia te kete ruru.

Katahi a Ranginui ka ki atu:—"E tama! Waiho te awa nei, a Te Awa-kairangi, hei whakamaharatanga mo ta tatau korero ko Heretaunga." Koia a Heretaunga awa.

Na, me hoki ano ta tatau korero ki te ope taua a Te Kopara o Mua-upoko ra. Ko te tino take i whakaae ai a Nga Rauru, a Ngati-Ruanui ki taua amio i a ratau hei taua ngaki mate mo Pukehou, he pirangi huia, kakahu Maori, mako mau taringa. Katahi ka haere mai; kaore i pai tenei wahi o taku rongo; he ahakoa, i rongo au i haere mai taua ope ma runga waka, e wha nga waka, he waka taua anake. I u mai ki Porirua nei, ka noho i Papa-kowhai i te taha rawhiti o Porirua nei, tatari atu ai ki a Mua-upoko. Ka tae mai a Mua-upoko i te wa e pua nei te kowhai. Ka tae mai ki te taumata i Te Wharau, ka kite i nga ahi e kaka ana i Te Wai-hirere, i Te Aka-tarewa, i Uruhau, i Te Whetu-kairangi, i Pae-kawakawa, i Motu-haku, i Makure-rua, i Wai-komaru, te pa a Tukapua o Ngati-Mamoe, era pa e rua; i te taha ki Te Rimurapa enei pa e rua. Ka ui atu a Tamatea-kopiri:—" Hei hea tatau o enei ahi e kaka ake nei?"

Ka mea:—"Waiho tatau i te ihonui i te wahi kaihora"—ara i te wahi e noho wehewehe ana nga tangata te noho. Ka whakaae te taua nei.

I te po o tetahi rangi noa ake ka moemoea a Kauhika, he whaea no Te Rangi-kai-kore tenei, he wahine moemoe hoki taua kuia. Ka moe ia, e nohoia ana a Te Wharau e te tangata—"I tahuna mai i reira te ahi nei tae tonu mai te mura ki Uruhau nei; wehi tonu mai au, oho tonu ake nei au."

Ka mea a Te Rangi-kai-kore:—"Me haere he tangata ki Te Wharau noho ai ki te taha ki te rawhiti o te matuaiwi, ki te tawhatitanga o te hiwi o te tau o Te Wharau noho ai ki tahaki, me kore e tupono te marua a po a te kuia nei."

Ka tonoa a Mohuia raua ko Kaipara, ka tae atu ki te wahi i tohutohutia atu ra e Te Rangi-kai-kore, ka noho i reira. Ka whanatu ka tairi te ra ki te huapae o te po, ka puta te ope nei e haere ake ana ki runga i taua hiwi i Te Wharau. Ka hoki mai aua tangata, ka mea, "He taua kei Te Wharau e matai ana ki te ahua o te kaka a nga ahi."

Tonoa tonutia e Te Rangi:—"Haere ki Te Aka-tarewa, ki Uruhau, kia tukua nga wahine me nga tamariki ki Te Whetu-kairangi; ka tono atu he tangata ki Para-ngarehu whakamohio atu ko te whakaariki tenei kei Te Wharau e matai ana mai."

Ka haere a Mohuia ki Te Whetu-kairangi, ka haere a Kaipara ki Te Aka-tarewa tae atu ki Uruhau. Ko nga waka o te tangata whenua ka whakawhitia ki te taha ki Motu-kairangi· Ka tikina ka tiakina te matuaiwi e tika ana mai i Te Wharau ma te taukahiwi e ahu whaka te tonga ana mai. Ka tonoa he tangata ki Pukeahu i runga ake o Hauwai ra, he ata marama hoki e ki ana te po. Ka kitea nga tangata e haere mai ana i te taha moana i Kumutoto ra e haere mai ana. Ka hoki mai nga toro o Pukeahu, ka ki mai:—" Kei te one i Waititi e haere mai ana te hiku, kei Kumu-toto nei a mua e haere mai ana. Me te uru ngahere te ruru o te tangata."

Katahi ka nohoia tonutia i Kaipapa, i te wahi i te taha rawhiti o Hauwai ra tiaki atu ai, mehemea era e peka ki tewhea pa; ka kite e haere tika ana ki Uruhau te taua nei whakaeke ai.

Ka rewa nga whetu o te ata, ka haere atu te tangata whenua o roto o Te Wai-hirere, ka tutaki atu ki nga tangata o Te Aka-tarewa. Katahi ka whakaputaia mai e te tangata whenua o roto o te pa i Uruhau ki waho. Kua taka tetahi wehenga o te taua ki te taha moana, ko tetahi wehenga i runga i te hiwi e awhi ana i te pa. Kua mohio tonu mai a Pakau ka mate taua taua i a ia, a me tona mohio tonu mai ki waho nga tangata o Te Wai-hirere, o Te Aka-tarewa whanga ana mai ki tona whakaputanga ki waho. Tera hoki a Tara raua ko Tautoki kua eke kei runga o te hiwi i Orongo; he ingoa tera no Tamatea-ariki i tona taenga mai ki Te Whetu-kairangi. Ka piki ki runga i taua hiwi matere ai ki roto i Te Whanga nui a Tara, ki tera motu hoki. I Te Awa a Taia e kato ana a "Takitumu," e aukaha ana, e pani ana ki te ware houhou i nga kowhao, ka oti katahi ka haere a "Takitumu" ki Arapawa, ara ki Te Wai-pounamu. Na Kupe tenei ingoa i tapa mo tera motu, nana hoki i kite te pounamu tuatahi ki Arahura i te taha mauru o tera motu.

Na, ka eke ra a Tara, a Tautoki ki te hiwi i Orongo ki reira taupua ai i te paahatanga o te taua ki Uruhau. Ka marama ka kitea atu te taua i te taha takutai i raro iho o te pa o Uruhau, a kua puta rawa te taanga whenua o roto o Uruhau ki waho. I rangona atu ki te waha o Pakau e karanga ana :—"Huakina! Huakina!" Kua wehe etahi o te taanga whenua ki te ara i te takutai, kua ara hoki te pakanga a tera ara. Ka apiti atu hoki te taanga whenua o Te Wai-hirere, o Te Aka-tarewa ki te pa ki Uruhau. Ka karanga a Te Rangi-kai-kore:—"Pakau E! Apitiria! Apitiria!" Ka rongo te taua, ka horo ki roto i te motu i te taha mauru o Uruhau. Katahi ka whawhai ko te ara ki tatahi, ka mate a Te Toko, tetahi o nga rangatira o te ope taua i te whawhai ki Waitaha i te takutai i te kurae i te taha mauru o Te Awa-a-Taia.

Ka po, katahi ka whakaaro nga tangata whenua, a Ngati-Hinewai, koi tahuri te taua ki te hauhake i nga purapura o a ratau maara kumara, kua pihi hoki te kumara, nga tipu. Katahi ka hutihutia i te po, ka waiho hei ingoa mo Ngati-Hinewai ko Ngati-Hutihuti-po. Ka mutu ka whakawhitiwhiti ki roto i Te Whetu-kairangi; tae rawa atu a Te Rangi-kai-kore, a Pakau, a Te Piki-kotuku, nga rangatira o nga pa o te tuawhenua, kua whiti nga wahine me nga tamariki, nga koroua ki Para-ngarehu e noho ana mai. Ko te toa hapai rakau anake e noho ana i roto o Te Whetu-kairangi, kī tonu taua pa, e ono topu hoki a Ngai-Tara i taua wa nei. Ko te ope taua a Ngati-Ruanui, a Mua-upoko, e wha rau takitahi.

I taua po ano ka tahuna a Te Toko, a Whakatau ki te ahi ki roto o Haewai, kei te taha mauru ma tonga o Te Rae-kaihau, taha moana.

I te ata ka tahutahuna nga pa, a Uruhau, a Te Aka-tarewa, a Te Wai-hirere, me nga whare paenga maara katoa i Pae-kawakawa, me era atu maara katoa o te tuawhenua. Ka tahuri te ope nei ki te mahi mokihi mo ratau hei whakawhitiwhiti mai i a ratau ki Motu-kairangi. Ka rupeke mai ki Te Motu-kairangi, katahi ka whakaawhitia a Te Whetu-kairangi, te pa. Kotahi rau i Takapuna, kotahi rau i Kirikiri-tatangi, kotahi rau i Te Mirimiri, kotahi rau i te taha ki Kaiwaka, te roto i te taha mauru o Te Whetu-kairangi; i penei te whakaawhitanga i Te Whetu-kairangi. Ka mahia mai te rarauhe i te tuawhenua hei whakapuru i te pa, kia tahuna ai ki te ahi iua puta te hau. Ka whakataetae ki te huri haere i nga powha rarauhe kia tata atu ki te pa;

kore rawa i tata atu i nga tangata o roto o te pa te werowero mai ki te manuka tarere mai i runga i nga puwhara o te pa. Tokowhitu nga tangata i mate i te tangata o roto o te pa, he mea tarere mai i runga i nga puwhara. He penei te ahua o tenei rakau, he mea whakakoi tetahi pito, te pito i kaniwhatia, e tu ki te tangata ka whati atu ki roto i te tangata ina tu, a ki te unuhia mai ka whati atu ki roto i te pito o te kaniwha, ka mau atu i roto i te tangata, a mate atu i tana kaniwha te tangata.

E kiia ana ka noho te iwi nei i waho, ka puta te hau tonga me te ua i tetahi po, ka mate te iwi nei i te ua, i te maeke, ao noa te ra. Ka mate hoki i te kai kore, kua pau hoki nga kumara whakatipu o nga maara te kai e ratau, nga purapura o ro oneone. Kaore e taea atu nga kai o te moana, te paua, te kuku, te pipi o Te Awa a Taia.

Katahi a Tara ka ki atu ki ona toa taua :—"Kia awatea rawa apopo ka whakaputa ki waho. Kia tokotoru ki te taki i te matua, ma muri e pēhi atu; kaua hei waiho; e kore e roa e whawhai ana ka ngenge i te mate kai, i te mate i te marangai hoki."

Ka whakaae katoa te tangata o roto o Te Whetu-kairangi. I waenganui po e taka ana te kai, e kai ana ka awatea. Katahi ka whakaputaina atu a Te Whetu-kairangi ki waho. I te nui o te puaheiri o taua po tae noa ki taua ra i puta atu nei nga toa nei, kite rawa ake kua pau atu te ono rau takitahi ki waho o te pa. Ka horo te taua nei ki te taha mauru ki Te Awa a Taia, tae atu ki reira nga mea i tae, na te tai kato mai ka matemate ki roto i te wai etahi, ko etahi na te patu a te tangata whenua. Ka mate a Tamatea-kopiri, a Marohi, ka mutu nga rangatira; ko tetahi o nga rangatira i mate ki roto i te wai, ka pae mai ki tahaki. Ki te korero he nui ano nga mea i puta, ara i whiti i te ia o Te Awa a Taia, te whakatere atu ki tetahi taha o te awa; tae rawa atu te kai patu ki te taha o Te Awa a Taia kua whitiwhiti etahi, te nuinga. I mohiotia ki nga mea i mate, he kotahi rau tuma, e kiia ana no Mua-upoko te nuinga o enei i mate nei. Ka mutu tenei pakanga.

Na, i muri o tenei pakanga, ahua roa ano te wa, ka tae mai a "Takitumu," ka noho i reira noho ai. I haere mai i Hokianga, i Muri-whenua, i a Ngapuhi ra. Kati, kua korerotia ake ra e au te nohoanga o Tamatea-ariki me te haerenga ki te Wai-pounamu, haere a Tamatea, a Te Rongo-patahi, a Kohupara, a Puhi-whanake, a Kaewa, a Maahu, a, he maha nga tangata a Ngati-Waitaha. Ka hori atu a "Takitumu," ka tae mai a Mapouriki, a Te Hooroa, a Te Kahawai, na Whatonga i tono mai ki te toro mai i te whanau, mehemea kei te pewhea te noho.

I konei ka wehe a Tautoki me tona iwi ki Wairarapa noho ai, ka tuturu ko Tara me ona iwi ki Te Whanga-nui-a-Tara noho ai, tae atu ano ki Wai-rarapa. Engari ko Tautoki ka tino wehe ia ki Wai-rarapa anake, ahu atu ki Tamaki, ahu atu ki Te Rerenga o Mahuru, ka mutu mai; ka tapahi ki roto ki Akitio awa, ka puta ki te moana

nui, ka haere mai i te takutai tae mai ki te Whanga-nui-a-Tara. Ka
rere i roto o Heretaunga tae atu ki tona kauru, tae atu ki Te Rere a
Mahanga (i te pae maunga, taha ki te mauru o Pae-tumokai
[Featherston] e tata ana ki Te Toko o Houmea), tae atu ki Kau-
whanga, ka makere ki roto o Manawatu, ka ahu ki uta, ka tae atu ki
Kai-mokopuna, he mokopeke, ka tutaki taua rohe i konei. I a raua
tahi ko te tuakana ko Tara me a raua uri, heke mai nei ki tenei
whakatipuranga e mau ana te mana o nga uri ki nga wahi i mau i a
ratau. Ko etahi wahi hoki he mea tuku na raua, tae mai ki o raua
uri me a raua mokopuna.

Na, ko te taha hauauru, ka rere i roto o te awa o Heretaunga tae
atu ki te kauru, ka mau atu ki Te Rere-a-Mahanga, ka whati ki te
mauru, Taumata-o-Korae, ka rere ki roto i te kauru o Otaki, rere
tonu i roto tae noa ki te moana, ka whakawhiti ki Kapiti, rere mai ki
te rae o Para-ngarehu, ka rere i te tahataha o te moana, tae noa ki te
ngutuawa o Heretaunga. Ka mau tenei wahi ki a Tara anake me ona
uri me ona iwi ake.

TE HAERENGA MAI O NGATI-MAMOE.

I a Tara ano e ora ana ka tae mai a Ngati-Mamoe, ka noho ki Te
Whanga-nui-a-Tara. Ka tukua atu e Tara te taha ki Pahua, tae noa
ki te moana, tae noa atu ki Te Rimurapa, tae noa atu ki Wai-pahihi e
hangai atu ana te ngutuawa ki Arapawa, ka rere i roto o taua awa, ka
puta mai ki te poho o Te Wharangi, he taukahiwi e takoto atu ki te
takiwa ki Porirua; ka rere mai ki te taha rawhiti nei o Te Wharangi,
ka makere ki roto i te awa o Waikohu, ka ahu whaka te rawhiti mai
ki Te Whanga-nui-a-Tara nei, ka tae mai ki te kauru o taua awa, katahi
ka ahu whaka te tonga, ka eke ki runga o te te hiwi ki Te Kopahou,
ka maro te rere i runga i te hiwi ki te moana waitai taha tonga ki Te
Hapua, taha mauru o te wahi e kiia ra ko Airana Pei (Island Bay), ko
reira a Te Hapua; ka rohe mai te wahi i tukua ki a Ngati-Mamoe i
konei i taua wa. No te wa i heke a Ngati-Mamoe ki Arapaoa ka
mahue te whenua, ka riro mai ano i a Ngai-Tara taua whenua katoa.

*   *   *   *

TETAHI KORERO MO TE INGOA NEI TE WHANGA-NUI-A-TARA.

He mea tango mai i tetahi pukapuka i tuhia mai e Hone Wairere,
o Whanganui.

Pari-whaiti, Oketopa 18-1911.

E hoa, tena koe, ko te whatu ngaro i a koe e ngaro nei i te matau
roa nei.

E hoa, i rongo au he tangata whakamine korero koe ki roto i te
rahu takai puni. Ana etahi mo roto i to rahu; engari, ki te kore e
marama i a koe aku *reta*, e taea hoki te aha; kā pā he whakairo rawa

na aku tipuna, e taea te tauaki ki te ataata rau nui. Kati enei . . .
. . . Ka haere mai a Tara me taua wahine, a Te Umu-roimata, ki
Heretaunga nei, tae mai ki te moana o Poneke nei, ka noho i te
moutere i waenganui o nga wahapu e rua. Ka mahia tona pa, a Te
Whetu-kairangi, kei te taha ki te ra; kei reira ano te puna wai
whenua, a Te Puna a Tinirau. Ko Te Roto-kura te roto kei te taha
mauru, he roto tuna na Wakanui. . . . .

No tetahi takiwa mai ka tapā te ingoa o taua moana e Te Umu-
roimata, wahine a Tara. Ka mea atu ia ki tona tane:—"E koro!
Ko wai he ingoa mo te moana nei?"

Ka mea mai a Tara:—"Ko Tawhiti-nui."

Ka mea atu a Te Umu:—"E! Waiho tonu ko koe he ingoa."
Koia Te Whanga nui a Tara i aranga ai.

Ka mea ano a Te Umu-roimata:—"Me waiho te awa e puta nei
i te taha rawhiti nei ki te moana ko Te Au a Tane."

Ka tapatapaia e taua ruruhi nga ingoa katoa o taua takiwa. Ko
Porirua, mo te ruanga o nga moana te take, koia a Porirua. He maha
atu nga ingoa a taua wahine i tapā ai.

E hoa, he mihi tenei ka uruki atu na ki a koe— Tena hoe, te mata
hapara o te kai taua.

(To be continued.)

THE GREAT MURU.

By a Taranaki Veteran.

DURING the Summer of 1873 I was living at Opunake, being manager of the Opunake Company's flax mill, and being in charge of the Europeans in that part of the district, as they worked at the mill, matters were brought more prominently to my notice than they otherwise would have been, and I had special facilities for seeing the full workings and effect of the *muru* of Te Namu *kainga*, the greatest *muru* that had been known on that coast in the memory of the oldest Maori.

Our mill and dwelling houses were situate on the south bank of the Otahi stream, and on the north bank, not far from the spot where Miss Dobie was afterwards murdered, was a Maori *kainga*, or village, of some twenty-five or thirty houses, usually called Te Namu *pa*, though it was not the real Te Namu, famous for Wi Kingi's defence against the Waikato war-party in about the year 1835; that was an intrenched position near the mouth of Otahi stream, about half-mile more to seaward.

One morning, about seven o'clock, while I was at breakfast a Maori woman rushed into the room crying out, "Kahui has run away with Lydia." As our ideas of Maori morality were not of a high order, the news caused but a mild excitement, and I simply said, "Well, what then?" The woman, astonished at my indifference, drew herself up, and in an angry tone repeated, "What then, what then, why there will be a big row, that's 'What then,'" and stalked indignantly out of the room. I laughed, went on with my breakfast, and thought no more about the matter. About the middle of the morning, however, some of the leading men of the village came to Mr. Black—our storekeeper and paymaster—and myself, and told us, with grave and anxious faces, there was sure to be trouble over this escapade of Kahui's; that as the parties concerned were of high rank, the relatives, friends, and connections (other than those living in Te Namu) of the guilty parties, intended to *muru* Te Namu, that is, rob the inhabitants of the village of all they possessed as *utu* (payment) for Kahui's offence, he being of high-rank in the village. One of the men who came to us with the news, was a regular old savage, a real old man-eater, and though he knew he would be robbed of all his belongings, he was in ecstasies at the prospect of the revival of a good old custom ; he danced around, he leaped and yelled, he quivered his hands and smacked his thighs, "Aha! Aha!" he cried, "the Maoris of this day think they know all about *muru*, they think when a horse or a cow, or a pig is taken, that is a *muru*.   But you and they will see a sight that has not been seen on this coast for a hundred years ; you will see a real *muru*," and, carried away by his feelings, he cried out, "O it is good to have lived to see this day," and quivered and shook and turned up the whites of his eyes and lolled out his tongue in a most diabolical manner. We were intensely amused at the antics of the old savage, but began to have a dim perception that a *muru* after the manner of the good old-times, might not be a matter for universal rejoicing.

And now I will digress for a moment to explain what all this fuss was about.

Kahui te Kararehe was a young and handsome chief of high rank in the Opunake district, and lived at Te Namu. He was already taking a leading position in the district, being clever, energetic, and possessing a soft and winning voice, and persuasive tongue. Lydia was a handsome half-caste, tall and graceful, and fair in colour, and Kahui was madly in love with her, and she returned his passion. Kahui wanted to marry her, but having years previously been betrothed and married to a half-negress named Betty, a daughter of black Davis (who boasted he was the first *white man* who came to Taranaki) the chiefs would not allow him to have Lydia. Whilst Lydia—to use a Scotch expression—was married on to Aperama, a young chief of high rank living in Parihaka. Kahui's marriage with Betty was not a happy one, nor was Lydia's with Aperama, and the trouble culminated in Kahui's eloping with Lydia. As both Kahui and Aperama were of considerable consequence—prospectively—in the district, the chiefs within a radius of fifteen to twenty miles of Te Namu, decided the event should be marked in an emphatic manner, by reviving in its full power and consequences, the ancient law of *muru*. Hence the dread and down caste looks of the Maoris who came to us, and the exultant delight of the old savage.

That afternoon those of us who were at times outside the mill, saw the Maoris from the nearest *kainga* (Matakaha—about a mile to the south of Te Namu) both men and women, troop past on their way to Te Namu, and after a time return, laughing gaily, and laden with old clothes, blankets, boxes, kits, eel-baskets, cooking utensils—and in fact all the moveable possessions of the village on which they could lay their hands. Our Maoris—as I may term them—were left with nothing but the clothes they had on them, and their guns and some food they had hidden. After dark the men came to Mr. Black and handed him in their guns, asking him to hide them away, as should any of the *muru* parties find them they would at once be taken possession of, as part of the spoil; and they also requested him on no account to return them until the *muru* was ended, for said they, "We may be hard pressed, more than we can bear, and we might be tempted to use the guns, and that would be bad for us, and for you." Mr. Black accordingly promised to hide away the guns, and give them up to neither friend nor foe, until the trouble was over; but he little knew the difficulties in store, nor the pressure he would have to resist.

The next morning (the 2nd day) the Maoris from Umuroa, Nuku-te-apiapi and Waitaha villages, to the northward of Te Namu, came trooping in, and spent nearly the whole day in raiding every fowl, duck, goose, turkey, and pig in the vicinity of or on the lands belonging to the village; not a feathered biped or grunter was left, and our Maoris began to look exceedingly gloomy.

On the third day the Maoris from Taungatara, Punehu and Ouri villages—between Opunake and Oeo—came and took away every horse, bullock, cow and calf they could find, not a hoof was left; and we had to carefully muster our horses and working bullocks and pen them, for fear they also should be taken. Even the old savage looked glum, and thought the affair had gone far enough; but the *muru* was by no means ended. By this time they had been robbed of every moveable thing they possessed, excepting the hidden food, and the guns in Mr. Black's charge.

Early on the morning of the fourth day a runner came from Parihaka to Te Namu, with the news that an armed party had left Parihaka, and were coming to have their share of the *muru*. "But," said our Maoris, when telling us this, "what can they get, we have only our houses and our lives left, and they may be coming to kill us," and then they demanded from Mr. Black their guns back again, in order that if things came to the worst they could defend their lives and the lives of their wives and children; it would not have been etiquette for them to leave their *kainga* until all was over. But Mr. Black wisely refused their request, as in the event of fighting we would be between two fires.

We learned that the war-party—*taua*—would be at Te Namu by 11 a.m.; and as there was likely to be an exciting time, we closed the mill soon after ten o'clock, and went to Te Namu to see all we could.

Not a Maori was there but those belonging to the *hapu*, it evidently was not correct for any but the principals to be present. The Maoris tried to persuade us to retire, as they knew not what would happen, and we might—accidently—be shot; but we had come to see the show, and refused to budge. We—there were about 20 of us—posted ourselves on a slight eminence on one side of the village, where we could see all that would happen. Our Maoris occupied a slope just across a hollow which lay between us, and about twenty yards distant, the men in front squatting down, the women cowering behind. The side of the village towards Parihaka was left open. At about a quarter to eleven, we heard the Maoris coming along the track from Umuroa; we heard an occasional sound of a chant rising or falling as they passed over hills or hollows, and at times there were volleys from their guns.

They evidently desired to create an impression before their arrival. The track was hidden with a dense growth of flax, *tutu* and *toetoe*, and though we could hear we could not see. The noises continued until the war-party was within about one hundred yards of the village, and then there was silence; a long, painful, anxious silence.

I looked towards our Maoris, and the men were rigid and immovable as statues, but for an occasional quiver of a muscle, showing the intensity of the strain upon them, they might have been images of wood or stone.

Presently, amidst the stillness, we could hear an occasional faint rustle, and judged the enemy was taking up its position near the edge of the scrub surrounding the village, and again there was intense silence.

On a sudden the air was rent with screams, such screams as could emanate only from the throats of highly cultured female savages, and then two old hags, I verily believe the ugliest that could be produced in the district, sprang screaming, leaping and dancing into view. They were absolutely naked, and to add to their hideousness—if such a thing were possible—they had rolled themselves in the black mud of the *raupo* swamp. Each held in her hand a lighted torch, and each danced, screamed and reviled our Maoris in the choicest "Billingsgate" they possessed, and their vocabulary was an extensive one.

They worked themselves up to a pich of frenzy, tore their cheeks and breasts with their sharp nails, until the blood ran down over the filth on their bodies; and at last seeming to be able to control themselves no longer, each rushed to a *whare* and shoved the blazing torch into the sides and roof; the *raupo* and *toetoe*, dry as tinder, blazed up in a flash, and they ran from *whare* to *whare*, until every one in the village was in flames. A glance at our Maoris showed the awful strain upon them, they had drawn their blankets over their heads, and crouched forwards, their heads down almost to their knees.

The two hags having done their worst retired, and not a sign of the enemy could be seen, nor a sound heard. But their silence and immobility was in a moment to change into active life; a cry went up from one of our Maori women that an old bedridden Maori had been left in one of the *whares*, and was being burned to death. Men, both friends and foes, rushed forward and reckless of burnt hands, arms or bodies, commenced frantically to pull down the *whare*, but it turned ont to be a false alarm, and back each went to their places, our Maoris to their former position and attitude, and the enemy to their hiding places in the flax and scrub. The burning went on merrily, and in a comparatively short time nothing remained to show where the *whares* had stood, but so many heaps of smouldering ashes, and then when the last frame had fallen, when the last tongue of flame had died down, the war-party entered the village, headed by an old fighting chief named Tamihana, and took up their position—squatting, with their guns between their knees—opposite to our Maoris, a space of about ten yards separating them; a beaten track running down the hollow lay between the two parties; the chief marched up and down this path in a slow and dignified manner. He was a stately but excitable old warrior, tattooed to perfection, he carried in his hand a splendid *taiaha*, which he used to give point and force to his speech; he soon worked himself up to a pitch of frenzy, would march one way in a slow and dignified manner, turning at the end with a yell and spring, and ceme rushing back raving and dancing, waving his *taiaha*, then on reaching the end of his self appointed beat, would turn, walk quietly back, turn with a yell and spring at the end, and so on for nearly half-an-hour. At times he would violently revile the Maoris, at others would lament in pathetic terms the disgrace they—through Te Kahui—had brought upon, not themselves but, Parihaka. " Oh Parihaka, Parihaka," he once exclaimed, "my heart grieves for you, and for the shame brought upon you by this people." At last, having exhausted both his subject and himself, he sat down at the head of and in front of his men; and then (but it is hard for a mere Pakeha to credit this) the wives of our Maoris brought forward food they had cooked, and actually waited upon and feasted the wretches who had burnt them out of house and home. None but the enemy touched the food, our men sat perfectly still, and apparently unconscious of what was going on ; and when the food was consumed the enemy, without a word to our party or even a look at them, rose and departed by the way they had come.

Everything had been done in perfect order, and in accordance with the best of their old traditions.

When the last man had gone, and the sounds of their tramping had died away, our Maoris, with a sigh of relief, a long drawn inspiration, rose to their feet, and we went towards them ; "Well," we said, " the *muru* is now over, the enemy has done his worst, and you have nothing more to fear." But one of the chiefs said bitterly, " No, it is not over, Titoko-waru, and his warriors from Omuturangi, have still to come." " But," we said " of what use will be his coming, you have nothing left ?" "Yes," was the gloomy reply, "we have our lives."

That evening and the next morning were anxious times for all, the blood-thirsty, one-eyed Titoko was not the man to spare anyone until he had received full *utu* for his fancied wrongs. At about 9 o'clock the next morning (the fifth day of the Muru) the news came that Titoko-waru and a war-party had started from Omuturangi, and were on their way to claim their share of the *muru*. Our Maoris were in despair, and practically demanded back their guns, but Mr. Black, knowing the danger of a collision with Titoko, that we as well as the Maoris might be swept out of the district or from off the face of the earth, was firm and refused to show where the guns were hidden. At last, at about eleven o'clock, when the excitement had reached fever heat, a messenger came galloping in, his horse in a white lather, and cried out the danger was over. Hone Pihama of Oeo had intercepted Titoko-waru, and bribed him with a present of bullocks to turn back, that Tito had graciously accepted the bullocks in full payment of his claim, and that the *muru* had ended, without the shedding of blood.

And whilst all this trouble was on, Kahui and Lydia were spending their honeymoon in an old clearing some miles up the Oeo stream, and a few days after the *muru* was over they returned. Kahui all smiles and jubilant at having won his old flame, and Lydia dignified, but a little shy of the new honours which had come to her.

Kahui was very pleased at having been able to confer lasting honour upon his *hapu*, in making them the victims in such a splendid *muru*, the greatest on record; the fact that they were homeless and lost all they possessed did not trouble him in the least, it was but a temporary inconvenience which would soon pass away, but the honour would last for all time. On meeting him I asked, "Well, Kahui, what is to become of Lydia now?" "Lydia," he exclaimed,"why Lydia is my wife, I bought her with the *muru*." "How can that be," I said, "Betty is your wife." "No, no," he replied, "Lydia is my wife now, hang Betty, she can go and get another man." On making further enquiries I found that what Kahui had told me was true; the *muru* had dissolved the marriges of Kahui and Betty, of Aperama and Lydia, and had soleminized the marriage of Kahui and Lydia; she became his legal wife according to Maori custom, and she remained his wife so long as he lived.

FURTHER NOTES ON THE *HEO* OF THE SOLOMON ISLANDS.

BY THE REV. C. E. FOX.

MASITAWA AND HEO.

WITH regard to the remark in my first paper to the effect that *heo* could have been derived from *masitawa*, this was an error, as, now that I have thoroughly examined the *heo*, I know they were not built up gradually in the way I suggested. The following description of the *heo* will make this clear.

HEO.

Heo are usually quite small, about fifteen feet by ten feet, and very often two or three feet in height. It is only occasionally that one sees large *heo*. The largest I have seen is not more than sixty feet by forty feet at the base, almost perpendicular, and fifteen feet in height. Along the coast they are made of large blocks of limestone, enclosing a rubble of smaller stones; but in the bush they are built of reddish earth. I shall describe in more detail three *heo*: two on the coast at Tawaniora and Tawatana, and one in the interior at Mwanunu.

1. THE *HEO* AT TAWANIORA.

This is a solid stone structure built round a core of natural limestone rock under which there is a large cave. It is about ten feet in height, and about thirty feet from east to west, and slightly longer from north to south, so that it is an oblong lying north and south, which seems true of most at any rate of the *heo*. It is so built up round the solid core as to leave a shaft running down to the mouth of the cave, but the shaft had been filled up with large blocks by the last users of this *heo*, and I did not get down into the cave, which however, some of those with me had done in former times. On top of the *heo*, and to the south of the shaft, was a dolmen of two flat upright stones, and a large stone slab across, but this is now destroyed; smaller stones placed on edge round this converted it into a kind of box, a receptacle for the bones of the dead. On the dolmen burnt sacrifices of dog and bonito were offered, but not of pigs or

anything else. These were not private sacrifices, but for the whole
clan. The dead man was lowered down the shaft into the cave, in
which he lay on a bed. The body was carried frequently to running
water; carried on the shoulders of a living man*; and the flesh
stroked away from the bones. When the flesh was all gone the bones
might be left in the cave, or (especially the skull or jawbone), might
be placed in the dolmen. The latter is called *hau suru*, i.e., the raised
or exalted stone. To the west of and alongside the *heo* was an *oha*, a
sacred building which women could not enter, and here first-fruits
from the gardens were hung up, and boys lived for three years
secluded, learning bonito fishing. To the north was the men's
dancing ground. The *heo* had a guardian serpent. On the top were
planted a sacred tree, *tabi*; and sacred *dracaenas*. At one corner was
a sacred coconut, where private sacrifices of pigs were offered. On
the *hau suru* was a sacred stone of *nagi* (flint) round in shape.

2. THE *HEO* AT TAWATANA.

The *heo* at Tawatana is also a solid stone structure but without a
core of natural rock and a cave, and it is therefore more typical of
heo in general. It is about fifty-five feet by thirty-three feet and runs
north and south; the height is not more than six feet. It has no
shaft running down into a cave, but to the north of the *hau suru* is a
shallow pit three or four feet deep, in which was a bed, on which the
dead man was placed, and a roof was built over the pit—of thatch.
The *hau suru* is a fine one, the large flat slab being about four feet by
two feet, with two large slabs at each end and smaller stones round.
It contained chiefly skulls. The burial rites were the same as at
Tawaniora. To the east of this *heo* is a large oblong cleared space
called a *hera*, and this is normally found in this position; but the
word *hera* is also used for the *heo* itself, and seems to mean merely an
oblong enclosed space. The *oha* was alongside, and I think on the
west side of the *heo*, but I did not make a note of its position.† The
first-fruits of the gardens were hung up in this *oha* as offerings to the
snake spirit (*hiona*) and sacrifices were offered on the *hau suru* to the
hiona. Only people of the Araha (chief's) clan were buried on these
two *heo*. The Araha are connected in many ways with the sun, and
when one of them dies his widow often "marries the sun."

3. THE *HEO* AT MWANUNU.

This is a typical bush *heo*, but larger than most. Its sides are
almost perpendicular, and, since it is now much decayed, it cannot
formerly have been less than fifteen feet high, judging from the

* As in Torres Islands.
† Possibly it was in the *hera*.

accounts of those who remember it when in use; but it is now perhaps about twelve feet high (I could not measure the *heo* exactly). It is almost square, about fifty feet by fifty feet. On the top there is the usual pit, now fallen in, but said to have been about eight feet deep, and widened at the bottom to form a cave, in which the dead were buried. I saw no *hau suru*, and could not find out if one had formerly existed. Only *araha* men or women were buried in this *heo*, and by the mouth of the shaft was a small house, for the husband or wife of the dead person, who lived there for ten days till the mourning ceremonies were concluded. The shaft was lined to-prevent the earth falling in. The dead person was carried on the shoulders to running water, and bathed (on the shoulders of the living) by a man who stroked off the flesh with the palms of his hands. There was no *oha*, and sacrifices of first-fruits were hung on the branches of sacred trees growing on the *heo*. The *heo* stood right in the middle of the village with houses all round it; not some little distance away as in most coast *heo*.

VERY LIKE SCALP-TAKING.

By S. Percy Smith.

THE following account of a Maori custom in war was told by an old Maori friend who was well up in their old customs. It is worth preserving as it has not been mentioned elsewhere so far as I know.

In a battle where the enemy is routed and flees, the *toas* or braves of the victorious party dash forward in pursuit, each bent on killing as many of the enemy as possible. Many a warrior would, on overtaking his victim, give him a blow on the head with his *mere*, or other weapon, and leave him there for others to finish the work, whilst he dashed onward to secure others in the same manner. After the fight, and when the victorious party were in their camp, it was customary for each of the warriors to boast of his deeds (called *korero-whakatu*). Each would say, "I killed so and so with my weapon, etc." and describe all the blows given and received, with minute details. After the victory of Tai-karamu, fought somewhere on the East Coast, all the victors were boasting in the above manner, some declaring they had killed more of the enemy than anyone else. A warrior named Tu-kokoru then stood forward, and untying his girdle let it fall to the ground, when it was seen that there were a great number of *koukou*, or top-knots such as each warrior wore, some with feathers stuck in them, others without. He said, "You are all boasting of the number you have killed. Behold my *hokowhiti*," i.e., his seventy *koukou*. Then the top-knots were counted, and there were found to be seventy. So all agreed that Tu-kokoru had killed the most men. On striking down his man each warrior would lay hold of the *koukou*, and using a chip of obsidian, which he carried in his belt, cut off the top-knot below the lashing, stick it into his belt, and then dash on after the fleeing enemy, all the time repeating his charms to cause the enemy to stumble and fall. In Tu-kokoru's case these charms were named "Tu-mania" and "Tu-paheke." Another name for a similar charm is "Pa-whakaoho."

Tu-kokoru lived five generations after the well-known ancestor Pou-heni, and therefore seventeen generations ago, or in the end of the fifteenth century.

RANGI-HUA-MOA.

A LEGEND OF THE MOA IN WAITEMATA DISTRICT, AUCKLAND.

By Geo. Graham.

IN the "Transactions of the New Zealand Institute" for 1916, page 425, appears an article by Mr. T. W. Downes, dealing with the vexed question of the probable period at which the Moa became extinct in New Zealand. After reading it I at once turned to an old memorandum book, wherein I had made an entry in 1910, of a legend in respect of the Moa in these parts—my informant being old Mereri. The old lady and myself had been talking of the ancient times, as was oft our wont, she being my informant of much ancient lore in which she was well versed. It was from her I obtained a version of "The Korotangi Myth," *vide* this "Journal," Vol. XXVII., page 86, where also appears her *whakapapa* on page 89, and which is supplemented by a further *whakapapa* at end hereof. As is often the case in obtaining this kind of information, it was a casual question of mine as to the meaning of her daughter's name, Rangi-hua-moa, that led her to give me the following :—

RANGI-HUA-MOA.

"This daughter of mine I named so at the request of my relative of Te Aki-tai *hapu.* It was Taka-anini who asked me to so name her; it was the name of an ancestress of us both. Such was the Maori custom; that naming gave the right to the guardianship as to marriage in due course, of children so named. Hence was my daughter Rangi-hua-moa named, and she ultimately married a younger relative of Taka-anini, when she came of age. Thus were inter-tribal relations cemented, and marriages into foreign tribes discouraged, thereby securing lands and other heirlooms, and preventing a depletion of tribal-membership.

Rangi-hua-moa was named after the mother of Te Ika-maupoho, who married Te Tahuri; these were the parents of Kiwi Tamaki, from whom Taka-anini is descended (as shown in *whakapapa*). This is the meaning (*putake*) of that old ancestral woman Rangi's name. She was at Te Pani-o-poa-taniwha at the head of the Paremoremo creek, a branch of the Wai-te-mata. Her parents were there catching and drying eels for a feast. Such was that place at Paremoremo—a place where at certain seasons they resorted to catch eels, birds; also to collect the edible flower of the *kiekie*, then plentiful in those parts; and the leaves thereof for mat-making.

On the day Rangi was born a nest (*kohanga*) of Moa eggs was found by Huri-aka (a *mokai* or slave of Hine-korako's). The eggs provided a feast; the last time such a feast was held, for no Moa eggs were found after that time. In a few days the child was called Rangi-hua-moa (the day of the Moa eggs). The tracks (*ara*) of the bird can still be seen on the ridges it formerly frequented, for it avoided the gullies and deep forests, and the ridges lightly forested and open places were its habitat (*nohoanga*). There on the ridges (*hiwi*) of the hill top of Te Pani-o-poa-taniwha, is the old *poka* (pit) wherein that bird was trapped. A Moa having been located on the ridges, a party of hunters gradually drove it along towards the pit; a party also approached from the opposite direction until they drove that bird into the pit where it was easily killed with spears and clubs; for it never attempted to escape into the gullies, nor, if slowly followed, would it run back through the line of hunters. The reason it was so killed was the great speed at which it would run, if too quickly chased, as also the fear of its power of kicking (*whana*).

When our people first saw the foreign birds brought by Governor Grey to Te Kawau,[*] we called it the Moa, and my cousin, Te Hemara, made a speech to those birds and cried, and we all there cried, for we remembered those old proverbs and laments concerning the past, which likened the disappearance of our dead parents and ancestors to the extinction of that bird, the Moa.

In some parts they hunted the Moa with the long spear (*tao-roa*), similar to that with which the pigeon was speared. In districts where there were swamps, the bird was driven therein. In Kaipara is a swamp known as the Te Toreminga-Moa (near Te Kapoai at Helensville). A name our people had for the Moa was Te Manu-pouturu (the bird on stilts), because of its peculiar walk, hesitating and awkward, like a person walking on stilts, and looking round every now and again before walking further. Te-rau-a-moa, at Pirongia, is not a name-place given after the Moa itself. At that place a battle was fought, and the slain lay about like the bodies of so many Moas after a Moa hunt, hence that name, 'The hundreds like unto the Moa.'"

---

[*] Sir George Grey had a flock of Emu imported and placed on the Kawau Island, where they are still found, and gave several to John Reid, of Motutapu, where is also a flock of Emus still to be found.

Such was Mereri's account of the Moa. I regret I did not keep a record of several proverbs and *waiata* she recited, but my recollection is that they were on very similar lines to those otherwise on record. I recollect, however, she told me that garments of the feathers of the Moa were prized because of their warmth, and that the feathers of the Kiwi and Moa were woven into the flaxen garments in a different manner to other garments, all the feathers being so woven that they stood in tufts outward, and not so that they hung downwards, as with the pigeon and other feather garments.

The pit on the ridge referred to, I have often examined with curiosity, it is about twenty feet by eighteen and perpendicular at the sides, and about five feet deep. There is nothing like it in the neighbourhood. Several years ago crossing from Okura to Paremoremo, I came across a similar pit on the ridges near the Pukeatua trig station.

The explanation of the naming of the ancestress Rangi-hua-moa, after the last recorded find of Moa eggs in these parts, is interesting, and I see no reason to doubt the truth of the legend. All Maori names of persons and places are derived from some such domestic or tribal event. I am inclined to place the time of Rangi's birth about 1660, allowing thirty years[*] for each generation to the present time. Apparently the feast of Moa eggs was a "red letter day," from which we may conclude that at that time the Moa was at least in the district of Waitemata-Kaipara districts, on the verge of extinction; otherwise the event would hardly be remembered as the birthday of an important chieftainess.

I have never been able to discover any remains of the Moa myself in these parts, except those relics known as *Whatu-moa* (Moa stones) and *Tutae-moa* (Moa droppings), which are the crop-stones of the bird and are found in most districts all over New Zealand. These stones are particularly plentiful on the ridges along which, as Mereri states, are still to be found what are certainly tracks, and where it was not conceivable that there ever was any very extensive human traffic. These tracks are still fairly well defined among the scrub, and are known here, as elsewhere, as *Ara-moa*, and resemble abandoned sheep and cattle tracks. Old natives assure me that they existed in their youth; before ever cattle came into these districts, and it is along these tracks that the so-called "Moa-stones" are very numerous in small patches of a dozen or more.

---

[*] Since 1893 the Society has adopted twenty-five years to a generation (not thirty years) in calculating dates. To make Mr. Graham's date conform to this rule, it should read 1675.—EDITOR.

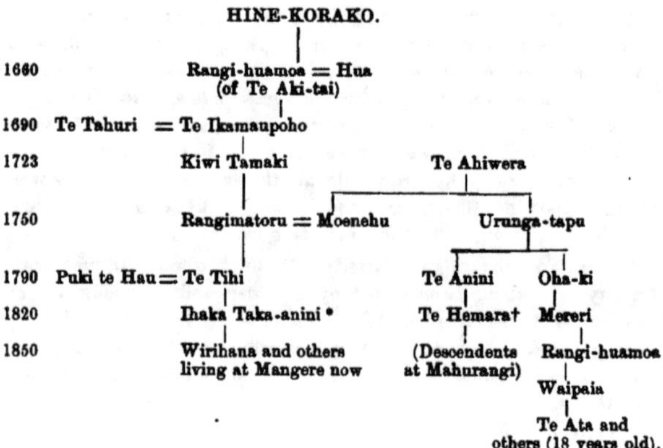

The above *Whaka-papa* agrees very closely with such parts thereof as appear in Fenton's "Judgments," and is supplementary to Mereri's *Whaka-papa* given in Volume XXVII., page 89 of this "Journal"—see "A Legend of Old Mahurangi."

* A fine, handsome old chief in 1860, who lived near Papakura, Auckland. He was supposed to convey information to the enemy Waikato during the Maori war of 1863, and was consequently interned at Mangere.—EDITOR.

† Another very fine chief of the Ngati-Rongo tribe living at Puhoi and Mahurangi in the early sixties of last century.—EDITOR.

THE ACCOUNT OF KUPE AND TAINUI.

By Geo. Graham.

[It is obvious that this account of Kupe refers to the second of that name, and not
to the original discoverer of New Zealand, who flourished some ten generations
before Toi, mentioned herein. See our "Memoirs," Vol. IV., for the account
of the original Kupe.—Editor.]

THE following is a short account of some incidents connected with
the arrival of Kupe in New Zealand, his return to Hawaiki,
and the subsequent arrival of the canoe "Tainui" at Tamaki,
Auckland, and of the early connection of that district with the
immigrants who came in that canoe.

KUPE'S VISIT TO NEW ZEALAND.

It was Kupe who first came here to New Zealand bent on
exploring lands he had heard of from his elders, and known to still
more ancient times. Such is the story as told me by my elder Tati
Wharekawa.

Kupe and his people discovered people at various places. These
people were the Mamoe, the Turehu, the Tahurangi, the Poke-
pokewai, the Patupaiarehe, the Turepe and the Hamoamoa. They
lived on the fronds and berries of the trees, and the roots of the earth.
They were expert in preparing such foods, and in snaring and
spearing the birds in forest and fish in stream. They also prepared
food from the tender parts of the *nikau*, the *tikoukou*, the *para* and the
mamaku (tree ferns). Another name that people were called by was
Te Tini-o-Toi-kai-rakau (the multitude of Toi, eater of trees). Toi
being an ancestor of a section of that people. They dug the roots
with long *ko* (spades), an implement unknown to the Maori before we
came to those islands, and found those people just as Kupe had
described them. Kupe was attacked by, and in return attacked those
people of Karioi, near Raglan, and Aotea on the West Coast. These
people were the Ngati-Matakore so-called, not the tribe of that name
now living here in this island, who descend from us of "Tainui."

Now Powhe-te-ngu,* his slave, he left with some companions at
Aotea. His daughter he had left in that other island (South Island)
at the place he called Taomui-a-Kupe (the eastern head of Queen
Charlotte Sound), where he had first landed in that island, and at

* Is this not Po-whete-ngu? Editor.

Rangitoto, D'Urville Island (Cooks Straits).   He left Po to look
after this island and his daughter to look after that other island ; for
he knew others would come and claim those parts if he did not thus
name places and leave people and signs of possession before he
returned homeward.   Kupe ordered Po not to follow, but to remain
in possession, and to ensure this he left the surging seas off the West
Coast at Marowhara.

POWHE-TE-NGU ATTEMPTS TO RETURN TO HAWAIKI.

Now Po lamented after the departure of Kupe, nor did he remain
willingly, for he feared the hostility of the original people of the land.
Therefore he built a canoe to return and follow Kupe to Hawaiki.
He called that canoe the "Rewa-atu."   He thereby disobeyed the
injunction of his head chief Kupe.   He gave out a report that the
canoe was for fishing, but it was not so, it was for the purpose of
returning to Hawaiki.   When the canoe was complete, he and his
companions secretly loaded it with stores of fern-root and started
forth.   But the *kawa* (ceremonial incantations) performed by Kupe to
prevent Po returning caused the seas to surge and the winds to blow
adversely ; Po's canoe capsized and he and his companions perished.

That canoe was turned into stone, also that man, and they may
still be seen at the Wahapu-o-Aotea (harbour entrance of Aotea, West
Coast, North Island.)   Hence the proverb applied to disobedient
servants who do otherwise than as commanded by their masters, " *Ko
te mahi o te uri o Powhe-te-Ngu*" (" The doings of the descendants of
Powhe-te-Ngu.")

THE BUILDING OF "TAINUI."

The multitude in Hawaiki heard of this Island on Kupe's return ;
then it was that Whakaoti-rangi asked for the *mauri* (emblem of
divine assistance) of Puanga, which was the *rori* of the house of
Uenuku, and of his father Memeha-o-te-rangi.   Her request was
granted, and the *tohunga* Rata-o-Wahie-roa undertook to build a
canoe to come hither from Hawaiki.   The three sacred adzes of
Hine-tua-hoanga were brought, and their names were :—

> " Hauhau-te-po "—the felling axe
> " Paopao-te-ra "—the splitting axe
> " Manu-tawhio-rangi "—the smoothing or finishing off axe.

Thereupon Rata, after proper ceremonial, began the building of
" Tainui."

(Then follows the account of the felling of the tree, and the
building of the canoe " Tainui " therefrom ; much on the lines of the
usual accepted narrative.)

When the canoe was finished, and was being tried in the water, it
was Marama-kiko-hua who called out to Hotu, " E Hotu, your canoe
is " Tainui "—hence she was so called.

Many sacred treasures were brought in "Tainui," including the above adzes.

"TAINUI" VOYAGES FROM HAWAIKI TO RAROTONGA.

From Hawaiki they came with "Te Arawa" canoe.; Ngatoro-i-rangi was the "Tainui" navigator.

When they arrived at Rarotonga [*sic*] the people of that place were urged to come along also, that is to say, the people called Te Aitanga-o-Whakaahu, younger brother of Puanga; but those people said "No"—they would not agree to leave their ancestral home and come hither—so they were left behind; also Rakataura of the "Tainui" crew, because of his thievish habits. Riu-ki-uta was now the navigator, because Tama-te-kapua had taken away on his canoe the "Tainui's" navigator Nga-toro-i-rangi, also that man's wife Kea-taketake.

"TAINUI" ARRIVES AT WHANGAPARAOA.

When the "Tainui" canoe approached the shore at Whanga-paraoa, it was surrounded by the sea monsters who were led by their leader Makawe-nui-o-rangi. To appease these monsters, they recited the appropriate incantations known as the *tua* and the *takamate*. To prevent a disaster on landing in the surf, the *tohunga* Riu-ki-uta first jumped into the water, recited an incantation to appease the monsters, plucking forth a lock of his hair, he threw the same together with his red feather plume (*rau-kura*) into the sea.

The sea monsters then departed, and they landed in peace. They performed many other appropriate ceremonies before they wandered over the land. For the deities of the land and forest and the rivers thereof would not be forgotten, and the land must first be freed from *tapu* (*whaka-noa* to be made fit for common use.)

RAKATAURA'S STRATAGEM.

To their surprise then stood forth that thief Rakataura; he had got there by a stratagem. That man had turned himself into a rat, and had hidden in the interior of the canoe. Hence the proverb applied to that man, "The new rat twice killed," an expression now applied in contempt when a person is quarrelling with his descendants.

HAPOPO'S FEATHER PLUMES.

As to the story of Hapopo, of the "Tainui" crew, it was he who first threw his red feather plume into the sea and first plucked the bloom of the *pohutukawa* (Christmas tree) to replace the same. This plume of feathers drifted ashore, and was found by Mahina; hence the name of any treasure cast up by the sea, "*He kura-pae na Mahina.*" (The cast up treasure from the sea, of Mahina.) Our forefathers called all red stone on the sea-coast "*Nga Tai-apa-kura*," another name being "The great plume of Hapopo." The *kura* of Hapopo was treasured and kept by the descendants of the "Tainui's" crew for many generations, for it revived the memory of the ancestral home at Hawaiki. All the other plumes thrown into the sea, in order to replace them by *pohutukawa* blooms, were lost, only Hapopo's was found and preserved by the descendants of Mahina, at Kawhia. It was the custom to bring it forth in order that it might be lamented over when friends long absent arrived from distant parts, or when the people were assembled to weep over the dead. Such were the treasured things (*taonga*) of old and the customs of our olden days.

"TAINUI'S" VOYAGE NORTH TO HOKIANGA.

"Tainui" arrived at Whanga-paraoa on the East Cost of the Bay of Plenty; at that place occurred the incident of the whale claimed by "Te Arawa" canoe party whom they met there. "Tainui" then explored northward till she rounded Muri-whenua (Land's End, i.e., North Cape) and entered Hokianga Harbour. From there they returned, not being able to proceed further southward because of the great seas left there by Kupe as before-mentioned.

"TAINUI" EXPLORES HAURAKI.

They then returned to Hauraki and came to the mouth of the Piako River. Here they sounded the water to try the depth, the oar stuck fast. The canoe drifted on, leaving the oar standing up in the mud. Hence the name of that district even to these times—"Te Hoe-o-Tainui"—Tainui's oar.* This oar was left as a token to those coming after them of Tainui's previous claim by discovery, and an act of taking possession. Now this oar was preserved by the descendants of Maru-tu-ahu until recent times. From Piako the "Tainui" came to Wharekawa on the west side Hauraki Gulf. Here Marama left the canoe with some other companions and some slaves, and journeyed onwards by land to that river at Otahuhu, so called now-a-days, but in olden times known as Whangai-makau.

"TAINUI" EXPLORES WAI-TE-MATA.

"Tainui" voyaged on from Wharekawa to Wai-te-matā, or Auckland Harbour. They rested at Takapuna† (North Head) on the

---

* The name of a place a long way up the Piako River, not far from Morins-ville.—EDITOR.

† Takapuna.—This I understand is not the actual name of North Head. Auckland Harbour, which is no doubt forgotten; but the name of a still existing spring of water on the western slope of the hill, near Mr Watson's home there. There are several places so named in New Zealand.

beach there below the Kurae-o-Tura* [*sic*].   Here seeing the flock of
sea birds coming from the west, they thought thus, "Yonder is the
sea—let us go and explore." So they departed hence to the westward.
Te Horoiwi remained with the people of that land.   Hence the name
of the headland *pa* eastward of Wai-pareira (St. Hellier's Bay) called
Te Pani-o-Horo-iwi (Horo-iwi's head), and the name of that *hapu*
(clan) of his who dwelt thereabouts.

TAI-KEHU SENT TO EXPLORE MANUKA.

And so they sailed on to the Tamaki river and rested there.
Tai-kehu and some others went on overland to explore. They
proceeded to various parts of the western district. They found the
waters of that sea called the Manuka (now Manukau) teaming with
fish, and caught many mullet (*kanae*). So great was the plenty of
mullet, they could catch one with each hand at a time. Hence the
proverb applied to the "Tainui" descendants of Tamaki as a motto
(*pepeha*): "*Nga potiki toa a Taikehu.*" (The brave young children of
Tai-kehu-nui). He was also the ancestor from Hawaiki of those
tribes of Takapuna and surrounding districts known as Ngati-Tai.

"TAINUI" VOYAGES FROM MANUKA TO KAWHIA.

Tai-kehu and his party returned to Tamaki and reported on their
discoveries of the seas of Manuka, and of its opening into the ocean
to the west. So they decided to drag that canoe "Tainui" into that
sea over the Otahuhu isthmus. Now Marama had arrived from her
overland journey, hence they called that place on the Tamaki, near
Otahuhu, "Te Whangai-makau." (The awaiting for one loved.)

From here "Tainui" was dragged into Manuka after the proper
ceremonies to counteract the effects of Marama's loose conduct during
her absence from her party.

Then "Tainui" floated on Manuka and passed on to Kawhia.

But that story is well-known; I will not here recite it.

"TAINUI" PIONEER SHELTERS AT TAMAKI AND HAURAKI.

Now the people of "Tainui" canoe who remained or came to live
at Waitematā and Tamaki were: Riu-ki-uta, Pou-tukeka and his
wife, Hapopo and his wife, Te Uhenga and his wife, and Hautai and
his wife. These lived with the people of those parts, and their
descendants were all important chiefs of the Tamaki tribes, who were
thus connected with relatives at Kawhia and Hauraki. Hence it was
that Titahi of Taranaki, and also in later times Maki, came hither
from the south to see his ancestrally connected tribes, but he

* Kurae-o-Tura.—Tura's headland—a *pa* in olden times; it is now almost
excavated out of existence for roadway and quarrying purposes. It is near the
Ferry Coy.'s workshops (Devonport). Tura's identity is not now possible to
ascertain.

quarrelled with and fought and conquered them.   Hence it was also that Hotunui, insulted because of a false accusation of theft, came from Kawhia and lived with his relatives of Tainui at Wharekawa; his son Marutuāhu, who afterwards came to seek him, also settled there.   Hence the tribal name Marutuāhu applied to all the kindred Hauraki people.   That is the name which links those people with Kawhia of "Tainui."

ORIGIN OF THE NGA-OHO TRIBE.

Now the old tribes of Tamaki were known as Nga-oho.   This is their *whakapapa* :—

Hamoamoa was an ancient ancestor of those people ; he was born of Rangawhenua, his father being a god.   Hamoamoa gave the name to those ancient people who were the *tangata-whenua* of those parts— Tamaki and Waitematā.

From Hamoamoa was descended Maheu,

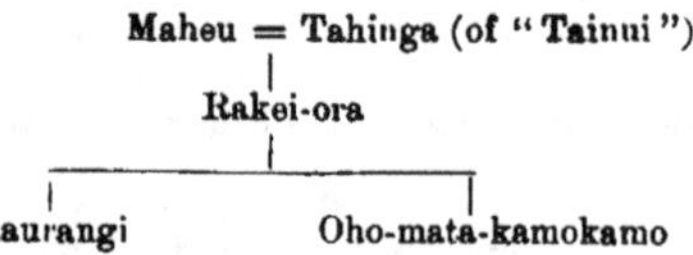

These two brothers quarrelled over their tribal areas at Rarotonga (? Mt. Smart, near Auckland);   and a long war resulted, each having many thousands of followers. Hence they are known as "*Nga tamariki hikuroa a Rakei-ora.*" (The long-tailed children of Rakei-ora.)   A *hiku-roa* being a name given to a chief who had a large following.

So great was the loss of human life, and the destruction of villages and cultivations, that this warfare has given rise to the well-known proverbs, "*He māra-pungarehu*" (a cultivation become an ash-field, i.e., a fruitful area become a desert); also "*Te Pokuru nui a Ruarangi, me nga namunamu o Hurihuri*" (the great stopped-up flow of Ruarangi—even as the sand—flies of Hurihuri." (The loss of lives being likened to the flood of waters and the numbers involved as numerous as sandflies on the sea-beach at Hurihuri.)

After a long and devastating struggle, Oho drove Ruarangi and a remnant of his followers into the Owairaka *pa* (Mt. Albert).   Here he besieged them.   Ruarangi and his people eventually evacuated the *pa*, escaping by a secret cavern, and went away to Waitakerei.

Oho remained the victor, and gave his name to that olden people of Tamaki known as Nga-Oho.   (The actual distinction from the Tainui people and Ngati-Whatua people of the north, as well as Wai-o-hua, is hard to define, owing to the extensive intermingling by marriage and so on—they were indeed a much mixed people.)

THE VISIT OF DENTRECASTEAUX
TO THE NORTH CAPE, NEW ZEALAND,
IN MARCH, 1793.

IT will prove of interest to members of our Society to learn something of the visit of the French Expedition in search of M. de la Pérouse, who had sailed from France in 1787, on a voyage of discovery, and had disappeared completely after his departure from Port Jackson for the Solomon Islands and those parts. Many years afterwards it was discovered by the Chevalier Dillon that Pérouse's two frigates, the " Boussoulle " and the " Astrolabe," had both been wrecked on Vanikoro Island of the Santa Cruz or Queen Charlotte Group, lying to the south-east of the Solomons.

On the 9th February, 1791, the " Assemblée Constiuante " of France addressed the King asking him to dispatch two vessels in search of Pérouse, and in consequence the frigates " Recherche," under the command of General Dentrecasteaux, and the " Esperance " commanded by Major Huon Kermadec, sailed from Brest on the 28th September, 1791.

The history of this voyage has been written by the celebrated naturalist, " Citoyen " Labillardière, and was published in Paris, in two quarto volumes and a volume of plates, in the year VIII. of the Republic of France (1780).

The doings of the expedition during the earlier part of the voyage do not concern us just now, so we commence our translation at Chapter XII. of Vol. II. The two vessels were at that time in Tasmania, and had been there some time exploring the coasts, along which they left many names which are in evidence to-day. Of course this was before Tasmania was colonized.

" We made sail from the Bay of Adventure at 9 a.m. on the 10th Ventose (March), 1793, and were forced along by strong breezes from the south-west, and were not long in passing Cape Pillar, behind which we saw many fires lighted by the Savages. We then directed our course to the north, we were about eight " Myriametres " in the offing, leaving to the west the Bay of Oysters, afterwards we laid our course for the Friendly Islands.

The 22nd, from daybreak we sighted the isles named Les Trois Rois (The Three Kings). At 8 a.m. we were in longitude 169° 56′ west (of Paris), when we sighted to the north at a " demi-myriametre " of distance, the middle isle of that group, and we determined the latitude to be 34° 20′ south. We noticed three principal rocks (isles) of a moderate elevation, placed nearly on the same parallel of latitude and not very far apart, and surrounded by many other rocks very much smaller. In spite of the haze that arose we saw others towards the north that form part of the same group. They appeared very arid, and we presume they are not inhabited. Nevertheless, a strong column of smoke above the most eastern isle announcing the presence of the Savages. No doubt they have chosen their sojourn there because of the facilities for fishing among the reefs.*

Towards 10.45 a.m. we perceived the land of New Zealand, which we gradually approached by aid of a breeze from the N.N.W. The natives had lighted a great fire on the most elevated of the hills that bordered the sea, and which advanced towards the North Cape. By 5.30 we were not very far from that Cape, when two canoes were seen to approach from the shore. They were not long in reaching us, and remained some time astern of us before daring to board us; but after judging that our dispositions towards them were friendly, they approached with confidence; besides, these Savages knew quite well that the Europeans which had visited their coasts had never been the first aggressors. They showed us at once some bundles of the flax of New Zealand (*phormium tenax*) by shaking it to let us see its fine quality, and offering it for exchange. It was with signs of great satisfaction that they received from us stuffs of various colors, and always with the greatest scrupulousness returned the price agreed on. They gave to iron a very great preference to all other objects we offered them. That metal is of so great value to this warrior people that they burst out in joyous shouts so soon as they found that we possessed the article, although we did not at first show but a small quantity of it, and at a distance. Nevertheless they recognised it perfectly by the sound made by two pieces struck one against another.

These people gave us in exchange for our things almost everything they had in their canoes; we regarded it as a great mark of their confidence in us that they made no difficulty in depriving themselves

---

* The Three Kings were sometimes inhabited for years together by members of the Au-pouri tribe, when they had suffered defeat at the hands of the Rarawa, or other tribes living to the south of them. The middle island is not nearly so arid as the narrative makes out. In 1887, when Mr. Cheeseman, of the Auckland museum, and I visited the island we found quite a number of New Zealand trees, or shrubs, growing there, and apparently a large space sloping to the south had at one time been cultivated. There is water just below this spot, and it was just off there that Tasman attempted in 1642 to land and obtain water, but the attitude of the natives was so hostile that he decided not to attempt it, though much in want of water. There is a species of *karaka* growing there that has berries as large as a hazelnut, and another plant, the nearest habitat of which is China. The Maori name of the group is Manawa-tawhi.

of their arms in our favour.   The longest of their spears we got were
not more than five metres long with a thickness of four centremetres—
the smallest were half as long.   They were all made of a single piece
of very hard wood and perfectly polished.

They gave us lines and fish-hooks, to some of which were attached
feathers in place of bait that they use to attract the voracious fish.
Many of these lines were very long with, at the extremity, a piece of
hard serpentine which they attach to cause them to descend to great
depths.   We admired the fine polish they had given to the stones,
which were of a spherical form, surmounted by a protuberance
through which they had pierced a hole for the cord.   It must be very
difficult for these Savages to pierce such hard stones, and no doubt it
takes a long time, but they have plenty of leisure to devote to such
work, for their wants are not many, and the sea supplies them
abundantly with food.   They sold us plenty of fish they had caught;
there are such great quantities along the coast that during the short
time we laid-to we saw many shoals of them on the surface of the sea,
agitating it over wide spaces, producing the effect of currents, and
during calms they might be taken for shallows.

These Savages even deprived themselves of their clothing in order
to procure our objects in exchange.   Some young men had ear-pendants
made of serpentine of a very great hardness; they were cut in ovals,
and most of them were about a "decimetre" (four inches) in length.

The men had hanging on their breasts a species of human
"cubitas" (? bone of forearm) at the end of a cord passed round their
necks (see plate 25).   They attach a great value to these ornaments.

It is known that these people eat with avidity human flesh, and all
that incites in them a similar idea causes them great pleasure.   One of
the sailors offered to one of them a knife, and, wishing to explain its
use, he pretended to cut off one of his fingers, which he immediately
carried to his mouth, pretending to eat it.   Immediately the Savage,
who had observed all the sailor's movements, expressed an extreme joy,
and we saw him laugh for some time with his throat open and rubbing
his hands.   All of these people were very tall and very muscular.   They
left us shortly after sunset.

·   At the same time a third canoe arrived from the nearest shore,
manned by twelve islanders, who immediately demanded some hatchets
in exchange for their things.   After one of them had obtained one,
another addressed us in a loud voice, shouting with all his power, "*E
toki*" (an axe), and he ceased not until he got one.

It was now night.   The "Esperance" was too distant from our
vessel to be seen, so we made flares in order to ascertain her position;
but we saw with surprise that the natives, far from showing any fear
at the effect of gunpowder, continued their exchanges.   It was more
than an hour after dark that they paddled away to the coast.

While we lay-to the lead was cast several times; the soundings always showed a sandy bottom at sixty to eighty-three metres.

23rd March. To the land breeze, which was felt feebly during the night, succeded at daylight a wind from the north-west. We were still very near the coast, and it would have been easy to have anchored in Lauristan Bay, but the sad event that had occurred to Captain Marion, and afterwards to Captain Ferneaux,* determined the General to pass on.

Nevertheless, I believe it my duty to express how important it would be to obtain in New Zealand the plant known under the name of *phormium tenax* (the flax of New Zealand) to transport it into Europe, where it would succeed perfectly. The firbe obtained from its leaves has a strength much superior to all other vegetable products which are employed in rope making; the cables made from it would resist every effort to break them. No one more than the Commandant of our expedition appreciated the utility of that plant for our marine. Nevertheless we continued our route towards the Friendly Islands by directing our course to the north-east."

Thus ends Labilliardière's account of their visit to New Zealand.

On the 26th of the same month they discovered the rock—for it is really nothing more—which they called L'Esperance after the ship commanded by Huon Kermadec, whose name they also applied to the group, of which L'Esperance is the southern member.

Both Dentrecasteaux and Kermadec died of scurvey on the way home. It is strange to find these sailors bearing Military titles—General and Major—while Labilliardière calls himself "Citizen," all, no doubt, due to the changes introduced by the French Revolution.

---

* This refers to the massacre of Ferneaux's boat's crew in Queen Charlotte Sound no doubt.

NOTES AND QUERIES.

[288] Malayo-Polynesian.

In the Transactions of the Fiji Society for 1918, page 4, Mr. Coleman Wall refers to the Polynesians under the above title. In an interesting paper Mr. S. W. Dutton, on page 18 of the same publication, refers to the Polynesians as Malayan. It is a pity these gentlemen in both these interesting papers continue to refer to a theory long since obsolete. It is now recognised that the Malays are a Mongolian race, while the Polynesians are a branch of the Caucasian.

[289] The Pacific Story of Jonah and the Whale.

In Mr. Coleman Wall's paper, referred to in the last notes, he gives the Fijian version of a tradition, somewhat analogous to that of the Biblical story of Jonah and the whale ; but in this case it was a woman who was swallowed by a big shark, and who eventually became the ancestress of a line of chiefs. The people of Niuē Island have very nearly the same story, the incidents are very similar, except that the woman became an ancestress of some Tongan clan, for it was on Tonga that she landed and cut her way out of the big fish. So far as is known this story is not common to Polynesia, and the finding of it in Fiji and Niuē, again shows that the latter people have a considerable element of the Melanesian in them, as insisted on in " Niuē and its People "—published by this Society.

PROCEEDINGS.

POLYNESIAN SOCIETY.

———

A MEETING of the Council was held at the Library, Hempton Room, on the 25th June, when current business including correspondence was dealt with.

New members elected :—
R. Clinton Hughes, New Plymouth.
Dr. W. M. Thompson, M.A., M.B., B.C.L.

The following corresponding members were also elected :—
Thos. G. Thrum, Honolulu, in recognition of his work in translation of the four volumes of Fornander's " Hawaiian Antiquities."
Stephen Savage, Rarotonga, in recognition of his translation of " Rarotongan Traditions."

Papers received :—
Further Notes on the *Heo*. Rev. C. E. Fox, Solomon Island.
Gilbert's account of Easter Island. H. D. Skinner.
The Gods of Maori Worship. Hare Hongi.
Traditions and Legends of Murihiku. Part X. H. Beattie.
Polynesian Linguistics. Part IV. Sydney H. Ray.
Traditions and History of Rarotonga. Parts VI. and VII.

The death of our Corresponding Member, M. A. Leverd at Tahiti, from influenza, was reported, and the following resolution relating thereto was placed on the minutes :—" That the Council has learned with great regret of the death of M. A. Leverd at Tahiti, and places on record its appreciation of M. Leverd's contributions to Polynesian Ethnology—a subject in which he showed more than ordinary interest and ability with great promise for the future. And the Council further desires to extend to the relatives of the deceased its sincere sympathy in their loss."

M. ARMAND LEVERD.

Died at Tahiti, of influenza, 9th December, 1918.

THE LAND OF TARA
AND THEY WHO SETTLED IT.

THE STORY OF THE OCCUPATION OF TE WHANGA-NUI-A-TARA
(THE GREAT HARBOUR OF TARA) OR PORT NICHOLSON,
BY THE MAORI.

By ELSDON BEST.

PART VIII.

(Continued from page 96, Vol. XXVIII.)

THE MAORI TEXT.

TE HEKENGA MAI O NGATI-IRA.

Na Rua-wahine Tawake i ki atu ki tona mokopuna:—"Haere ki o kainga noho ai, ka watea hoki te whenua." Mo Waimatā, mo Hikuwai, mo Tauwhare-parae, mo Huiarua, mo Te Ahi-kouka, mo Wai-ngaromia, koia nei aua whenua i ki atu ai a Tawake.

Ka utua e Te Wha-kumu te kupu a tona tipuna ki a ia:—"Waiho o kainga hei haehae i a koe, ina au e kainga nei e te matao. Ka haere tenei au ka whakamau atu ki te uru o te tonga, ki te whare i maru ai au." Mo Tutaporu, i moe i a Rerekiokio, tona papa.

Ko te putake tenei i heke mai ai a Ngati-Ira i te pa tahuri i Pakaurangi, e kiia ra ko Te Pueru-maku, noho rawa mai ko Tapuwae-tahi-o-Rongokako i te pito ki te tonga o Whangara, i te taha rawhiti o Turanga-uui. I reira te pa ka mahia e Ngati-Ira, ka oti, ka nohoia taua pa e ratau. E rite te rahi o te wahi i nohoia e Ngati-Ira i roto i taua pa i Te Tapuwae ki te maara nei; ka titiro atu matau ki taua maara, era pea e tae ki te whitu *eka* te nui. E ki ana a Rihari i te tau 1837, e tu tonu ana nga awakari o taua pa i te taha tonu o te moana nui. Ka hui a Ngati-Ira ki reira mahi ai i te kai, kumara kao, ika maroke, paua maroke, koura maroke, kao korau maori, aruhe parahou, aruhe kopuwai, ko nga aruhe pai tera, momona. Katahi ka wahi a Ngati-Ira, ko tetahi wahanga ka hoki ano ki runga i te whenua noho ai; ki Tauwhare-parae, ki Huiarua, ki Waimatā, ki Hikuwai, ki Taumata-patiti, ki Anaura, ki Te Ahikouka, ki Wai-ngaromia.

THE LAND OF TARA
AND THEY WHO SETTLED IT.

THE STORY OF THE OCCUPATION OF TE WHANGA-NUI-A-TARA
(THE GREAT HARBOUR OF TARA) OR PORT NICHOLSON,
BY THE MAORI.

By ELSDON BEST.

PART VIII.

(Continued from page 96, Vol. XXVIII.)

THE MAORI TEXT.

TE HEKENGA MAI O NGATI-IRA.

Na Rua-wahine Tawake i ki atu ki tona mokopuna :—" Haere ki
o kainga noho ai, ka watea hoki te whenua." Mo Waimatā, mo
Hikuwai, mo Tauwhare-parae, mo Huiarua, mo 'Te Ahi-kouka, mo
Wai-ngaromia, koia nei aua whenua i ki atu ai a Tawake.

Ka utua e Te Wha-kumu te kupu a tona tipuna ki a ia :—" Waiho
o kainga hei haehae i a koe, ina au e kainga nei e te matao. Ka haere
tenei au ka whakamau atu ki te uru o te tonga, ki te whare i maru ai
au." Mo Tutapora, i moe i a Rerekiokio, tona papa.

Ko te putake tenei i heke mai ai a Ngati-Ira i te pa tahuri i
Pakaurangi, e kiia ra ko 'Te Pueru-maku, noho rawa mai ko Tapuwae-
tahi-o-Rongokako i te pito ki te tonga o Whangara, i te taha rawhiti
o 'Turanga-nui. I reira te pa ka mahia e Ngati-Ira, ka oti, ka nohoia
taua pa e ratau. E rite te rahi o te wahi i nohoia e Ngati-Ira i roto i
taua pa i Te Tapuwae ki te maara nei; ka titiro atu matau ki taua
maara, era pea e tae ki te whitu *eku* te nui. E ki ana a Rihari i te
tau 1837, e tu tonu ana nga awakari o taua pa i te taha tonu o te
moana nui. Ka hui a Ngati-Ira ki reira mahi ai i te kai, kumara kao,
ika maroke, paua maroke, koura maroke, kao korau maori, aruhe
parahou, aruhe kopuwai, ko nga aruhe pai tera, momona. Katahi ka
wahi a Ngati-Ira, ko tetahi wahanga ka hoki ano ki runga i te whenua
noho ai; ki Tauwhare-parae, ki Huiarua, ki Waimatā, ki Hikuwai,
ki 'Taumata-patiti, ki Anaura, ki Te Ahikouka, ki Wai-ngaromia.

Ko nga taina o Tane-ka-tohia, ara ko Rua-wahine me te tungane, me Tama-kauwae.

Na, ko tetahi wahanga o Ngati-Ira ka ki e kore ratau e hoki atu ano ki ena whenua noho ai, ka haere ratau ki te wahi i u mai ai nga waka o nga kaumatua i te haerenga mai i Hawaiki ki Whanga-paraoa; koia tera e noho mai ra a Te Tatana, a Tikitiki-rangi. me o ratau iwi o Ngati-Ira e noho mai ra i Opotiki ra.

Na, ka ki te wehenga ki a Te Wha-kumu, a ko ia me ona hapu me haere ki te pu o te tonga, ki Wairarapa.   Koia tenei te Ngati-Ira i a Tane-katohia e noho nei i Wairarapa nei ki a Te Miha-o-te-rangi, ki a Te Manihera Rangi-takaiwaho, ki a Tutapakihi-rangi; kati nei aku e whakahua ake i naia nei.   Na, ko nga uri a Rua-wahine ko Te Aitanga-a-Mahaki, ko Te Aitanga-a-Haniti, tae atu ki a Te Whanau-a-Rua i Tokomaru. Na, ko nga uri a Tama-kauwae koia tera a Ngati-Purou e pae mai ra i Tawhiti huri noa ki roto o Waiapu tae noa ki Whare-kahika; kati mai i konei taku whakahuahua.   He iwi nui tenei iwi a Ngati-Ira, nona tenei whakatauki :—" He pekehā ki te moana, ko Ngati-Ira ki uta "; he iwi toa hoki ki te pakanga.   Kati taku whakamarama ake i tenei take; kā pā he tere koe ki te tuhi, ko tenei ka taka te marama i a taua e mahi ana kaore ano i paneke i a koe.

Na, ka haere mai te ope a Te Wha-kumu, ka tae mai ki Here-taunga, ka mahia tona pa, ko Nga Whakatatara te pa, kei rawahi atu o Te Pa-whakairo tana pa.   I te tau 1853, i te tuwhera tonu nga awakari o taua pa.

Ka kite nga iwi o Orotu, e, he iwi hou tenei kua hanga pa rawa ki runga i to ratau whenua, a katahi ka whakawhaiti Tini o Orotu, ara a Rangitane, ka whaiti ki roto i Te Puketapu pa, i rawahi mai o Omahu i Heretaunga ra.   Katahi ka mea a Paewhenua, a Te Hau-te-rangi, a Te Kowhaiwhai, nga rangatira a aua iwi, kia kotahi te matua e tuku ma roto i Tutaekuri, ko tetahi me tuku ma te hiwi i Te Tauwhare heke iho ai ki Nga Whakatatara pa o Ngati-Ira taupoki iho ai i te pa. Na, tetahi o nga matua me tika atu ma te parae ki Te Wai-o-hiki tau ai, kia marama ai te titiro atu ki te putanga mai o te matua i roto o Tutaekuri, o runga hoki o Tauwhare, hei poa hoki i a Ngati-Ira kia haere mai ai ki waho o tona pa, kia riro ai te pa Nga Whakatatara i te matua e heke iho ana i Tauwhare, kia watea ai te matua i roto o Tutaekuri hei awhina i a ratau ka whakaeke ra ki Te Wai-o-hiki pae ai.   Koia tenei nga whakaaro i roto i a Rangi-tane, i a Ngati-Awa, i a Ngati-Mahanga.

Na, i te poka whakatata ki te whakaeroero nga whetu i te ata hapara, ka wehewehe nga matua e toru nei, he ran topu ki te matua kotahi.   Na, ka hapara te ata whakaao marama, ka puta atu a Te Ahipara, a Te Horipu ki waho noho ai, ka kitea atu te matua tangata e haere mai ana i te mania, ko te kirikau anake.   Ka hoki ki roto i te pa, ka karanga:—" Ko Tu-mataenga!   Ko Tu-matauenga!"   Ka karanga tetahi o aua tangata:—" Ko te whakaariki!   Ko te whaka- ariki!"   Ka karanga tetahi:—" Kei te mania."

Ka puta mai a Te Wha-kumu ki waho o te pa matakitaki atu ai. Ka mea nga toa o te pa o Ngati-Ira kia tikina kia whawhaitia taua ope.   Ka mea a Te Wha-kumu:—" Kia mau, waiho kia ukiuki te whenua, akuanei e whakaputa ana ki Te Puketapu, kua kore he tangata o roto, he wahine, he pangore anake kei roto.   Kia wha rau e kawhaki ki reira, ko te tokomaha e noho hei ora mo te pa nei.   Kaua rawa hei puta kei waho, waiho kia awhi ana i te pa nei.   Ko tena e haere mai ra he ahi hunuhunu, ana ano te matua kei te ngaro i a tatau. E hara tena, he patoi kia puta atu tatau ki waho, ka manukawhaki ai, ko reira te matua huaki ai.   Koi pohehe ki tena ahua arataki matua."

Ka noho katoa a Ngati-Ira, tane, wahine, tamariki, i roto i te pa noho ai.   Ka piki a Te Wha-kumu ki runga i te puhara noho ai, mataki ai.   Ka mea ia ki ona toa:—" Whakaarahia he puhara moku, kia kotahi ki te taha ki uta, kia kotahi ki te taha ki te awa nei, kia tiketike."

Kua takoto nga rakau, ka whakaarahia, ka ara ki runga aua puhara e rua.   Ka eke a Te Wha-kumu me nga toa tokorima ki te puhara o uta; ko te puhara i tai ka eke a Te Whanonga me nga toa tokorima hoki, me a ratau tokotoko, me a ratau manuka kanoi, me a ratau pukoro kowhatu hei whakaruru ki te taua nei.

Na, i penei te ahua o te pa nei me te tu a nga puhara nei.   Ko nga waha ngutu tera i raro iho o nga puhara e rua.   Ko te tu a nga puhara e rua nei he tiaki i aua waha ngutu e rua, koi uru te tangata ki roto i te pa nei.   Tuarua o nga take he whakaatu i te ahua o te mahi a nga taua awhi i te pa, whakaeke ranei, tukituki ranei i te parepare o waho, ki nga toa o roto i te pa.   Na, ko te kuwaha o te parepare o roto, kotahi tonu te kuwaha e tomo atu ai i te parepare o waho ki roto i te parepare o roto.   Ko taua waha ngutu he mea hou atu i raro i te whenua, ka puta ai ki roto o te parepare tuarua.   Na, pera ano te waha ngutu o te parepare tuatoru, he mea hou ma roto i te rua e uru ai ki roto; ko nga parepare e toru katoa.   Na, e kite ana koutou i te parepare kokoti o roto rawa; ko tera he rohe mai i nga wahine, i nga tamariki, i nga koroua ki te wahi whaiti noho ai.   Ko te waha ngutu kei roto i te whenua ka puta atu ki roto ano i te pare- pare paku na e puta ai ki roto i te wahi o roto rawa me hou ano ma roto i te whenua i te waha ngutu.   Na ko tetahi wahanga o to roto he marae tera no nga tane anake e takatu ai ki te tiaki i nga parepare o te pa nei, ara ko te wahi e tenei (?).   Ko te parepare o waho rawa e kiia ana e toru whanganga te tiketike; ko te awakari o waho a taua pare- pare e wha whanganga te whanui me te hohonu o te awakari.   Na, ko nga parepare katoa o roto mai i to waho, kaore he awakari, engari e rua whanganga te tiketike ake i te papa o te pa nei, e wha te papa whanga (?), e rua a runga, haere tonu ai nga tangata i runga, ara nga toa.   Ko te parepare o waho rawa kotahi te whanganga te matara o tetahi i tetahi, ara o to waho rawa i to roto mai, i peratia ai mo te uru te taua ki roto kaore e tika tona wero i tona tokotoko, huata ranei, i te apiapi o aua parepare, a kei runga ra hoki nga toa i te parepare o roto e haereere ana, e werowero ana i nga tangata e uru ana mai, ina uru ki roto i taua pa.   Kati aku whakamarama i te ahua o te pa nei.

Na, ka roa e noho ana ka whakaputa mai te wahanga o te taua i ma roto mai i Tutaekuri awa.   Na, e heke iho ana hoki te matua i heke iho i runga i te hiwi o Tauwhare, kua whakawhiti mai hoki te wehenga i Te Wai-o-hiki ra, ka karapotia te pa nei ka tahuri ki te whakauru ki roto i te pa nei.   I te nui o te mahi a nga tangata o te taua ki te whakauru, kore rawa nei i taea i te wehi i nga puhara e rua nei, a tokotoru rawa nga tangata i mate i te werohanga ki te tokotoko, ki te huata hoki, ko Te Horeta, ko Hauparua, ko Te Iwi-katea, koia nei nga mea i mate o te taua i tenei ra.   Ka po hoki, ka heke te taua ki te taha o te awa noho ai i taua po nei.

Na, ka tonoa e Te Wha-kumu nga tangata e rua rau topu ki Te Puketapu pa i runga i te puke.   Ka tahuri taua pa, ka riro herehere mai nga wahine, nga tamariki, nga kaumatua.   Ka mate i reira a Koura, a Te Awapara, a Te Kirirua, a Poupou, a Tangi-akau, me era atu e maha, era pea e tae ki te whitu tekau, neke ake ranei.

Na, ka hoki nei te iwi nei, tera tetahi wahine kua puta i te taua nei, kaore i kitea, i roto i te rua kumara e moe ana.   Ka warea te taua ki te hopuhopu i nga tangata o te pa nei, ka heke te wahine i te puke i runga ake i te *piriti* o Omahu, ka tae ki te taua ka ki atu kua tahuri a Te Puketapu.   Ka maharatia he taua na Ngati-Whiti-kaupeka no Patea, no Rangitikei ranei.   Ka whati te taua nei i konei, ka tae ake nga tutai ki a Te Wha-kumu, ka mea:—" Kua tae mai te karere o te taua ki Te Puketapu, kua tahuri te pa.   Kati, kai te whati te taua nei ki reira."

Ka mea a Te Wha-kumu ki a Te Okooko, ki a Kokau:—" Haere korua, kia wawe korua ki te taha ki mua o te taua i whati nei, whakatitaha ai i te ara hokinga mai ma uta ma runga hiwi, kia hori atu te taua ka heke iho ai ki te ara nui ; ka whai atu hoki matau."

. E korero ana ka kitea atu ka koori (? koiri) te au o te ahi o te weranga o Te Puketapu i te ahi, na Te Nanara i tahu.   Katahi ano ka rere nga toa nei, ka mea a Te Wha-kumu kia rua rau topu e haere ki te whai i te iwi nei.   Ka whaia i te po, ka tae atu ki Te Awatapu, kua kino te whati a te taua nei, kua marara noa atu te haere i te whawhai, kia wawe te tae.   Ka timata te karapoti o te rua rau topu ; ka patua haeretia te iwi nei ; koia tenei parekura a Marae-kakaho.   No te hora haere i te parae o te tangata, kaore rawa i taea taua pa e te taua te pa horo.

Na, ka roa, ka pae he kai ma ratau, katahi ka haere ki Wairarapa.
Kaore i ea tenei matenga i a Ngati-Awa, i a Ngati-Mahanga, i a
Rangitane hoki.

Ka tae te taua nei ki Whareama, a Ngati-Ira, kaore i homai he
waka hei whitinga i te awa o Whareama. Ka noho i Wai-mimiha, i
te ngutuawa o Whareama; katahi ka whakaturia te haka e te wahine,
nawai ra ka eke mai i runga i nga waka kia tata mai ratau ki te taha
matakitaki ai. Ka neke te haka a nga wahine o Ngati-Ira ki uta,
katahi ka u mai nga tangata ki uta matakitaki ai ki a Ngati-Ira e
haka ana. Katahi ka huakina mai e te taua ma roto i te tahataha o
te awa, ka mau e wha nga waka. Ka kokirikiri nga tangata ki roto i
te wai, ka kau ki te taha tonga o te awa o Whareama. Katahi ka
whakawhiti a Ngati-Ira i Whareama, kotahi mano topu taua taua a
Te Wha-kumu; koia te whakatauki na:—" Tena, tera a Ngati-Ira te
haere na i uta me te mea tera he tere pekehā i te moana." Mo te nui
o te tangata o taua ope.

Na, tera kua tae te rongo o te taua nei ki nga wahi katoa, me te
nui o te wehi o te tangata. Kua omaoma nga tangata noho tahora,
me nga hapu me nga iwi ki roto i nga motu o uta o te tuawhenua,
i te nui o te wehi. Ka whakaturia te pa mo te whawhai ki a Te
Wha-kumu me tona iwi. Ko te Pa o Rakai-tauheke tetahi, kei uta o
Whareama; i tu ai ki reira, i maharatia era taua ope e tika atu ma te
ara e tika ai ma uta ki Wairarapa; ko Ihutu te pikitanga tiketike o
taua ara. Kia tae atu ki reira ka whawhai ai a Rangitane, a Ngati-
Whatumamoe, koia nei nga iwi kua hui ki roto o taua pa. Kotahi o
nga pa, ko Nga Wahine-potae, kei runga i te maunga e tu ana, kei te
taha rawhiti o te awa o Mangapakia; tenei pa i aua iwi ano. Kaore i
mamao te Pa o Rakai-tauheke i Nga Wahine-potae.

Na, ka mahia tetahi pa ki te taha tonga o te ngutuawa o Whareama, ko Oruhi te ingoa, he karapuke nei te tunga o taua pa; no
Rangitane ano taua pa. Ka mahia tetahi pa ki Tupapaku-rua, ki uta,
ko Take-whenua te ingoa, he pa nui kei te huanui e ahu mai ai ma uta
ki Maungarake nei. Engari he pa tahito enei pa e rua, a Oruhi, a
Take-whenua; ko te Pa o Rakai-tauheke, he pa hou tenei; ko Nga
Wahine-potae he pa tahito tenei no Ngati-Wairehu, no Ngati-Takawa.
Enei hapu, iwi hoki, no Whata, koia te rangatira o enei iwi e rua, e
aranga Te Kai-hinaki-a-Whata i Te Waipukurau ra o Heretaunga ra.
Kati, ka marama mai koe ki enei take.

Na, ka kite koe kua haere te ope taua a Te Wha-kumu ma Whareama ki te ngutuawa,; ka whiti katoa te taua nei ki te taha tonga o te
awa nei. Katahi ka whakaeketia a Oruhi, kaore i roa ka horo taua
pa, ka horo i te po, ka mau a Te Poki, a Kaikore, a Te Whatu-rakau,
a Te Hau-taruke, koia tenei nga rangatira o Rangitane i mate ki
reira. Ka horo atu etahi ki roto i Take-whenua i Tupapaku-rua, i
kiia ake ra e au.

Ka roa e noho ana ki te mahi kai moana ma ratau taua ope o Ngati-Ira, ka pae te kai moana, te aruhe, te mahi. Ka mea etahi o nga herehere ki a Ngati-Ira:—" Kei uta o Whareama nga pa e rua e tatari ana mai ki a koutou i te nui o to koutou rongo toa e hau mai nei i te whenua; ko te Pa o Rakai-tauheke, ko nga Wahine-potae, ka oti tera te kowhiri ko ia toa anake o Rangitane e noho mai nei. Kati, kotahi o nga pa tauwhanga i a koutou ko Take-whenua, kei uta o te pae maunga nei, kei konei anake te toa o tenei takutai moana e whanga ana mai ki a koe."

Ka mea a Te Honoiti ki a Te Wha-kumu :—" Kua pae te ora o te tangata ; pewhea tatau ? "

Ka mea atu a Te Wha-kumu ki a Te Honoiti me Ngati-Ira katoa:—" Tenei te whakaaroaro ake nei te ngakau ki nga rongo korero a te herehere nei, kei nga huarahi e tauwhanga mai ana nga pa tuwatawata tutaki i a tatau, whakatau hoki i to koutou rongo toa o te riu o Heretaunga, haere mai nei ki tenei. Kati, ki te titaha tatau i te Pa o Rakai-tauheke me Nga Wahine-potae ka whai kupu a Rangitane, a Ngati-Mamoe—'hei aha nana ra i titaha penei takoto wharoro ana ratau i konei.' Koia tenei te ahua o te kupu ma ratou ki a tatau, koia ahau i whakaaro ai me wahi ki a koutou kia wha rau topu ki Nga Wahine-potae, kia wha rau topu ki te Pa o Rakai-tauheke, whakaeke ana tetahi me tetahi. I te mea kua tae te rongo kua titaha tatau i aua pa e rua, kua marara te noho a te tangata o roto, ka whakaeke ngawari noa atu te taua. Kia wha topu e waiho hei tiaki i nga wahine, i nga tamariki nei i konei, ko tatau e haere ki era pa e rua."

Ka wehea te haere a nga matua nei, ko tetahi ka ahu ma te taha tonga o Whareama, ko tetahi ka haere ma te taha rawhiti marangai o Whareama, a ka tata atu ki te Pa o Rakai-tauheke, ka noho i reira kia tae tetahi matua. Ka tae te matua ma Mangapakia, he awa tera, tae atu ki Te Papa-kowhai i raro iho o te pikitanga o Ihupiri, ka noho kia awatea. Ka huaki i te po, ka whakaawhitia nga pa nei, ka tatata ki te puao nui ka kitea tetahi tangata e haere ana i waho mai o te pa, me te wahine ; ka hopukia, ka mau, ko Kapukapu me Hine-whiri aua tangata, no roto i te Pa o Rakai-tauheke. Ka uia atu :—" Kei te aha a roto i te pa nei ? "

Ka kiia mai :—" Kua hokihoki te tangata ki uta whenua ki nga kainga noho tahora, ki nga wahine, ki nga tamariki."

Ka uia atu ano :—" Kei te pewhea a Nga Wahine-potae ? " Ka utua mai :—" Kua pera ano te ahua o te tangata." E mahara ana a Kapukapu raua ko Hine-whiri he taua whakauru tera no Rangitane ake ano. Katahi ka ui atu a Kapukapu :—" Kua hori te ope taua a Te Wha-kumu me tona iwi, a Ngati-Ira, ma Tupapaku-rua ? "

Ka mea atu te tangata o te taua :—" Koia ra tenei te taua a Te Wha-kumu e ki mai na koe."

Ka kanakana nga whatu kia oma ia; ka mea atu a Te Honoiti:—
"E! kaua hei oma, koi patua koe, ata noho kia ora ai koe."

Ka whakaura te haeata o te ata ka whakaeke na te Pa o Rakai-
tauheke, ka mate a Rakai-tauheke i konei. E kiia ana he nui ano te
tangata i mate i reira, he tane anake te nuinga. Ka mauria te upoko
o Rakai-tauheke; te take i mauria ai he pai no te ahua o taua tangata,
e kiia ana he tino tangata pai rawa atu te ahua; ka mauria te upoko
hei whakaatu ki te iwi o Ngati-Ira.

E tahuri ana tenei pa ka wera mai hoki a Nga Wahine-potae i te
ahi. Pera ano kaore i maha nga tangata o roto; i roto, ki roto i te
awa o Mangpakia te nuinga o te tangata, i reira e paepae ake ana te
taua a Ngati-Ira, i wehea ko etahi hei whakaeke i te pa, ko etahi hei
te taha ki te awa noho ake ai.

Ka hoki nga matua taua nei, ka tae ki Oruhi, ki to ratau nuinga.
Ka mea atu a Te Wha-kumu:—"Kati. Tuku atu a Kapukapu me nga
herehere mai o Nga Wahine-potae, o te Pa o Rakai-tauheke kia haere."

Ka tukua katoatia nga herehere kia haere. Ka mea atu a Te
Wha-kumu ki a Kapukapu me era atu o nga herehere:—"Haere! ki
atu ki a Rangitane me era atu iwi, whakawatea ki tahaki i te ara
moku i Tupapaku-rua. E haere ana au ki Potaka-kura-tawhiti, ki Te
Wharaunga-o-Kena, ki aku matua ki a Te Whakamana, ki a Te
Rerewa. Kaore au i haramai ki te patu tangata; i mate ai te tangata
i au e haere nei, he whakawatea naku i taku huarahi; i peka ai au ki
uta o Whareama nei, he wawao naku mo te kupu he wehi i titaha ai
taku ope ma Tupapaku-rua. Mo tena whakaaro anake i peka atu ai au
ki te whakatau i Rakai-tauheke me nga Wahine-potae. Haere!
koi tahuri mai o koutou kanohi ki muri nei; kia maro te haere ki
tahaki o te huarahi."

Ka haere a Kapukapu me ona hoa e rua rau tuma, te tane, te
wahine, te tamariki. Ka nui te koa o nga herehere mo te tukunga i a
ratau kia hokihoki ki o ratau kainga. Ka mea a Kapukapu, a Te
Whao, nga tangata o nga herehere ra:—"Haere! ma maua e haere
ake ki Take-whenua nei whakaatu ai i to kupu. Ki te whakaae mai,
tena maua e hoki mai ki a koe; ki te kore e whakaae mai
ka hoki matau ki Puketoi kei uta o Whareama, o Mataikona, o
Owahanga hoki," he maunga tera wahi a Puketoi.

Ka po rua e whanga ana te ope haere a Ngati-Ira ki a Kapukapu
raua ko Te Whao, kua kore e tae mai. Ka mea a Te Wha-kumu ki a
Te Honoiti:—"Whakatika tatau ka haere."

Katahi ka haere, ka tae ki waho mai o Take-whenua, ka pa mai te
reo o te tangata o roto o te pa:—"Ane ki au! E koro ma, e! Te
takoto kino mai ra i ro o Whareama .. e .. i."

Koia ra te maioha a nga wahine o te tangata whenua. Ko te ahua
o taua maioha e maioha ana mo nga tangata i mate ki nga pa i kiia
ake nei o roto o Whareama. Engari kaore ano i puta atu te taua nei

ki waho o te putaanga; i ki atu a Te Wha-kumu:—"Ko te haere, me tutira te haere, kia kotahi rau topu te matua ki mua, me tane anake; kia kotahi rau topu te wahine e maka ki waenganui. Ka aua atu tera, ka tukua ake kia kotahi rau topu te tane; ka aua ake tenei ka tuku ake kia kotahi rau topu ano te wahine; me pena tonu, a mutu noa. Kia wha rau topu te matua tane ki muri hei tutaki mai i muri."

Koia tenei nga tohutohu a Te Wha-kumu ki tona iwi ki a Ngati-Ira; na, ka pera te haere a te iwi nei.

Ka whanga nga tangata o roto o te pa ra kia kitea te hiku o to ope nei. Ka pena tonu te haere o te tangata, a ahiahi noa e haere ana. Ka mea nga tangata o roto i Take-whenua:—"Ka tika ano te toa o te iwi nei e hau mai nei te rongo ki a tatau, ina te ahua me he uru ngahere tera te nui o tenei ope." Ka tau te wehi ki nga tangata o roto i Take-whenua, kaore rawa i korikori te tane, ko te wahine anake e maioha mai ana ki o ratau tupapaku i mate ra i Oruhi, i te Pa o Rakai-tauheke, i Nga Wahine-potae.

Ka tae te ope nei ki Wainuioru, ka tae atu a Kapukapu raua ko Te Whao ki te puni o Ngati-Ira, ka korerotia kaore i whakaaetia te take o ta raua haere mai, kia kana hei whawhai:—"Kotahi tonu te whakaaro o te tane, o te wahine, ko te puta tonu mai ki waho ki te whawhai ki a koe, e Ngati-Ira! Na te kitenga i te ahua o te rere a te tangata, a ahiahi noa, kaore e mataki te haere o te tangata, katahi ano ka mate haere te whakaaro o nga toa whakaputa o roto o Take-whenua. Kati, kua mutu, haere noa atu koe, e tokoto nei ki te riu o Wairarapa, kaore he aha o mua i a koe. Kei Potaka-kura-tawhiti anake te tangata, i to rongo, nana i whakawhaiti te noho a te tangata ki reira. E tae e koe ki Maunga-rake, e noho i kona; tukua he tangata mau ki o matua i roto o Potaka, kia wawe ai ratau te mohio mai ko koe."

Ka mea atu a Te Wha-kumu:—"E pai ana." Ka mea atu ano a Te Wha-kumu:—"Ko taku whakaaro me noho korua, ko korua tonu he karere maku ki roto o Potaka."

Ka whakaae a Kapukapu, a Te Whao. Ka tae te matua nei ki runga o Maungarake, ka marama te kanohi ki roto o Wairarapa, mai i te moana tae noa ki te kauru. Ka noho te ope nei i reira, ka tukua a Kapukapu raua ko Te Whao kia haere. Ka tae a Kapukapu ma ki Potaka-kura-tawhiti, ka uia mai e Te Whakamana, e Te Rerewa, me o raua iwi:—"I nu tai?" Ka mea a Kapukapu:—"Ko Te Wha-kumu! Ko Te Wha-kumu te ope haere nei!"

Ka mea ano a Te Whakamana:—"E Kapu! Hokia ano!" Ka mea ano a Kapukapu:—"Ko Te Wha-kumu! Ko Te Wha-kumu a Tu-tapora te ope haere o Ira."

Ka tukua mai nga taina o Te Whakamana me to ratau tuahine ki te kawe kai mai ma Te Wha-kumu, hokorima topu te ope pikau kai mai ma te ope haere mai o Te Wha-kumu. I konei ka tae mai ki

Maungarake nei te ope mai o Potaka-kura-tawhiti, koia nei nga mea i
tonoa mai, haunga nga kai pikau kai.   He kao korau, he kao kumara,
he piharau, he tuna hao maroke, he ika paka, he koura mahiti, he
paua maroke, he pepe whinau, he pepe inanga, he taha huahua, koia
nei nga kai.

I muri i iho i tenei ka ki atu a Hine-tuwawe, tuahine o Te
Whakamana, ki a Te Wha-kumu:—"E tama!   Me haere tatau ki te
marae i o matua, o o tipuna, o o taina, kia wawe te ta o ratau ngakau
ki a koe, e homai nei to rongo me he mura ahi tera e taoro ana to mahi
ki te patu haere mai i a Rangitane, i a Ngati-Awa, i a Ngati-
Mahanga, haere mai nei koe i te takutai nei kaore he morehu e tu ana
ki to aroaro.   Kati ra te patu i te tangata, kei hea he whakaruru hau
mou i patua ai koe."

Ka mea atu a Te Wha-kumu:—"E hine!   He tika to kupu, ka
mutu taku, he karo patu, me i kore hoki au e karo i te patu moku, e
kore au e kite i a koe."

Katahi ka whakaae atu a Te Wha-kumu kia haere ratau, ka mea:—
"Ko te rakau nei he rata tona ingoa o mua, me ki i naia nei ko Te
Rata o Te Wha-kumu."

Ka tae ki Potaka, ka moe a Te Wha-kumu i a Hine-ipurangi,
tetahi tenei o nga tino wahine rangatira o Wairarapa nei o aua ra.

TE TANGI A NUKU I TE MATENGA I PEEHIKATIA, MO TE
OHONGAITUA, MO TE RANGI-TAKUARIKI.

"Haere atu ra, e tama ma e!
I te mata o te rakau a Tu-matauenga
I patua ai Kaupeka i roto o Kauwhata-roa
Ka tangohia te manawa, ka poia ki a Aitupawa
Ki a Rehua, ki a Tahurangi
I te mata takitaki i tupea ai a Rangi
Ki te poho o Rangi-tamaku i Tahuaroa
I hikaia ai e Tupai, e Tama-kaka
Ki te ahi tapu na Rangi-nui
I takahia ki Tauru-rangi-atamai
Ka tu tona ahi, koia te ahi tapu
Koia te ahi toro, koia te ahi tipua
Ka puta ki te hou matapu
Ka ea ki te ao nei—e tama ma, e!

Haere ra, e tama ma, e!
I te ara ka takoto i Taheke-roa
Kia karangatia mai koutou ki te Muri ki te Waihou
I to koutou tipuna, i a Ruaumoko
E whakangaoko ra i Rarohenga
Ka puta te hu ki te taiao

Koia Hine-puia i Hawaiki
E tahi noa mai ra i te kauhika
Ki waho i te moana
Ka tere Hine-uku, ka tere Hine-one
Ka tere Para-whenua-mea ki a Hine-moana
E tu mai ra i Tahora-nui-atea
Ka whakapae ki uta ra, koia Hine-tapatu-rangi
E haere atu na korua
E tama ma . . e . . i."

[The allusion above to volcanic action in Polynesia in past times is interesting. Hine-puia is the personified form of volcanic activity; Hine-uku and Hine-one, representing earth and land, together with Para-whenua-mea, representing water, as streams, etc., move into or are engulfed by Hine-moana, personified form of the ocean. Tahora-nui-atea, Mahora-nui-atea and Marae-nui-atea, are all expressions denoting vast ocean expanses, the waste of waters, sometimes alluded to as the *marae* or plaza of Hine-moana.

The above allegory reminds one of a tradition preserved by the Takitumu folk of the submergence of certain lands in Polynesia in former times, caused or accompanied by a tremendous eruption that destroyed a mountain named Maunga-nui, in which catastrophe whole tribes perished.]

HE WAIATA NA NUKU.

Mo te korenga o nga tangata o Wai-rarapa e hoki mai ki te whakatau ki te whawhai ki a Ngati-Awa, ki a Ngati-Mutunga, ki a Ngati-Raukawa, ki a Ngati-Toa.

" Nei ka noho i te ra o te waru
Ka haramai e tamaroto ka pupuke ake
Me ko Rua i te pukenga, ko Rua i te wananga . . e
Rua i te rururu, e, ko Rua i te wetewete, e
Ko Rua i te horahora ki tukemata rau, e
Waiho ra, e, me ata kaupeehi iho, e
Kia ata tukutuku ra, e, i te ahorangi, e
Me ui pea e au ki te makau tangata o te waotu, e
E hara tenei kei te pokiki he paewai, e
Me ui pea e au ki te mata ngaro i a Rangi, e
Kaore te ki mai te waha
Ka whanatu tenei au, ka whetoki haere ki tai ra
Me ko te punga i te toroa a punga
Ka whai i te pua tuhi no Tawhiti-nui
No Tawhiti-pa-mamao, e
Kia whitirere ake au me ko te ata i marama

Marama te ata i Hotu-nuku, e
Ko Tane te waiora . . e . . i."

HE WAIATA TANGI MO NUKU.

Na Te Whare-pouri i Nukutaurua.

"Tera Tariao ka kokiri kai runga
Ko te rite i ahau e whakawhetu nei
Wairua i tahakura nou nei, e Nuku
Kei te whakaara koe i taku nei moe
Kia hua ake ai au ko to tinana tonu
Me he wai wharawhara te tuturu o te roimata i aku kamo
E tangi, e manu, kia mohio roto
Ma te hau tonga au e whiu
Nga puke iri mai o Rangitoto i waho ra
Kia whai atu au i to tira
Ka wehe rawa ia koe i ahau
Tera pea koe ka iria he maunga a tai
E horo e manu kahu i raro ra
Ki nga puhi raia ki Wainuku
Maruao ki Marianuku
Te huri rawa mai to wairua ora
Ki ahau i konei . . e . . i."

HE WAIATA.

Ka mau a Ripeka Te Kakapi, tamahine a Te Whare-pouri, me
nga matua, ka tae ki Nga Umu-tawa, ka poroporoaki tera, koia tenei
tona tau :—

"E tama ma, e! Tenei au te rapa noa nei,
Te hahau noa nei
I te mate waiora na Paikea
Kia ea ake ana ko Hikurangi nga morehu, e
Tenei ia ka pahunu te tangata, ka pahunu te whenua
Ka rapa te waewae i te manawa ka nguha
Ki te takapau whare ki te whenua
Ka hurihia ake nei ki muri
He hau taua e topetope mai nei i te whenua, e
Tenei he koronga ka tu ki roto o Makauri
I whiua mai ra ki uta hei tohu mo Mahaki
Kia kata noa mai te kikitara
Kotipatipa kohurehure titipounamu
E tangi haere ana ki tona whenua
Ka tipuria nei e te maheuheu
Tangi kau ana te mapu . . e . . i."

HISTORY AND TRADITIONS OF RAROTONGA.

By Te Ariki-tara-are.

PART VI.

Translated by S. Percy Smith.

ABOUT TANGIIA AND TE NGA-TAITO-ARIKI.

[In the following part (which is a continuation of Part IV.) the
Sage, while professing to give the history of the celebrated
Rarotongan chief, Tangiia-nui, also in reality gives a brief sketch of
the history of the people right away from the first ancestor known to
them down to the same Tangiia, who settled in Rarotonga in the
thirteenth century. Tangiia's adventurous voyages, his wars, and
his loves will form another part of these papers.

As in all these old Polynesian legends we are carried back to that
stage of development in human progress, when it was the common
belief that the gods took part in the affairs of mankind, a belief by
no means exclusively Polynesian.

The scene of most of the following story is laid in Savai'i and
'Upolu of the Samoan Group, the former of which islands is known
to the Rarotongans as Avaiki, while Avaiki-raro is a general name
for the Samoan, Fiji, and other islands in their neighbourhood. In
some of the proper names it is difficult to understand whether the
Sage refers to gods or men, for they often have identical names. The
story of the Ruru (White Heron) and the Sea-snake is also to be
seen in our " Rarotonga Records," and the two stories whilst agreeing
in the main, should be read together, for each contains detail not
shown in the other. Some remarks on the genealogies are referred to
in the general introduction to this series of papers.]

THIS is a word about Te Nga-taito-ariki, who was a son of Te Tumu (from whom descend the following generations of men):—

[1] 95	Te Tumu		74	Te Tarava-enua
	Te Nga-taito-ariki			Te Rua-enua
	Mna			Te Rua-mata-iko
	Eanga			Te Punupunu. Te Utarei (e
	Maina			uanga ika ia. Anau akera
90	Maeata			ta Rua-mata-iko).
	Makaro			Ara-kapua
	Te Marama		70	Te Ara-o-nga-atua
	Te Eanga-ki-te-ao			Toi
	Tangata-kato			Pungaverevere (ka ngaè ki te
85	Te Atu-tanganga			Ara-o-nga-atua).
	Te Atu-te-ngangata			Manu
	Te Atu-te-ki			Manu-kaiaia
	Te Atu -		65	Manu-kavakevake
	Tiki			Ore
80	Taito-rangi-ngunguru			Turanga ma Te Ruru
	Taito-rangi-ioio			Rongo-rua
	Taito-kuru-angiangi			Rira (or Rina)
	Taito-kuru-ma-rakamea		60	Te Irapanga [3]
	Vaitakere [2]			Tu-tarangi
75	Te Tarava		58	Etoi

TU-TARANGI AND HIS WARS.

254. Tu-tarangi (generation No. 59 above) caused a great war, the reason of which was as follows: He owned certain birds [probably trained sea-gulls] named Aroa-uta and Aroa-tai; they were trained birds that did work for him, they obtained food, and fished for him. On a certain occasion, Tane-au-vaka sent a messenger to Tu-tarangi asking for the use of his birds, but Tu-tarangi would not consent at first, but in consequence of frequent applications he at last allowed the bird that lived ashore (Aroa-uta) to be sent to Tane-au-vaka. But the bird would not act (for its new master) so it was killed. Tu-tarangi was then applied to for the other bird, and he finally consented to lend Aroa-tai to Tane-au-vaka. This time the bird did his work and caught fish; but it was not treated properly, it was not fed, and so when it was sent to fish along the shore, the bird refused to work because it had no stamina.

1. The numbers show the generations back from the year 1900.

2. In the times of Vaitakere we learn from other documents that the people were living in that Avaiki which has been identified with either Java or Sumatra.

3. Te Irapanga is in all probability the navigator shown in our "Memoirs." Vol. IV., p. 32, who led the migration from Tawhiti-nui (? Borneo) to the Hawaiian Islands, but who apparently settled finally in either the Lau islands of the Fiji Group, or in Savai'i of the Samoan Group.

255. Then Tane-au-vaka became angry with the bird, and killed it. When Tu-tarangi learnt that both his birds were dead, great was his anger, and he despatched his son Etoi to fell the tree named " Te Ii-matoa-i-avaiki " [to make arms of]. So the son went, and felled the tree, and when it was down he returned and reported to his father. The father then said to his son, " Go thou, and lay the matter before [the god, or perhaps a learned man] Tāne."

256. Then Etoi took the wood to Tāne, and on his arrival, Tāne said, " Return! and tell Tu-tarangi to send hither a priest." In accordance with this command, Tu-tarangi sent Rauru-maoa with an offering of food; it was cold (uncooked) food, and was (?) named after that tree "Au-makariri." On Rauru-maoa's arrival, Tāne directed him, saying, "O the powers of earth! turn over this wood. O the powers of the land! split the wood, named "Te Ii-matoa-i-Avaiki," hew it in pieces, shake it; gnash the teeth, be nimble, glare the eyes; that it may return to the breast of Rongo-ma-Tāne! "[4]

257. After the wood had been split up, eight weapons were dubbed out of it, and the following names given to them : the spear was named by Tu-tavake after his own teeth—" Nionio-roroa " ; the *aro* was named " Te Aroaro-rangi," the *kounga* was ' Te Pivai-rangi,' the *mata-tupa* was ' Te Mata-tua-rere,' the *rupo* was ' Te Poopoo-rangi,' the *korare* (the javelin) ' Te Iti-rarerare,' the *akatari-kuri* (a barbed spear) ' Puapua-ai-nano,' the *tao* (lance) ' Rau-tiare.'

258. After all the weapons were completed they were deposited in the house called Oro-kete, which was the ediface at the back part of house [? of Tu-tarangi], where was the *ataata-itu* [? altar] to the god Rongo-ma-Tāne. When all the weapons had been placed in due order, the priest, Rauru-maoa, reported to Tu-tarangi that all was complete. Tu-tarangi asked, "Are they really good weapons ? " to which the priest replied, " One only is deficient, ' Nionio-roroa,' which Tu-tavake has placed on the altar of Rongo-ma-Tāne."

259. When Tu-tarangi learnt this, he sent a messenger to Kuru —his leading warrior—instructing him as follows : " Go thou, and take possession of the weapons now with Rongo-ma-Tāne." In consequence Kuru proceeded to the presence of the god, when Tāne said to him, " O Kuru! Welcome! O Kuru, what have you come for? You have a strange appearance, thy eyes are (?) staring!" Kuru replied, " I have come to fetch the weapons." Tāne spoke to him, " Enter then!" After Kuru had entered the house all the weapons of Tāne moved or wriggled ; then he proceeded to examine them all, to find which best suited his purpose, even that on the altar

4. These cryptic sayings are difficult to understand (as were also the Greek oracles), but the object appears to have been to facilitate the conversion of the wood into spears, and to give the latter *mana*.

of Tāne named " Nionio-roroa."   He decided on that particular one, when Tāne said, " O Kuru! that is a cursed weapon (of evil omen). It will be the death of (the people of) the land, and also destroy the land."   Kuru replied, " This is the one I choose " (prefer).

260.   Kuru then came forth from the house, and holding up the weapon he cast it into the hands of the several gods (i.e., he called on those gods to give his weapon power) saying, " The weapon that shall stand in the battle, whose shall it be?   By Rongo, Tāne, Rua-nuku, Tu, and Tangaroa! " (shall my weapon be guided).   He then seized the weapon in his hand, and with it cut off the heads of the children of Tu-tavake named Ti-tape-uta and Ti-tape-tai.   The boast (accompanying the action) resounded afar, when Tāne asked, " O Kuru! what is that?"   " It is the effect of the sacredness of the weapon." " I said to you, ' O Kuru! it is a cursed weapon.' "

261.   Kuru then went out again and met the sisters (of those already killed) named Titi-kereti and Tata-kerero, both of whom he killed.   The sound spread, and then Tāne asked, " O Kuru! what is that?"   " That is the woman-consuming power of the weapon!" Then said Tāne, " It is Tu-the-relation-eater.   Go, O Kuru! I have done with it, and do not return; thine is the *tapakau,* the *rau-ota* and the *moumounga* (? wastefulness)."

262.   And then Kuru departed for the other side of Avaiki and ' there fought (the people); and succeeded in catching Tane-au-vaka and all his many men.   So Kuru killed Tane-au-vaka.   Thence Kuru proceeded to another part and fought there, even unto Amama [5] the place of Maru-mamao, who with his many men fought from daylight until the evening. (In the battle) Maru-mamao and his party held the coast line, while Kuru and his party were by the road side inland, and so his eyes were completely blinded (? by the sun), and then Maru-mamao struck Kuru in the face with an axe, and killed him. Thus the celebrated weapon " Nionio-roroa " became the property of Maru-mamao.

UI-TE-RANGI-ORA AND DISPERSION OF THE PEOPLE.

263.   There were born unto Etoi (Tu-tarangi's son, the following descendants):—

<pre>
57   Etoi
     Etai
55   Emaunga
     Erangi
     Ui-tamua
     Ui-taringa
51   Ui-te-rangiora
</pre>

5.   Amama is one of the islands mentioned in Part V. hereof, as being adjacent to Futuna (Horne Island), north of Fiji.   But it may be a local name on Savaii, where this scene is laid.

It was the latter who built a (celebrated) *pai* [or sea-going canoe], and the timbers of the canoe were men's bones.[6] The keel of the canoe (? and the canoe itself) was called "Te Ivi-o-Atea." The whole of the canoe was built of men's bones, and because no bone was long enough to form the *kiato* [or connecting supports of the outrigger], the tree named "Te Tamoko-o-te-rangi" was felled for that purpose. This tree was a reserved (and sacred) tree belonging to Taa-kura and Ari. When these two found out that Ui-te-rangiora had cut down their tree, they commenced a war with his party and many men were killed, but they secured eight portions of the tree, which were dubbed into drums, *tutunga*, [*tapa-beating* logs] and boards. The drum was named "Taka-enua," and was used in the *akaariki* ceremonies at Avarua,[7] while the *tutunga* was named "Tangi-varovaro."

264. Then Ui-te-rangiora proceeded to complete his vessel, and launched it on the sea. This was the first occasion of seeing the *pai* and canoes (? of that kind), and the (commencement) of the scattering of all Avaiki to the various islands. Due to the wars originating in Avaiki through Kuru, Taa-kura and Ari, were the people scattered to all the islands; to Avaiki-runga [Eastern Avaiki—Tahiti, Paumotu, etc.] to Iti-nui, Iti-rai, Iti-anaunau, Iti-takai-kere [some of the Fiji group, no doubt the eastern or Lau islands], Tonga-nui, Tonga-ake, Tonga-piritea, Tonga-manga, Tonga-rara, Tonga-anue [the Tonga, or Friendly Islands] to Avaiki-raro [Savai'i], Kuporu ['Upolu], Manuka [Manu'a], Vavau [North Tonga Group], Niva-pou [Niua-fou] and Niua-taputapu [Keppel's Island, both north of Tonga Group].

265.   Ui-te-rangiora's descendants were :—

<pre>
51   Ui-te-rangiora
     Makua-ki-te-rangi
     Te Rangi
     Ata-o-te-rangi
     Tara-o-te-rangi
     Te Paku-o-te-rangi
45   Te Uka-o-te-rangi
     Uu
     Ane
     Taipu
41   Tuna-ariki
</pre>

6. Thus the original reads, but it is a strange statement which has some meaning not apparent. Perhaps the canoe was ornamented with bones let into the wood.

7. It would be interesting to learn where this Avarua is, either in Savai'i, 'Upolu, or perhaps the Lau Group. It is mentioned in several traditions, and is not that one at Rarotonga or Ra'iatea. The *akaariki* is the appointment of a high chief to his office.

In Tuna-ariki's time a war commenced between him and Tu-ei-puka, about Avarua. Tuna-ariki insisted that it belonged to him, whilst Tu-ei-puka equally claimed it. So Tuna-ariki killed Tu-ei-puka, and the *au*, [the chieftainship] devolved on the former. In the end he was killed by a pig, an *uru-kivi* [? striped] pig, which ate that *ariki*.

266. After his death the government devolved on Kati-ongia, about whom is the saying, "Kati-ongia became ruling chief, and Kuporu ('Upolu) ruled." He was a son of Tu-ei-puka who had a brother named Māru. Kati-ongia's [8] descendants were :—

40 Kati-ongia
    Kapua
    Atonga (also known as Otenga-atua and Tauira-rangi-o-Avatea).
37 Te Aru-tanga-nuku

ABOUT THE VESSEL OF TE ARU-TANGA-NUKU.

267. Te Aru-tanga-nuku very much desired to have a canoe of his own; he was incited thereto by his parents (probably uncles) Oro-keu, Oro-i-nano, and Oro-taere. The reason of this strong desire was the scarcity of food, for the food allowed them by Atonga [the ruling chief who is said to have had two natures, one a spirit (*vaerua*) and the other a physical one (*kopapa-tangata*)] was very deficient, very little was given to them or their child (? nephew). Hence they incited the elder son (of Atonga)—Te Ara-tanga-nuku to build a vessel in order that they might go to other lands [than Kuporu, or 'Upōlu].

268. After their minds had been made up, they prepared the axes, made the customary feast, and next morning shouldered their axes and proceeded to prepare a tree as a keel for the vessel. They went to the mountains, where they met a *ruru* [the white heron] and an *aa* [snake][9] striving together. The *ruru* said to Oro-keu, "O the chief! O Oro-keu! Separate (or end) the fight of the *ruru* and the *aa*." The *aa* said, "The scarlet-belted chief must go on his way and leave the *ruru* and the *aa* to their mutual struggle." And so Oro-keu went on his way.

269. After the above appeared Oro-taere, to whom the *ruru* addressed himself, "O the chief! O Oro-taere! end the fighting between the *ruru* and the *aa*! Now Oro-taere felt sorry for the *ruru*

8. This Kati-ongia is no doubt identical with 'Ati-ongie of the Samoan genealogies.

9. Snakes of a harmless kind, but sometimes over 12 feet long are found in Samoa: but this was the sea-snake, or *pu*. For the cause of this strife, see "Rarotonga Records," p. 83.

because he was an elder brother of his, one of Ore's children.[10] His anger grew towards the *aa*, for he supported the cause of the *ruru*, and he therefore cut down the *aa* with his axe, and then lifted down his relative the *ruru*, and, placing it in front of him, wept over him, and healed the wounds made by the *aa* As soon as this was accomplished, the *ruru* asked Oro-taere, "What is your object here?" "I am going to fell a tree to make a vessel for the *ariki*." Then said the *ruru*, "Go to my tree at Ara-punga-verevere; I did not tell Oro-keu and Oro-i-nano about this [because they would not help me in my struggle with the *aa*]. Probably they are dead on the ridge by this time." So Oro-taere went on and found the tree, a Maota-mea was the kind,[11] which he felled and commenced shaping out [as a canoe], then fixed the hauling ropes (*kaka*) and left it.

270. Now, at this time there came Tangaroa-iu-mata [? the owner of the forest] and behold! there laid the fallen tree. He asked [to himself], "Who has fallen my tree?" But he could not find out; so he went to the guardian of the place—Rata-i-te-vao[12]—and asked him, "Who has been felling one of my trees?" Rata replied, "I do not know!" Tangaroa then proceeded to enquire of every one who dwelt near those parts, Titiri, Tata-rara, and Tu-enua-i-te-vao-tere, but they all replied they had no knowledge of the circumstances; and then he came to the conclusion he would not be able to ascertain who was the delinquent. So Tangaroa returned to the fallen tree, and re-erected it, saying to the tree, "Stand up thou *maota-mea*, be erect, be girded on thy bark." At this the bole of the tree stood erect again, and then he addressed the top (*tamoko*) of the tree, saying, "Stand there, O thou head of the tree! the large and small branches of the tree! the chips and the leaves return to your places! Adhere, gird on, the bark!" At this the tree stood erect as it was previously, and Tangaroa-iu-mata returned to his home.

271. Sometime after the above, Oro-taere and his party returned to their work, and on arrival at the the place where the stump ought to have been—it was not there; the tree stood erect; nothing but the hauling ropes suspended on a tree were to be seen. They searched and then found the tree by a white place from which a piece of bark had been taken down to the sea by them [when they felled the tree]

10. This looks like the Samoan custom of claiming relationship with certain birds, etc.—a species of incipient totemism But probably it was a fight between two clans, of whom the heron and sea-snake were the totems, or gods.

11. Maota-mea is the *Dysoxylon alliaceum*, a very handsome tree that grows in the Samoan Group. There was a beautiful clump of these trees in front of Robert Louis Stevenson's house at Vailima, on the hills behind the town of Apia, the lower branches of which he had cleared away, leaving a charming view of the town and the sea under the upper branches, as seen from the house.

12. Rata-i-te-wao is known to Maori traditions.

in consequence of the sacredness of the tree [and over which ceremonies to remove the *tapu* of the tree had to be performed]. They all
returned to the shore, and again Oro-taere consecrated his axes, the
tapu of which had been destroyed in killing the *aa*, and hence it
became possible for Tangaroa to re-erect the tree again. After this
had been done they returned and again felled the tree, barked it,
fixed the hauling ropes, and commenced dragging the log to the
place where Atonga the priest lived.

272. The [13] food was prepared for the priest, for Atonga, the
riaria and the other parts were cooked, but the heap of wood was left,
it had not been shaped. On another day Te Ara-tanga-nuku said to
his wife, Pori-o-kare, "You must go and take some *papaia*, [pounded
and baked *taro*] for the priest." She proceeded to cook some, and
before long took it to Atonga, and after he had eaten and was satisfied,
he said to Pori-o-kare, "Return, and say unto the *ariki* he must
build a house. To-morrow the vessel will be completed, and when
the house is finished let all Kuporu be seated there so they may
behold the vessel being dragged along by the birds."

273. After Pori-o-kare had departed, Atonga summoned Tupua-
ki-Amoa [14] and said to him, "Haste, and say to the *ruru*, it is to go to
the Pirake-akaruirui-rangi,[15] and assemble all the birds to come and
drag the vessel of the *ariki*." He went off and gathered all the
many birds. When daylight came all the birds surrounded the vessel,
the *moamoa* [? ground birds] took hold of one side, others helped from
inside. The Kakaia, the Ngoiro and Katikatika families, the quick
flighted birds on the out side. And they said, "With the wings
strike the stern; shake the log; lift it; shake the bows; together,
hasten the ' Ivi-o-Atea.' Gathered together are the many of Kuporu,
to see the sight; thou will win O Oro-keu! O Oro-i-nano." It was
the Kati-rori bird who recited the song. And now the canoe arrived
at the house built by the hands of Te Ara-tanga-nuku. Tupua-ki-
amoa had been sent to fetch the vessel, but he failed through want of
food. [Another story says that he took off the figure-head of the
canoe and hid it, but Atonga recovered it.]

274. This is the explanation about that vessel: It was dubbed
out in the night by Atonga-vaerua [Atonga-the-spirit] and his work-
men, and these are the names of those shipwrights: Iu-mata, Aa-ngu,

---

13. There seems as if a part of the story had been ommitted here. *Riaria*
means refuse, but the sentence is apparently incomplete. The *riaria*, we learn
from another narrative, were demanded by Tupua-i-Amoa, as his perquisites, but
the woman refused to give them, and hence Tupua's subsequent action in taking
off the figure-head of the canoe.

14. Tupua is an old family name in Samoa. Amoa is a place on the north-
east coast of Savai'i Island.

15. Pirake is a bird noted for its soaring habits.

Na-ora, and Na-oti, who built one side of the vessel, while Tupa, Tupa-ake, Tupa-aki, and Uri-reka built the other side; there were eight builders, Atonga being the ninth. Atonga named the vessel "Taraipo" [built-in-the-night],[16] while the birds also gave it a name, "Te Manu-ka-tere."[17] When the canoe reached the home of the *ariki*, the birds returned inland, but Atonga stopped the *ruru*, and asked it, "Where is a tree suitable as a *rakau-tukara* for the *ariki* ?" The *ruru* replied, "At Te Po-amio." "Where is that place ?" said Atonga. "At the Ara-pungaverevere, at the place where I live." And then the bird went away.

275. Atonga· now instructed Tupua-ki-Amoa, saying, "Go thou and cut down Te Po-amio," and explained where it was. So Tupua went off to enquire of Rata-i-te-vao (the guardian of the forest), saying, "Where is Te Po-amio ?" "Beyond there," said Rata, so Tupua went on and inquired of Tupi-riri, who replied, "Further on." So he went on, but could not find it. Then he descended to Tupa-raro and asked him, who said, "A long way on"; but he still did not find the place. He then went to Tu-enua, in the great forest, who explained to him, "There it is." Then he went on and searched, found it, and cut down the tree which was named Ipi-rere. He brought it down to the village and shaped it, and on completion named it "Te Amio-enua." He then delivered it to the *ariki*, who took the weapon and placed it in the canoe, and then the vessel was named "Te Pore-o-kare."

TE ARA-TANGA-NUKU'S VOYAGES.

276. The vessel was now launched into the sea, and proceeded on its voyage to Iva (the Marquesas Islands). The name given to the vessel at Iva was "Te Orauroa-ki-Iva" [the long voyage to Iva]. From there it went to Rapa-nui [Easter Island] and on to Rapa-iti [or Oparo, south-east of Rarotonga in lat. 27° 30′ south, another name for which is Rapa-hue], where Irei (or Ivi) was left on account of his bad navigation of the vessel. From there they sailed to Avaiki-runga [Tahiti and neighbouring groups] and all the islands near there. At Avaiki-runga the vessel received a further name, "Te Ara-ki-Avaiki."

277. The great desire of the *ariki*—Te Ara-tanga-nuku—and all the crew, on the completion of the vessel, was to behold all the wonderful things on the ocean which had been discovered and reported by Ui-te-rangiora [see par. 263] the man's-bones canoe (Te Ivi-o-Atea) in former times. The following were those things: The rocks growing out of the sea beyond Rapa Island; the monstrous

16. Compare the New Zealand Maori story of the canoe of the same name, and built under somewhat similar circumstances.

17. A name by which, I was informed in Tahiti, this celebrated canoe was known in that island.

waves; the female dwelling in those waves, with her hair waving and floating on the surface of the ocean; and the *tai-uka-a-pia* [the frozen sea], the deceitful animal seen on the sea, which dived below the surface; a very gloomy and dark place, where the sun is not seen. There is also there (a kind of) rock whose summit pierces the sky with steep bare cliffs, where vegitation does not grow. Such was the work of this vessel at that time; and also to convey people to all the islands. It was this vessel, "Te Ivi-o-Atea," that discovered all these great and wonderful things on the ocean, and all the surrounding islands.

[The inference to be drawn from the foregoing statement is, that Te Ara-tanga-nuku followed in the footsteps of the other great navigator, Ui-te-rangiora, who flourished fourteen generations, or 350 years before him, and that he visited, some at least, of the " wonders" discovered by Ui-te-rangiora, in the seventh century (using the generation herein given as chronology). There can be little reasonable doubt that the " wonders" described above refer to the Antarctic regions, "a very gloomy and dark place where the sun is (rarely) seen," the " rocks whose summits pierce the sky," being icebergs, while the " deceitful animal " is probably either a walrus or sea-lion, while the " hair waving on the surface " is probably the bull-kelp, which these people would not see in the tropics. The " Tai-uka-a-pia" is the ice, or frozen sea, like *pia*, the scraped arrowroot, which is exactly like snow, and is just the kind of description these people would give to snow or ice, with which they would not be acquainted with, except perhaps traditionally. *Uka* is the equivalent of the Maori *huka*, ice, frost, snow. Such, expressed in the poetical language of the islanders of the tropics, is the description of the regions south of Rapa, where the ice is frequently to be found about latitude 50°. The Tongans have also traditions of the frozen ocean, which they had visited in ancient times.]

278.   Te Ara-tanga-nuku had the following descendants :—

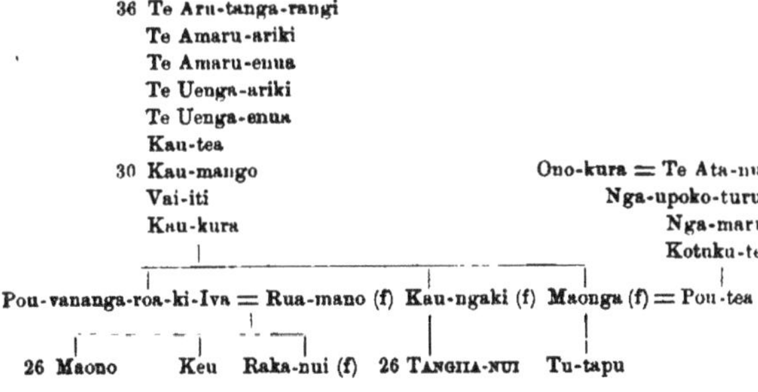

[Here we leave these generations of adventurous voyagers and emigrants, for in the times of Tangiia-nui the twenty-sixth generation from the year 1900, we enter upon an important epoc in Polynesian history. The time covered by this Part VI., saw the spread of the so-called "Tonga-fiti" branches to nearly all parts of the Pacific, and it was four generations after Tangiia that the last migration to New Zealand took place, i.e., in the middle of the fourteenth century.]

NO TANGIIA E TE NGA-TAITO-ARIKI.

253.   E tuatua no Te Nga-taito-ariki; e tamaiti na Te Tumu, anau akera tana ko Te Nga-taito-ariki :—

```
95   Te Tumu
     Te Nga-taito-ariki
     Mua
     Eanga
     Maina
90   Maeata
     Makaro
     Te Marama
     Te Eanga-ki-te-ao
     Tangata-kato
     Te Atu-tangangu
     Te Atu-te-ngangata
     Te Atu-te-ki
     Te Atu
     Tiki
80   Taito-rangi-ngunguru
     Taito-rangi-ioio
     Taito-kuru-angiaugi
     Taito-kuru-ma-raka-mea
     Vai-takere
     Te Tarava
     Te Tarava-enua
     Te Rua-enua
     Te Rua-mata-iko
     Te Panupunu, Ko Uta-rei (e uanga ika ia) Anau akera ta Rua-mata-iko
70   Ara-kapua
     Te Ara-o-nga-atua
     Toi
     Punga-verevere-ku-ngaè-ki-te-ara-o-nga-atua
     Manu
     Manu-kaiaia
     Manu-kavakevake
     Ore
     Turanga, ma Te Ruru (e manu ia)
     Rongo-rua
     Rira
     Te Ira-panga
     Tu-tarangi
57   Etoi
```

254. Kua akatupu a Tu-tarangi i te tamaki; tera te mea i tupu ei taua pekapeka ra—e puke manu na Tu-tarangi, ko Aroa-uta, e Aroa-tai; e puke manu rave angaanga nana; e rave kai nana, e tautai ika nana. E tae ake ra ki tetai tuatau, kua unga maira a Tane-au-vaka i te karere i aua nga manu ra ki a Tu-tarangi, kia omai aia i aua nga manu ra nana. E kare akera i tika i a Tu-tarangi. E, no te putupntuanga i te tiki mai, kua oatu aia i te manu noo uta na Tane-au-vaka—koia a Aroa-uta. Kare i keu ki te angaanga, kua ta aia i te reira manu. E kua tiki akaou mai i tetai—kua pati rai ki a Tu-tarangi, e kua oatu a Tu-tarangi i a Aroa-tai ki aia. E, kua rave taua manu ra i tana angaanga, kua tautai i te ika nana. E kare ra aia i takinga-meitaki i taua manu ra; kare i angai ki te kai; e kia tono ra aia i te manu ra kia tiki i te ika ki tatai, kare te manu e keu. No te mea, kare ua e kaponga a te manu.

255. Kua riri iora a Tane-au-vaka i te manu, e kua ta iora, mate iora. E kia kite ra a Tu-tarangi e, e kua mate nga manu, kua tupu iora te riri o Tu-tarangi; kua tono atura i tona tamaiti, i a Etoi, ei tipu i te rakau, i a Te-Ii-matoa-i-Avaiki. Kua aere atura te tamaiti, kua tipu atura i te rakau; e topa iora ki raro, kua oki maira e akakite ki te metua. Kua karanga atura te metua ki te tamaiti, "Ka aere! kavea ki a Tane."

256. Kua aere atura a Etoi, kua apai i te rakau ki a Tane. E tae atura ki a Tane, kua tuatua maira a Tane, "E oki! e karanga atu ki a Tu-tarangi, kia unga mai aia i tetai taunga." Kua akaunga atura a Tu-tarangi ia Rauru-maoa; kua keri iora i te kai ei taonga. E kai makariri i topaia i te ingoa o taua rakau ra, ko Au-makariri. E tae atura a Rauru-maoa, kua tuatua maira a Tane, na-ko-maira, "E te atu papa e! e kia uriuriia akera te rakau nei, E te atu-enua! kia vavai akera te rakau nei, ko te Ii-matoa-i-Avaiki; kia tutuki, kia ungaunga, kia ru, kia tete, kia ngavari, kia inana. Kia koki ra e, ki roto i te uma (? rima) o Ronga ma Tane e."

257. E oti akera te rakau i te vavaiia, kua tarai iora e, e varu rakau. Teia te ingoa o taua au rakau ra; Ko Te Tokotoko; koia tei topaia e Tu-tavake ki te nio nona—koia a Nionio-roroa. Ko Te Aroaro-rangi; koia te aro. Ko Te Pivai-rangi—koia te kounga. Ko Te Mata-tua-rere—koia te mata-tupa. Ko Te Poopoo-rangi—koia te rupo. Ko te Iti-rarerare—koia te korare, e Rau-tiare—koia te tao. Ko Puapua-ai-nano—koia te akatara-kuri.

258. Kua ma te au rakau kua kave ki roto i te are, ko Oro-kete—koia te orau i te tuaroa o te are; ko te ataataitu ïa o Rongo ma Tane. Kia oti te au rakau i te akapapaia kua aere atura te taunga ra, ko Rauru-maoa ki a Tu-tarangi, "E rakau meimeitaki ainei?" Kua karanga atura aia, "Okotai rai taka i te rakau; ko Nionio-roroa tei i a Tu-tavake, tei runga i te ataata-itu o Rongo ma Tane."

259. E kite akera a Tu-tarangi i tei reira tuatua, kua tono atura aia i te karere ki a Kuru—ko tona ïa tumu-toa—kua na-ko-atura a Tu-tarangi ki aia, "Ka aere koe, ka tiki i te are rakau i o Rongo ma Tane." Kua aere atu a Kuru, aere atura, e tae atura ki o Rougo ma Tane. Kua kapiki maira a Tane, ki a Kuru, na-ko-maira, " E Kuru e! ina! ka oro mai, E Kuru! e aa te aerenga. Kua tu ke koe E Kuru! Kua ioi o mata." Kua karanga a Kuru ki a Tane, "E tiki au i te are rakau." Kua kapiki maira a Tane ki a Kuru, "E na roto mai." E. tei to Kuru tomoanga atu ki roto, kua keukeu atura te are rakau a Tane i a Kuru; e tae atura aia ki roto kua akara aere iora aia i te au rakau ravarai e tau i aia; mari ra ko te rakau i runga i te ataata o Tane, ko "Nionio-roroa." Kua kiriti maira aia i taua rakau ra; kua kapiki maira a Tane, "E Kuru e! e rakau kanga. Ka mate te enua, ka nina ua te enua." Kua karanga maira a Kuru, " Ko taku rakau rai teia ! "

260. Kua tomo atura a Kuru ki vao, kua akatu akera i te rakau ki runga, kua titiri atura i te rakau ki te rima o te au atua, na-ko-atura, "Ko te rakau e tu i te taua naai? Na Rongo, na Tane, na Rua-nuku, na Tu, na Tangaroa." Kua opu aia i te rakau, kua taki akera ki runga i tona rima, kua tipu iora ki nga tamariki a Tu-tavake—i a Ti-tape-uta e Ti-tape-tai. Kua vavaro atura te iio; kua ui maira a Tane, "E Kuru e! ko te aa tena?" "Ko te tapu tena i te rakau," "O, i karanga atu na au ki a koe, 'E Kuru e! e rakau kanga!' "

261. Kua oki akaou atura a Kuru, kua aravei atura i nga tuaine, i a Titi-kereti, e Tata-kerero; kua mate ia tokorua; kua vavaro mai te iio; kua ui atura a Tane, "E Kuru! ko te aa tena?" "Ko te kai vaine teia i te rakau." Kua na-ko maira a Tane, "Ko Tu-kai-taeake tena. E Kuru! e aere; kua oti taku. Aua e oki mai. Naau atu te tapakau, e te rau-ota, e te moumounga." Kua aere atura a Kuru ki tetai pae i a Avaiki, kua tamaki atura; kua rauka iora taua ariki ra ko Tane-au-vaka ma tona tini tangata katoa. E kua ta iora a Kuru i taua ariki ra, i a Tane-au-vaka, mate iora.

262. Kua aere atura aia—a Kuru—ki tetai pae, kua tamaki. E tae ua atura ki Amama ki o Maru-mamao. Kua tamaki maira a Maru-mamao ma tona au tangata i aia i te akirata i te popongi. Ko Maru-mamao ma tona au tangata, i a ratou a tai—i te tapa tai; ko uta a Kuru i te tapa-ara. Kua tamaki iora, kua verovero maira te rä ki nga mata o Kuru; kua poiri kerekere iora nga mata o Kuru. Kua pari maira a Maru-mamao i nga mata o Kuru ki te toki; mate iora aia. Kua riro atura taua rakau ra i a Maru-mamao.

263.   Anau akera to Etoi, ko :—

        Etai
    55 Emaunga
    .   Erangi
        Ui-tamua
        Ui-taringa
    51 Ui-te-rangiora

Kua tarai aia i te pāī, e ivi tangata te rakau i taua pāī ra.   Ko te
ivi o Atea te takere ı taua pāī ra.   E oti ua ake taua pāī ra e ivi
tangata anake.   No te mea ra kare e ivi tangata roa ei ova, ei kiato,
no reira i kotia ei a te "'Tamoko-o-te-rangi" ei kiato, ei ova.   E
rakau raui na Taa-kura e Ari.   E kite akera a Taa-kura e Ari e,
kua motu taua rakau ra, i a Ui-te-rangiora ; kua tamaki atura, kua
mate iora te tangata, kua riro maira te rakau i a raua.   E ono
potonga i riro mai, kua tarai iora ei pau, ei tutunga, ei papa.   Ko te
ingoa i te pau ko Taka-enua—koia te pau akaariki ki a Avarua.   Ko
te tutunga ko Tangi-varovaro.

    264.   Kua rave akaou a Ui-te-rangiora i te pāī, kua akaova, e
kua ri, kua aau i te kiato ; kua oti, kua tuku ki te tai.   Ko te
kiteanga akera rai 'ia i te pāī e te vaka.   Ko te pueu-rikirikinga teia
i a Avaiki ki te pa enua.   No te tamaki i tupu i Avaiki e Kuru, e
Taa-kura e Ari, kua pueu-rikiriki atura Avaiki ki te pa-enua
ravarai ; ki Avaiki runga, ki Iti-nui, ki Iti-rai, ki Iti-anaunau, ki
Iti-takaikere, ki Tonga-nui, ki Tonga-ake, ki Tonga-piritia, ki Tonga-
mauga, ki Tonga-raro, ki Tonga-anue, ki Avaiki-raro, ki Kuporu, ki
Manuka, ki Vavau, ki Niva-pou, ki Niua-taputapu.

    265.   Anau akera ta Ui-te-rangi-ora ko :—

    50 Makua-ki-te-rangi
        Te Rangi
        Ata-o-te-rangi
        Tara-o-te-rangi
        Te Paku-o-te-rangi
        Te Uka-o-te-rangi
        Uu
        Ane
        Taipu
    41 Tuna-ariki

Kua tupu te tamaki i a raua ko Tu-ei-puka ; Tera te ara ; ko
Avarua.   Te manono nei a Tuna-ariki nona a Avarua ; te manono mai
a Tu-ei-puku nona.   Kua ta iora a Tuna-ariki i a Tu-ei-puka ; mate
iora.   Kua riro maira te au ki a Tuna-ariki.   I te openga iora kua
mate aia, kua pou i te puaka, e uru-kivi te puaka i keinga i (? ai)
taua ariki ra.

266. I muri iora i aia, kua riro te au ki a Kati-ongia—i tuatuaia ai e, "Kua ariki Kati-ongia, kua au Kuporu." E tamaiti aia na Tu-ei-puka. E teina a Māru no Tu-ei-puka:—

    40 Ko Kati-ongia, anau taua ko
        Kapua
        Atonga (known also as Otenga-atua and Tauira-rangi-o-avatea)
    37 Te Aru-tanga-nuku

NO TE PAI O TE ARU-TANGA-NUKU.

267. Kua akakoro a Te Aru-tanga-nuku ei vaka tona. No nga metua tane te manako no Oro-keu e Oro-i-nano e Oro-taere. Tera te tupuanga i taua manako ra, e aue kai. Ki te kai a Atonga e kai ua maira, kare e omai na ratou ma ta ratou tama. No reira ratou i akakoko ei, ki te tama ariki—ki a Te Aru-tanga-nuku—kia tarai i tetai pāī ei ara no ratou ki te pa-enua.

268. E taka akera te tuatua, kua rango iora i te toki; kua moe i te angai e popongi akera, kua apai te toki ki te tipu i te rakau, i te takere i te pāī. Kua aere atura ratou e tae atura ki te maunga, kua aravei iora ratou i te Ruru e te Aa, te taiapiapi ua ra. Kua kapiki maira te Ruru ki a Oro-keu, "E te ariki, E Oro-keu! e vaoa te taua a te Ruru ma te Aa." Kua tuatua maira te Aa, "E aere rai te ariki Maro-kura i tana aere e vao rai te Ruru ma te Aa kia taiapiapi marie." Aere atura aia i tana aere.

269. Kua mama atura a Oro-taere; kua kapiki maira te Ruru, "E te ariki, e Oro-taere! a vaoa te taua a te Ruru ma te Aa." Kua tupu akera te aroa ki roto i aia, no te mea, e tuakana te Ruru noua—ko tetai tamaiti ya a Ore. Kua tupu akera tona riri ki te Aa, kua tauturu atura aia i tona taeake, kua tipupu iora i te Aa. E mate atura i taua taeake noua ra, ki raro, ki mua i aia, kua aue iora ki runga i te Ruru. E oti akera kua rapakau iora ki te vai, kia papa te etietinga a te Aa i aia. E oti akera tei reira, kua ui maira te Ruru ki a Oro-taere, "E aa to aerenga?" "E koti rakau toku aerenga; e pāī no te ariki." Kua na-ko maira te Ruru, "E oro ki taku rakau, i te Ara-pungaverevere; kare au i akakite ki a Oro-keu e Oro-i-nano. Tera raua kua mate ki runga i te kaivi." Kua aere atura a Oro-taere e tae atura ki taua rakau ra, e Maota-mea te ingoa i te rakau. Kua tipu iora, e kua pari, kua tamou te kaka, e vao kia vai.

270. Kua aere maira a Tangaroa-iu-mata, e ina! kua motu te rakau. Kua ui maira na-ko maira. "Naai i tipu taku rakau?" E kare akera i kitea; kua aere atura ki te tiaki i te kainga—ki a Rata-i-te-vao—na-ko atura, "Naai i tipu taku rakau?" Kua karanga maira, "Kare au i kite." Kua ui tatakitai aere atura ki te au tangata ravarai i vai tata mai ki taua kainga ra, ki a Titiri, ki a Tatarara, ki a Tu-enua-i-te-vao-tere, kua na-ko-maira ratou, "Kare rava matou i kite." E kite akera aia e, kare i kitea. Kua oki atura

aia—a Tangaroa-in-mata—kua akatu akaou i te rakau, e kua kapiki
atura ki te rakau, na-ko-atura, " E tu te maota-mea e, ka tu mai ki
runga; kia kiri; kia taka." Kua tu maira te tumu ki runga i reira;
kua kapiki akaou atura aia, ki te tamoko o te rakau, na-ko atura,
" Ka tu mai koe, e te kauru o te rakau! e te manga o te rakau ; e te
atava o te rakau; e te rara o te rakau, e te ungaunga o te rakau, e te
rau o te rakau. Kia piri! kia kiri! kia taka!" Kua tu te rakau ki
runga, kua aere atura aia ki tona kainga.

271.   E miringao i te reira, kua aere atura a Oro-taere, e tae
atura aia ki te tumu i te rakau—kare ua; kua tu ki runga. Ko te
kaka ua tera e tarava ua ra; kua kimi iora ratou, e kitea iora ki te
ngai kiri e tea ua ra; ko te ngai kiri ïa i tuoia ki tai, i te tapu
i te rakau ki o te iiotanga. Kua oki atura ki tai, kua rango i te
toki, no te mea, ko te ara ïa i akatuia te rakau no te toki i tipuia ki
te Aa—kua noa ki reira te toki. E kia oti, kua oki ratou, kua tipu i
te rakau ; kua motu ki raro, kua pari, kua ma ; kua tamou te kaka ;
kua kika ; kua tōtō atura ki o te taunga, ki o Atonga.

272.   Kua tau atura i te kai na te taunga—na Atonga. E ope ua
atura nga riaria e te enua i te tau atu, te vai ua mai rai te ututua
rakau, kare akera rai i taraiia. E tae akera ki tetai ra, kua tuatua
atura a Te Aru-tanga-nuku ki tana vaine, ki a Pori-o-kare, " Ka aere
koe, ka rave i tetai papaia na te taunga." Kua aere atura aia, kua
tau ; e maoa iora, kare i mamia kua apai atura ki a Atonga ; kua kai
iora aia, e pangia akera, kua tuatua maira aia ki a Pori-o-kare, na-ko
maira, "Ka aere, ka akakite atu ki te ariki, kia anga i te are; Apopo
kua oti te pāī. E kia oti te are, akanooia a Kuporu ki raro, kia
matakitaki i te pāī i te totoanga mai a te manu."

273.   Tei te aerenga o Pori-o-kare, kua karanga atura a Atonga
ki a Tupua-ki-Amoa na-ko atura, " Ka oro koe, e karanga atu ki a te
Ruru; kia aere koe ki a te Pirake akaruiruirangi ei oro i te manu
tini ei kika i te vaka o te ariki." Kua aere atura aia ki te oro i te
manu, e katoa akera te manu tini ; kua tae ki te popongi, kua iri te
manu ki runga i te vaka ; kua pakipaki iora te aronga moamoa na tai
pae, na tai pae, i te papaki i te manu ki roto i te vaka. Ko te Kakaia,
e te Ngoiro, e te Katikatika—ko te aronga oro ïa i vao. Kua kapiki
iora, na-ko atura, " Pakia i miri vaka, ueuea te tumu ; ka maranga-
ranga, ka ruea (? niea) te iu o te vaka ; ka tere, ka maoru (? maeru)
ki te Ivi-o-Atea. Ka topokipoki e te tini o Kuporu, ka matakitaki ;
ka re koe e Oro-keu e Oro-i-nano; Oro-keu, Oro-i-nano." Na te
Katirori i tumu te amu. Kua tae atura te vaka ki roto i te are, ta te
rima o Te Aru-tanga-nuku i rave. Kua unga iora a Tupua-ki-Amoa
i te tiki i te vaka, tera te ara, e aue kai.

274.   Teia te tu o taua vaka nei ; i taraia i te po, na Atonga-
vaerua i tarai ma te aronga rima-rave. Teia taua aronga ra: Ko

Iu-mata; ko Aa-ngu; ko Naoti—ko te aronga taunga ia i te rave i tetai pae i te vaka. Ko Tupa; ko Tupa-ake; ko Tupa-aki; ko Urireka—ko ratou te rave i tetai pae; tokovaru taunga, ko Atonga ka tokoiva. Kua topa iora a Atonga i te ingoa o taua vaka ra, ko Taraipo; kua tapa te manu i ta ratou ingoa, ko Te Manu-ka-rere. E riro atura te vaka ki o te ariki kua oki te manu, kua tāpu atura a Atonga i te Ruru, kua ui atura ki aia, na-ko atura, "Tei ea ake te rakau ei rakau tūkava na te ariki?" Kua tuatua maira te Ruru, "Tei te Po-amio." Kua na-ko maira a Atonga, "Tei ea ia ngai?" "Tei te Ara-pungavere-vere, i te ngai taku e noo nei." E kia riro atura te manu kia aere.

275. Kua karanga atura a Atonga, na-ko atura, ki a Tupua-ki-Amoa, "Ka aere koe, ka tipuia te Po-amio." Kua ui akaou atura a Tupua-ki-Amoa, "Tei ea ia ngai?" Kua tuatua maira a Atonga, "Tei te Ara-punga-verevere." Kua aere atura aia ki a Rata-i-te-vao, kua ui atura ki aia, "Tei ea a te Po-a-mio?" Kua na-ko maira aia, "Tei ko atu." Kua aere atu aia ki a Tupi-riri, kua karanga maira aia, "Tera atu." Kua aere atura aia ki reira, kare rai. Kua topa atura aia, ki o Tupa-rara kua akakite maira aia ki aia, "Tera roa ai." E tae atura aia ki reira, kare ua rai. Kua aere atura aia ki o Tu-enua, i te vao-tere, kua akakite maira a Tu-enua i te vao-tere ki aia, "E tera." Kua aere atura aia, kua kimi; e kitea iora, kua tipu atura. E ko Ipirere te ingoa i taua rakau ra. Kua apai maira ki te kainga, kua tarai iora, e oti akera kua topa iora i te ingoa, ko Te Amio-enua. Kua apai atura, kua tuku ki te rima o te ariki. Kua rave te ariki i taua rakau ra, kua aao ki roto-i te pāī; kua topa iora i te ingoa o te pāī ko Pori-o-kare.

276. Kua tuku atura i te pāī ki te tai akatere atura ki Iva. Ko te ingoa o taua pāī ra ki Iva, ko Te Oraurea-ki-Iva. Aere atura ki Rapa-nui, e Rapa-iti, akaruke iora a Irei (? Ivi) ki reira. No te akatere kino i te pāī i akarukeia. Me reira, kua aere ki Avaiki-runga, e ki te pa enua katoatoa e pini ua ake. Ko te ingoa ki Avaiki-runga i taua pāī nei, ko Te Ara-ki-avaiki ïa.

277. Tera te akakoroanga a te ariki—a Te Aru-tanga-nuku—ma te au tangata, i te otinga i te pāī, ko te au mea i te moana ko tei kitea e te pāī ivi-tangata, i muatangana. Tera taua au mea ra; ko te mato tupu i te moana—tei tai-rua-koko ra, te peru ua ra i te rauru i roto i te moana, e i runga i te kiri-a-tai; e te tai-uka-a-pia; e te puaka pikikaa i runga i taua tai ra, ko tei ruku ki raro i te tai—e ngai ave ua e te popoiri, kare e kitea e te ra. Tera tetai, e mato rai, kua tae roa te take ki roto i te rangi, e pare-moka ua, kare e ngangaere e tupu. Ko te auganga ïa i raveia e teianei pāī i taua tuatau ra, ko te tari i te tangata ki te pa-enua ravarai. Ko te Ivi-o-Atea te pāī i kitea ai te au mea katakata numui ki te moana, ma te pa-enua e pini-ua-ake.

278.　Kua anau akera ta Te Ara-tanga-a-nuku ko :—

```
        36  Te Aru-tanga-rangi
            Te Amaru-ariki
            Te Amaru-enua
            Te Uenga-ariki
            Te Uenga-enua
            Kau-tea
        30  Kau-mango                        Ono-kura = Te Ata-nua
            Vai-iti                          Nga-upoko-turua
            Kau-kura                         Nga-maru
                 |                           Kotuku-tea
         +-------+--------------------------------+            |
         |                                        |            |
Pou-vauanga-roa-ki-Iva = Rua-mano (f)  Kau-ngaki (f)  Maonga (f) = Pou-tea
         |           |                       |            |
   +-----+----+------+-----+                 |            |
   |          |            |                 |            |
26 Maono     Keu     Raka-nui (f)   26 Tangiia-nui    Tu-tapu
```

TRADITIONS AND LEGENDS.

COLLECTED FROM THE NATIVES OF MURIHIKU.
(SOUTHLAND, NEW ZEALAND.)

BY H. BEATTIE.

PART X.
Continued from Volume XXVIII., page 51.

WHEN the collector of these traditions had gained the confidence of the aged southern Maoris, information gathered in surprising volume, so there is a good deal of additional matter on hand relative to items already published, and as it is mostly from hitherto untapped southern sources no apology is required for its appearance, although it is somewhat belated no doubt.

In regard to Te Rakitauneke * (who flourished about 1650) he was caught by a Kai-Tahu *waka-ariki* (my informant said this was a battalion, while a *taua* was an army) and supposedly killed, and they left him on the ground and went on to his *pa*, where they found him standing in the gateway and they were beaten. That was the work of his *atua* or god named Matamata. When Rakitauneke died (continued my informant, who had received his information from Tare Wetere te Kahu, a descendant of Rakitauneke) his body was buried, in accordance with his dying instructions, in a cleft in the rock on the summit of the Bluff Hill, with his face to the rising sun, so that he could overlook Murihiku. Hence the name of that hill is Motu-poua (*motu* = island, *poua* = an old man). When the narrator was a boy there were bones in a crack in the rocks, but he did not think they were Rakitauneke's; but it was a *tapu* spot until the Pakehas levelled the top of the hill to build the pilot observatory. The famous Tu-te-makohu was a descendant of Te Rakitauneke.

In the account of Te Rakitauneke, as published (Vol. XXIV., p. 138), the collector would add that the then narrator used no fewer than six terms in describing Matamata, or the god, four being Maori and two being English. The text does not make this quite clear.

---

* See "Journal Polynesian Society," Vol. XXIV., p. 138.

THE FIGHT AT MOKAMOKA.[*]

When the Kai-Tahu chief Waitai, who settled at Mokamoka, near the Bluff, in the seventeenth century, was killed by his Kati-Mamoe foes, all his men except four shared his fate. Kaiapu and Tamakino escaped and eventually reached Kaikoura, and the other two, Rere-whakaupoko and Potoma were not actually in the fight. They were coming from the Mata-au (Molyneux river) and saw the defeat of their companions and bolted into the seaward bush. They crossed to Ruapuke with their wives, and were the first inhabitants of that island. Subsequently, two Kai-Tahu men visited them, but insulted their wives so the two visitors were slain, cooked, and potted with *titi* (mutton-birds). A layer of *titi* was placed in a *rimu* (kelp bag) and then a layer of human flesh and so on alternately. Some of the rest of the tribe came to reside on the island, and were regaled with the "potted meat." They praised it, asking was it *pakake* (seal), but when they found what it was they threw it away. Although some were relatives of the slain men nothing was said, and my informant never heard of any warfare over the affair.

AN OLD-TIME DUEL.[†]

In regard to the killing of Tu-takahi-kura by Tu-te-makohu, an old Maori tells me it did not happen at Taukohu (Nuggets Point), but at Paekohu, which is a hill between the Taieri Plain and Blueskin Bay. The hill is noted as a weather-glass; fog on it being a sign of rain. Another old man said:—"There were two chiefs called Tu-te-makohu, so one is known as Tu-te-makohu-a-Karapohatu, and the other as Tu-te-makohu-a-Korekore. It was the former who pursued Tu-takahi-kura when this chief ran off with his two wives and his children. He overtook them at Waitete (now called Waitati), where they were encamped, and he camped near them. He did not sleep at nights, but sat brooding over his troubles. Then he challenged Tu-takahi-kura to a combat, arranging that the latter's men should let him go with his wives and children if he killed their chief. The latter was a big powerful man, while the challenger was low in stature. They fought with the *taiaha* (also called *maipi*), and Tu-te-makohu killed his tall opponent and took his own wives and children back to O-taupiri (Hokanui Hills), while the people of the slain chief went on to their home at Kaiapohia." My informant added, "When the Kati-Mamoe were plentiful they were a quiet and peaceful people, and the Kai-Tahu did as they liked with them; but once they were reduced in numbers and in land they roused themselves and fought like tigers."

[*] See "Journal Polynesian Society," Vol. XXIV., p. 139.

[†] See "Journal Polynesian Society," Vol. XXV., p. 15.

RELATIONSHIP OF TE WERA TO TAOKA.[*]

In the narrative the relationship of Te Wera and Taoka is given as undecided, but one of my informants quickly dispelled the mist of doubt.

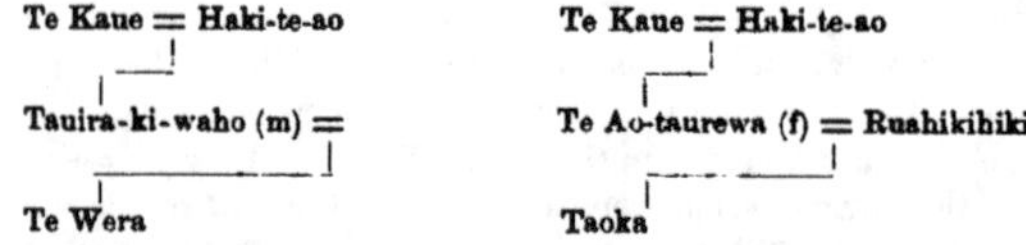

Listen to my informant :—" Te Kaue was a famous Kai-Tahu chief up Kaikoura way. [See Stack's "South Island Maoris," pages 45, 56 and 66.] He married Haki-te-ao and had three children, the first a girl Te Ao-taurewa, the next a girl Te Hikaiti, and the last a boy Tauira-ki-waho, who married a woman whose name escapes me, and whose son was Te Wera. Te Hikaiti married Ruahikihiki (a son of Manawa's) and begat Te Matauira, Moki and Ritoka. Her elder sister Te Ao-taurewa married a man called Te Ao-taumarewa and begot Manaia. Then her husband died and she married Ruahikihiki and begat Taoka, and her sister became jealous and with her own newly-born babe jumped over the cliff at Hakaroa and was killed. Therefore Te Wera and Taoka are first cousins because they were the children of a brother and sister."

MORE ABOUT TE WERA.[†]

In regard to the warfare between these two famous cousins one of my informants made a correction regarding the killing of Taoka's son, Roko-marae-roa, by Te Wera. He said :—"It was not Te Wera himself who killed the eldest son of Taoka, but his people, and he got back in time to assist in eating the body. The place was not at Timaru, but near the mouth of the Waitaki river. You can see the spot from the railway line, and it is still called Ka-umu-o-Roko-marae-roa." One of my informants considered that Te Wera's friend who was killed at Mapou-tahi was named Puke-hau-kea.

Two old men at Stewart Island said, "When Te Wera came to Rakiura (Stewart Island) he found the Kaiarohaki *pa* on the Moutere (island) of Turi-o-Whako (near The Old Neck) deserted, as there was no water on the island. A *pa* on the mainland near there was Taunoa, but there was no one in it. Then Te Wera went round to Pu-tatara *pa* at Raggedy, but there was no one there to fight. [The inhabitants of this *pa* under Tukete were killed by Tu-wiri-roa two generations before this, as narrated earlier in these articles.] Te Wera died there—

---

[*] See "Journal Polynesian Society," Vol. **XXV.**, p. 15.

[†] See "Journal Polynesian Society," Vol. **XXV.**, p. 56.

not at Kawhakaputaputa, near Colac Bay, as is sometimes said—and was buried at Putatara, a valuable piece of greenstone being buried with him. Except Putatara *pa* being captured by Tuwiriroa, there was no fighting on Rakiura, nor was there ever any on Ruapuke as far as we know."

WARFARE AT KINGSTON.

One of Tu-te-makohu's wives had two relatives named Te Papatu and Korapa, and these men were in a party which attacked Tu-te-makohu on the Waimea Plains. The fight stopped when Tu-te-Makohu got a spear thrust (by a man named Tawhana) through his arm, and Te Papatu and Korapa tended to his wound. Tu-te-makohu told them there had been enough fighting, but they persisted in going to attack Marakai. They said they would kill the chief and fill a kelp-bag with his cooked body. Marakai was living at the south end of Lake Wakatipu, so Tu-te-Makohu sent a lad to warn him, and Marakai laid a trap for his attackers. He built a *takitaki* (a yard and fence) outside his house, and laid in a stock of firewood. He told his men to tell the visitors he was at the Mataura (where Garston now is), but would soon be back. When he saw them coming he went inside, and they came to the *takitaki* and hung their weapons on the fence. After dark Marakai crawled out of the window of the *whare* to where some flax was heaped. This he wound round him, and then he sat with his enemies and talked to them. He put wood on the fire and then retired while they went to sleep. Next Marakai silently took the flax that enwrapped him and tied all the weapons securely to the *takitaki*. Then the killing commenced, the suddenly-roused men tugging at their weapons and falling easy victims to their wily adversary. This killing led to further fighting of which the collector has not got the details.

THE KILLING OF MARAKAI.*

One of my informants says that the words said by the Marakai to Matauira were as follows :—" *Me he mea naku, na ka to ake kauaka ki Waipahi ko tenei kua kukure noa atu,*" and says that the place referred to as the "ford of the Waipahi" is on the old road between Clinton and Mataura, and even to this day the natives call the spot where the road crosses the stream Te-kauaka-o-Waipahi. Another of the old men tells me that he thinks Marakai and Tu-te-Makohu were related, and that Tu-wiri-roa was also connected by blood ties with both these celebrated chiefs. Another of my informants wrote down the last remarks of Marakai as follows:—" *He hara i au na te Marama inini ki ka whetu mea nahaku ka kauaka ki Waipahi kua kukura noa atu.* The latter

* See " Journal Polynesian Society," Vol. XXV., p. 54.

half of these words mean—if it was me at the crossing at Waipahi they would be exterminated long ago." Seeing that the collector's ignorance of the Maori tongue led him slightly astray on his former account of the speech of Marakai, the above represents his mentor's efforts to put him right.

THE CAPTURE OF TAREWAI.*

The narrator said :—" When the Kati-Mamoe caught Tarewai on the Otago peninsula they killed a Kai-Tahu chief and *tohuka* called Kahutupunei.   The chief of the Kati-Mamoe was Tiroko-takanewha. Stack calls him Whaka-taka-newha, but the other name is right.   The practice of *ohu* is to get people to help you with work and you feed them.   The Kati-Mamoe got the Kai-Tahu to help build a house. After the feed they began to wrestle in fun at a place called Ka-puke-turoto.   The *atua* of Kahutupunei told him to say, ' *Toki whakaruru te mate,*' and someone said, 'it must be that *toki* that Tiroko has,' but Tiroko said it was an axe to chop firewood.   The men were wrestling in detached lots, hidden from one another, and the Kati-Mamoe killed several, and one escaped and gave the alarm.   He called out to Kahutupunei, ' *E Kahu ! te whana* ' (start a charge), but Tiroko, who was sitting beside that *tohuka*, said, ' *E Kahu ! tiki ko to ure* ' (a vile taunt), and struck and killed him.   All the rest were killed save Tarewai, whom they laid out to cut open with a ' *mata* ' or ' *parahi pohatu* ' (rude stone knife).   They had not made much progress when his guards, deceived by his quietness, relaxed their hold, and he gave a yell and jump and darted into the bush.   In the bush he did ' *tahu-tahu,*' or put hot fat in his wounds. [See Stack for narrative, page 85.] . . . " When he made his famous leap he threw his *patu* up, and it had a string on it and this string curled round a *kokomuku* shrub (called also *koromiko* in North Island), and he clambered up and got into the Kai-tahu *pa*.   I do not know whether Tiroko was killed or died naturally, but Te-waha-o-te-marama an *iramutu* (nephew) of Tarewai was killed with him at Preservation Inlet.   The party went round in two big double canoes, and Terewai's got there first and anchored off the Kati-Mamoe *pa*.   A man swam out and tied a rope to the canoe, and it was hauled in and the crew were invited into the *pa* and installed in a *whare*.   The people made an oven and called to Tarewai to come out.   His nephew was going, but Tarewai stopped him and went and was killed after a brave fight, and the rest were killed easily. The other canoe came in next day, and one of the crew acted as a seal and they captured the *pa* and stayed round there."

* See " Journal Polynesian Society." **XXV.**, p. 59.

MORE ABOUT THE DOUBLE CANOES.*

To the notes supplied by the collector on this subject an editorial footnote was appended. The collector must plead guilty to a looseness of phraseology, which rightly drew the editorial correction. He was aware that some of the canoes of the 1350 migration were double canoes, but that the North Islanders allowed this method of seafaring to fall into desuetude, whereas the Southerners adhered to it. Since his notes were published three old men described these canoes to the collector, and he will here give further details. One said, " In double canoes the larger one was called *unua*, and the smaller *tawai*. The space under the deck between the two canoes was called *aroa*, and men got under there and heaved with their shoulders to help the canoe being hauled up on shore. The man who swam out to Tarewai's canoe made fast the rope to the *aroa*." Another informant said :— " My son was a sailor and has told me of the canoes in the South Sea Islands having outriggers, but with our double canoes both were proper canoes. Beams were laid across the canoes, and on these decking was built between the canoes. The mast did not rise from either canoe, but from the centre of the decking. The mast was called *hua*, and now shipmasts are called by this name. Cordage was called *taura*, and sails *ra*. I think this name *ra* came about because when you hoisted the sail against the sun you could see the rays showing through the *tiaka* of which it was made. The hollow of the canoes was called *te-riu-o-te-wakatere*, the paddles were called *hoe-tia*, and the steering oars were *hoe-whakatere*. A steerer usually stood in the rear of each of the canoes, and was called a *takata-whakatere*. Another old man said :—" The bigger canoe was *unua*, and the smaller *waka*; the platform was *orau wawa*, the mast *hua*, the sail *ra*, and the seats in the canoes *iraka*. The beams were put in *rua* (holes) in the sides of the canoes and lashed with *whitau* (flax). The space underneath the platform was called *arowa*. [Note—He wrote the word down *aro-wa*.] I was once on a double canoe. The Mata-au (Molyneux) was very rough and we wanted to cross. My father and brother were drowned in that river, so Rakitapu chopped *manuka* for beams, and made a platform between the two canoes to avoid a capsize. It was a rough-and-ready *waka-unua*, but it kept us quite safe."

THE FATE OF TAHUNUNU.

One of my informants said:—"Tahununu was killed at Waikakahi (Little River) by a *taua* from the south. Hinehaka a prophetess on Ruapuke Island foretold his doom in these words—' *Tahununu i Hakaroa e taki ra ki Waikoau, apopo ia o iwi taki ana ka turaka Potaetu ki te pa tete a te hoa o Whakatepe kotahi te ika i kai mai ko takii mako e.*' "

* See " Journal Polynesian Society," p. 60.

[Which was translated to me as "Tahununu at Hakaroa you had better cry for Waikoau, as by-and-by your bones will cry on the groper-grounds on the fish-hooks of the husband of Whakatepe. One fish took my bait—my shark."]   "And," continued the old man, "sure enough his bones were brought south and made into hooks and used for fishing at Potaetu, the groper-ground off the New River Heads."

It may be added that Waikoau was Tahununu's home, and that the husband of Whakatepe was callee Kuao. The affair took place at the time of the Kaihuka feud, and Whakatepe died an old woman at the Bluff about 1861.

ANOTHER FAMOUS DUEL.

Puneke was the youngest son of Turakautahi by the latter's second wife Tawharepapa. Two men from Mokamoka reported that the Kati-Mamoe had killed Kai-Tahu people there, so a Kai-Tahu party went up to Lake Wanaka to kill some Kati-Mamoe in revenge. They captured a Kati-Mamoe chief called Raki-amoamohia and asked who would fight him in single combat. Puneke volunteered, and a duel with *patu-paraoa* resulted. Puneke was a youth and short in stature, but wiry and strong, while his opponent was big and heavy. They fought on and on with no advantage, until both were so tired that they had to have a spell. The sun was high when the duel started, but it was going down when the spell occurred. After the combatants had rested a while the old people said, " You had better start again as the sun's legs are hanging down" (i.e., over the hole where it disappears every night). After this advise Raki advanced to where his opponent was sitting on a tall stump. Puneke made one great bound and although his foe stepped back, the latter movement was just a fraction too late as Puneke's weapon caught him under the jaw and killed him. Puneke married two sisters, Hinepiki and Te Waiata (daughters of Tuna and Marama), and by the former wife he had fifteen children, and by Te Waiata five, so it can be seen he did his part in keeping up the census returns in ancient Maoridom.

A SOUTHERN PAKEHA-MAORI.

The story of James Caddell (the Pakeha-Maori) is well-known. In "Murihiku" (R. McNab) it is stated that the chief who killed the crew of the "Sydney Cove," near South Cape, was Hunneghi, and that Caddell married Tougghi-Touci. One of my native informants said, "James Caddell (better known as 'Jimmy the Maori,' because he was tattooed by our people, or 'Jimmy the Boy,' because he was so young when captured) was taken prisoner near South Cape (Opehia or Puhi-waero) by Maoris from Ruapuke under Te Pahi. I will tell you the lineage of that chief. Hau-tapu-nui-o-Tu married Taumata and had a daughter, Te Whakaraua, and two sons, Honekai

and Pukarehu. Te Whakaraua was an ancestress of the late chief
Topi. Honekai married Kohu-wai, a Kati-Mamoe woman of high
rank, and begat Kura (who was the mother of Tuhawaiki) and
Whakataupuka. This last chief was very ugly, and was called "Old
Wig" by the whalers. He was good to the Europeans, but cruel to
his own people. His children all died, and that ended his line.
Pukarehu married Koko and begat Te Pahi, whose only child was a
son, Te Kaha, who was drowned with a canoeful of people in Foveaux
Straits (Te Ara a Kiwa) and ended that branch. Te-Pahi had a
young sister, Tokitoki, and it was she who threw a mat over 'Jimmy
the Boy' and saved his life. She afterwards married Jimmy, and
went over to Sydney with her husband. Te Pahi went over later, and
both died in Parramatta, and thus ended that branch."

It will be noticed that this statement bears out Rutherford's
account about the way Caddell's life was saved, the other accounts
stating that the boy ran to an old chief and happening to touch his
ka-ka-how (*kakahu*—a garment), his person was then held sacred. The
name Hunneghi evidently stands for Honekai (an uncle of Te Pahi),
and Tougghi-Touci for Tokitoki. This latter weird-looking mis-
spelling is perhaps more understandable when we remember that the
Maoris in the south often pronounce "k" as "g."

(To be continued.)

AN ANCIENT CARVED *PARE*.

THROUGH the courtesy of Mr. T. F. Cheeseman, F.L.S., curator of the Auckland museum, we are enabled to publish a photo of a very beautiful *pare*, or architrave, used by the Maoris in old days to ornament the doorways to their *whare-punis*, or principal houses. Mr. Cheeseman says, in his annual report for 1918-19, . . . "it is evidently of great age, and in perfect condition. It was dug up in a peat swamp in the Hauraki plains [Thames district], and has been deposited for a lengthened period by the finder, Mr. L. Carter."

It seems probable that the *pare* had been hidden in the swamp to preserve it from the enemies of the tribe to whom it belonged, and it may be suggested that it was during the numerous raids of the northern Nga-Puhi tribes into the Thames district in the early years of the nineteenth century, that the *pare* was hidden away. Swamps were common hiding places for wood carvings under similar circumstances, for they were always well preserved there.

The central figure is a female; but what it represents is difficult to say. We suggest it may be intended to delineate the goddess Hine-nui-te-po, who presides over Hades, and " who drags mankind down to death," the smaller figures right and left of the large one being human spirits in the process of being drawn to "the great-lady-of-night," as was the hero Māui when he attempted to destroy death on earth, and himself fell a victim to Hine-nui-te-po. The *pare* is eight feet long, and the delicate carving, especially that to the right and left of the lower part of the central figure, is the best we have seen.

ANCIENT CARVED *PARE*.

TRADITIONS OF AND NOTES ON THE PAUMOTU OR (TUAMOTU) ISLANDS.

*Collected by the Rev. Père Hervé Audran, of Fakahina,
Paumotu Islands.*

TRANSLATED FROM THE FRENCH BY R. H. ROCKEL, M. A.

PART IV.
(Continued from Vol. XXVIII., page 38.)

FAKAHINA OR PREDPRIATIE ISLAND.
DISCOVERY AND GEOGRAPHICAL SITUATION OF THE ISLAND.

1. According to Rienzi the Island of Predpriatie was discovered in 1824 by Kotzebue. He found it peopled by a vigorous, olive-coloured race. Pretty huts, built of branches, were seen here and there under the trees. The swell and the attitude of the natives prevented him from landing. The island is low-lying and wooded, and has an interior lagoon. It is four miles in extent from E.N.E. to W.S.W. Its geographical position, as ascertained by that navigator, is 15° 58′ S. and 142° 39′ W. [west of Paris]

2. According to "The Physical and Political Geography of the French Possessions of Oceania," by M. F. V. Piquenot, Fakahina or Fakaina or Predpriatie is 540 sea-miles, as the crow flies, from Motu-uta in the roadstead of Papeëte. He notes Fakahina as an island that produces but little copra. This is a great mistake, as the whole crop might amount to some 600 tons annually. He further states that the area of the island is four miles by four, and that the population is 131 souls. All these figures are incorrect.

3. According to the French map, No. 1716, of the Tuamotu Archipelago, Fakahina is situated E.N.E. of Tahiti, from which it is distant 580 miles in a straight line, and 660 by a detour viâ Hao. The actual landing-place of the island, situated on the east, is in lat. 16° 1′ S., and long. 142° 29′ W., near the great rock of Tenanako, which has given its name to the whole of this part of the island.

TOPOGRAPHICAL DESCRIPTION OF THE ISLAND.

The situation of Fakahina is incorrectly marked on maps of the Archipelago. Not only is this the case, but it is assigned a form which it does not possess at all. It is almost circular instead of being oval. Thus the egg-shape given it is incorrect. In form it is an elongated crown almost without indentations. Unlike most of the islands of the Paumotu group, whose S.E. coasts usually exhibit only a few clumps of trees, scattered at rare intervals, and seemingly given by Providence as a guide for captains who are in the habit of sailing these seas, this island is planted and well wooded over the whole of its area. Kereteki of Fakahina—to employ the specific term used by the natives to designate this part of the island—has only one *hoa* (channel), which communicates with the open sea. With the exception of this *hoa*, and of one or two other spots, where the soil is poor, the whole island is planted. The south-east part of the island constitutes the fourth division for the production of copra. But, as it is from time to time invaded and submerged by the high tides prevalent during the equinoxes, its productivity is less than that of the other divisions.

AREA.

In length the island measures from east to west and from reef to reef, seven miles, five of which are occupied by the lagoon. Its breadth from north to south is five miles, of which four are occupied by the lagoon. The strip of cultivated land which surrounds the island varies in breadth. From the western reef, where a landing is usually effected, to the dry stone wharf constructed on the edge of the lagoon, measures about half a mile. At Te Matahoa the distance is greater. It was at this spot, apparently, that M. Garnier, who had been sent to deepen and improve the channels in the Tuamotu Group, effected the triangulation of the island. Possibly it is as a result of M. Garnier's labours that it has been ascertained that the situation of the island has been "incorrectly marked on the maps."

The former name of Fakahina was, according to an ancient song, Niuhi, "the isle of the coconut." As a matter of fact, the word *niu*, which is pure Maori, means "coconut." The final syllable *hi* is only a suffix added to round off the word or as a "glide" formed by the fall of the voice. The real derivation is possibly, rather, from the Polynesian *niu*, "coconut," and the Marquesan word *ehi*, also "coconut." The final syllable of this word being suppressed, we have the compound word signifying "rich in coconuts." Niuhi bears out, to a letter, the signification of its name. It is, in fact, at the present time one of the most prosperous islands of the archipelago. Here more than anywhere else we can admire the beauty of the tropical scenery. The numerous *motu* (islands) covered with a luxuriant vegetation seem so many baskets of verdure cast by Providence into the midst of the Pacific. The whole is but a veritable forest of coconut palms. It is so extensively planted with this fruitful tree that it seems to the wondering gaze a huge unbroken crown of exuberant verdure, surrounding its tiny lagoon, from the surface of which rise gracefully several islets. These are veritable clumps of dark *mikimiki* of a velvety emerald-green edged by the strip of sand sparkling in the first rays of the rising sun.

The name Fakahina, according to the elders, is comparatively recent; and the author and cause of the change are quite unknown to-day. In my opinion the name is of Marquesan origin. If the Marquesan Dictionary of Mgr. Dordillon be consulted, the following derivation may be made out; *faka* in Polynesian signifies "to make," and *hina* signifies conquered, vanquished, overthrown, defeated. The word *hina*, pronounced *hinga* signifies in Tuamotuan the same thing, and has exactly the same sense.

The following is a song describing Niuhi, i.e., Fakahina:—

<table>
<tr><td>

Ko Niuhi te fenua tukau matagi,
tere te vaka i tua kiriti hia
tere te vaka i aro kiriti hia
kia hipa hia tura e koe
te tika ia o te henua o Niuhi
kua taka pipita raufara
ka to ihoiho
ka to gahegahe
fakarua te matagi
paupau taku manava.
E horo te kaiga Niuhi te fenua i te
    fatatapua Nuku o
rarahiva
Hiva tautua

</td><td>

This is the land of Niuhi, where blows the gale so strongly, that when a canoe sails in the offing it is driven out to sea, and also when sailing homewards it is driven out to sea.

Would you mark the form of Niuhi you will see that it is like a roll of *raufara* (pandanus leaves rolled on a stake) at the hour when daylight dies, and a great calm fills the broad horizon, a calm broken from time to time by light breathings of wind from the north-east. But I can sing no more; my breath is failing.

O fair land of Niuhi!

</td></tr>
</table>

(Hiva tauaro, western portion of the Taumotu Group; Hiva tautua, eastern portion.)

In this ancient lay we are told in clear and impressive terms that Niuhi is a land of violent and irresistible storms, which carry out to sea both canoes which are making for the island and those which are leaving it. But when the storm is over and perfect calm reigns, and when the gentle breeze from the north-east breathes in the brilliant sunshine, so round does Niuhi appear that it bears a striking resemblance to a roll of pandanus leaves.

ORIGIN OF THE FIRST MAN AT FAKAHINA.

With respect to the first man who inhabited Fakahina, I have been unable to gather any information at all definite. That the first inhabitants were numerous is evident from the fact that several old men, when questioned on the point, quoted the names Tane-tupu-hoe, Mahinui, Maui and Mapu-te-agiagi, Te-mapu, Te-agiagi (first migration.)

Are these people autochthones? It is difficult to believe this. In my opinion all the tribes of the Tuamotu Group are immigrants. In the case of the inhabitants of Fakahina, as of many others, tradition preserves a complete, or nearly complete, silence. Of their original home, the cause of their coming, the name of their *pahi* (vessel), their wanderings by the way, the time of their arrival there is not a word. In a word, all is uncertainty with regard to the first inhabitants of Fakahina and their origin.

There are, however, two different opinions. It is claimed by some authorities, but without any proof in support, that the first inhabitants came from the west, that is, from Tahiti, or, at least, from the islands near Tahiti. Others, with more probability, claim that they came from Mangareva. Te-mapu Te-agiagi, one of the very first inhabitants of Fakahina, was certainly a native of Mangareva. He was, no doubt, a son or grandson of Te-agiagi, high-priest of Gatavake, youngest son of Anua-motua, who came from the Sandwich Islands.

The great migration which peopled Reao, Pukarua, Takoto, Vahitahi, Hao, Fakahina, Fagatau, and, to some extent, Hikueru, by giving them wives, took place in the reign of the celebrated Ape-iti XXV., king at Rikitea at Mangareva, conqueror of Taku. From Ape-iti to Gregorio Maputeoa, the last king of the Gambier Islands, who died on June 20th, 1857, there was a succession of kings, ten in number, who reigned in Rikitea. Now, if an average of twenty years be allowed for each reign, we should have about 220 plus 60 years, a period which would yield the year 1637 as the date of this great migration. In a war which broke out between the districts of Rikitea and of Taku at Mangareva the latter was victorious. Rather than submit and accept the conditions imposed by Ape-iti the former people preferred to migrate elsewhere and preserve unimpaired the freedom which was their dearest possession. The then reigning sovereign of Taku was Tupou. He was conquered by Ape-iti, and almost all his tribesmen slain. He took refuge with such of his people as survived in the Tuamotu Group. They escaped on seven rafts. (See Mangarevan-French Dictionary, p 22, s.v. Ape-iti, and this "Journal," Vol. XXVII., p. 130.) Some years ago (1883) an old man of Taravai informed the present chief of Fakahina, Bernard Mahui, that the first inhabitants of Niuhi came from Mangareva. The reason for this migration was, according to this old man, a bloody war in which they had been conquered. They had no alternative but to flee or be taken, slain and sent to the ovens.

A further fact, more recent perhaps, is that the elders of Fakahina understood and spoke perfectly the Mangarevan dialect. The following incident is a proof of this: In the days of paganism at an unknown date, but many years before the arrival of the Catholic missionaries, a Mangarevan *pahi*, or canoe, put in, and the crew landed. In the island everyone was on the alert and expecting war. The new-comers were asked if they had landed as friends or enemies. Meanwhile both sides made active preparations and had already made their dispositions for battle. Just as a bloody strife was about to commence challenges in good Mangarevan were made from camp to camp. This was sufficient to calm those spirits which were already too eager for the combat. It may be remarked that to land without a safe-conduct on the reefs of one of these islands, where cannibalism was still rife, was to risk being sent to the oven. No mercy was shown to a foe. Therefore, before landing, a crew had to hail from a distance, that is, from the canoe, the inhabitants who were standing ready with their arms on the reef. It was first necessary to establish one's *parau-tupuna*, that is, one's genealogical tree so as to find in the island an old relative, some ancestor, who *ipso facto* became a protector and a guardian. As soon as the relationship was established by the inhabitants of the island, the visitors could land without danger. They were *fetii*, or relatives, and received as such. The voice of blood was always respected.

HAS FAKAHINA BEEN LONG INHABITED?

I have investigated this question, employing the genealogical records of several families, who have willingly placed them at my disposal and permitted me to prosecute my researches, although among our natives this is a great and carefully guarded secret. I have examined and carefully studied seven different genealogical tables.

The longest of these, that which begins from Tane-paku and Kai-haruma, his wife, counts only twenty-three generations. Now, reckoning, on an average of thirty years for a generation, as is done in Europe, we should have 690 years, bringing us back to the year 1227.* The genealogy of the Gati-Mahinui, which begins with Panoko and his wife Kuhi, reckons fifteen generations. This would give us 450 years and bring us to the year 1467. That beginning with Marere and his wife Te-Pogi, contains from twelve to fifteen generations, brings us to 1467 or 1557, according to the line of descent followed. From Marere and his wife Manuia, are descended nineteen generations, giving 580 years and bringing us to the year 1347. The line of descent which claims

---

* The Polynesian Society, after ascertaining the views of those most capable of judging, decided from the very first to adopt 25 years as the length of a Polynesian generation; and Père Audran's ought to be altered to agree with this scale, and thus allow of comparison with dates in other groups. —EDITOR.

Manava-rere-tu-te-unu for *tupuna* (ancestor) reckons only ten generations. No doubt it was this Manava-rere who landed on the island of old, and the whole of whose crew was surrounded, captured and slain: but it is not said that Manava-rere himself was killed. Evidently he alone was spared, and afterwards became the founder of a branch of the race. The *parau tupuna* of Tane-matavai and his wife Kapu-roro reckons twelve generations down to the children of J. Tagaroa and R. Hura, giving 360 years and bringing us to 1557. The *parau tupuna* of Rata, that is. beginning from Kuhi and Panoko down to their descendants Pakora and Haroagi, reckons eight generations and brings to the year 1677. From Rutua and his wife 'Te-Fakaruru have sprung ten generations.

According to an ancient and persistent tradition it was Tehu, the son of 'Te-Tahoa and Te-Ahio, who on one of his voyages to Tahiti or to some of the islands to the west, in his famous *pahi*, " Katau," brought to Fakahina the first coconuts, *taro* and *ape*. On the shore of the island he lost his anchor, a large, flat, round stone resembling a mill-stone, pierced with a hole in the middle. This stone encrusted with coral is still visible. From Tehu have sprung six generations extending, according to our average, over a period of 180 years.†

It may be said that the coconut, which covers the greater part of the cultivable area of the island is the chief source of the wealth of the whole archipelago. The copra from the Tuamotu Group is of much superior quality to that produced in Tahiti, and commands a higher price. It is owing to the quality of the former that Tahitian copra is so well-known and so eagerly sought after. Some 9,000 tons, valued at 4,400,000 francs have been placed on the European market. Of this quantity the island of Fakahina furnished a large proportion. The following table is given for the purposes of information :—

Years	..	1912	1913	1914	1915	1916
Tons	..	170	490	296	400	395

These are the official figures for the island, but in reality they are too low. Of a certain amount no official record is taken. The chief or his deputy is quite unable to supervise all the weights and exports. Again, a certain amount of evasion goes on, the supercargoes giving whatever figures they please. The fact is well-known and cannot be disproved. The island is one of the most prosperous in the archipelago at the present moment. Considering its small area it surely holds the record for an annual yield. It is possible to make the circuit of Fakahina in less than a day at a leisurely walk.

---

† We omit here, for want of space, the author's description of the uses to which the coconut is applied, as they have often been described in the pages of this " Journal." EDITOR.

The following is a list of the different coconuts found in the
Tuamotu Group :—

1. The Mamagu :—The fibre is dark green, almost black ; the
kernel when cut dries very quickly.

2. The Kaipoa :—The husk is so tender and sweet that it is eaten
whole. The natives are very fond of it, especially the children,
who are always nibbling at it or sucking it.   There are the
ordinary Kaipoa and Makire-Kaipoa, that is, the one which
yields enormous crops.   From it a salad can be prepared.

3. The Uakuru :—This is a variety of Makire, that is, a coconut
yielding an abundance of fruit..

4. The Takaveatika :—In this the spathes are not branched, the
fruit being closely packed and usually attached directly to the
bough itself.

5. The Koheko :— The fruit is almost yellow.

6. The Uriuri :—The fruit is almost as green as that of the Mamagu.

7. The Fafatea.

The coconuts whose stripes are very long and very high are called
Hakari a Eva.

I estimate that, at the lowest computation, there must be 48,000
coconut trees on the island.   My estimate is based on the following
calculation.   Eighty coconut trees are necessary to produce annually
one ton of copra. Now, Fakahina, I feel sure, can produce 600 tons
annually.   This gives 48,000 trees, as above.   If we take an annual
yield of 350 tons, we should get 28,000 trees ; but in 1913 the yield
was 490 tons.   Many coconuts are eaten by the inhabitants or given to
the pigs.   I have seen hundreds of folk dressed in silk (?) and well skilled
in the husking of the nuts and exposing them to the sun, end up by
breaking the nut and then eating it.   At least half a ton of copra
disappears in this way in a single day.   Moreover, there are thousands
of coconut trees which never bear a nut the whole year round, as they
are smothered by the larger trees.

For the purposes of the coconut harvest the island is divided into
four *rahui*, or sectors.   At the entrance of each sector the established
rule, accepted by everyone, is to remove the husk carefully before
cutting the nut and making copra.

Immediately on their return from Mangareva, the people of
Fakahina planted only the interior of their *maite*.   They vied with
each other in planting the largest number of trees, and in doing so the
most rapidly.   Consequently, the plantations of this period are lacking
in symmetry, and are planted too thickly.   In their ignorance many
natives are persuaded that the more trees there are the better.   In
many of the islands it is still very difficult to remove this prejudice,
and to make the natives understand that it is in their own interests,
and that of the community, to allow sufficient space between the trees.

(To be continued.)

POLYNESIAN LINGUISTICS.

IV.—POLYNESIAN LANGUAGES OF THE SANTA CRUZ ARCHIPELAGO.

By Sidney H. Ray, M.A., F.R.A.I.

1. Introduction.
2. The Languages of the Santa Cruz Archipelago.
3. A Pileni Grammar.
4. A note on the Tikopia Language.
5. A Vocabulary on the Pileni Language.
6. Pileni Texts.

I. INTRODUCTION.

THE Santa Cruz Archipelago consists of four groups of islands in the Western Pacific, lying between 9° and 12° south latitude and between 165° and 171° east longitude. The south islands of the Solomons are due east from Santa Cruz, the Torres and Banks Islands lie to the south, whilst far away east is Rotuma, and in the south-east, Fiji.

The four groups are :—

1. The Duff or Wilson Group in the north, consisting of Taumako and several smaller islands.

2. The Reef or Swallow Islands in the north-west, including the islands of Nibanga, Banepi, Lomlom or Fonofono, Fenua Loa, Matema, Nufiloli, Pileni, Nukapu, Nalogo and Nupani, with the island and active volcano of Tinakula about twenty-five miles south-west of Matema.

3. The large island of Santa Cruz (Ndeni or Indenni) about 25 miles long and from 10 to 12 miles broad, with the smaller islands of Trevanion close to its north-western corner, and Lord Howe Island off the south-east coast. The native name of the northern side of Trevanion Island is Te Motu, that of the southern side is Nimbi.

With these may also be included the islands of Utupua,
about forty miles south of Santa Cruz Island and Vanikoro,
or Vanikolo, about 25 miles south of Utupua.

4. Nearly 150 miles south-east of Vanikoro is Tikopia, with
Cherry Island (Anuta) about 80 miles to the north-east,
and Mitre Island (Fataka) about the same distance east-
north-east.

Santa Cruz was discovered by the Spanish navigator Alvaro de
Mendaña on his second voyage to the Pacific in 1595, in search of
the Islands of Solomon, which he had discovered on his first voyage
in 1567. Having lost his bearings in thick weather, one of his ships,
the "Almiranta," disappeared off the island of Tinakula during the
night of September 7th, and next morning the mainland of Santa
Cruz was in sight. This was at first thought to be one of the Solomon
Islands, but when the mistake was discovered Mendaña named the
new land Santa Cruz. He tried to establish a colony, but a mutiny
broke out amongst his·crew, and the murder of a friendly chief,
Malope, by the mutineers aroused the hostility of the natives.
Mendaña died of fever, and his lieutenant Quiros led the expedition
back to the Philippines.

In 1605 Quiros revisited the Pacific and discovered Taumako.
From the chief of this island, named Tamay, he obtained information
of Chicayana (i.e. Sikaiana) and other islands in the west. Among
these were Fonofono (Lomlom), Nupan (Nupani), and Pilen (Pileni)
in the Reef Islands; Tucopia (Tikopia) and Manicolo (Vanikolo).[1]

In 1767 Carteret in the "Swallow" rediscovered Santa Cruz. He
visited the Reef Islands and named them after his ship. Thirty-one
years later Captain Wilson, conveying the first Protestant missionaries
to Tahiti, passed Taumako and gave the name of his ship the "Duff"
to the Group, to which it belongs.

In 1785 the French frigates "Astrolabe" and "Boussole," under
the command of La Pérouse, left Brest on a voyage of discovery in the
Pacific. They arrived at Botany Bay in January 1788, and left in
February. Then for nearly forty years their fate was unknown, till in
1827 Captain Peter Dillon, of the Hon. East India Company's ship
"Research," ascertained that the ships and their crews had been lost
off Vanikoro. Meanwhile Captain Edwards in 1791, in the "Pandora,"
had passed between Utupua and Vanikoro and discovered Cherry and
Mitre Islands. The French government sent an expedition in search
of La Pérouse in 1791, in the ships "Recherche" and "Esperance,"
under the command of General D'entrecasteaux. In 1793 these ships
called at Santa Cruz. Mr. Woodford notes that "in one of the

---

1. Cf. "Journal Polynesian Society," XXI., 1912, p. 167, and XXVI., 1917,
pp. 34, 35.

canoes which came alongside a portion of a joiner's chisel fitted to a wooden handle, was observed. It is possible, and even probable that this chisel came from one of La Pérouse's ships, since the distance from Santa Cruz to Vanikoro is only sixty miles, and communication by canoes is not infrequent, but the clue was not followed up."[2] Dillon first came upon relics of La Pérouse in 1813 at Tikopia, but the fate of the expedition was not fully established till 1827.[3] Confirmation was obtained by Dumont d'Urville in 1828. The same navigator revisited the islands ten years later.

· The modern history of the Santa Cruz Archipelago began with the first visit of Bishop G. A. Selwyn in 1852. He did not then go ashore, but four years later tried at Santa Cruz to make friends with the people. His knowledge of Maori enabled him to make himself understood a little at Nukapu in the Reefs. He also landed at Utupua and Vanikolo.

In 1862 Patteson, then Bishop of Melanesia, went ashore at Santa Cruz at seven different places. In 1864 two members of the Melanesian Mission, Edwin Nobbs and Fisher Young, were killed at Graciosa Bay, Santa Cruz. Patteson revisited Nukapu in 1870, and again in 1871 when he, the Rev. J. Atkin, and a native named Stephen were killed. In 1875 Commodore Goodenough was killed at Carlisle Bay, Santa Cruz. The taking home of some Nufiloli men who had been cast ashore in the Solomons in 1877, led to the re-opening of the mission, Wadrokal, a Loyalty islander, being the first teacher. Since that time the attitude of the islanders to white men has sensibly changed, and Christianity has made some progress in Pileni, Nufiloli, and Santa Cruz.

The anthropology of the people of these islands has been partially dealt with by Gaimard[4] and Dr. Codrington,[5] and short but vivid sketches of native life have been given by the Rev. W. O'Ferrall.[6] The sociology of Santa Cruz, Vanikolo, the Reef Islands and Tikopia has been discussed by Dr. Rivers,[7] that of Tikopia and Santa Cruz

2. Handbook of the British Solomon Islands Protectorate. Tulagi, British Solomon Islands, 1911, pp 11-13

3. Cf. P. Dillon. " Narrative and successful result of a voyage in the South Seas," London, 1829.

4. Gaimard. "Voyage autour du Monde." Paris, 1833. Tome V , p. 108 ff, and pp. 304-312.

5. R. H. Codrington. "The Melanesians: Studies in their Anthropology and Folk-lore." Oxford, 1891

6. W. C. O'Ferrall. "Santa Cruz and the Reef Islands." Melanesian Mission.

7. W. H. R. Rivers. "The History of Melanesian Society." Cambridge. 1914. pp. 217-231 and 298-362.

more briefly by Rev. W. J. Durrad[8] and W. Joest.[9] The island trade
is dealt with by Thilenius.[10] Graebner has published a long account
of the Santa Cruz people.[11] The "Folk-Lore" has been exhibited by
Rev. W. O'Ferrall[12] and Dr. Codrington.[13]

In physical features the Santa Cruz islanders are Melanesian, but
in Taumako and some of the Reef Islands there appears a strong
strain of Polynesian blood, whilst in Tikopia the people are Polynesian
with traces of Melanesian admixture. Additional evidence of this
mingling of races is found in the language, and in the freer intercourse of the sexes. The natives of all the islands chew betel. Kava
is only used in ceremonies in Vanikolo, Utupua and Tikopia, and not
at all in Santa Cruz and the Reef Islands. The canoes, some of very
large size, are dug-outs with outriggers, and not plank-built as in the
Solomons. The Taumako people are said to be the best canoe
builders, and the Matema people the best sailors.

Native money (*tavau*) is made from small red feathers. Mats are
woven on a loom in Santa Cruz and Nufiloli, but not in Vanikolo,
Utupua or the Reef Islands. The fibre is obtained from the stem of
the banana, a black-stemmed variety being used in forming a pattern.
Weaving was seen by the Spaniards in 1595, and is no doubt of
ancient use. "Native tradition is that it was invented by a woman,
but insomuch that it kept her from the less interesting and more
arduous labour in the gardens, the invention was appropriated by her
lord and master."[14] Though almost identical in form[15] with the loom
used in the Polynesian Solomon Islands and in the Carolines, there is
no evidence of its introduction from those places. The loom and its
parts have each their distinctive names in Santa Cruz and Nufiloli,
but these are entirely different from the names in the Solomon and
Caroline Islands. The Polynesians in the Reef Islands have no looms
and can only describe the apparatus and its parts in common terms as
" sticks " or " strings."

8. Rev. W. J. Durrad. "Southern Cross Log " 19.

9. A. Baessler. " Neue Südsee Bilder," 1900, p. 386.

10. Dr. G. Thilenius. " Ethnographische Ergebnisse aus Melanesien " I.
Halle, 1902.

11. F. Graebner. "Völkerkunde der Santa Cruz Inseln. Ethnologica."
(Städt-Rautenstrauch-Joest-Museum.) Köln I., 1909, pp. 71-184.

12. Rev. W. O'Ferrall. " Native Stories from Santa Cruz and Reef Islands,"
" Journal Anthropological Institute," XXXIV., 1904, pp. 223-233.

13. R. H. Codrington. "Melanesian Folk-tales. Folk-lore," IV., 1893,
pp. 509-511.

14. O'Ferrall. "Santa Cruz and the Reef Islands. Mat making."

15. Cf. pictures in O'Ferrall and Parkinson, " Dreissig Jahre in der Südsee."
Stuttgardt, 1907.

The distinction between chiefs and commoners is very definite in Tikopia,[16] but in Santa Cruz the authority of the village headmen "does not extend beyond that village, though their influence may do so," and there are "no powerful chiefs such as are found in the Solomons."[17]

Each village in the group has its club house, (Santa Cruz, Mandai; Vanikolo, Manggore; Nufiloli, Japulau; Pileni, Afalau) in which the unmarried men live, and where male visitors from other villages are entertained. Each has also its "ghost-house," (Santa Cruz, Ma-nduka; Nufiloli, Niekipejalikive; Pileni, Faleatua[18]) containing wooden stocks or posts, "ghosts" (Santa Cruz, Nduka; Nufiloli, Ndekilavo; Utupua, Nduo; Vanikoro, Leñoe; Pileni, Atua) carved and painted to represent a dead person who in his lifetime possessed great power, influence or skill. (Santa Cruz, Malete; Nufiloli, Kinaa; Utupua, Ana; Pileni, Mana.[19])

After death Santa Cruz spirits go to Mbluka,[20] those of Nufiloli to Patanee, those of Pileni to Thalafali. These names are equivalent to the Mota and Banks' Islands Panoi.

II. THE LANGUAGES OF THE SANTA CRUZ ARCHIPELAGO.

The first word recorded in the language of this region of the Pacific was obtained at Santa Cruz by Mendaña. Figueroa[21] states that the chief Malope, who came on board, called himself Tarique, a word which is, no doubt, intended for the Polynesian Te Ariki. Its use on Santa Cruz, where the language is Melanesian, may be accounted for by the fact that the Spaniards in order to obtain interpreters had sent to kidnap some boys from the Reef Islands. These were said to be more intelligent than the people of Santa Cruz, a supposition confirmed by native admissions to Dr. Codrington.[22] Thus, instead of the Santa Cruz word for chief, Mbonië, the Spaniards obtained the Reef Island interpreter's Te Ariki or Te Aliki. Gaimard gives a form of Te Ariki used in Tikopia. During Dumont d'Urville's

16. W. H. Rivers. "The History of Melanesian Society," Cambridge, 1914, p. 305; and Rev. W. J. Durrad, "Southern Cross Log," 1911.

17. Rev. W. O'Ferrall. "Santa Cruz and the Reef Islands." Introduction.

18. Dumont D'Urville gives "Baito Atoua, Baito Tapou, Maison des esprits," op. cit., p. 169, but these words are in the language of Tikopia, and show that he probably had a Tikopian interpreter. The Vanikoro equivalent would be Moeleñoe.

19. Cf. W. H. R. Rivers, op. cit., I., p. 230.

20. According to Dr. Codrington, "Melanesians," p. 264, the dead assemble at a place called Netepapa and thence go to Tamami, the volcano Tinakula.

21. Cf. Dalrymple. "An Historical Collection of Voyages." London, 1770-71. I., p. 81.

22. Islands of Melanesia. R. H. Codrington, D.D. "Scottish Geographical Magazine," 1889.

visit to the group, his naturalist, M. Gaimard, collected vocabularies
of three dialects of Vanikoro (Vanikoro, Tanema, Taneanou) and of
Tikopia. He also obtained the numerals of Utupua (two dialects),
Fonofono (Lomlom), Mami (probably a village in [omitted by Mr.
Ray]), and Indeni (Santa Cruz).[23] A discussion of the affinities of
Vanikoro, based on these, was made by Lesson[24] and D'Eichthal.[25]

Inglis obtained the numerals of two dialects of "Vanikolo, Queen
Charlotte's Island."[26] The first of these is Polynesian, resembling
[omitted by Mr. Ray], and the second resembles the Tanema of
Gaimard.

A short vocabulary of Vanikoro is to be found in the Journal of
Commodore Goodenough, with one word from Santa Cruz.[27]

Dr. Codrington has published short grammars and vocabularies of
Santa Cruz (Nelua on the central north coast) and of Nifiloli (Nufiloli)
in the Reef Islands.[28] The Rev. C. E. Fox has published longer
vocabularies of Santa Cruz (Te Motn on the north coast of Trevanion
Island) and Vanikoro.[29] The Rev. W. J. Durrad's vocabulary of
Tikopia, edited by Archdeacon H. W. Williams, has been published
in the "Journal" of this Society.[30]

A few books in the Santa Cruz language, and one in Pileni, are
used in the Melanesian Mission.

Some of the languages in this region are Polynesian and some
Melanesian. A Polynesian language is spoken in Taumako, and the
same language is spoken in the Reef Islands Fenua Loa, Pileni,
Matema, Nukapu and Nupani. The language of Tikopia is also
Polynesian, but differs slightly from the Pileni. The statement made
by Thilenius that the language of Utupua is Polynesian is incorrect.[31]

The remaining languages of the group, so far as they are known,
appear to be Melanesian of a very distinct type, differing a good deal
from one another and from the Melanesian of the Solomon Islands

23. Voyage de l'Astrolabe. Philologie. Tome II. Paris, 1883. pp. 165-174.
24. P. A. Lesson. "Vanikoro et ses habitants." Revue d'Anthropologie V.,
1876, pp. 252-272.
25. Not given by Mr. Ray.
26. Report of a Mission Tour in the New Hebrides. By Rev. John Inglis.
Auckland, 1871. Also in "Journal Ethnological Society" III. 1854.
27. Journal of Commodore Goodenough.
28. "Melanesian Languages." Oxford, 1885. pp. 39-52 and 486-498.
29. "Vocabularies of Santa Cruz and Vanikolo." "Melanesian Mission
Press," 1908.
30. "A Tikopia Vocabulary." "Journal Polynesian Society" XXII., pp.
86-95 and 141-148.
31. Ethnographische Ergebnisse aus Melanesien. I. Die Polynesischen
Inselr., Halle 1902, p. 23. "In Sikaiana beschrieb mir ein Eingeborener die
Inseln Tikopia, Lineniua, Tagnu, Utupua kurz dahin, all same men, one talk."

and New Hebrides. Words are difficult to write because of the uncertainty and shifting nature of the sounds, which give the appearance of great differences in the vocabularies. Words are often quite unlike their equivalents in other Melanesian languages, and the grammars also differ considerably. But nothing appears which would definitely mark any of the languages as other than Melanesian in structure.

The following vocabulary of all the languages known to me will exemplify their great variety. The numerals which follow will show some of the difficulties experienced in recording the sounds.

For comparison I add the nearest language of the Solomon Islands (Wango, San Cristoval), the nearest Melanesian to the south (Tegua, Torres Islands), the Rotuma almost due east of Tikopia, and as representatives of Polynesian, Tonga and Maori.

COMPARATIVE VOCABULARY.

ENGLISH	1. TE MOTU	2. NELUA	3. NUFILOLI	4. VANIKOLO	5. TANEMA
Areca nut	Kavla	—	—	Namue	Boin
Arm	Mu	Mu	(Nimen)	Me	Menini
Arrow	Nipna	(Nipna)	Niepa	Puri (Abione)	Punene
Banana	Mbepi	Mbepi	Noi	Puna	Unra
Belly	Nela	Mbole	Nuora	Janane	Jenana
Bow	Netev	Netevu	Jinpa	Ore (Tennanu)	Ora
Chief	Bonie	(Bonie)	—	Teligi, Aligi	Taligi
Ear	Ndetu	Ndole	Nugon	Mabalewi, Mambaheuhi	Rañewo
Eye	Ma	Mu	(Nimbaeai)	Mala	Maleo
Fire	Nie	Ñie	Nie	Nebie	Ñava
Fish	No	No	(Si)	Niene	Ane
Hair	Nuwi-nae	Niwi-nave	Niluu	Wienbaja, Wenbañanlli	Valau-baja
Head	Nae	Vo (Nae)	(Nuota)	Baja	Baja
Leg	No	(No)	Nike	Kele	Alenini
Man	Nepala	Nepala	Sime	Lamoka	Ranuka (Ranaka)
Moon	Tema	Tema	Nepe	Mele	Malaula
Nose	Notn	No	Nota	Nele (Nole)	Nele
Road	Nati	Naji	(Numbatage)	Nene	Nana
Sand	Ndauo	Ndauo	Nikeninno, Numbo	Uteka	Ouolo
Stone	Apla	(Alpa)	Niva	Vaka	Vaka
Sugar-cane	Nalu	—	(Nawu)	Tolo	Rova
Sun	Nawn	Nawn	Nale	Woie (Noie)	Woin
Tongue	Nalapu'	Lapu	Nalimbia	Mea	Min
Tooth	Nuwi	Nine	Nuotende	Ufie	Kole
Water	Luwe	Luwe	(Nuei)	Wire	Nira
Woman	Ovla	Ovla	Sineda	Venime	Vauime

ENGLISH	6. TANEANU	7. VANIKOLO	8. UTUPUA	9. WANGO	10. TEGUA
Areca-nut	Buaka	Fenere	—	Bua	— a
Arm	Maini	Me	Namana	Ruma	Pini
Arrow	Puene	Pure	Kotho, Vogono	—	Liwe
Banana	Unro	Puna	Wuo	Hugi	Vetal
Belly	Jaene	Sa	Mbasela	Ahu	Tokwe
Bow	Vijane	Ore	Katomono	Ba'e	Nu
Chief	Teligi	—	—	Mneraha	—
Ear	Tañaini	Mambelen, Tañia	Sino	Karina	Ndeline
Eye	Mataeo	Mala	Nduna	Mna	Mete
Fire	Iaua	Nepie	Nivio	Eu	Nav
Fish	Namokho	Namaga	Nono	I'a	Nige
Hair	Vieu-Baja	Wie Ne Mbaza	Niviniola	Warehu	Ul
Head	Baja	Mbaza	Jinio, Ndinio	Ba'u	Kwutu
Leg	Aeleda	Kele	Nagana	Uwa	Rono
Man	Amualigo	Lamuga	Tumuo	Noni	Tela
Moon	Metele	Mele	Jolo	Hura	Magage
Nose	Neleo	Nele	Nomboouni-vla	Barisu	Mundu
Road	Anaoko	Nene	Nduinene	Tara	Mejale
Sand	Ouele	Wutega	Nene	—	Nin
Stone	Vijiboko	Vaga	Foio	Hau	Vot
Sugar-cane	Ton	Lembie	Tovio	Ohu	Te
Suu	Aeve	Woie	Nuo	Sina	Elo
Tongue	Mimiaeo, Miniako	Men	Mamela	Meamea	—
Tooth	Ije	Wuñe	Uju	Riho	Liu
Water	Ero	Wire	Nio	Wai	Pe
Woman	Vinivi	Neme	Aimio	Urao	Lekwavine

ENGLISH	11. ROTUMA	12. PILENI	13. TIKOPIA	14. TONGA	15. MAORI
Areca-nut	—	Pua	(Kaura)	—	—
Arm	Siu	Lima	Lima	Nima	Rina
Arrow	Kas	Nau	Fana, Nasau	Nahau	Pere
Banana	Per	Tavel	Futi	Fuji	—
Belly	Efi	Manava	Afirana	Kete	Kopu
Bow	Fan	Loku	Fana-kalolo	Kau-fana	Kopere
Chief	Nanaja	Aliki	Ariki, Aliki	Eiki	Ranatira
Ear	Falina	Talina	Tarina	Telina	Tarina
Eye	Maf	Mata	Kafimata	Mata	Kanohi
Fire	Roh	Keu	Afi	Afi	Ahi
Fish	I'a	Ika	Ika	Ika	Ika
Hair	Leva	Laulu	Rauru, Raulu	Louulu	Makawe
Head	Filo	Piso-ulu	Poko-ulu	Ulu	Upoko
Leg	La	Vae	Vae	Vae	Waewae
Man	Fa	Tai, Tanata	Tanata	Tanata	Tanata
Moon	Hula	Akafu	Marama	Mahina	Marama

ENGLISH	11. ROTUMA	12. PILENI	13. TIKOPIA	14. TONGA	15. MAORI
Nose	Isu	Iu	Isu, Kauisu	Ihu	Ihu
Road	Sala	Ala	Ara	Hala	Ara
Sand	Fanfan	One	One	Oneone	Onepu
Stone	Hof	Fatu	Fatu	Maka	Kowhatu
Sugar-cane	—	Tolo	Toro	To	—
Sun	Asta	Vela	Ra	Laa	Ra
Tongue	Alele	Alelo	Alelo	Elelo	Arero
Tooth	Al	Nifo	Nifo	Nifo	Niho
Water	Taun	Vai	Vai	Vai	Wai
Woman	Hone	Fafine	Fafine	Fefine	Wahine

NUMERALS.

	1. TE MOTU	2. NELUA	2A. INDENI	3. NUFILOLI	3A. PONOPONO
1.	Eja	Eja	Teja (Beja)	Nigi	Nigi
2.	' Li, Ali	Ali	Ali (Odi)	Lilu	Lelu
3.	Tu	Atu	Adi	Eve	Eve
4.	Apue	Apue	Abuni (Abuni)	Uva (Uvae)	Uve
5.	Navlunu	Navlunu	Narune	Vili	Idi
6.	Eja-me	Eja-me	Teïamua (Teiamera)	Polegi [Welegi]	Pulegi (Puveage)
7.	Eli-me	Olime	Eduma	Polelu	Polelu
8.	Etu-me	Otu-me	Ebuema	Pulee	Pole
9.	Epue-me	Opue-me	Napu	Polouva [Polove	Polohue
10.	Napnu	Navlu	Ekaton	Nugolu (Nukolu)	Nokolu Hokolu

	4. VANIKOLO	5. TANEMA	6. TANEANU	6A. VANIKOLO	6B. VANIKOLO
1.	Tilu	Kero	Iune	Riro, Tasi	Keru
2.	Taru	Lalu (Lahu)	Tilu	Lal, Rua	Lalu
3.	Telu	Raru	Teve	Raru, Toru	Rava
4.	Tava	Rava (Iava)	Teva	Rava, Fa	Leli
5.	Teli	Teri	Tili	Seli, Rima	Roo
6.	Tawo	Ro	Tuo	Ro, Ono	Roembi
7.	Tembi	Rumbi	Timbi	Ruambe, Vitu	Embidua
8.	Tawa	Lembidua Laubidua	Tua	Imbitua, Varu	Duariudi
9.	Tanru	Tuarendi	Tindi	Taurine, Siwa	—
10.	Kauluga	Indonolo Huiduholo	Tenaulu	Edonolo, Nofuru or Nafulu	Longolo

	7. VANIKOLO	7A. TUPUA	FENUA GALAIO 7B. (TUPUA)	8. UTUPUA	9. WANGO	10. TEGUA
1.	Ti Liogo	Tuo	Jika	Sika	Tai	Vu Jie
2.	Ta Ru	Buiu, (Biun)	Iu	Iu	E Rua	Vu Rue
3.	Te Lu	Bogo	Too	Thoo	E'Oru	Vu Tel
4.	Ta Va	Mabeo	Jiva	Sivia	E Ha'i	Vu Vat
5.	Te Li	Kaveri	Jini (Jun)	Sin	Rima	Teva Lime
6.	Ta Wo	Kaveri-Juo	Juo (Jaeo)	Suo	Ono	Levi Jie
7.	Te Mbi	Vio	Timbi	Timbi	Bi'u	Leve Rue
8.	Ta Pwa	Viro	Ta	Ta	Waru	Leve Tel
9.	Ta Dru	Reve (Rove)	Tujo	Toju	Siwa	Li Vat
10.	Gau Uluga	Anaru	Navi (Hunoi)	Navi	Tanahuru	Henewul

11. ROTUMA	11A. MAMI (MATEMA)	12. PILENI	13. TIKOPIA	14. TONGA	15. MAORI
1. Ta	Tai	Tai	Tasi, Tasa	Taha	Tahi
2. Rua	Lua	Lua	Rua	Ua	Rua
3. Folu	Tolu	Tolu	Toru	Tolu	Toru
4. Heke	Fa	Fa	Fa	Fa	Wha
5. Lium	Lima	Lima	Rima, Lima	Nima	Rima
6. Ono	Ono	Ono	Ono	Ono	Ono
7. Hifu	Fitu	Fitu	Fitu	Fitu	Whitu
8. Walu	Paru	Valu	Varu, Waru	Valu	Waru
9. Siau	Iva	Eva	Siva	Hiva	Iwa
10. Sahulu	Kadua	Kado	Fuuafuru	Honofulu	Tekau, Nahuru

These Vocabularies are written in a uniform alphabet. a, e, i, o, u as in Italian, *a* as English a in "bat," *e* as French e in "le," *o* as French eu in "leur," *u* as French u in "lune," *n* as English ng in "sing," *g* as English ng in "finger," j as English j in "jail."

In transcribing the French vocabulary I have written w or u for ou, *n* for nh, j for dj and tch, and ñ for gn.

These vocabularies are derived from the following sources :—

1 and 7. Rev. C. E. Fox. Vocabularies of Santa Cruz and Vanikolo. 1908.

2, 3 (in square brackets) and 9. Rev. R. H. Codrington, D.D. Melanesian Languages. 1885. Words in brackets in No. 2 are from the Santa Cruz Prayer Book.

3. MS. Rev. H. N. Drummond. In brackets from a MS. written by J. Sau for Rev. C. E. Fox.

2a, 3a, 4, 5, 6, 7a, 7b, 11a. Dumont D'Urville. Voyage de l'Astrolabe. Philologie. Tome II. 1830-34. Words in brackets are from P. A. Lesson in Revue d'Anthropologie. 1876.

6a. Rev. J. Inglis. Report of a Mission Tour in the New Hebrides. Journal Ethnological Society. 1854.

6b. Journal of Commodore Goodenough. 1876.

8. MS. Rev. B. Teilo.

10. MS. written by A. Towia for Rev. C. E. Fox.

11. MS. W. L. Allardyce, C.M.G.

12. MSS. Rev. J. W. Blencowe, Rev. H. N. Drummond and N. Vane.

13. Rev. W. J. Durrad. Tikopia Vocabulary. Journal Polynesian Society, XXII. Words in brackets from W. H. R. Rivers. History of Melanesian Society.

14. Rev. W. Shirley Baker. English and Tongan Vocabulary. 1897.

15. Rev. H. W. Williams. Dictionary of the Maori Language. 1917.

GILBERT'S ACCOUNT OF EASTER ISLAND.

By H. D. Skinner.

THE present writer was stationed in England during 1916 and part of 1917, and spent part of his spare time in collecting information relating to the ethnographic material from the Pacific brought to England by the members of the three expeditions led by Captain Cook. In the British Museum and at the Records Office, Chancery Lane, London, he found the logs and journals of a number of officers who sailed on one or another of the voyages, documents which, in so far as they relate to New Zealand, have already been published by the late Dr. Robert McNab.* The far larger part of them, however, which relates to Polynesia, Melanesia, North America, and Alaska, but especially to the first-named region remains unpublished. It seemed to the writer that if funds were available the publication of these journals ought to be undertaken by the Polynesian Society in the form of a Memoir or Memoirs uniform with those they have already published. Publication in some form is called for, first by their historic interest, and secondly by the amount of new ethnographic matter they contain.

The following extract and sketch were copied from the journal of Jos. Gilbert, master of the " Resolution," and are of unusual interest in that they relate to Easter Island, which on account of its great statues has attracted keener public interest than any of the smaller islands of the Pacific. At the Royal Naval College at Greenwich are the originals of a number of portraits by Hodges, including two of Easter Islanders, engravings of which were published in the first edition of the second voyage.

The relevant part of Gilbert's journal is as follows:—

> " Wednesday, 16th March, 1774.

" The natives are of a middle stature, well made, of a copper colour complexion, with a brisk and lively countenance, very active and audacious. Some wearing a light garment over their shoulders, others quite naked, women few have been seen, those kind and obliging wearing a thin light covering round their waist hanging carelessly down to their knees. Both men and women paint with a bad kind of vermillion; besides heavy, exceedingly curious figures and lines marked upon their faces, legs, arms and different parts of the body by a black liquid punctuated thro' the skin.

The islanders throughout the Pacific Ocean have this custom, and in general their rank in life distinguished by different characters.

* " Historical Records of New Zealand." Vols. I. and II.

At Otaheiti the young women were not permitted to marry till this ceremony is performed, which is from the loins round their hips, and is continued to the lower part of the thigh behind; curious and exceeding handsome, nay, so becoming in those people that to an European they would appear naked without it.

The land is extremely poor, the hills full of stones, of an hungry dry soil incapable of cultivation. Some plantations of potatoes and plantains to be met with in the valleys, which are the principal productions. No trees of any size sufficient to make more than the helve of an axe, nor any kind of vegetable useful for refreshment. Water exceeding scarce and indifferent throughout the island. The inhabitants do not I believe exceed a thousand men. During our stay here we got five tuns of bad water, some plantains, potatoes, and a few fowls. The wind changing to the westward the captain thought it necessary to put to sea, otherwise we might have purchased a sufficient quantity of roots to have served the ship's company four or five weeks. Cocoanut shells and Otaheiti cloth are the best commodities for traid; old hats, rags and bottles are not bad things. Fish seem scarce, we caught none; no quadruped animals except rats. Providence has even denied them the pleasing service and companionship of the faithful dog. What I have seen of their habitations are of an ovil form about 10 or 12 ft. in length, in height 4 or 5 ft., made of rushes, reeds and plantain leaves, strengthened with a few sticks fastened in a platform of stone on which they are built. At one side is added a small porch through which they creep into the hut; no furniture observed within, only a little straw, on which they compose themselves at night.

Their canoes are as indifferent as their huts. From 20 to 25 feet in length and a foot and a half in breadth, quite open, made of thin boards, badly put together. We have some reason to believe these islanders to have once been in a more flourishing state. There remain some vestiges of exceeding curious workmanship, which to appearance must have been executed some centuries back, and seem impossible for those people in their present helpless situation to equal. These are statues of a monstrous size erected along the seashore. Time having brought several to the ground; some 27 feet in length, breadth in proportion, one solid mass of stone, the weight having been calculated to exceed 20 tons. It required great ingenuity to have erected these prodigious images without the knowledge of machine power; the wedge, lever, pulley and screw are not in their possession. Neither does the island visibly produce materials to make them. And what is more extraordinary these figures are capped with a stone larger than the circumference of the body altogether, making a very formidable appearance. Before these images a square out of stones artfully fitted into each other, raised 6 or 7 feet in height in a direct line from 30 to 40 feet betwixt the facings."

NOTES AND QUERIES.

[990] The Wanaka District.

Mr. Richard Norman, of Oamaru, formerly of Wanaka, tells me that when the first white settlers visited the Makarora Valley, they saw there a number of birch trees, the bark of which had been scored down one side by the Maoris, the intention being to cause the heart-timber to rot while the outer timber continued growing, thus half forming a canoe. On the bank of the Clutha there were conspicuously placed a number of white quartz boulders, each about the size of a loaf. The Maori shearers explained these as a message indicating that a party of Maoris had passed, going to Hawea, and would return. Of a large lagoon on the east side of Lake Hawea the following story was told: A *tohuka* was fishing and caught a huge eel. In carrying it home he became tired and cut it in half, taking one half home. On returning for the other half he found it had turned into the lagoon, and that its blood was represented by the stream which flows into Lake Hawea.

These fragmentary notes are worth recording as we know almost nothing of the Wanaka district in pre-European times.

H. D. SKINNER.

PROCEEDINGS.

POLYNESIAN SOCIETY.

A Meeting of the Council took place at the Library, Hempton Room, on the 3rd September, when there were present: The President in the chair, and Messrs. J. B. Roy, P. J. H. White, G. H. Bullard, M. Fraser, W. W. Smith, W. L. Newman.

After the minutes of the previous meeting had been read, the following new members were elected :—

> John Baillie, Director, New Plymouth Museum.
> George N. Curtis, Stratford.
> H. M. Good, Stratford.
> Alfred Snowball, The Manse, Ormond, Gisborne.
> The Invercargill Public Library, Invercargill.
> Onehunga Carnegie Public Library, Onehunga.
> G. T. Kronfeld, P.O. Box 405, Auckland.
> Wm. McKay, F.R.C.S.E., 45 Guinness Street, Greymouth.
> James McKay. L.S., P.O. Box 55, Greymouth.

The following papers were received :—

> History and Traditions of Rarotonga.   Parts VIII., IX., X., XI., XIII., XIV.
> Native Names of Birds, Mangaia Islands.   F. W. Christian.
> An Ancient Maori *Pare*.
> Traditions and Legends of Murihiku.   H. Beattie.
> The Rua-kopiha.   G. Graham.

It was agreed to exchange with the Museu Paulista, Coixa g. San Pedro, Brazil.

The death of one of our original members, the Hon. Sir John Dennison, was reported ; and the resignation of Mr. Drummond was received.

A list of books, etc., received in exchange was read.

HISTORY AND TRADITIONS OF RAROTONGA.

By Te Ariki-tara-are.

PART VII.

Translated by S. Percy Smith.

[In Part VI. of this series the lives, emigrations and voyages of the ancestor of the great Rarotongan chief, Tangiia-nui were recorded so far as the information to hand allowed. That part brought the history down to the thirteenth century, when Tangiia's immediate forbears had settled in Tahiti. This, Part VII., will describe the life and adventures of Tangiia-nui from his birth to the time—probably in his middle age—when he settled down in Rarotonga. Perhaps the distinguishing feature of this portion of his life is the number of voyages he made in his celebrated vessel, "Takipu" (afterwards renamed "Taki-tumu," though this latter name must not be confounded with another vessel of the same name that came to New Zealand in the middle of the fourteenth century).

Tangiia's voyages illustrate in a striking manner the ability of these South Sea vikings to make very extensive voyages, by which, as their own historians say, they became able navigators, and that at a period when no other nation in the world had accomplished anything more than what may be termed coastal voyages. Our historian treats of these voyages in a manner to indicate that the people thought nothing of starting off on expeditions covering some thousands of miles. No details of the voyages are given; even the class of vessel employed is not stated, any more than that they were *pā‘i*, which we know to mean a large, built-up canoe, generally a double one with a platform between them; though from what is stated in paragraph 307 the inference is that Tangiia made most of his voyages in an outrigger canoe. The following brief abstract of Tangiia's voyages will show the extent of his travels :—

Paragraph.	Extent of Voyage.	Approximate Nautical Miles.
282-3	Tahiti to Mauke	480
284	Mauke to Tahiti	480
285	Tahiti to Savaii, Samoa	1320
285	Back to Tahiti	1320
294	Tahiti to Samoa and Avaiki (to Savaii)	1380
300	Avaiki and back to Uea Island......?	
300	Uea to Upolu	270
300	Upolu to Uea and back	540
301	Upolu to Fiji (? Lau Islands)	480
302	Fiji to Easter Island	4200
303	Easter Island to Moorea Island	2400
304	Moorea to Huahine and Porapora	150
310	Porapora to Fiji	1680
313	Fiji to Paumotu Islands	2400
316	Paumotu to Taha'a Island	720
317	Taha'a to Rarotonga	540
		18,360

To this considerable mileage—measured in an air-line, though there is no doubt the course taken against the trade winds would involve much longer distances—we may fairly add the distance run to the south of Rarotonga when they missed that island and found the sea-water very cold—probably another 800 or 1000 miles at least. Again there was the voyage to Avaiki, and as the position of this particular Avaiki is doubtful, we cannot estimate a mileage for this, probably the longest voyage of all. The name is given both as Avaiki and Avaiki-te-varinga (the ancient Avaiki), and it is clear that this was not Avaiki-Atia, the original Fatherland of the people (more generally called Atia). In the book "Hawaiki," it was attempted to identify this Avaiki with Java or Sumatra, but certain considerations lead me to think it may have been some other of the Indonesian islands, perhaps the Celebes or Gilolo, or even Borneo. But this is not the place to discuss that question.

I fear I have not always understood some of the detail in the Sage's story.]

TANGIIA'S BIRTH AND DISPUTES AT TAHITI.

WHEN Tangiia was born his grandfather, Ka'u-kura, gave him the name of Rangi, and when his uncle, Pou-vananga-roa, learnt that his sister, Ka'u-ngaki, had given birth to a son, he adopted the boy for his own, and renamed him Tangiia-nui. The uncle also adopted the son of his other sister, Maonga, named Tu-tapu, as a second child. They thus became the adopted children of Pou-vananga-roa. [We learn from other sources that Tangiia's original name was Uenga.]

279. This is the line of descent to Tu-tapu (on his father's side): Nga-upoko-turua-o-'Taie and 'Tai-rauu were the sons of Onokura by his wife 'Te Ata-nua.[1] The first named son had Nga-maru, who had Kotuku-tea, who had Pou-tea, who married Maonga, the sister of Pou-vananga-roa, and their son was 'Tu-tapu, who was thus an elder brother (really first cousin) of 'Tangiia, while Maono (eldest son of Pou) became the *ariki*, and his brother Keu a priest.

280. This is the history of these children of Pou-vananga-roa:[2] He appointed his children to their various functions, Maono to be *ariki*, or head chief, Tu-tapu was also to be an *ariki*, while Tangiia was to be a *tavana*, or minor chief. Hence grew up dissensions because the latter objected that he was not also made an *ariki*. Tu-tapu was an *ariki* of Iva (the Marquesas), while Maono was an *ariki* of Tahiti. Tangiia became much enraged, and seized the insignia of rank (or usurped the position) of the *ariki* at the *marae* at Avarua, and performed the functions, driving Maono away to the mountains. The village now became his and part of the *kuru* (probably the first fruits of the breadfruit, as a right of the chiefs). Maono fled through this persecution to the hills, and then the evils commenced. When Tangiia had seized the power and the lands, his younger brethren awaited (in vain) the distribution of part of the lands and some of the power for themselves to be given to them by Tangiia; and this remained a source of evil between them. These are the names of those people: Nuku, Ai, Ika, Mere, Uki and Maraka.

281. The second cause of trouble between Tangiia and Tu-tapu, was a stream, Vai-iria, a sacred stream of Tangiia's. Trouble broke out over that stream in which Tu-tapu bathed, and fighting followed at Patu-te-ere-tiki and Umu-toto-tatatou, where Tangiia's "teeth were broken" and the plumes of Te Tua-ki-taaro were smashed. This is the meaning of Te Tua-ki-taaro, it means (the people of) Avaiki, while Te Tua-ki-taa-poto means the (people of) Iva and Tahiti.

1. Onokura is a very celebrated ancestor of these people, whose adventures fill forty-seven closely written pages of the documents we are translating, and these we hope to translate later on.

2. There is a very strange story embodied in the MSS. from which these traditions are taken, relating to one Kiri-paru, a descendant of the above Pou-vanangaroa-ki-Iva (which is his full name, and may be translated as Pou-of-the-lengthy-recitation-at-the-Marquesas Islands). During one of the numerous intertribal disputes on the question of ritual at the *maraes*, Kiri-paru, who appears to have been a member of the people living at Rangi-atea on the N.E. coast of Rarotonga, in order to accomplish his object stayed the course of the sun in its orbit! This same Kiri-paru seems also to have been endowed by great powers of sorcery, as we shall see later on when we come to deal with his family.

282. The third cause of trouble was about the two fish, the *raratea* (the shark tribute) and the *onu* (the turtle tribute). Tu-tapu insisted that when a shark was killed the head was his tribute, while the tail-end was for Tangiia, and that the turtle should be divided one part for him, one for Tangiia. But Tangiia would not consent to this; and further trouble arose between them, leading to their separation. Tu-tapu then returned to Iva (Marquesas) while Tangiia started on a voyage to Mauke Island (of the Cook Group), to visit the daughters of Te Tata-uru-ariki, and his wife Te Puaranga-uta, which daughters were named Pua-tara and Moe-tuma.

TANGIIA VISITS MAUKE ISLAND.

283. When Tangiia reached Mauke Island he landed in the district of Utaki, where is the *koutu* (or sacred place of religious ceremonies, meetings, etc., etc.) named Rangi-manuka. He went to look for the girls, and found them by the path beating out bark (for cloth). He stealthly drew near to them, through the bushes, and as he approached he felt inspired and composed the following love song :—

[Which song I do not feel competent to translate—see the original.]

WAR AT TAHITI BETWEEN TANGIIA AND TU-TAPU.

284. After these proceedings he returned to Tahiti.[3] His sister asked him about the *kuru* (breadfruit tribute). He replied, "I did not pluck it." She had thought that Tangiia had it, and was not aware that Tu-tapu had taken it away with him to Iva. In consequence of this a quarrel arose between the brother and sister in front of the *marae*, which grew in violence between him and Maa, the sister's husband [other sources give the husband's name as Uki-mara].[*] Tangiia snatched part of the turtle from the hand of Maa, and this caused ill-feeling on the part of the latter. So the sister (named Raka-nui) took the canoe named "Kai-oi" and departed for Huahine Island, accompanied by Maa.

285. Tangiia now dwelt at Tahiti [from what follows, it must have been for some years], and then he fitted out the canoe named "Tuna-moe-vai," which name had been given by his grandfather, Ka'u-kura [who had also been a noted voyager see "Journal Polynesian Society," Vol. IV., p. 102, where, however, Mr. Stair calls

---

3. The narrative does not say if Tangiia was successful in his love making to these two ladies, but we shall learn further on that he had children by them. Their names were Moetuma and Puatara.

* From the same source we learn that these two were the parents of Tarionga, an ancestor of the Taranaki tribe of New Zealand.

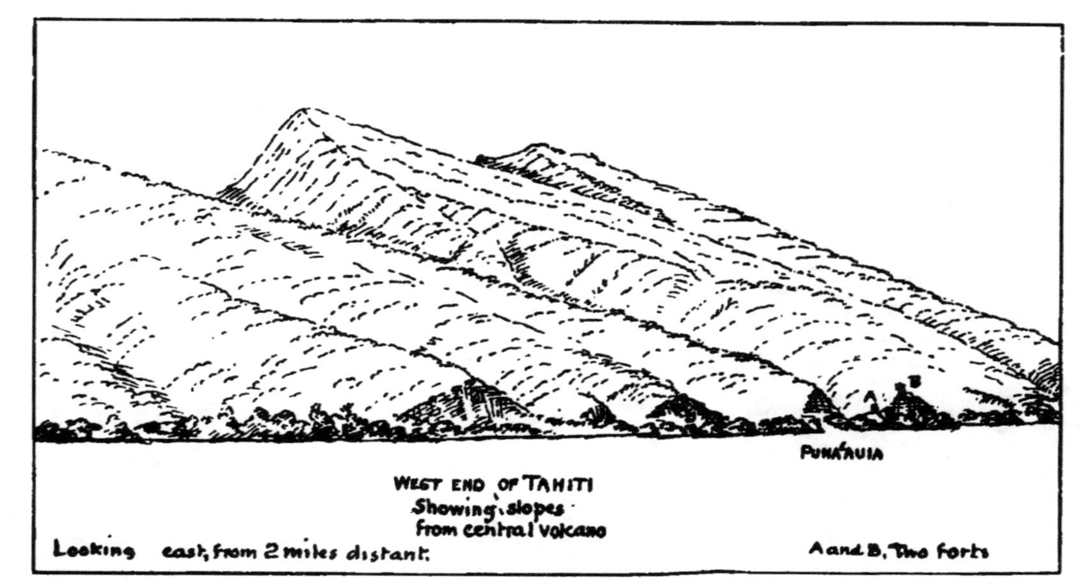
PUNA'AUIA
WEST END OF TAHITI
Showing slopes
from central volcano
Looking east, from 2 miles distant.
A and B, Two forts

the voyages there described "Samoan Voyages," though in reality they were made by these people we are dealing with], while his sister named it "Te Tika-o-te-tuaine." On completion Tangiia renamed it "Taki-pu," and then he visited Avaiki (Samoa) and many other islands. On his return to Tahiti he dispatched Tino-rere to fetch his children from Mauke Island.

286. On the latter's return from Mauke, Tu-tapu and his host had arrived from Iva (Marquesas). The object of Tu-tapu's expedition was to make war and to secure the celebrated weapon named "'Te Amio-enua" [4] from Pou-vananga-roa (his adopted father), and the *rara-roroa* [emblematical for a man? for sacrifice]. But Tangiia emphatically refused to concede these things, the weapon and the two "fish"; Tu-tapu holding that they were his [by righ of seniority], but Tangiia was obdurate. Tu-tapu then abandoned these things and demanded the *rara-kuru* [the breadfruit branch—some right of a chief, not known to the translator], and this Tangiia conceded in order to pacify Tu-tapu, but it had no effect on the latter.

287. And now war commenced; Tangiia assembled his clans the Kaki-poto, the Atu-taka-poto, the Kopa, the Tavake-moe-rangi, the Tavake-oraurau, the Neke, the Ataata-apua and the Tata-vere-moe-papa.[5] There was now a separation of the people, Tu-tapu and his army retiring to Tautira [a beautiful place on the north shore of the eastern peninsula of Tahiti], while Tangiia retired to Puna-auia* [a river and district at the extreme west part of Tahiti].

288. Tangiia then composed the following lament for his land:— [See the original, I cannot translate it, though the sense can be made out. Tangiia evidently forsaw disaster to his party in the war about to commence, and hence the lament.]

289. The war now commenced and great was the destruction; one side of Tahiti was full of Iva people. Tangiia retreated, followed up by the Iva forces. So Tangiia gathered all his people together, and prepared their vessel, launched her, and placed on board all their property, including the (emblems of the) gods Tonga-iti, Rongo-ma-

---

4. For the origin of this weapon see Part VI. hereof. It is clear that for part of his life Tu-tapu lived at Afareaitu on the east side of Moorea Island, for in 1897 I was shown the stone foundation of his house.

5. It seems probable from many circumstances that these clans, or some of them, were Melanesians, brought from the west as crews of the vessels. See the description of some of the Ra‘iatea people of this period in our "Memoirs," Vol. IV.

*The accompanying sketch shows Te Fana-i-Ahurai district at the extreme west end of Tahiti, and Puna-auia, Tangiia's home there, and the hills that were set fire to. There is a level flat along the sea, varying from a quarter to a half mile wide. The forts were used by the French in their war with the Tahitians in the forties of last century.

Tane, Rua-nuku, Tu, and Tangaroa. Two of the gods had been taken by Tu-tapu, viz., Rongo-ma-Uenga and Maru-mamao. The chief's seat named "Kai-au-unga" was also secured. After all these things had been placed on board, they returned and continued the fighting, and then, on the mountains, fell his children Pou-te-anuanua and Motoro.

290.   This was the cause through which his children fell. During the course of the battle instructions were given to his cousins Uki and Maraka, as follows: "At Vai-tietie, my cousins! place your company."   To Ika and Mere he said, "Station yourselves, your young relatives and your companies at Vai-pa-ekeeke."   To Nuku and Ai, "At Vai-pikira you and your juniors and companies station yourselves."   These streams were the fighting places, where the assault took place, and here the ridges were set fire to [? by Tu-tapu's people] and caused the death by burning of Pou-te-anuanua.   All Tangiia's fighting streams were taken, and he (and his people) were driven into the sea.   Tangiia reached the sea, and waded over the shelving reef, got on board the canoe.   From there he beheld all inland covered with fire and smoke, right up to the upper mountain spurs.

291.   Now, the goddess Taa-kura, looking down on the raging fire, saw Motoro [Tangiia's son] enclosed by the fire.   She said unto the god Tangaroa, "Alas! this *ariki*! He will be burnt by the fire!" Tangaroa replied, "What is to be done?   You are a god; he is a man."   "*Eia!*   I will haste and fetch my husband!" said Taa-kura. Then Tangaroa urged her, saying, "Haste thee to Retu[6] and ask him to give you a *pakoko-ivi* (a thick cloak worn on the shoulders) to cover him with."   She also asked for a gust of favourable wind in which to hide herself in her descent, and then the south-east wind was sent, into which the goddess entered and covered Motoro with the cloak; then seizing him she took him off to A'ua'u [the island now called Mangaia, where Motoro was afterwards deified.   For reference to him see "Rarotonga Records," p. 28].   It was the Muu and the Pepe (the latter is the butterfly) who carried him there.   And hence (? were these names) given to Tinomana.   [But other stories differ from this.   They say that Motoro remained in Tahiti for many years, until he was brought from there to Rarotonga after the war, described in Part IX., by Keu the priest, after calling at Mangaia Island, where another son of Tangiia's, named Te Rei, had arrived from Mauke Island.   Motoro became the ancestor of the Tinomana family which still lives at Arorangi on the west side of Rarotonga.]

6. It is not known who this personage is—probably a god.

292. After Tangiia had gazed for some time at the (burning) land, he lamented it as follows :—

> Great is my love to my land
> Tahiti that I am leaving
> And geat is my love to my *koutu*
> At Pureora, that I am leaving,
> Great is my love for my drinking springs,
> Vai-kura-a-mata and Marama-ata-kai
> That I am leaving,
> My bathing places, Vai-iria and Vai-te-pai
> That I am leaving,
> My own district, Puna-auia and Papeete
> That I am leaving,
> For my mountains, Tikura-marumaru
> And Aorangi, that I am leaving
> And for my dear children
> Pou-te-anuanua and Motoro now dead
> Alas! Alas! O my children!
> My children O! Alas!
> O Pou-te-anuanua! Alas!
> O Motoro O! O Motoro!

293. After this, Tuiti and Nukua-ki-roto were sent to the *marae* to fetch a wreath and some red berries, and certain white *tapa* [used in the *marae*] which things were gods of theirs. But they did not go to fetch those things, but rather to steal the god Ronga-ma-Uenga to be taken on board the vessel. It was in consequence of this theft that Tu-tapu so persistently pursued Tangiia [as we shall see].

TANGIIA STARTS ON HIS VOYAGES.

294. The vessel now departed to the west to all the islands there, to Avaiki (Savai'i, Samoa), Tangiia still lamenting the loss of his children and his home. His grief for his children was something extraordinary. Pai [Tamarua-pai, see Part VI. hereof] joined in this expedition, for Tangiia had taken him as his chief warrior (and navigator). It was his function to navigate the vessel to Avaiki, and Tangiia gave him the name of Tei-vao-ariki.[7]

When the vessel reached Avaiki [not Savai'i, but in Indonesia probably], the trumpets and the drums were heard, and Tangiia asked, " What are these trumpets and drums sounding for ? " Pai replied, " They are trumpets and drums denoting the appointment of a chief, and the *takurua* feast, and the accompanying ceremonies and dances ; a gathering of the many gods to the feast, with their priests. It is that which we hear."

---

7. It would seem from this that Tamarua-pai had already visited this distant Avaiki, which is certainly not Savai'i of Samoa.

THEY INTERVIEW THE GODS.

295. They then went ashore, and there Te Mata-iri-o-puna and Pai were sent to (the gods) Tu-te-rangi-marama, Rua-i-te-kari, Tu, Tangaroa, Rua-te-atonga, Taakura, Tupua-nui, Rangatira, Tu-vaero-kura, Kura-akaipo, Aronga, Tu-Avaiki, Tu-tavake, Rongo, Uenga, Maru-mamao, Kau-kura, Tonga-iti, Nge-mua and Mumai-io. Their gathering was the celebration of the *takurua* [presentation of first fruits] at this time, and it was just then that Tangiia arrived at Avaiki from Tahiti after the war with Tu-tapu, and death of his children.

296. Tu-te-rangi-marama asked of him, " Why have you come to Avaiki ? " Tangiia replied, " My coming is due to misfortune; Tu-tapu and I have been at war, and my children Pou and Motoro are dead, whilst I had to flee from Tahiti with all my property. As for this, I am at a loss what to do." Then all that gathering proceeded to enquire of him, " What was the cause of your war ? " He confessed to them, " It was the government, the *ariki*-ship ; the fish-tribute ; the turtle-tribute ; the shark-tribute and the human-tribute ; besides the weapon " Te Amio-enua "—these were the fruits [causes] of our war."

Tu-te-rangi-marama then spoke, saying, " It was lucky you were *tapu*, and were not struck " [? wounded or killed]. Then they consulted among themselves, saying, " Let us give unto him great powers, and set aside some particular land for him to dwell in." Then Tonga-iti said to Tangiia, " There is a home for us two, named Tumu-te-varovaro [Rarotonga, an ancient name] ; go thou to that land, and there live till thou diest." And then they gave unto him great *mana* [power, wisdom, prestige] which is the *ira*[8] of the gods, the meaning of which is that he would always conquer in war—he would always win.

297. After this he begged of the gods that they would come with his expedition.[9] These are those companies and their armies and their followers : Tangaroa and his company ; Tu-te-rangi-marama and his, and the same for the following gods—Tu-tavake, Rua-i-te-kari, Kau-kura, Mumai-io (who is the same as Tou-tika, and his descendants, seven in number, three sons and four daughters). Rua-te-atonga, Ari, Tupua-nui, Taa-kura, Kura-akaipo, Tonga-iti, Rangi-puta-rua, Ai-marie, Maru-mamao. And now for the first time did Tangiia possess all these properties.

8. *Ira*, in Maori means the " spark of life," but here it probably means supernatural powers.

9. Apparently this means that some figures of the gods were to be given to him.

[The whole of paragraphs 296 and 297 are difficult to understand. The Sage writes as if Tangiia had actually interviewed the gods themselves, whereas it probably means that he visited the priests of those gods in this distant Avaiki, which is not Savaii, but very likely Java (Hava, Ava, Ava-iki), or some other part of Indonesia where there were still living some of their own race, left behind when the great migration took place—see introduction to this part. These 'gods' he brought away were probably figures of them such as are used by all Polynesians.]

298. Tangiia then begged (of the gods) for all things connected with the *takuruas*, which application was consented to. These are those various things :—

Te eiva, five kinds	The *peu* au *eiva*
A *kaara*	The *akaingo*
A *puapua-aki*, or *tioi*	The *pau*
A *tutaumaa*	A *kapo-rakau*
An *era-tipa*	A *puputa*
A *Taumua poupou*	A *pare-eva-tipa*

[These are various kinds of posture-dances, drums, etc., some of which are described in Par. No. 369.]

299. When these things came into his possession Tangiia ordered Taote and Mata-iri-o-puna to take charge of the trumpet and the drum. And to Tavake-oraurau he assigned the charge of the things pertaining to the *takuruas*, the *ara o nga atua* (?), and a drum to Avaiki. Anga-takurua took Tangiia's place in the direction of the *takurua* (ceremonies) and Te Avaro, from Rangiraro Island, took charge of other trumpets on board the vessel. Tangiia had now secured all there was to be got at Avaiki, and hence is the saying, "*Ko te tere a te tumu*" (the expedition that cleared out all down to the bottom—Free translation).

THE EXPEDITION RETURNS SOUTH.

300. The vessel now returned, and on its way called in at Uea [or Wallis island, north-east of the Fiji Group; another name for this island is Varehao]. Here they beat the drums and sounded their trumpets. On departing, Te Avaro left behind one of the trumpets. The vessel came on from there and reached Kuporu (Upolu, Samoa), where they again beat their drums and sounded the trumpets. Behold! there was no trumpet because Te Avaro had left it at Uea. They returned at once to Uea to fetch it, and on securing it Katu joined them. Back again to Kuporu came the vessel and there beat the drums and sounded the trumpets, whilst the following song was composed. [Though I cannot translate the song in full, the meaning of parts is quite plain. It refers to the acquisition of the drums, etc., and states that one was made from the tree cut down by Ui-te-rangiora, etc., etc.]

301. The expedition sailed for Iti [Fiji—probably the Lau Islands—where no doubt some of their compatriots were still living] and here they met Iro [Whiro, a well-known ancestor of Rarotongans, Tahitians, and Maoris]. Tangiia asked him, "Where is thy child whom I want as an *ariki* (for my people)?   My children are dead." Iro replied, "O! He is away at distant Rapa Island; I have settled him there." Tangiia then said to Iro, "I shall go there and take him as an *ariki* for my people." To this Iro consented, saying, "Go then, and take him."

EASTER ISLAND.

302. The vessel now went right away to Rapa-nui [Easter Island, which name was given to it to distinguish it from Rapa-iti, south-east of Rarotonga, and from the latter island it is said some of the Easter Islanders sprung.   But the native name of the island is Te Pito-te-henua, also Vaihu, Mataki-te-rangi and Kairangi].   On their arrival they found this boy, by name Taputapu-atea, who was on the reef diving for shell-fish, to whom Tangiia addressed himself, saying. "Who art thou?"   He replied, "I am Taputapu-atea!" Then said Tangiia, "It is well, let us go, for I have come for you, and will make you an *ariki*."   And so that child was taken on board the vessel, which then departed.

TANGIIA AND HIS SISTER MAKE PEACE.

303. The vessel then proceeded to Moorea Island [just fifteen miles to the west of Tahiti, the most beautiful island in the Pacific], but they found that Iro had not arrived, so a message was left, "If Iro should come here, tell him that Tangiia has taken his son to make of him an *ariki*."

The vessel now sailed for Uaine [Huahine, about eighty miles W.N.W. of Tahiti], and on arrival Maa [Tangiia's brother-in-law[10]] came on board to see Tangiia, and said to him, "You had better return, for thy sister Raka-nui has prepared and dried the firewood to cook you with."   Tangiia replied, "I shall not return, I am the priest Unutea, and my assistant is Marotai, I insist on going ashore." When he had entered the channel (in the reef), Raka-nui and her daughters came and began to abuse him [it will be seen in paragraph 284 that they had parted in anger when they last met] saying, "O thou great big headed eel! fall down and grovel in the water. Behold! O my brother! You have been brought here to my place, in the great ocean.   That is the direful result, my brother! of evil."

10. According to the "Tuatua no Tangiia-nui," p. 2, the husband of Raka-nui was Uki-maraka, probably another name for Maa, and their son was Tarionge, an ancestor of the Taranaki Maoris.

Then those on board the vessel answered the abuse of those on shore, to the Papaka-tueraera, saying, "It was thou who brought (the trouble?) to Huahine and Ngangana. Uki and Rakamea dwelt with the woman Raka-nui, and gave birth to Tarionge and Te Ariki-oa-ngata, that searched for some *para* at Tahiti. This is I, Tangiia, a priest Unutea, whose assistant is Marotai. I have a very fine canoe now, so was the way to Huahine made easy to my sister Raka-nui. Let me go ashore. Keu [their brother] is ashore there." On this the sister cried over Tangiia and rubbed noses, and then they went to the village.

- [The greater part of par. 304 is very obscure, and probably I have missed the meaning of these emblematical sayings. It is interesting to note the name of Tarionge, who was one of the ancestors of the Taranaki people of New Zealand, many of whom at this period were dwelling in the neighbouring island of Rangiatea (Ra'iatea).]

305. When they arrived at Raka-nui's house, a feast was prepared for Tangiia and the crew of the vessel, and after hunger had been satisfied, Raka-nui questioned Tangiia as follows, " What has caused your delay ? What have you been doing ? How is our home (in Tahiti) ? Where is our *rara-kuru*, and our gods ? Where is the weapon, 'Te Amio-enua' ? and our children, and our father?" [In reference to the *rara-kuru*, or breadfruit tree branch, I was told, by the Rev. W. Wyatt Gill I think, that in the times of Tangiia the population of Tahiti had become so dense that the product of bread-fruit trees was divided and owned by separate families—no one was allowed to own the whole of the fruit from one tree. And that a dispute between Tangiia and Tu-tapu over a *rara-kuru* was one of the causes of their subsequent war. It is probably this that is referred to above. It is to be remembered that the breadfruit is not indigenous to the Pacific, but was brought by the people from Indonesia, and hence perhaps in Tangiia's time it had not had time to become so plentiful as in these days.] Tangiia replied to his sister, "I have been delayed by my long voyage over the ocean, to assuage my anger [at his defeat, see par. 290-291, etc.] and to mourn the loss of my children." The sister asked, " Are your children dead ? " " Both Pou-te-anuanua and Motoro are dead ; the land has been conquered ; our *rara-kuru* is gone ; as also one of our gods." " But where then is the weapon ? " " It is with me ! " Said the sister, " What then has been the real cause of your delay ? " Then Tangiia explained to her, " I was a long time at Avaiki-te-varinga." " A ! have you really been to distant Avaiki ? What is the news from there ? " Tangiia replied, " This is the news that I have gathered at Avaiki ; there was a great *takurua* (feast and ceremonies) going on when I arrived there, accompanied by all kinds of games and amusements."

306.   Then Raka-nui asked of Tangiia, "Describe those things which you brought back from there." Tangiia replied, "These are the whole of them; we brought away everything; there is nothing left." Raka-nui asked, "Where is the *eva-tipa* (ceremonial dance)?" "It is here."   "O! let us see it!"

Then the sister tried to persuade Tangiia to remain there at Huahine, saying, "Let us both live here. You on one side of the island; I on the other." But he replied, "Not so! I cannot remain, I must go on to Tumu-te-varovaro [old, or spirit-name of Rarotonga], which (the god) Tongo-iti has told me of. I am going on there to live till I die." "What land is that?" asked the sister. Said Tangiia, "What land indeed! I have never seen it."

Then Tangiia explained to his sister, "With me is the son of Iro, whom I have brought along to make an *ariki* of." "Why is he left with you? are you not an adult yourself?" But Tangiia replied, "That will not do; I am going to set him up as an *ariki*." But the sister objecting, argued with her brother, saying, "Don't do that! There are plenty of *mataiapo* [minor chiefs], and priests suitable for the office." But the brother insisted that (the boy) should be an *ariki*. To this the sister (eventually) agreed.

307.   Then the sister Raka-nui asked, "Who is he to be the *ariki* of?" Tangiia replied, "He is to be *ariki* over Te Neke, Te Kaki-poto, Te Atu-taka-poto, Te Ataata-pua, Te Tavake-moe-rangi, Te Tavake-oraurau, Te Tata-vere-moe-papa, Te Kapa-tavarivari, and Te Mana-une." [These were the clans, or divisions of Tangiia's people, and, as already remarked, they probably included many Melanesians taken as sailors, slaves, etc., by the Polynesians. The Mana-une (or Mana-hune) are known traditionally to the Maoris; the word means a cicatrice, such as the Melanesians mark their bodies with. A tribe of that name lived in Mangaia Island, and also in Tahiti, while in Hawaii they were known as Mene-hune.] The sister then approved, saying, "It is right!" She then asked, "What is his name?" to which the reply was, "Taputapu-atea!" To this the sister agreed; and then new names were given to the lad, "Te Ariki-upoko-tini." [The chief of many heads, or ruler over many people] and Ta-i-te-ariki [a name borne not long ago by one of the West Coast, N.Z., chiefs]. After this Raka-nui gave her canoe into the hands of Tangiia, saying, "Here is a second canoe for your vessel." When this canoe, named "Kai-oi," was delivered to him, it was taken to the sea-shore and served to convert the original vessel into a *purua*, or double canoe; the work being done by the navigator (and naval expert) Tamarua-pai. When this work was completed, all Raka-nui's property was taken on board, and she, her husband Maa, and their children joined Tangiia's party. In consequence of this joining of

the two canoes (to make it a double one—*parua*) Pai received the
name of Purua. And now Tangiia and his sister broke out into song,
and sighs [being somewhat anxious as to whether] death or salvation
[laid before them].

308.   [The song will be seen in the original, but cannot be
translated, though much of it is clear.]

TU-TAPU IN CHASE OF TANGIIA.

309.   News was now received that Tu-tapu was near; so the
expedition left for Porapora [forty miles W.N.W. of Huahine, a
somewhat low island with a beautiful precipitous peak on it].   On
their arrival there they commenced to consecrate the *ariki* [Iro's son],
but the ceremony had not reached the stage of girding with the
scarlet belt, when Tu-tapu arrived on the scene, in full pursuit of
Tangiia.   The latter then composed the following, expressive of his
love [to Iro's son; for which see the original].

310.   The expedition now left Porapora and sailed for Rangi-atea
[Ra'i-atea Island a few miles S.E. of Porapora], where the two
vessels (of Tangiia and Tu-tapu) closed, and passed along the coasts
together, those on Tu-tapu's vessel shouting out, "Give up my god!
Give up my god!"   [It will be seen in paragraph 293 that
Tangiia's messengers had taken Tu-tapu's god Rongo-ma-Uenga].
And now night fell, and a gust of wind [and ? mist] arising, which
hid them, and their courses separated.

311.   Tangiia now returned to Fiji [a distance of 1,730 nautical
miles, due east to the Lau Islands, to which no doubt, they went.   It
would not take them long as the trade wind would be abaft the beam
all the way].   On arrival all hands were ordered ashore the better to
enumerate the crew (and passengers), and it was ascertained that
they totalled two hundred men, whose place on board was to be the
katea [the main one of a double canoe], while to the women and
children was assigned the *ama* [or lesser canoe, the word usually
means an out-rigger].

312.   At this time the following song was composed [which seems
to be a sort of prayer for good fortune in the future].   And then this
name of "the two hundred" was given as a name for Tu-pa-moa-ariki,
thus, "Te Rua-rau."   [= two hundred, but all Polynesians counted
men by pairs, so it means four hundred, rather a numerous crew for
a Polynesian *pai*, or ship.]

TANGIIA MEETS KARIKA.

313.   After the above the expedition visited many islands exhalting
the fame of the vessel [—its name was "Taki-pu"], even those
islands towards the sun rise. When they were at the island called

Maketu[11] they met (the Samoan chief) Karika. On sighting this canoe, Tangiia called out, "There is a vessel." So Tu-iti and Nukua-ki-roto climbed up the mast to see it better. As soon as they discovered that it was Karika, they reported to Tangiia, saying, "It is Te Tai-tonga! [another name of Karika's[12]] and you will be killed." Tangiia asked, "How many men has he?" "A great many! A great many!" was the reply. "What is to be done?" said Tangiia. "What indeed? There is only one course open, you must deliver up the *rangi-ei* (the head plumes) on your head [i.e., must give up the supremacy to Karika].

314. Soon Karika's vessel drew near, quite close to the other, and Karika came on board that of Tangiia. Tangiia had already sent below all the able bodied men, leaving none but slaves, children and the decrepit on the deck of the vessel, so that Karika might not see them (the men). Tu-iti and Nukua-ki-roto now urged, "Give up (your) *rangi*! Deliver over the supremacy!" So Tangiia took off the red plume from his head and was about to hand it to Karika, when Pou-te-are rushed up and knocked it out of his hand, and then took charge of it, climbing up the mast, and placed it on his own head. Then Pai [the navigator of the vessel] rushed after him and knocked it off Pui's head, and it fell down (? on the gunwale).

11. Mr. Savage informs me this is not Maketu—now called Mauke—of the Cook Group, but one of the Pau-motu islands. It is not, however, shown in Mr. J. L. Young's list of those islands. See "Journal Polynesian Society," Vol. VIII., p. 264. In my opinion the island is not in the Paumotu Group—properly so called—but is the island called on the charts Ma'itia, situated some 60 miles to the east of Tahiti. This island was formerly called Tuhua; it is of volcanic origin, and is some 1,600 feet high. At the present time the island is named Me'etia (which is the same as the chart name Ma'itia), but was formerly also called Me'etu, but in consequence of the word *tu* in the last syllable entering into the name of one of the *tapued* chief's names, the last syllable was changed to *ia*. As the Tahitians do not pronounce the letter *k*, and as *o* and *e* are universally interchangeable, we have the name Maketu, as the island was known to the Rarotongans. This is an interesting example of the letter changes in Polynesian languages: it is more interesting perhaps to know that under its name Tuhua it was known to Maori tradition, and also as Maiteka in the Taranaki tradition of the "Aotea" canoe. See "Journal Polynesian Society," Vol. IX., p. 213. The island is known to the Paumotu people as Mekiteka, and its European name is Osnaburg Island. I would remark here that probably this is the island known to Maori tradition in which a violent volcanic eruption took place some time before their ancestors left those parts in the fourteenth century. The name Tuhua, the meaning of which is now lost, evidently meant a volcano, or volcanic eruption formerly. Thus we have Tuhua island in N.Z. an extinct volcano, Tofua in the Tonga Group, Tofua-tuana'i in Upolu, Samoa, Tofua, Savaii in Savaii Island, Samoa, all extinct volcanoes.

12. Karika came from Manu'a Island in Samoa, where his descent is retained on the archives of that island. It is probable that a feud already existed between him and Tangiia.

Hence is this circumstance called "Au-topa" [the fallen plume, or fallen supremacy].

315. Then Pai went on to the *ova* or sea-board of the canoe and seized the emblem of peace; this was the second time the plumes had been taken; hence is this circumstance called "Rua-kake-ova." This is what happened when the *rangi* was [attempted to be] given to Karika at that time, at Maketu.

316. And now commenced fighting; and Mū-tokerau and Mū-tonga [? names of winds, used emblematically for the fury of the fight], came and fought for the supremacy, and evil nearly befell them through the paucity of men, for only the decrepit were [? on deck]. The vessels were fastened close together; the paddles were seized, when Tangiia called out to his men, "Hold fast you men, take the paddles, the whole of them." It was in consequence of his expression *taki-pu* and *taki-tumu* that his vessel received the names "Taki-pu" and "Taki-tumu" [which I think means "destroy root and branch"]. Fear now fell on all men [the enemy], and Karika was in great trouble, whilst Tangiia's men felt their spirits rise. Each man now took to the paddles, and towed Karika's vessel from Maketu to Maiau. And so Karika decided to make peace with Tangiia, and [to cement it] gave him his daughter Mokoroa-ki-aitu in marriage. And then the canoes separated. [The next sentence appears to indicate that this was at Ta‘a, perhaps Taha‘a near Ra‘iatea, but it is not clear.]

TANGIIA SETTLES AT RAROTONGA.

317. Tangiia had asked of Karika [who was a great navigator. Dr. W. Wyatt Gill says he made eight voyages from Rarotonga to Samoa], saying, "Where is Rarotonga?" Karika then explained, "There." [Another tradition is more full than this (which appears to have something omitted), and describes the course Tangiia was to take to the south and west to find Rarotonga.] The vessels now separated, Karika going his way, and Tangiia on his. But the latter missed his mark and reached those parts [in the south] where are great waves and currents, and he thought, "This is the 'Tai-rua-koko'" [place of monstrous waves, reported by Ui-te-rangi-ora, see par. 277, Part VI. hereof. Another account says they knew they were too far south by dipping their hands in the sea and finding it intensely cold]. From (those parts) they returned north, and then discovered Rarotonga, and finally reached the land [which was to be Tangiia's home ever afterwards. Another account says that the name of this beautiful island is derived from Karika's directions to Tangiia; he was to go *raro* (west) and *tonga* (south). Here we may leave the expedition while the Sage describes the first inhabitants of Rarotonga, see Part VIII., and take up Tangiia's adventures later on].

KA NOO A TANGIIA-NUI I TAITI.

Kua anau maira a Tangiia, ko Rangi te ingoa ta Ka'u-kura i topa ki tona utaro. E kite akera a Pou-vananga-roa i te tama a te tuaine —a Kau-ngaki—kua rave aia nana; kua topa aia i te ingoa o tana tamaiti ra ko Tangiia-nui. Kua rave katoa maira i ta tetai tuaine tamaiti—i a Tu-tapu—ei tokorua i aua nga tamariki nana ra ko Tu-tapu; ko ta Kau-ngaki ïa ko Tangiia, ko ta te teina ïa, ko ta Maongo, ko Tutapu ïa. E riro roa rai maira na Pou-vananga-roa aua tamariki.

279. Tera te aerenga mai o te kapionga ki a Tu-tapu: Ko Nga-upoko-turua o Taie ma Tai-ranu—ta Ono-kura i anau i te vaine, i a Te Ata-nua. Auania e Nga-upoko-turua ko Nga-maru. Anau akera tana ko Kotuku-tea; anau akera tana ko Pou-tea: kua rave aia i te tuaine o Pou-vananga-roa ei vaine nana, ka anau mai ei a Tu-tapu, i riro ei a Tu-tapu ei tuakana no Tangiia, i riro ei a Tangiia ei teina, no te mea, e tuakana a Kau-ngaki, e teina a Maongo. Ko te ariki a Maono, ko te karakia te teina, a Keu.

280. Teia te tuatua i taua au tamariki nana ra, a Pou-vananga-roa ra. Kua akataõnga aere aia i aua nga tamariki nana ra; ko Maono, ei ariki aia; ko Tu-tapu ei ariki aia; ko Tangiia ei tavana aia. Kua tupu iora te pekapeka i aia, koia kare i akaarikiia. Ko Tu-tapu, e ariki ïa ki Iva. Ko Maono, e ariki ïa ki Taiti. Kua riri akera a Tangiia, kua ao atura i te taõnga i mua i te marae, i Avarua: kua tavaitai maira te anu nana, kika atura a Maono i runga i te kainga, aere atura ki te maunga. Kua riro maira te kainga ma tetai pae i te kuru ki aia—ki a Tangiia. Kua peke a Maono i te nekeneke ki te taru-pakuivi; ka tai te kino ka tupu. Kia tavaitai mai te taõnga ma te kainga ki a Tangiia, kua tatari mai nga teina i tetai tapa kainga ma tetai taõnga na ratou, kia oronga mai a Tangiia no ratou; kua vai tei reira ei kino ki roto i a ratou. Teia taua aronga ra—ko Nuku, e Ai, e Ika, e Mere, e Uki, e Maraka.

281. Teia te rua o te pekapeka i a Tangiia e Tu-tapu; ko te vai, ko Vai-iria; e vai tapu no Tangiia. Kua tupu te tamaki ki taua vai ra, ka pa'i ai e Tu-tapu, ka tamaki ki reira, ki Patu-te-ere-tiki e Umu-toto-tatatou. Kua ati te nio o Tangiia, e kua ngaa te tia a Te Tua-ki-taaro. [Tera te aiteanga o Tua-ki-Taaro, ko Avaiki ïa, ko Te Tua-ki-taa-poto, ko tei kore ia i ngaa, e te aiteanga o Te Tua-ki-Taa-poto, koia a Iva e Taiti.]

282. Teia te toru o te kino, ko nga ika e rua, ko te Raratea e te Onu. Kua manono mai a Tu-tapu, e tipu te mango, uana te mimiti, na Tangiia te iku; e vãi te Onu nana tetai pae na Tangiia tetai pae. Kare ra e tika i a Tangiia, kua tupu iora te kino i a raua, ma te ke ki tetai ki tetai. Kua oki atura a Tu-tapu ki Iva, kua aere atura a Tangiia ki Mauke, ki nga tamaine a Te Tata-uru-ariki, ko Te Pua-ranga-uta tana vaine; ko Pua-tara e Moe-tuna nga tamaine.

283. E tae atura a Tangiia ki Mauke kua kake atura ki uta ki te
tapere ra, ko Utaki, ko Rangi-manuka te koutu. E kite atura aia i
aua nga vaine ra, te noo ra ki runga i te renauga, te tukai ra i te ara.
Kua akapiri aere atu aia na roto i te ngangaere; e tae atura aia i
vaitata, kua tae mai te au ki aia, kua atu iora i te pee, na-ko atura:—

> Ka tukaiia, ka tukaiia tau oki, rirerire e—
> Ki te ara-kura ua, Pua-tara e, ki au e—
> Ka moe noa te vaine, e Moetuna,
> E tungou o mata e te ariki
> Ka kite ra ia koe—e—
> Ka tukaiia ra, ka uka ia
> Ka ukaia mai ana.
> Kotai pakia ia, a paki akanui,
> Katakata noa koia 'e—
> Kua inga te ta urua, Puatara e—ki au e,
> Ka moe noa te vaine, e Moe-tuna,
> A tungou nga mata o te ariki
> Ka kite ra ia koe e, a kia mou a aroa.
>
> Akatae, akatae e rire taku au ki Mauke e—
> Ra Pua-tara ki au e—
> Ka moe noa te vaine Moe-tuna,
> Tungou nga mata ki te ariki
> Ka kite ra i a koe e—
> Ko akaa, akatere ki Mauke e—
> Ki a Tama-tino-rere, kua rere ua
> Ki te rangi tapu e rire e—
> Ko te rei o Tangiia, Pua-tara e, ki au e—
> Ka moe noa te vaine Moe-tuna,
> A tungou o mata ki te ariki,
> Ka kite ra i a koe e—
> E poupou pou ra ki tai e—
> Ko te tai o Kori-mata oki
> Ko te kau ra tena ra,
> Ki te tama rirerire e
> Ki te kape uti i a Pua-tara e, ki au e—
> Ka moe noa te vaine e Moe-tuna
> Tungou nga mata ki te ariki,
> Ka kite ra i a koe, e—
> E ko ikiiki iki na runga ki te tai
> Opukia ko te kauranga tena ra
> E te tama a ki runga i te koko
> Ki taku uutia ua, Pua-tara e—ki au e—
> Ka moe noa te vaine Moe-tuna
> Tungou nga mata o te ariki
> Ka kite ra i a koe, a kia mou aroa—e—

284. E oti akera tei reira, kua oki atura ki Taiti. Kua ui maira
te tuaine ki aia i te kuru. Kua karanga atura aia, " Kare au i aaki."
Kua manako aia e, tei i a Tangiia, kare aia i kite e, e na Tutapu i
aaki, kua taria ki Iva. Kua tupu ia pekapeka i a raua ma te tuaine

ki mua ki te marae; kua tupu ia pekapeka ki reira, ki a Tangiia rai e Maa. Kua anna e Tangiia te tonga-na onu ki te rima o Maa—ko to Maa puku ia ki a Tangiia. Kua rave atura te tuaine i te vaka, i a "Kai-oi," kua akatere atura ki Uaine! kua aru atura a Maa i reira.

285. Kua noo iora a Tangiia i Taiti, kua aro i te vaka, i a "Tuna-moe-vai." Ko ta Ka'u-kura ia ingoa i tana vaka ra; ko ta te tuaine ingoa, ko "Te-tika-a-te-tuaine" ia. Kia oti te vaka kua topa a Tangiia i tana ingoa ko "Taki-pu," kua akatere atura ki Avaiki ma te pa-enua ravarai. E oki maira ki Taiti kua unga atura i a Tino-rere ei tiki i nga tamariki ki Mauke.

286. Kia oki mai i Mauke, tera a Tu-tapu kua tae mai ki Taiti, mai te tangata katoatoa. Tera to Tu-tapu aereuga, e tere tamaki, e aō i te rakau, i a "Te Amio-enua," ki te metua, ki a Pou-vananga-roa; e te rara-roroa—koia te tangata. Kare roa akera i paria e Tangiia ana nga apinga ra e toru; me te rakau, e nga ika e rua. Kua tupu iora te taumaro i a rua, e keta a Tu-tapu nana; kare a Tangiia e pa. Kua akaruke i tei reira a Tu-tapu, kua pati ki' nga rara-kuru. Kua tuku atura a Tangiia i nga rara nona ei akamaru atu i aia: e kare rava akera i maru mai.

287. Kua tupu iora te tamaki, kua koi iora a Tangiia i tona tangata, i Te Kaki-poto, e Te Atu-taka-poto, e Te Kopa, e Te Tavake-moe-rangi, e Te Tavake-oraurau, e Te Neke, e Te Ataata-apua, e Te Tata-vere-moe-papa. Kua mavete i teianei, kua taka a Tu-tapu ma tona nuku ki Tau-tira, kua taka a Tangiia ki Puna-auia ma tona nuku.

288. Kua tangi a Tangiia ki te enua, kua tumu aia i te pee :—

> E turina koia, i runga a poi noa e—
> Ka rere po, rere ra e—
> Patiu te oro e, pua ara ua,
> Ko te mate e—
> Patiū te oro e, ka naku oi au e—
> Ko Taiti akarere e, ka rere e—
> Ka rere poi rei reira e—
> Patiu te oro e rai,
> Akua ara ua ko te mate e—
> Patiu te oro e rau akatea,
> Te mate noa ruru—e—
> E te pua ra oti ake ooia e—

Ko te ua teia :—

> Ka kapiki ana e tamaki e—
> Ko tua rau enua ra
> Ko te aere mai nei, katoa ra,
> Te area tai e, ka rere poi rei ia.
> Pati te oro e, e pua rau ua,
> Ko te mate e.

Pati te oro e, ko te aere mai nei e,
Ko te area tai oki, kua kapikipiki e—
Ko iku i Taua-roa e—
Kua topa a Vaimoko—
Te aro ua ake nei te tamaki,
A Tangiia, ki runga kau-aka ïa,
Ka rere po rei ia,
Pati te oro e pua rau ua,
Ko te mate e.
Pati te oro e, ua a Tane nana e,
Ko Akamatu kua e, kia mate
Te marama rei iri e—
Ko te kaa ia na te taunga,
Na Keu-totoa e tataa ki Motu-tapu
Ka rere poi rei ia,
Pati oro e, e pua rau ua,
Ko te mate e—
Pati te oro e rau aka ia
Te mate uoa ruru e
E te pua, oti ake ooi e.

289. Kua ta te tamaki, kua maata te kino, kua ki tetai pae i a
Taiti i te Iva; kua peke a Tangiia. Te aere ua maira te Iva. Kua
rave iora a Tangiia i tona au tangata ma te pāī, kua tuku atura ki te
moana, kua tari i tona apinga ki runga i te pāī: i te atua ko Tonga-
iti, e ko Rongo ma Tane, ko Rua-nuku, ko Tu, ko Tangaroa. Kua
riro e rua i a Tu-tapu a Rongo-ma-Uenga, e Maru-mamao. Kua apai
i te nooanga, i a Kai-au-unga, ki te pāī. Kia ope te apinga ki te pāī,
kua oki, kua ta i te tamaki; topa atura nga tamariki ki te maunga—
ko Pou-te-anuanua e Motoro.

290. Teia te mea i topa ai nga tamariki, no te kotinga i te tamaki,
i te ikuikuanga ki nga teina, ki a Uki e Maraka, "Ei Vai-tietie
korua, e nga teina! noo ei ma to korua tini." Ki a Ika e Mere.
"Ei Vai-pa-ekeeke korua e nga teina noo ei ma to korua tini." Ki
a Nuku e Ai, "Ei Vai-pikira korua e nga teina noo ei ma to korua
tini." Ko nga vai tamaki teia—I eke, i tauna ai te tuaivi, i mate ei
tetai tamaiti a Tangiia i te ka ki te āī—koia Pou-te-anuanua. Kua
eke katoa ta Tangiia vai tamaki, kua topaia ki roto i te tai, kua iro
atura a Tangiia na runga i te arakaoa ki runga i te pāī. E tae akera
aia ki runga i te pāī, kua akara ki uta; kua ngaromia te enua i te
auāī, kua ka te tua-ivi.

291. Kua akara katoa maira a Taa-kura, ki raro i te āī e ka ra.
Kite iora i a Motoro i roto i te āī; kua kapiki maira ki a Tangaroa,
no-ko maira, "Aue! teia ariki e, ka ka nei i te āī e." Kua kapiki
maira a Tangaroa, ki aia, "E akapeea! e atua koe, e tangata tera."
"Eia! ka oro au ka tiki i taku tane." Kua akaunga atura a Tangaroa i aia, na-ko atura, "E oro ki a Retu, kia omai i te pakoko-ivi ei
tapokipoki ei." Kua pati atu i tetai takao-matangi ei uuna i aia, kua

orangaia maira te matangi-nui; kua na roto aia i reira; kua tapoki
iora, kua apai atura ki A'ua'u; na Te Muu e Te Pepe i apai atu.   No
reira i topaia ai ki a Tino-mana.

292.   Kia oti te akaraanga a Tangiia ki te enua, kua iriea iora ki
te enua na-ko atura :—

> Ka aroa mea ra e, ki taku-enua,
> Ko Taiti ka vaio nei
> Ka aroa mea ra e, ko taku koutu,
> Ko Pure-ora, ka vaio nei
> Ka aroa mea ra e, ko taku vai inu,
> Ko Vai-kura-a-mata, e Marama-ata-kai, ka vaio nei,
> Aku vai pai ko Vaiiria, ko Vai-te-pia, ka vaio nei,
> Aku tapere ko Puna-auia e Papeete, ka vaio nei,
> Taku maunga, a Tikura-marumaru,
> E Ao-rangi, ka vaio nei,
> E ae oki aku tamariki,
> Ko Pou-te-anuanua e Motoro i mate nei.
> Aue tou e! aku tamariki e,
> Aku tamariki e, Aue tou e!
> E Pou-te-anuanua e, Aue tou e!
> E Motoro e! E Motoro e!

293.   I muri ake i tei reira, kua akaunga atura i a Tuiti e Te
Nukua-ki-roto ei tiki i tetai iri, koia te iriiri i te marae, e poreo, e te
tikoru.   Taua apinga ra ei atua no raton.   Kare atura raua i aere ki
tei reira; kua aere atura ki te keia i a Rongo-ma-Uenga kia riro
maira ki runga ki te pai.   No ana nga atua ra i aru aere na ai a Tu-
tapu i a Tangiia.

294.   Kua akatere atura te pai ki raro i te pa enua ravarai, e tae
na atura ki Avaiki, i te kairau aere i nga tamariki ma te enua.   E
mamae tu ke to tona ngakau i nga tamariki.   Ko Pai tei iri ki runga
i tana aerenga ra, kua rave a Tangiia i aia ei toa nona.   I aia te
akatere i te pai ki Avaiki.   Ko Teivao-ariki to Pai ingoa i topaia ei e
Tangiia.   E tae atura te pai ki Avaiki kua eaau maira te pu e te pau,
Kua ui maira a Tangiia, na-ko maira, "E pu ea? E pau ea! e kaara
ea?"   Kua tuatua maira a Pai, " E pu akaariki; e akaau takurua;
e pau e akaau takurua; e kaara, e akaau takurua; e evatapu, e akaau
takurua; e eiva e akaau takurua; e tere na te atua tini, e akaau
takurua; e ara-maora, e akaau takurua; e ui-taura, e akaau takurua;
ko taua au mea ra i a taua e akarongo nei."

295.   Kua kake atura ki uta i te enua.   E tae atura ki uta kua
akaunga atura i a Te Mata-iri-o-puna kia aere raua ko Pai ki a
Tu-te-rangi-marama, i a Rua-i-te-kari, i a Tu; ia Tangaroa; ia
Rua-te-atonga; i a Taakura; i a Tupua-nui; i a Rangatira; i a
Tu-vaero-kura; i a Te Kura-akaipo; i a Aronga; i a Tu-avaiki; i a
Tu-tavake; i a Rongo; i a Uenga; ia Maru-mamao; i a Kau-kura;
i a Tonga-iti; i a Nge-mua; i a Mumaiio.   Tei te akaau takurua

anake to ratou nipaanga i teianei ; ko te tuatau ïa i tae atu ai a Tangiia
ki Avaiki mei Taiti atu nei, ka oti ei te tamakianga a Tangiia ma
Tutapu i te mateanga o Pou-te-annanua; ko te mua ïa o te tamakianga.

296. Kua ui maira a Tu-te-rangi-marama i tona aerenga, na-ko
atura, " E aa koe i topa mai ei ki Avaiki nei?" Kua tuatua maira a
Tangiia ki aia, " E oro-kanga toku aerenga; e ta maua ma Tu-tapu.
E kua mate aku tamariki, ko Pou-te-annanua e Motoro; e kua peke
au i Taiti e te au mea katoa, kua ope. E teianei, kare na aku ravenga."
Kua ui maira tana aronga katoa ra, na-ko maira, "E aa te ara i ta
korua tamaki?" Kua aaki atura aia, na-ko atura ra. "Ko nga
taõnga; ko te ariki; ko nga ika; ko te omu, ko te raratea; ko te
rararoa ; ko te rakau—ko Te Amio-enua ; ko nga pua ïa i ta maua
tamaki."

Kua karanga maira a Tu-te-rangi-marama, na-ko maira, " Mari
rai koe kua tapu, kua kore e pa." Kua karangaranga iora ratou,
ratou ua-o-rai, na-ko akera, "Ka akamana tatou i aia, e ka akataka i
tetai enua nona." Kua kapiki maira a Tonga-iti ki a Tangiia, na-ko
maira, "Tera to taua enua—a Tunu-te-varovaro—ka aere koe ki
reira, e ki reira koe mate ei." E kua tuku maira i te mana nona—
koia te ira o nga atua. Tera te aiteanga, ka au-tu-roa aia i te tamakianga katoa, ka riro ra te re ki aia.

297. E muri ake i tei reira kua pati atura aia i te au atua ravarai,
kia uta ratou ki runga i tona tere. Teia taua aronga ra, i to ratou au
nuku ma to ratou au tere: Ko Tangaroa, ko tana tere ma tona au
nuku. Ko Tu-te-rangi-marama ko tana tere ma tona au nuku. Ko
Tu-tavake, ko tana tere ma tona au nuku. Ko Rua-i-te-kari, ko tana
tere ma tona au nuku : Ko Kau-kura, ko tona tere ma tona au nuku :
Ko Mumai-io, ko tana tere ma tona au nuku—(koia a Tou-tika i
muriugao e tumu-toa, e tapakia, e uka, e reko, e maai-a-nuku, e maai-
a-rangi ; ko te anaunga ïa a Mumai-io, tokoitu ratou — tokotoru
tamaroa, tokoã tamaine). Ko Rua-te-atonga, ko tana tere ma tona
au nuku ; Ko Ari, ko tana tere ma tona au nuku ; Ko Tupua-nui, ko
tana tere ma tona au nuku. Ko Taa-kura, ko tana tere ma tona au
nuku. Ko Te Kura-akaipo, ko tana tere ma tona au nuku. Ko
Tongaiti, ko tona tere ma tona au nuku. Ko Te Rangi-puta-rua, e
Ai-marie ko ta raua tere ma to raua au nuku. Ko Maru-mamao, ko
tana tere ma tona au nuku. Katai aua mea ka rauka i aia i reira.

298. Kua pati akaou rai aia i te takurua ma te au mea ravarai o
te takurua. E kua tika, kua riro maira tana au mea ravarai nana.
Teia taua au apinga ra: Ko te eiva: e rima tu o te eiva; ko te peu—
koia te eiva—e kaara, te akaingo; ko te puapua-aki—koia te tioi—e
pau tona akairo; e tutauuaa, ko te pokara tona akairo; ko te kapo-
rakau, e kaara tona akairo; na Tu-tavaki ïa eiva; ko te eva-tipa—
koia te kopuporeo ki mua i te kopu, e te kopu-porio ki nga rima; e te

puputa; e te tau-mua-poupou ma te peketue ki runga i te taukupu, e te pare-eva-tipa ki runga i te upoko, e te rauru ki muri i te tua, e te parae tia ki mua i te rae, e nga takakaravia ki nga taringa e te takumi ki te kautuai, ko te tua-a-manu ki muri ei akamanea ïa a muri i te pare.

299.   E taka maira taua au mea ravarai ki aia, kua akaunga i a Taote, Mata-iri-o-puna ei tari i te pu e te pau e te kaara katoa, ma te au mea katoatoa. E kua tono i a Tavake-oraurau ei apai i te anga mei te takurua—koia te ara o nga atua, e te kaa ki Avaiki. Ko Te Mata-iri-o-puna, ko te pau ia a Tangiia, ko te anga e te akaau takurua, ko Anga-takurua ïa.   Ko Te Avaro no Rangi-raro aia, nana nga eau pu i apai ki runga i te pāī.   Kua uri i te tumu, te tere a Tangiia mei raro, mei Avaiki, mei te urunga, mei te papa, mei te unga mei te potiki, i topaia e, " Ko te tere a te tumu."

300.   Kua oki maira te pāī, kua tapae ki Uea ; kua rutu te pāu ki reira, kua akatangi te pu.   Kua topa ki reira tetai pu i a Te Avaro ; kua aere maira te pāī mei reira mai e tae mai ki Kuporu.   Kua rutu te pāu ki reira, kua akatangi te pu.   Ina ! kare ua te pu, kua topa ki Uea i a Te Avaro.   Kua oki atura te pāī ; te tiki akaou ki Uea.   E riro maira, kua piri mai a Katu i reira. E tae maira te pāī ki Kuporu, kua rutu te pāu, kua akatangi te pu ki reira ; kua tumu te pee ki reira, kua na-ko akera :—

> Teia te pāu i runga i a Atea
> E karu pāu no te kotinga ïa
> Te Tamoko-o-te-rangi, ka paupau ra nga vaka e,
> E mate i te akama e
> E Rongo e ! kua oro ki Vai-nuku
> E ka paupau ra nga vaka e—
> I tuputupu ra i Avaiki e—i Avaiki mai ana,
> E papa ra, ko Akaotu, te etu taki riko e—
> E te purotu tama na Te Puta-i-ariki, e ariki e—
> Rutu i te pau i Kuporu e—
> Akatangi te pu mei Uea e—
> Ko te ape oki na te ariki Maro-kura ie ra,
> Ka paupau ra nga vaka e—e mate i te akama,
> E Rongo e ! kua oro ki Vai-nuku e—
> Ka paupau ra nga vaka e—
> I tuputupu ra i Avaiki e—i Avaiki mai ana,
> E rakau ko Te Tamoko-o-te-rangi e—
> I kotia ia e te ariki, e Ui-te-rangiora,
> Ei kiato, ei ova, i to pāī, ia Tei Ivi-o-Atea nei,
> Ka paupau ua ra nga vaka e—mate i te akama oki,
> E Rongo e ! kua oro ki Vai-nuku e.
> Ka paupau ua ra nga vaka, ka paupau ra,
> Nga vaka oki, e rue e—

301.   Kua aere atura te pāī ki Iti ; tei reira a Iro.   Kua ui atura a Tangiia ki a Iro, " Tei ea te tamaiti ei ariki noku ?   Kua mate aku

tamariki." Kua akakite mai a Iro, "E tei Rapa roa ai; kua aka-nooia e au ki reira." Kua karanga atura a Tangiia ki a Iro, "Ka aere au; ka taoi, ei ariki noku." Kua akatika maira a Iro, na-ko maira, "E aere! taoiia!"

302. Kua aere atura te pāī ki Rapa-nui; kua kite atura i taua tamaiti ra—ia Taputapu-atea, tei runga i te akau; te maruku ra i te pao i reira. Kua ui atura a Tangiia, na-ko atura ki aia, "Koai koe?" Kua tuatua maira aia, na-ko maira, "Ko Taputapu-atea au!" Kua kapiki a Tangiia, na-ko atu ra, "Aere mai, ka aere taua; e tiki au i a koe; ka taoi au i a koe ei ariki noku." E riro maira taua tamaiti ra ki runga i te pāī, kua aere atura te pāī.

303. E tae atura te pāī ki Morea, kare rai a Iro i tae mai; kua akakite atura ki reira e, "E kia tae mai a Iro e akakite atu kotou e, kua taoi a Tangiia i te tamaiti ei ariki nona."

304. Kua oro maira te pāī ki Uaine. E tae atura ki Uaine, kua eke maira a Maa, e kite maira i a Tangiia; kua kapiki maira aia, ki a Tangiia—kua tuatua maira, "E oki! kua tamatemate te vaiē a to tuaine—a Raka-nui—e kua maro; ei tau i a koe." Kua na-ko atura a Tangiia ki a Maa, "Kare au e oki, e taunga ko Unutea, e purii ko Maro-tai, ka aere rai au ki uta." E tae atura aia ki raro i te ava, kua eke maira a Raka-nui ma nga tamaine, kua amuamu maira i aia, na-ko maira, "E te tuna e! upoko nui, takiritia, topa ki raro, e ketu ana i te vai, e ketu ana i te vai. Ina! e taku tungane! kua takina mai na koe ki toku ngari (? ngai), ki te moana nei. Ko te amoinu tena, E taku tungane! o te kino." Kua tuatua atura to runga i te pāī ki te amuamu mai ki to uta, ki te Papaka-tueraera, na-ko atura, "Naau i taki mai nei ki Uaine e Ngangaua. Ko Uki ma Raka-mea, ka noo i te vaine, i a Raka-nui, i anau ai a Tarionge, ma Te Ariki-oa-ngata, e ketu mai i tetai para i Taiti. Ko au rai ïa, ko Tangiia, e taunga ko Unu-tea, e purii ko Maro-tai. E vaka mania taku i tuku atu ki a koe, a kua paraaraa te ara ki a Uaine, ki taku tuaine, ki a Raka-nui. Oatu au ki uta. Tena a Keu tei uta." Kua aue iora te tuaine ki runga ki a Tangiia, kua oongi iora, aere atura ki te kainga.

305. E tae atura raua ki roto i te are, kua tau iora i te umu-tara-kai na Tangiia, ma te aronga-a-vaka. E pangia akera ratou, kua ui maira Raka-nui, ki te tuugane, ki a Tangiia e, "E, e aa koe i roa ai? E aa te tupu i a koe? E tei ea o tatou kainga? Tei ea o taua rara-kuru? Tei ea o tatou atua? Tei ea te rakau—a Te Amio-enua? Tei ea nga tamariki? Tei ea to taua metua?" Kua karanga atura a Tangiia ki te tuaine, na-ko atura, "I roa au ki te tere ua i te moana, i te kaoe aere i taku riri; ki te akaevaeva i aku tamariki." Kua na-ko maira te tuaine, "Kua mate o tamariki?" "Kua mate a Pou-te-anuanua e Motoro; kua riro te enua; kua riro nga rara-kuru o taua; kua riro tetai atua." "Tei ea te rakau?" "Teiia." "E aa ra te mea i roa kitu ua i a koe?" Kua akakite atura aia e,

" I roa rava au ki Avaiki-te-varinga." "A, tae roa koe ki Avaiki ! E
aa te tuatua i Avaiki ? " " Tera te tuatua i Avaiki, taku i kite ki
reira ; e takurua i toku taenga atu ; te akaau takurua ra, ma te rave
i te au peu tu matini."

306.　Kua ui maira te tuaine ki a Tangiia, na-ko maira, " E,
tena taua au mea ra kua taoi mai e koe ? " Kua akakite atura aia ki
te tuaine, " Teia ravarai ; kua taki maira i te tumu, kare e toe."
Kua karanga maira a' Raka-nui, " Tei ea te eva-tipa ? " " Teia ! "
" O ! ka kite tatou ! " Kua tāpu maira te tuaine, " Ka noo taua i
kunei ; ei tai tara koe i te enua, ei tai tara au." Kua karanga atura
aia, " E ia, kare au e noo ; ka aere au. Tera toku enua ko Tumu-te-
varovaro ; kua akakiteia mai e Tonga-iti noku. Ka aere au ki reira
e mate ua atu." " Koai ia enua ? " " E koai oki ! kare ua au i kite."
Kua akakite atu ki te tuaine, " E tena ake te tama a Iro kua taoiia
mai e au ei ariki noku." " Ei aa i vao rai ki a koe ; kua tangata
metua koe." Kua na-ko maira a Tangiia, " Eia, ka aere rai au ka
iki ei e ariki noku." Kua tamaki maira te tuaine ki te tungane, " Eia,
E Tama ! e manganui te taōnga, e mataiapo, e taunga, e kaa." Kua
maro rai te tungane ei ariki rai. Kua akatika maira te tuaine.

307.　Kua ui maira te tuaine ki te tungane, " Ei ariki aia no te
aa ? " Kua akakite atura aia, na-ko atura aia, " Ei ariki aia no Te
Neke, no Te Kaki-poto, no Te Atu-taka-poto, no Te Ataata-pua, no
Te Tavake-moe-rangi, no Te Tavake-oraurau, no Te Tata-vere-moe-
papa, no Te Kapa-tavarivari, no Te Mana-une." Kua akatika maira
te tuaine, na-ko maira, " Kua tika ! " Kua ui akaou maira te tuaine,
ki a Tangiia, na-ko maira, " Koai tona ingoa ? " Kua akakite atura
a Tangiia, " Ko Taputapu-atea." Kua ae mai aia, " Koia ! " Kua
tapa iora i te ingoa, ko Te Ariki-upoko-tini, e Tai-te-ariki. E oti ake
tei reira kua tuku maira i te vaka ki te rima o Tangiia, na-ko maira,
" Tera te rua i o vaka ki to rima." Kia riro maira te vaka—a
" Kaioi "—ki te rima o Tangiia, kua apai atura ki taatai, kua purua
iora i nga vaka ; kua aau iora a Pai i te vaka. E oti akera kua tari
maira to Rakanui apinga ki runga i te pāī ma tana tane e te tamaiti.
No reira a Pu-rua i topaia ei i a Pu-rua ki a Pai. Kua eeva iora
raua, raua ua-o-rai, i te irieaanga ki te ora, ki te mate.

308.　Kua na-ko maira :—

> Ka'u-kura taku tupuna e—
> Eia mai to tika, te tama e—
> Te pa tuki-papa ki te ipo e—
> Ko Ka'u-kura a ariki,
> Ko tei anake nei e—
> Te pa tuki-papa, tiria io i runga e—
> E Rongo, E Tane, Rua-nuku,
> Ko Tu, ko Tangaroa, rei iri e—
> Ko te Ta-ei-rangi, kia rongo Tangiia,
> Ka tuku ua ra, tuku ua ake e—

> Te pa tuki-papa ki te ipo e—
> Ko Ka'u-kura ariki,
> Ko te anake nei e—
> Te pa tukipapa rua e.

309. Kua ee maira e, teia a Tu-tapu; kua oro atura ki Porapora. E tae atura ki Porapora, kua iki iora i te ariki ki reira. Kare i tatuaia te maro-kura kua rokoia mai e Tu-tapu. Ka arumakina ra e Tu-tapu. Kua tupu iora te aroa ki reira, kua na-ko maira :—

> E ariki iki ua ki Porapora e—
> Ka tuaru-makina e, pati te oro e—
> Kua reka ia i ta oi vare e—
> Ko te ariki ka tuaru-makina e,
> Pati te oro e, okotai koe, okotai au,
> Oro ua atu ua koe ki Avaiki
> E ka tuaru-makina e,
> Pati te oro e, tapaiia apai e,
> Ka tuaru-makina e
> Pati te oro rau aka ia, te mate noa
> Ruru e te pua, oti ake io e.

310. Kua akaruke maira i Porapora, kua oro atura ki Rangi-atea, kua kapiti nga pāī i reira, me to Tangiia e to Tu-tapu, i te tauani aereanga i tei reira ngai moana, ma te kapiki aere atu to Tu-tapu pai ki mua i to Tangiia e, "E omai taku atua! E omai taku atua!" E tei te poirianga iora, tuku maira te takao matangi ei uuna i a ratou—taka ke atura.

311. Kua oki akaou atura ki Iti-nui. E tae atura ki uta kua titiri atura i te tangata ki uta, kia taka meitaki te rainga o te tangata, kua akakatoutoaia iora e rua rau tangata, kua tuku oora (? iora) ïa ki a katea ; ko te vaine ma te tamariki kua tukua ïa ki a ama.

312. Kua tumu i te pee ki reira :—

> Ka uia katoa e, e rire,
> Ko te vaka ïa no Tangiia e—e riri e—
> E mii, e anau e, te metua vaine,
> Ko na te tokerau ooki ana
> Te omai ake tai aroa, e riri e—
> Ka uiuia ra ki Iti-nui,
> E kia taka meitaki te rua rau tangata o Tangiia
> E anau, e mii, e anau e, te metua vaine e—
> Kona te tokerau ooki ana
> Te omai etai aroa, e riri e—
> E mii, e anau oki, e rue e—

Kua tapa iora i taua rua rau tangata ra, i topaia ei ingoa no Tu-pa-moa-ariki koia a "Te Rua-rau."

313. E muri ake i te reira, aere atura te pāī ki runga, ki te pa enua ravarai, akateitei rava atura i te pāī ki te itinga o te rā. E tae atura ki Maketu, kua aravei atura ma Karika ; e kite atura a Tangiia

i a Karika, kua karanga atura ki te tangata, "E pāī teia!" Kua
kake atura a Tu-iti e Te Nukua-ki-roto ki runga i te tira, kua akara.
E kite atura ko Karika, kua akakite maira ki a Tangiia e, "Ko te
Tai-tonga teia! kua mate koe!" Kua ui atura a Tangiia ki a raua,
"E ia ona tangata?" "E rai! e rai!" "E, ka akapeea?" "E
ka akapeea oki, ko te rangi ei i to upoko taau e tuku."

314. Kua vaitata mai te pāī o Karika; e piri maira ki te pae,
kua kake a Karika ki ruuga i to Tangiia pāī. Kua tapoki iora a
Tangiia i te tangata ki raro i te pāī, kua vao uaorai i te unga ma te
tamariki, e te tangata apikepike ua ki runga ua i te oropapa i te pāī,
kia kore a Karika e kite. Kua raurau maira a Tu-iti e Te Nukua-
ki-roto, "E, tukua te rangi! tukua te rangi!" Kua kiriti akera a
Tangiia i te Au-kura i runga i tona upoko, ka tukua ki a Karika. E,
e kite akera a Pou-te-ari, kua oro maira aia, kua patu i taua Au-kura
ra i te rima o Tangiia, kua topa iora ki raro, e riro máira i a Pou-te-
ari, kua oro atura aia ki runga i te tira, kua pare ki runga i tona
upoko. Kua oro atura a Pai, kua patu i taua pare rai i runga i te
upoko o Pou-te-ari, kua topa iora ki raro—koia "Au-topa."

315. Ko te oronga a Pai i runga i te ova i te pāī ka arapaiia; ko
te ruaanga ia raua i te mou i te au, ko "Rua-kake-ova" ia. Ko te
tu ua ia o te rangi i tukuia ki a Karika i tei reira tuatau ki Maketu.

316. Kua tupu iora te tamaki i reira; kua rere mai a Muu-
tokerau, e Muu-tonga kua rere iora i te okoitu, ka tamaki no te au;
i tatakinoia ra e te kore tangata i te pāī, e apike anake. Kua aau
iora i nga vaka, kua kapiti kia piri; kua mou i te oe, kua kapiki iora
a Tangiia ki te tangata, na-ko maira, "Ka takipu ua mai kotou, ka
mou te oe, takitumu ua te oe i te vaka." No reira i topaia ai taua
vaka ra i a "Takipu" e "Takitumu." Kua io ra te mataku o te
tangata, kua tumatetenga roa akera a Karika, kua rere te mauri i te
maruaanga i te tangata o Tangiia. Kua mou iora te tangata i te oe,
tanao, tanao, kua oe atura, e riro maira to Karika vaka i te taoi mai.
E takipu mei Maketu mai e tae mai ki Maiau. Kua akaau maira a
Karika ki a Tangiia, kua omai i te tamaine, i a Mokoroa-ki-nitu ei
vaine na Tangiia. Ko te mataraanga i nga vaka, ko Taa ia
(? Taauga).

317. Kua ui atura a Tangiia ki a Kariki, na-ko atura, "Tei ea a
Rarotonga?" Kua akakite maira a Karika ki aia, "Tera!" Kua
matara nga vaka, kua aere a Karika i tona aerenga; kua aere maira
a Tangiia i tona aerenga. Kua taveva ke atura ki te ngai i uri-nui
ei te au; te na-ko aia e, "Ko te tai-rua-koko!" Kua oki maira mei
reira mai, kua kite maira i a Rarotonga, e tae maira, e vaitata ki te
enua nei, kua uru maira ki uta.

(Tera ia te roanuga tei te 332.)

THE PAUMOTU CONCEPTION OF THE HEAVENS AND OF CREATION.

With Notes by J. L. Young.

[Through the courtesy of Mr. Young we are enabled to reproduce a quite unique drawing made by Paiore, a man from the Paumotu Group, in 1869, representing the world, and the heavens above as conceived of by the branch of the Polynesians to which Paiore belonged.

The photograph from which the picture is taken is in two parts, each nine by seven inches, and from this a tracing was made for reproduction on a smaller scale. The photograph is too faint to admit of a further reproduction by that process. The drawings of the canoes in the second photo will be reproduced later on.

It is much to be regretted we have no further particulars as to the meaning of the various parts of the picture, beyond what Mr. Young has supplied, for no doubt, in former times the natives would have been able to explain the whole, but now alas! there is no hope of this.

It would appear that in the Paumotu belief there are nine spheres in the heavens above, whereas the Maoris have twelve, and other branches eight. It is peculiar too, that the Paumotu people recognise separate names for the two sides of the heavens, or, what is more probable, that the names written on the right hand side, refer to spheres or periods of development of the earth, and that these names should properly be written on the nine stages so encumbered by figures that the native draughtsman could not find room for them in their proper places. None of the Paumotu names for these spheres can be identified with those of the Maoris, though both peoples had the same ideas as to concentric spheres above the earth. Mr. Young's notes follow.]

I was unable on my late visit to Tahiti to sight the original drawing, which has disappeared because of the death of the former owner.

But from notes which I made at the time when the photograph was taken in 1892, and after consultation lately with certain aged natives of Tuamotu, I have arrived at the following as the probable text of the inscription which in the photograph before me, as in the one in your possession, is illegible in parts :—

> " Te mau parau hohoa i faaitehia e te feia tahito.   E hohoa no te ao atoa nei e te parau atoa na te hua raa, parau oia nana e faui te mau uri.   Tirara parau mau pona tiamu no te api ra ati tane, ati tohe, ati mau ni, te fanaua uri a ū na ati buaka, a hio i roto i te pipiria nei ia ite e papai."

Na Paiore, 1869.

Which with the assistance of the old men aforesaid, was translated as follows :—

> " The likeness (or description) of things made known to the people of ancient times.   The form of this our World and the account of our ancestors, and of the beginning of the movement of animal life.   This is the true and succinct description (literally a bundle tied up with a knotted string) of mankind which was confined in narrow spaces, and of the origin of things and of the various trees (or vegetation) and of the bringing forth of animals which suckle their young, such as four-footed animals.   These are to be seen in this sheet of paper as understood by the writer, I, Paiore, 1869."

The foregoing is written in the Tahitian dialect, but with an admixture of words in Tuamotu.   The writer seems to have put " i " and " a " instead of " e " in several instances.

I am not quite satisfied with the correctness of the translation as for example, " e faui te mau uri "—" the beginning of the movement of animal life ": and " no te api ra ati taue," " of mankind which was confined in narrow spaces ": but such was the interpretation of the old men referred to.   They also held that the words " mau ni " literally " all the coconut trees " means in the context, " all trees and vegetation."

The word " buaka "—a pig; was used by natives to signify any four-footed animal except a rat.   It is said that the drawing was made with a stick in the sand by Paiore, an aged *tuhunga*—wise man, who lived at Takaroa Island, but who was a native of Anaa, and that the drawing was copied by a young relative who had been to school at Papeete: the inscription it is said was dictated by Paiore in the Tuamotu dialect, but written by the young man in Tahitian.

NOTES ON THE DRAWING.

It is explained by the natives that the lowest division represents a period when the world was inhabited by animals not known to the Islanders, and when the sky hung low over earth and sea.   In the *third* division are shown the first homicide, the first burials, and the first canoe.

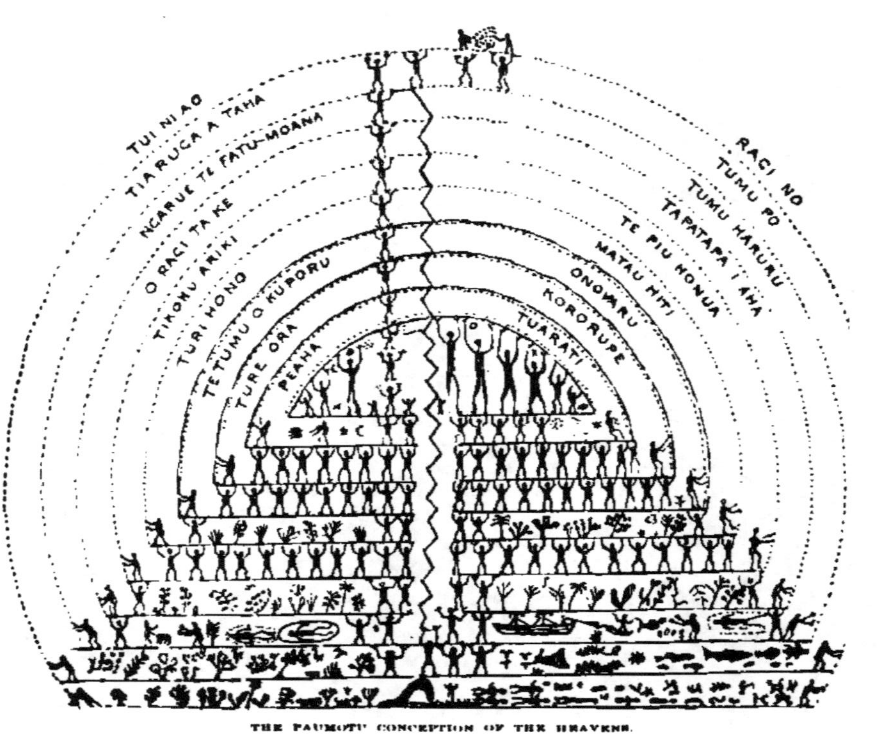

THE PAUMOTU CONCEPTION OF THE HEAVENS.

In the *fourth* the first coconut tree, pandanus tree, Puatea (*Tourne-fortia*) tree, and Tou (*Cordia Subcordata*) tree, &c., &c.

In the *ninth*, on right side, the Constellation Scorpio, and on the left side, the moon and a star and a man making an offering or sacrifice at a fire. The names written outside each circle are as follows:—

Outer Circle left side	Tui ni ao
Second	Tia ruga a taha
Third	Garu te fatumoana
Fourth	O ragi te ke
Fifth	Tikohu ariki
Sixth	Turi hono
Seventh	Te tumu o Kuporu
Eighth	Ture Ora
Ninth	Peaha
Outer Circle right side	Ragi no
Second	Tumu no
Third	Tumu haruru
Fourth	Tapatapa i aha
Fifth	Te piu honna
Sixth	Matau hiti
Seventh	Onovaru
Eighth	Kororupe
Ninth	Tuarati

The canoes* are those built by Rata; the inscription above the sail of the middle one is "Tutu nei tere a tetoira"—"Sailing with a light easterly breeze to the westward." Note the ladder-like masts which were those used on the Tuamotu sea-going *pahi* canoe of old.

I am doubtful as to the value of this drawing, as I think that the author was probably influenced by missionary teachings and by pictures which he had seen.

For instance, the figures of the Ass† and the Ape† in the lowest division: the homicide in the third suggests Cain and Abel: the offering (if it was intended to signify such) in the ninth suggests Abraham and Isaac.

Nevertheless, the general idea is that of ancient tradition: the raising of the heavens by human or rather superhuman effort. The names of the heavens are also interesting.

---

* The drawings of the canoes will be reproduced later on.— EDITOR.

† It is suggested that these figures represent a pig and a dog.—EDITOR.

TRADITIONS AND LEGENDS.

COLLECTED FROM THE NATIVES OF MURIHIKU.
(SOUTHLAND, NEW ZEALAND.)

By H. BEATTIE.

PART XI.

IN common with their northern brethren the Maoris in the south were exceedingly prone to superstition, and the collector of these traditions came across many instances of this characteristic. Several parts of Otago seemed to be specially haunted by ogres, judging by the nomenclature. Some hills behind Waikouaiti are called Pukemaeroero, while the hills behind Tautuku and the mountains to the west side of the lower end of Lake Wakatipu, also bear the same name. The Maeroero was a wild man of the woods, covered with long hair, and possessed of great strength and craftiness. The name Maeroero also seems to have been sometimes applied to elves and fairies, but the word usually implies monstrous beings, whose existence was implicitly believed in up to quite recently. One old Maori said to the collector:—"The Maeroero which lived in the Owaka forest was a fearsome creature. Two knobs in the Ratanui Range are called Puku and Miki after two sisters who were married to Te Waka-tau-puka, an uncle of Tu-hawaiki (and incidentally an uncle of the narrator also). One of these women wandered into the bush where she killed a *kakaruai* (robin), and the Maeroero pounced out and carried her and the dead bird away. She came back about a week later but was unable to relate her experiences owing to fright and collapse. Her friends made an *umu* (oven) and covered it with clay upon which the woman was laid. This act of *tao-whakamoe* was done to remove the spell and avert evil. 'It shifted the *tapu* off her and made her an ordinary woman again,' " concluded the narrator.

The mention of *tapu* recalls the fact that the late Rakitapu of Port Molyneux once had a pig which he named after Hau-matakitaki, a mountain near his birth-place at Lake Wanaka. Then some one recalled the fact that that mountain, and mount Kaki-roa near it, had been named after ancestresses of his, so the pig became *tapu*, and they could not eat it. A year later when the pig was in prime condition the elders consulted together, and decided that the naming

of the pig had been done unwittingly, and that the *māna* acquired
from the ancestral spirits had all gone to its head so the head was
carefully severed, and the rest of the animal was eaten.

SANDY AND THE MAEROERO.

In some notes which Mr. James Cowan kindly gave to the collector
to make use of as desired, occurs the story of Sandy's shooting
expedition. The collector was also told this tale, but as Mr. Cowan's
account is fuller it is herewith presented :—"In the very early days
Sandy, a *pakeha*, met a Maero on Puke-maeroero ('Fairy Hill'—
between Tautuku and Hakopa). The Maoris warned him that there
were fairies there, but he would go. Into the dense forests he went
shooting and firing at *kereru* (or *kuku*, pigeon). He hit a *kereru* and it
dropped flopping to the ground. Just as he went forward to pick it
up, suddenly a terrible figure—a wild, hairy man of the woods—
appeared and menaced him. Sandy immediately rammed down a
charge into his gun and hurriedly fired at the Maero at very close
range. The shot should have struck him, but he was no mortal man
to be killed by shot. He laughed loudly, snatched up the pigeon
and disappeared into the woods—*ka mauria te manu*—carrying the
bird. Sandy's shooting was over for that time, and he got out of the
bush with speed."

WARNING VOICES.

One of my Maori friends said :—"Down near where the 'Tararua'
was wrecked is the Whare-kaio landing-place. Here the rock has
kelp on it, and it is the only place along there where you can get kelp
for *pohas* or eel bags. When the natives had cut enough kelp a
voice from the bush would say, '*Kati, waihoki ina atatau.*' If you
didn't stop when you heard that voice you would die when you
reached home. If a Maori did not obey the spirits disaster would
overtake him."

"When the Maoris were at Tautuku, and the women went out to
cut flax," said another old man, "the Maeroero would warn them
when they had cut enough, and evil befell them if they did not heed
the warning. The Maeroero lived down there, hence are the wooded
hills there called Puke-maeroero. It was also said of other places
that spirit voices warned the people when they had caught enough
fish. These are all what the white man would call mere fairy yarns,
but they were believed in by the people of old."

Although no warning voice emanated from the Burning Plain
near Pomahaka, the wreaths of smoke from the lignite were a warning. Tradition says that the Maoris tried to cook on the steam
escaping from the ground but the food went black, and thereafter
the natives shunned the locality.

THE TAEPO.

What the *taepo* is the collector cannot define. The dictionary says it means " a goblin, a spectre," but in the south, at least, it seems capable of a wider use than this definition would imply. One old woman says that when she was a girl she saw one. It was at the winding part of the Taiari River, known as Te Rua-taniwha, which was said to be haunted by the ghost of a *karara*. The grown-ups said to the children, "Don't go there—that is where a *taepo* dwells," but the little ones in a spirit of fun went to that spot and shouted, "Taepo come out, Taepo come out! " and suddenly, said the ancient dame, they saw a fearsome kind of thing like a shark come out from a hole in the bank, and begin throwing water in the air with its tail. They waited for no more, but fled screaming from the spot."

An old man narrates that many years ago he went an eeling trip from Tuturau up to the Otama and Otama-iti lagoons, and that when camped at Whareoka (near Charlton) a violent earthquake occurred in the middle of the night. He woke up with a start and thought the *taepo* was abroad, or that the eels had come to life again and broken loose. Another tremor came, and when it passed he was quite relieved to find he was still on terra firma, whole and sound, and that the *taepo* had not got him.

TANIWHA AND KARARA.

The dictionary defines the *taniwha* as a water-monster, and the name has cropped up once or twice. A very old man said :—" There is a lagoon on Ruapuke Island called Wai-o-tokarire, and in it lived a *taniwha*. It was a *wairua* (spirit) or *taepo* and had long hair on it. When the people went to get water they could see it floating about. They tried to dig an outlet to drain the water, and after some water had got away the people could see the cave the *taniwha* had been living in but it had disappeared in the night. The place was *tapu* for a long time after that, and it is still regarded with awe."

If *taniwha* means a water-monster the term *karara* (*ngarara* in the north) must also mean the same in some cases, although it is also applied to a kind of big lizard in the south. From a roomful of Natives at Colac Bay the collector could only glean this meagre information :—"A kind of shark is called *taniwha*. There was a *karara* on the Mataau called Kopuwai, and it captured a girl called Kaiamio;" but they knew of no other *karara*, nor did they know of Maeroero, *taepo* nor *tipua* in Murihiku, but ghosts (*atua*) were plentiful in many places, they said.

Round near Orawia (which is correctly Orauwea) in a field some rocks can be seen, and these are said to be the petrified remains of a *karara*. It killed men who were out hunting *wekas*, and finally chased a man named Taiari. He ran zigzag to escape it, and it became jammed between two trees and was killed. Another account says its habitat was the west side of Hekeia (Bald Hill). It may be added that on the west side of the Waiau River at Clifden are caves called Te-ana-o-te-karara.

A demon fish lived in a hole in the Whawhapo Creek at Kaka Point. It could turn itself into an eel, a log or a minnow. It had a name which the narrator could not call to memory. A child fell into Lake Kaitiria long ago and disappeared. It was at a spot near where Mrs. Aitcheson now lives, and the people reckoned a demon had got it, hence they called that place Kai-takata (and this is the origin of the name Kaitangata as now given by the *pakeha*, thought the narrator).

The North Island is "The Fish of Maui," and some time after the Tarawera eruption of 1886, Tare Wetere te Kahu, of Otakou, visited the north, and in conversation with Wahanui, of the King Country, said he considered the great fish had become restive and given itself a shake with a result that a scale had flown out through Mount Tarawera, thus creating the eruption.

FAIRIES AND ELVES.

Not all the supernatural beings of the olden Maoris were grim monsters or fierce goblins; the fairies and elves are in a different category. The hill near Palmerston South, known as Puketapu, is sometimes swathed with fog as picnickers who have arranged to ascend it find out to their disappointment. The Maori legend avers that the mists only come on Puketapu when the spirits are holding high revel on its summit and sides. Their flutes and their musical voices gleefully singing and calling to each other can be heard through the white curtain they have imposed between man and themselves. My Maori informant added that curious *pakehas*, as well as inquisitive Maoris in the past, had sometimes tried to "beat the mist" but their endeavours to penetrate the veil of mystery shielding the elves had always been unsuccessful. One man said the fairy people are fond of playing the kind of flute known as *koauau*, and it is a female spirit who plays in the hills near Catlins. He reckoned these elfin musicians came in the canoe "Takitimu," but other natives considered that these spirit people came in a very much earlier canoe.

A FAIRY WOMAN.

Kai-he-raki was a witch woman who lived on the Takitimu Range —not an ugly old witch-hag, but a young and beautiful witch whose comeliness defied Time. She was *tapu*. A man out hunting *wekas* caught her, but the narrator forgot his name. The man said to his captive, "*Taku wahine pai*," and she answered, "*Taku tane pai*." He got his *kauati* out to make a fire to *ta whakumos* or remove the *tapu* from her.   He told her to put her foot on the *kauati* while he worked the *karimarima* on it.   Soon smoke came and a little flame kindled but she threw blood on it, putting it out.   She fled but the man overtook her and coaxed her back.   He wiped the *kauati* carefully and started again on his task, but the fairy woman repeated her previous performance and this time she escaped for good.   That was the only man who ever caught her.   She was seen afterwards high up on the mountains and finally she vanished.

Another account ends: — "The Takitimu Mountains are still haunted.   Kai-he-raki has been seen there in quite modern days."

TOHUKA (WIZARDS).

Merehau, a *tohuka*, who resided usually in the Port Molyneux district was living when the white settlers came.   He was a magician, said one of the collector's informants, and if offended could upset canoes which were out at sea, and he could do other magic.   He had a garden between O-marama and Te Karoro, and he called it Te-au-o-Hatane, which means "the gall of Satan," according to the narrator, who added, " He was not afraid of Satan as he always had his own *taepo* with him," and continued, " The powers of the *tohukas* were wonderful.   Matamata, a priest or prophet of the old times, was appealed to in storms at sea.   The *tohuka* would use a firestick, and say *karakia*, and two whales would come alongside the canoe and keep it from capsizing.   The *tohuka* would give each whale a hair of his head.   Rakitauneke was a famous *tohuka* of old, and had a guardian whale Tu-te-raki-hua-noa, and also sometimes one called Matamata.   One day the former of these whales appeared off Moeraki, and the children cursed it, and its owner in anger sent a tidal wave which drowned them.   The creek they were standing by had been fresh water till then but it has been brackish ever since.   Its name is Ka-wa."

There is a place at Stewart Island which, the collector was told years ago, was called Ringaringa because a Maori had lived there who suffered from leprosy of the hands, but a well-informed *kaumatua* (or elder) says it is named from a famous old wizard, Rikarika, who lived there long ago.

"Te Maraki was a *tohuka*, and was a cousin of Karaki who was the father of Matiaha Tiramorehu.   When Karaki died at Moeraki the people did not observe the proper burial customs, but went on working.   This offended Te Maraki and he brought whales and evil fairy fish roaring on to the land, where later they died.   The people were sorry for their actions, and in answer to their entreaties Te Maraki sent the great fish back to sea alive.   Since then the water, which before that had been fresh, has been salt in the Moeraki creeks."   (For comparison with this narration see "Journal Poly-nesian Society," Vol. XXVII., page 96.)

One of the old men was inclined to rank Rakaihautu as a magician or as an undoubtedly clever man. "Rakaihautu," he said, "was the first of the Waitaha tribe, and he went through the South Island planting some of his tribe at Oreti, some at Molyneux and so on. When he came along and a plain was dry, and he felt thirsty, he stuck in his *ko* (spade) and lo! he had a pool to drink from."

A DREAM AND A LIZARD.

A southern Maori who visited the Hokanui Hills on four annual *weka*-hunting trips (1867-70) tells the following story :—"His brother and he were camped on the Otamaten stream, and one night he dreamt he was fighting a big strong man (the narrator is himself a tall man) and that he finally threw a big stone at this man and killed him. He woke with a start, and his brother asked what was the matter, and he told his dream, and said he would know the place he dreamt about if he saw it. Next day as they were journeying he saw the place. The white men had built a sheep-dip near it. They looked to find the stone of the dream, and not seeing it they dug down and found two big stones one on top of the other, and charcoal and burns underneath. They were astonished and said *karakia*, which the narrator would not repeat or it would lose its *mâna*. Later that day they climbed a peak with a new trig station on top. Near the summit was a rock as big as a cottage, and in a crack facing the N.W. was the biggest lizard he ever saw. It was a *karara* probably two feet long. He picked up a big stone and hit it, and it jumped over the rock. Going round the brothers found it lying on its back, belly up, and they killed it. They lit a fire of scrub, and burning it left, in case other lizards might follow them. They came through the Waimumu Gorge, and reached Tuturau with as many *wekas* as their horses could carry. Old Karaka, a brother of Maiharoa and a man of *mâna*, was there and he told them that gorge was a place of worship where the old *tohukas* used to go. He said it was a good thing they had killed the lizard and so averted the evil of the dream." The narrator considered that the charred place where the two stones were found had been an *ahi-tapu* (sacred fire) in connection with the rites of travellers going that route. A part of that ceremony consisted in lighting a fire and burning a hair of the head.

In the old days, continued the narrator, lizards were kept as pets. One such was found at Motu-kai-puhuka, a clump of bush east of Kaitiria (now called Lake Kaitangata.) It was named Te-horo-mokai but it got away after some time, and was last seen in the creek Te-wai-a-kiri near there. A small ridge there is named after this celebrated pet. The narrator further said that some of the old Maoris ate lizards but he had no particulars of it. (See "Trans. N.Z. Inst." Vol. VII., p. 295.)

THE TIPUA AND PUKUTUORA.

"Up at Wanaka," said one of the old men, "is an island called Te Pae-karara. There is also another island called Taki-karara after a man who had a fishing station at the lake which was called Taumanu-o-Taki-karara. He stood on a clump of vegetation on a point of land, and one day the point floated away with a noise like a bird. Unknown to him there was a *tipua* under it, and it is said to still drift about. This is probably what started the story about the floating island. Taki-karara left the district as it was too uncanny for him."

Tipua is translated as a "goblin, ogre, monster, demon, fairy, spirit," so there is a wide choice of meanings. Mr. D. Monro, writing in 1844, says," "a floating island is said to sail about on one of the lakes at the source of the Molyneux." Huruhuru's map, drawn for Shortland, in 1844, says of Lake Hawea, "Here is a floating island shifting its position with the wind," and of a place on Hawea's shores, "Turahuka—the abode of a *tipua*." The question now remains— although an island in Wanaka is named Taki-karara, should not the floating island Taumanu-o-Taki-karara be located in Hawea, in accordance with Huruhuru's statement? The collector will endeavour to ascertain this point later on.

Mr. Monro also writes:—"The *pukatuola* is another wonderful animal of the southward, told of by the old men. Under a different name he is heard of in the north. A gigantic animal of the lizard species, most dangerous to humanity." The information the collector received was that the *pukutuora* was a kind of aquatic monster, and that one of them haunted Lake Wakatipu. Rawiri te Awha who guided a white party to the lake in January, 1859, was very much afraid to venture near the edge of the lake after dark lest the demon, which he called *pukutuola*, should seize him to his destruction.*

RAKAU-TIPUA.

The collector again has recourse to the interesting notes of Mr. James Cowan for the following item :—"At Te Muka stood the tree called 'Hine-paaka'—a *kahikatea* tree. It was *he rakau-māna-tapu* (a sacred tree) and was fenced round. Of this tree strange tales are told. A *pakeha* chopped it down but on returning to cut it up he found it standing erect again. Its god had raised it. No one could fell it ; no one could burn it. After all the bush around it had been felled and burnt it still stood unharmed."

* The Puku-tuora is, perhaps, identical with the Tuoro of the north. The Maoris describe this mythical animal (or fish) as being like a very large eel with a great lump in its tail. It was said to be eight or ten feet long, and as thick as a man's body. It gave chase to any one approaching the lagoons in which it lived, and the only way the Maoris had of escaping it was to cross land off which the fern had been burnt.—EDITOR.

The collector has heard rumors of bewitched trees which could move from place to place. So far he has no particulars of such, but his notes mention one or two trees which, although not in the miraculous category, may be mentioned here. One old man said, "There is a *totara* tree at the mouth of the Pou-mahaka (Pomahaka) River named Raki-ihia because that great chief camped under it and caught a lot of eels there. It is on the south side of the Pomahaka where it joins the Molyneux. A big *totara* tree grew close to a rocky face near the Mataura River below East Gore. Its name was Ota-karamu, but how it got that name I do not know. The hills round there are now called by that name. The *pakeha* cut that tree down." Another old man said:—"The tree Rata cut down for a canoe was a *totara*. This tree does not grow in *Kanaka* islands, so what land would it be? It is the chief of the forest trees and must be very ancient as it was the son of Mumuhako in the days of the gods."*

MAORIS VERSUS SEALERS.

The conflicts of the white sealers with the native inhabitants form an exciting chapter of early southern history, and were mentioned by some of the old men. One related these incidents:—"Up about Arawhata or Okahu (Jackson's Bay) on the West Coast was a *kaika* (village) with perhaps 200 or 300 inhabitants. The sealers were then at Arnett's Point further north than the *kaika*, and one night some canoes went up to the sealing station on a raid to try and acquire some of the white man's treasures. The Europeans were alert, however, and fired on them, but without killing anyone. In the scuffle the only man killed was a white man, one Perkins by name. The Maoris returned to their home and some time after the sealers, among whom was the famous Chaseland, pulled in to the shore fronting the *kaika*, and in revenge shot some of the natives from the boats. They then landed and slaughtered all who did not escape into the bush. When Chaseland was roused he became a frenzied fiend. Among his other acts he seized a child, Ramirikiri, whose father and mother had been killed, and dashed her head on a rock and left her for dead. After the sealers had done all the mischief they could they left and the surviving natives crept out of the bush and returned to their desolate homes. They found the little girl living and revived her and she died at Colac, an old woman, some fifteen or sixteen years ago. Often in past years did I hear her tell Chaseland what a savage brute he was when he was

---

* This refers to the story of the building of the celebrated canoe called Manu-ka-rere, which was hewed out from a tree in the forest of which Rata-i-te-wao was the guardian. The Rarotongans say the tree was a *Maota-mea* (which grows in Samoa), and that the tree was growing in the island of Kuporu, i.e., Upolu of Samoa. See this "Journal," Vol. XXVIII., p. 140, par. 270. This shows how incidents occurring in other countries become localized.—EDITOR.

young, and she would rebuke him for his part in the massacre. Chaseland did not like it but he had nothing to say in self-defence. But this is not the end of the story of the cruel deeds done them. The sealers pulled round to Milford Sound and there met natives from the south. The Maori name of Anita Bay is Tauraka-o-Hupokeka because the old chief named Hu-pokeka used to come round there for greenstone. These people were ignorant of the row between the sealers and the Westland natives, and they had done the sealers no harm, yet they were killed without mercy. The victims had only Maori weapons, and were shot down like rabbits. Hu-poheka was shot while standing on a rock in Anita Bay, and such of his people as were still living were placed in a canoe and towed by the sealers round to Whareko, the next bay south of Milford; and there to finish the sport the canoe with its helpless crew was let go in the surf. The breakers dashed it to pieces, and not a soul was left living."

FURTHER ATROCITIES.

"At Paringa, on the West Coast," said another of the old men, "the sealers killed some seals, and wanting to go after others they told the Maoris who were there to skin the seals and to do what they liked with the carcases. The sealers having said this departed after more seals. Unfortunately the language they had used was not plain and the natives did not properly understand it, so the Maoris made a big fire and singed the hair off the seals as they usually did. When the sealers returned they were very angry at what had been done, and they pulled their boat a little way out from the shore and fired at the people, killing one and breaking the arm of a chief named Kahaki. They then made off. The Maoris walked overland to Otago Heads where they considered the matter. A party left for Stewart Island to obtain revenge on some sealing gang or other, and eventually they caught and killed some white men at Murderers' Cove on South Cape Island. This is maybe, where the girl threw the cape over Jimmy the Boy. Wahia, a chief from Otago Heads, stopped the killing by saying they had had enough revenge and to fight no more. The Europeans playing tricks on the native women made trouble sometimes."

Another aged man said in passing:—"At Murderers' Cove on Taukiepa (South Cape Island) a massacre took place. Only two, a woman and her child, were saved and she hid when the crew were being killed. She was either a European or *Kanaka* woman, and the child and she were rescued by a later boat of sealers. As regards Caddell, or Jimmy the Boy, I think he acted as interpreter when peace was made at Rakituma (Preservation Inlet) between the Europeans and Maoris, and then he went over to Sydney with his own race."

The late Hon. Tame Parata said to the collector:—"At Whare-akeake (Murdering Beach) the Maoris and sealers had a fracas. Matahaere (the father of Rimurapa) although a small man seized a sealer and began carrying him, and calling on his people to come and kill the man. While they were struggling the boat escaped, leaving a boy Jimmy, and a *Kanaka* from Calcutta named Te Anu as captives. The only *pakeha* killed was the one on the back of Matahaere. The two prisoners were taken to Rakiura (Stewart Island). A girl threw a mat over the boy to save him, but I do not know her name. Jimmy was given a wife named Pi, but they had no children. Te Anu married a woman and had a son called George Turi, but no descendants are now living. Te Anu lived at Colac Bay where I can remember him. Jimmy went over to Sydney in the end and never returned. In regard to the killing in 1817, it was at Hobartown Beach, and was another affair altogether."

SWIMMING.

The question of acquatic sports cropped up in conversation with the old men, and here is what they said:—" When a Maori swam, with his shoulders out, we called it, ' *He kau tu.*' Sometimes the young people would assemble on the bank and one would call out '*ka ruku taua,*' and they would all dive together."

" There were two kinds of swimming our old people did as far as I know. One was with the body upright and working the legs, and the other was on the side with only the side of the head showing. At Ruapuke there were no surf beaches. The people swam in fresh-water lagoons; the men and women bathed together."

" Swimming was called *kau*. The younger people would bathe in the sea; the older ones preferred the warmer water of the lagoons. At Ruapuke there was no bathing in the open sea—the people bathed in the Tau-o-te-maku lagoon but not in the one called Wai-o-to-karire." (It was haunted—see *supra*.)

" The Rapuwai people when swimming lay on their bellies with their elbows close to their sides, and hit the water with their hands—hence their name. The old Maori way was to swim like a walk in the water with the water up to the armpits. You worked with your legs and elbows, and it was surprising how fast one could go. This style was called *kau-po*."

" When I was a boy I saw three kinds of Maori swimming—*kau-tu*, swimming upright; *kau-tahi*, swimming lying on the side; and *kau-tuara*, swimming lying on the back."

SURF-BATHING.

At least four of the old men mentioned the sport of surfing, as follows:—" The young Maoris would swim out with a short board, put it under the chest and shoot in on the waves. I remember round at Kakararua (Hunt's Beach, Westland) we were at it, and a white man named Baker would try it. He was a big, heavy man, and when he came in his board struck the shore and almost stunned him. His chest was rather severely hurt."

"The board used in surfing was called a *papa*, and it requires certain practice to use it. You must keep the end of it up just as you reach the beach or it will dig into the sand and perhaps break your ribs. The board was about four feet long perhaps, and came in like an arrow. I was round at the West Coast diggings, and the beaches there are very suitable for it. Another sport was when the boys would take a *tawai* (a kind of canoe) out and come in through the surf. They would capsize sometimes but that was all the more fun."

"I never saw the sport of surfing, but know that a *papa* or surf-board was used. I have heard that in the whaling days old Takata-huruhuru went surfing in the bay at Port Molyneux. He was a descendant of the people who came south in the Makawhiu canoe."

The late Tare te Maiharoa said :—"Take kelp off the rocks and dry it as for *pohas* or kelp bags [to preserve birds in]. Take two of these bags and tie them together about two feet apart. Blow them up, and having got them out beyond the surf, put one on each side of you from the armpits to the hips, lie on the flax connecting them, and come in with the breakers. It is fine sport and you cannot drown. This was an old pastime at Moeraki, Waikouaiti, and other good beaches, and was called *para*. (He pronounced it pālă.) In the old Maori days there were very few sharks about—they have only come in any numbers since the European fishermen throw the fish-heads back into the sea."

The names *papa* and *para* are interesting. The collector looked up Tregear's Dictionary, and in it he notes that in Hawaii a surf-board is called *papa*, and in Tahiti it is named *papahoro*. As for *para* the nearest appropriate meaning seems to be "the half of a tree which has been split down the middle" (and hence may be cut down into a surf-board) but perhaps Maori scholars could help to explain the term *para*.

TATTOOING.

Wishing to know about tattooing in the south, the collector asked about it and received these replies :—"The usual name for tattooing was *moko*, and the work of tattooing was called '*ta ki te moko*.' Some of the old people, I remember, were tattooed, but no one has been for many years now."

"The old man who brought me up was tattooed on one side of his face only—a thing we called *kane* or *kawe*.* Old Mrs. Paina at Colac,

* Kauae.—Editor.

was tattooed with two straight lines across her face with dots in the middle, but I do not know the name of that kind of tattooing." †

"Tattooing in straight lines is a very old way and is called *tuhi*. We call writing nowadays *tuhituhi*. The usual name of tattooing was *moko*, but the different tribes had different styles. That done on one side of the face from nose to forehead was called *tiwhana*, a pattern scroll all over the face was called *huritua*, while tattooing on the hips was *repe*."

"My father was tattooed in a single line across one cheek from ear to nose. This was called *tuhi*, although the ordinary face tattoo was called *moko*. He was tattooed on the arms also, and this we called *tiatia*. Old Koraka was tattooed on one side of his face only, and this made him look fierce. His body was tattooed in the *tiatia* fashion down to the waist, so that when he cast off his *kakahu* (cloak) and possibly his *maro* (waist-cloth) also—when fighting — the tattooing would show. The word *tiatia* really means 'pierced,' but it was applied to that tattooing."

JOTTINGS.

Tu-mataueka. In Mr. S. Percy Smith's "Maori History and Traditions of the Taranaki Coast," at page 537, we read of the murder at Kapiti of the southern chief Tu-mataueka. When news of this reached Ruapuke a descent was made on Tutaeka-wetoweto (Lord's River, Stewart Island) where two North Island Maoris were killed in retaliation. My informant said, "There is a beach at the mouth of Lord's River called Ka-one-o-Whitiora, after a Thames native who was killed there in revenge for the murder of Tu-mataueka, a brother of Haereroa Toheti, at Kapiti Island. Whitiora was with a *pakeha* called 'Scotch John,' who was building a boat. His brother, Ueka-nuka, was also killed, but another Maori escaped. Their father afterwards came down to Otakou and got some greenstone as *utu* " (or payment).

Turihuka. In the "Memoirs of the Polynesian Society," Vol. IV., page 242, we read that Turihuka, the wife of Tamatea, died (about 1350 A.D.) on a high ridge in the South Island (presumably in the Waitaki region from the narrative). In retailing some of the nomenclature of the lakes districts, an aged southerner said, "A big hill which the Europeans call 'Old Woman's Hill,' was called Turihuka after a woman who died there long ago." He was referring to the mountain which the surveyors named Breast Hill. It is 5,146 feet high, and lies close to Lake Hawea on the eastern side. This, to the collector's mind, identifies it as the place where the wife of Tamatea died. That Tamatea visited there is quite probable as he

† Probably *moko-kuri*.—EDITOR.

was evidently a great explorer and traveller, for his name is associated in tradition with Te Rua-o-te-moko, Takitimu Mountains, Dome Mountains, Waimea Plains, West Coast Sounds, etc., so it is likely he visited the lakes and also the Waitaki River.

Te Rua-o-te-moko is the Maori name of the densely wooded and mountainous country between the Waiau River and the Fiords. It was the retreat of broken tribes but, it may be noted in passing, these people are described as men, not as elves or phantoms as would probably be the case were the traditions ancient. The name of this vast tract of rugged land is sometimes given as Te Rua-o-te-moa but the former name is more probably correct, as it is said to have been named in commemoration of Tamatea having pits (*rua*) dug to get pigment for tattooing (*moko*) when he explored the Waiau country.

Te Au-kukume was the name of a *kaika* south of the Taieri mouth; it was a fishing camp of Te Raki in modern days. This is a name of some significance in Kati-Mamoe circles for Te Au-kukume was the wife of Hotu-Mamoe, after whom the tribe was named.

Timaka. "At Tautuku Beach there is an old burial ground," wrote the late Mr. W. H. S. Roberts, "in which are several Maori graves. At the head of one is a slab of Australian cedar, with the inscription: 'Sacred to the memory of Temuc who departed this life September 25th, 1846.'" One of my informants said, "Timaka was a woman who died at Tautuku and was buried in the whalers' cemetery there. Her mother, Kiwi, had died near Kaitangata and was buried in a *hapua* (lagoon) there known as Te Karohe. A man was fishing in that lagoon, and poking a stick under an overhanging bank her skeleton came up, and it was then buried in a landslip near Stirling. A boy named Temu died about the same time. He was out with an eeling and birding party, and going out alone failed to return. Search was made, and his body was found stone dead and was taken down to Port Molyneux and buried. The cause of death was unknown. This sudden fatality occurred near the falls on the Kaihiku River. The word 'Temuc' on the slab should be Timaka."

Haki-te-kura. The fact that this celebrated lady swam across Lake Wakatipu was mentioned in these articles (Vol. XXVI., page 83) but one of the old men has given further details. She swam from about where Queenstown now is, and apparently she must have set out in darkness, for she steered her course by Cecil and Walter Peaks whose tops in the dawning light she watched twinkling and winking at her like two eyes, hence their name Ka-kamu-a-Haki-te-kura. She landed on Refuge Point and lit a fire, and that is why it is known to the Maoris as Te-ahi-a-Haki-te-kura.

The voice. Either the voices mentioned were exceptionally stentorian, the hearing of the Maoris extremely keen, or the localities possess great acoustic properties if the following *bona fide* narration by an aged Maori is accurate. "The celebrated Kati-Mamoe chief Raki-ihia had a voice that could be heard from Wharepa right over to the hills east of Kaitiria (Lake Kaitangata). In case you scarcely credit this, I may mention that my brother's voice was once heard at a distance of eight miles. He was standing on the hill Uhi-whitau (near Kaitangata) and his voice carried to Akatorea. Raki-ihia had a very powerful voice, and he could shout at Wharepa and be heard at Uhi-whitau."

Obituary. It is with regret that the collector notes the narrowing of the circle of his aged native friends. Hone te Paina, Ratimira te Au, Wiremu te Awha, of Colac Bay, and Tuhituhi te Marama, of Bluff, have all gone during the last year or two. Tuhituhi was a brother of John Topi te Patuki, and the newspapers gave his age as 110, although the collector figured it out as about 90. He and the late Mrs. Gilroy (died at Bluff, aged 86) gave much valuable information about ancient Maori place-names. There died the other day at Puketeraki, Ria Tikini, aged 105, she being seventeen years old in 1831, when Te Rauparaha captured Kaiapohia. The collector called on her in 1915, but found her very deaf. She was tattooed in the *tuhi* style, each side of her face being adorned with two straight lines from temple to mouth and from mouth to ear. Tare te Maiharoa has passed away in South Canterbury in his 70th year. He gave much information that has appeared in these articles, and was a great stickler for accuracy, he was always most anxious that the correct history should be preserved. The collector always found him a mine of information and was looking forward to further interviews, but a fall from a stack cut short a life that, as far as health and activity went, seemed destined to continue for years. He was the greatest authority left on the Waitaha lore, and his death leaves an irreparable blank.

(To be continued.)

NIUĒ FOLK-LORE.

By G. N. Morris.

THE STORY OF THE VEKA AND THE KALE.

THE home of a Kale was in a cave which is known as Anakale, and a Veka lived at Tukaiavi nearby. The Kale went to visit the Veka but on arriving at Tukaiavi there was a quarrel between the two. The Kale said, " The long-leaved banana and the sugar-cane are for me alone. For you there is plenty of filth where the flies gather in the open spaces." The Veka was angry at the insulting words, and he sought a plan to kill the Kale. The Veka went down to the reef to a place where a Clam lived, some twelve feet from the foot of the high cliff at Tukaiavi. The Veka put his feet near the Clam-shell, and there danced and sang to entice the Kale to come down from the top of the cliff where he was sitting. This was the Veka's song :—

> Come, come O Kale, come, come O Kale,
> Here is a fine place for your feet,
> Come here and be tickled,
> O come and be tickled!

So the Kale came down to the Veka and the Clam, and put his feet into the Clam-shell which closed upon them and held them fast. Then the Kale cried and screamed to the Veka for help, struggling this way and that to free himself but unable to do so. The Veka ran up the cliff and danced in his gladness. He sang a second song in mockery :—

> O Kale, O Kale,
> Now chew your sugar-cane,
> Now eat your bananas,
> You tried to fool me into eating filth,
> O filthy Kale, O filthy Kale!

But afterwards the Veka began to be sorry for the Kale, and he sang another song to help him to free his feet :—

> Rise quickly, O Tide,
> Rise quickly, O Tide!

And the tide came in and the mouth of the Clam opened so that the
feet of the Kale were freed. He came up with an incoming wave
which the Veka did not see, but he was surprised to see the Kale on
the top of the cliff. The Kale caught hold of the Veka and struck
him on the head with a branch of the Toi tree. The Veka begged
for forgiveness, calling the Kale by his honorific name, Manatafeiki,
but the Kale would not forgive the Veka and continued to strike him,
splitting his head in several places so that the marks of the strokes
and the blood can be seen to this day. Afterwards they made another
agreement about the food. The Veka agreed to let the Kale have
the bananas and the sugar-cane, but the open places, where the flies
live, were to be for himself. That is to say filth was to be the Veka's
portion.

NOTES.—The Veka (Maori, Weka) is long extinct in Niuē having
been exterminated by wild cats and dogs. The bird was evidently
not particularly dainty as to its food.

The Kale. This bird is still plentiful and is similar to the New
Zealand Pukeko. It plays havoc with the sugar-cane and banana
plantations, and is the only bird not protected by law in Niuē.

Tukaiavi is the place where the Government Jetty at Alofi now
stands. The cliff is just to the north of the jetty.

The native version was written by Harry Lupo, Government
Interpreter, from information obtained from Togiafulu, Uea and
others.

KO E TALA KE HE KALE MO E VEKA.

KO e kaina ne nofo ai e Kale, ko e ana, ti ui ai e ana ia, ko
Anakale. Ko Tukaiavi e kaina he Veka, ti fano e Kale ke
feleveia mo e Veka. Kua hoko atu a Kale, ke he kaina a Veka, ko
Tukaiavi, ne taufetoko e Kale mo e Veka, ti pehe e Kale: "Ka
lauleleva mo e lau malikalika, haaku a ia; ka momolago he malamalaega, haau ia." Ti ita e Veka he kupu kelea e Kale mo e kumi
lagatau ke mate ai e Kale. Ti hifo e Veka ke he uluulu i tahi ke he
mena ne tu ai e Gege; hogofulu ma ua e futu he vaha mamao mo e
pokoahu, e mena ne tu ai e Gege; ko Tukaiavi e higoa he maga tahi
ia. Ti uta e ia e tau hui haana mo e fakaeleele he gutu Gege i tafo
mo e koli; ti uhu ai e Veka a lologo ke fakaohoohoaki e Kale ne nofo
he feutu ke hifo age. Pehe e lologo :—

<blockquote>
"Kale, Kale, ō hau ke
"tamai nove fakatu
"he mena malie ē
"nukua maineine noa
"kua maineine noa."
</blockquote>

NIUĒ FOLK-LORE.

By G. N. MORRIS.

THE STORY OF THE VEKA AND THE KALE.

THE home of a Kale was in a cave which is known as Anakale, and a Veka lived at Tukaiavi nearby. The Kale went to visit the Veka but on arriving at Tukaiavi there was a quarrel between the two. The Kale said, "The long-leaved banana and the sugar-cane are for me alone. For you there is plenty of filth where the flies gather in the open spaces." The Veka was angry at the insulting words, and he sought a plan to kill the Kale. The Veka went down to the reef to a place where a Clam lived, some twelve feet from the foot of the high cliff at Tukaiavi. The Veka put his feet near the Clam-shell, and there danced and sang to entice the Kale to come down from the top of the cliff where he was sitting. This was the Veka's song:—

> Come, come O Kale, come, come O Kale,
> Here is a fine place for your feet,
> Come here and be tickled,
> O come and be tickled!

So the Kale came down to the Veka and the Clam, and put his feet into the Clam-shell which closed upon them and held them fast. Then the Kale cried and screamed to the Veka for help, struggling this way and that to free himself but unable to do so. The Veka ran up the cliff and danced in his gladness. He sang a second song in mockery:—

> O Kale, O Kale,
> Now chew your sugar-cane,
> Now eat your bananas,
> You tried to fool me into eating filth,
> O filthy Kale, O filthy Kale!

But afterwards the Veka began to be sorry for the Kale, and he sang another song to help him to free his feet:—

> Rise quickly, O Tide,
> Rise quickly, O Tide!

And the tide came in and the mouth of the Cave opened so that the bed of the Kalo were food. He came up with an incoming wave stick the Veka did not set, but he was surprised to see the Kalo on the top of the cliff. The Kalo caught hold of the Veka and struck him on the head with a branch of the Ti tree. The Veka begged for forgiveness, calling the Kalo by its honorific name, Manutaleki, but the Kalo would not forgive the Veka and continued to strike him, splitting his head in several places so that the marks of the strokes and the blood can be seen to this day. Afterwards they made another agreement about the food. The Veka agreed to let the Kalo have the bananas and the sugar-cane, but the open places, where the flies live, were to be for himself. That is to say filth was to be the Veka's portion.

NOTES.—The Veka (Maori, Weka) is long extinct in Niue having been exterminated by wild cats and dogs. The bird was evidently not particularly dainty as to its food.

The Kalo. This bird is still plentiful and is similar to the New Zealand Pukeko. It plays havoc with the sugar-cane and banana plantations, and is the only bird not protected by law in Niue.

Tukaiavi is the place where the Government Jetty at Alofi now stands. The cliff is just to the north of the jetty.

The native version was written by Henry Lega, Government Interpreter, from information obtained from Togiaduki, Usa and others.

KO E TALA KE HE KALO MO E VEKA.

KO e kaina ne nofo ai e Kalo, ko e ana, ti ai ai a uta ia, ko Anakalo. Ko Tukaiavi e kaina he Veka, ti fano e Kalo ke folevela mo e Veka. Kua heko atu a Kalo, ke he kaina a Veka, ia Tukaiavi, ne taufetoko e Kalo mo e Veka, ti pehe e Kalo: "Ka lauleleva mo e lau malikaliko, haaku a ia; ka tonudogo he malamalaoga, haau ia." Ti ita e Veka ke kupa helea a Kalo mo e kuai laguloa ke uncle ai e Kalo. Ti kite e Veka ke he nimelu i tahi ke he tonoi ne fai ai e Gogo, langohia mo ia e hana ke mama taumau mo e pokoulu, e nava ke fai ai e Gogo; ko Tukaiavi e kupa ke maga tahi ia. Ti uta a ia e tau hui haana ma e lalewaloa ke gutu Gogo; folo mo e halli; ti uta ai e Veka a Lago ke lave oneadaahi a Kalo ne nofo ke tonu ha mile aga. Pehe e Lago:—

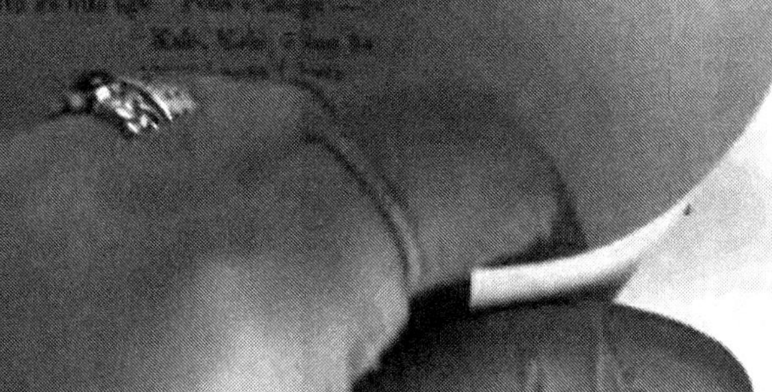

Ti hifo e Kale ke he mena ne nofo ai e Veka mo e Gege, ti faka-olo e ia e hui ke loto he Gege ti kati ai e gutu he Gege ti apitia ai haana hui. Ti ui atu e ia ke he Veka ke hau ke lagomatai a ia hakua tagi fakatutu a ia, kapa ki he, kapa ki ko, ai maeke. Fakakopa a Veka hake nofo he feutu mo e koli he fiafia ti uhu foki ni he Veka taha lologo fakafiu. Pehe lologo :—

> " Kale, Kale, ō gau ho to
> " kai ho futi fakavaiaki
> " ti vala te.   Tetekale, tetekale."

Kua mole ia ti tupu ai e fakaalofa a Veka kia Kale, ti uhu ai e ia e lologo ke maeke ai e hui he Kale.   Pehe lologo :—

> " Tahi hokohoko vave.
> " Tahi hokohoko vave."

Kua hoko e tahi ti mafa e gutu he Gege, maeke agataha e hui he Kale.   Ti hake a ia he peau, ai kitia he Veka, ka e ofo ne Veka kua hoko hake tuai e Kale.   Ti tapaki e ia e Veka, tamai e la Toi fahi aki e ulu, ka e ole atu e Veka kia Kale pehe : " Manatafeiki, Mana-tafeiki " (ko e taha higon lilifu ia he Kale he vaha tuai).   Ka e fahi ni he Kale e Veka ti maihiihi loga haana ulu; ko e mena ia ne avaava ai haana ulu mo e kula he toto ke hoko mai ke he vaha nai. Mole ia ti liu taute ai foki e laua e pulega ke he tau mena kai. Pehe a Veka: Ka lauleleva mo e lau malika, ha Kale a ia, ko e futi a ia mo e to; ka momolago he malamalaega, ha Veka a ia, ko e te a ia.

Ko e mena ne tu ai e Gege, ha he mena kua toka ai e uaafu ai nai, ke he faahi tokelau.

NOTE.—The Hindus have a very similar story to this, but I cannot place my hand on the reference.—EDITOR.

THE MAORI BELIEF IN THE SUPERNATURAL POWERS OF CERTAIN AXES.

THERE are many references in past numbers of this "Journal" to some of the celebrated stone axes of former times, which were supposed to be endowed with supernatural powers; they were in fact looked on as gods. These notes are intended to show that a very similar belief was in very ancient times common to other races. But first it may be as well to recall the traditional history of the two most famous of these Maori axes.

These two axes were named "Te Awhio-rangi" and "Whiro-nui." An attempt at the translation of these names may be made, and it will be seen that they both embrace the same general idea. The first name means "The heaven-encircler," the second "The great twirler." And when we learn the purpose for which, according to tradition, they were first used, the meanings seem somewhat appropriate. The axes are first mentioned in Maori tradition in connection with the earliest dawn of their history and mythology. After Rangi-nui (the Sky-father) and Papa-tua-nuku (the Earth-mother) were separated by their offspring the Whanau-rangi, the minor gods, it was found that they clung together in lingering embrace which prevented the full enjoyment of the light of the world by the gods, and to a certain extent nullified the object of the separation of their parents, which was to allow of their offspring proceeding forth from the æons of darkness represented by the close embrace of their parents, to the *Whai-ao* and *Te Ao-marama*—the world of being and of light. These celebrated axes were then used to sever the arms of the two parents, and cut the "props" which were erected—principally by the god Tāne—to support the Sky-father in the position he now occupies as represented by the dome of the sky.

According to Maori belief these same axes were brought away from the Father-land—the site of creation—and accompanied the migrations in their wanderings in the Pacific to the time when one of the migrations that had charge of them settled down in Tahiti at a date which is somewhat uncertain, but probably about the tenth century of our era.

The next we hear of the axes is when the "Takitimu" canoe, on her voyage from Tahiti to New Zealand about the year 1350, met with a gale of wind at that part of the ocean called "Tuahiwi-nui-o-Hine-moana" (The-great-ridge-of-Lady-ocean), when the same axes were used by the priests to "slay" the gale. In our "Memoirs," Vol. IV., p. 224, is this statement: "When the canoe arrived at this place the priests took the axes 'Te Awhio-rangi' and 'Whiro-nui' from the depository in the stern of the canoe, where they were kept in a calabash named 'Ahuahu-te-rangi.' These two axes were very *tapu*, and were used in the *poipoi* (or 'waving ceremony') offered to the gods Kahu-kura (and others). Tupai (the priest) took hold of 'Whiro-nui' axe, and the following is the *karakia* (invocation) used by those priests to 'fell' the easterly seas of Tahiti." Then follows the long invocation in which the names of the axes are mentioned more than once. After this the narrative goes on (p. 226): "Then were the two axes used to chop the waters by Te Rongo-patahi and Tupai (priests); and thus were the seas severed and spread abroad..." Herein we observe the supernatural powers accredited by the Maoris to these celebrated axes.

When the migration above referred to visited the Whanganui River, they met people of one of the other migrations, and a marriage was arranged between a chief and chieftainess of the two parties, in which the "Awhio-rangi" axe was given to the latter's tribe as a marriage gift (see p. 244, *loc. cit.*). From that time this axe remained as a most valuable property with the Nga-Rauru tribe of Wai-totara. Seven generations ago, during some tribal stress probably, the then custodian, Rangi-taupea, hid the axe away, and it was not discovered until the year 1887, when some great ceremonies accompanied its exhibition to the tribe, as described in this "Journal," Vol. IX., p. 229. The axe is now preserved with the utmost care by the tribe, and is hidden away so that only its guardians know where it is. It is so sacred that no white man has ever been allowed to see it, though a description has been obtained, from which it would appear to be one of the large axes made by the Polynesians, all over the Pacific, from the giant Trydacna shell.

Of course the story of these axes having been used to sever the limbs of the Sky-father and Earth-mother, has been applied to them to give the axes additional *māna*, or power, prestige, etc. But there can be little doubt one, at least, was brought here in the "Taki-timu" canoe in the fourteenth century. About "Whiro-nui" there is some doubt. One account says it was left in Tahiti.

It is tolerable clear from the above that these axes were endowed in the belief of their owners with supernatural powers by which miracles were worked, that in fact they were gods. One of our most learned Maoris says of these axes that they were possessed of *māna-atua*, that is, god-like-powers.

That other races had similar beliefs the following quotation will show. We all know of the most interesting and valuable discoveries made during the last twenty-five years in the island of Crete, in the Mediterranean, during which the ancient Minoan civilization was first brought to light. In a book by Prof. R. M. Burrows published a few

years since entitled "The Discoveries in Crete," p. 113, he remarks
on the sign of the double axe form on many of the building stones in
the ancient ruins of Knossos, and says, "The evidence is overwhelm-
ing from every site in Crete that the double axe, like the sacrificial
'horns of consecration' with which it is often found, was intimately
connected with religious worship; and it is highly probable that, like
the pillar, and less commonly the shield, it was originally regarded
as the visible habitation of the divine spirit. . . . its appearance
finally among the cult-objects in the sacrificial procession on the
sarcophagus from Hagia Iriada (south coast of Crete) is evidence
enough and to spare."

"Starting as a kind of fetish in early Aniconic days, the axe
survived as an object of worship throughout the transitional stages
when the divine spirit first began to be represented in human form . ."

It would not be right to say of the Maori, or indeed of any
Polynesian, that they *worshipped* the axes. Polynesians did not
worship "sticks and stones"; but they addressed the god or spirit
which for the time being, and at the call of the priests, took up their
residence in such things as these sacred axes, and it is possible this
was the attitude of the Minoan people of Crete. This is born out by
the following sentence copied from the article "Crete Archæology,"
in the 11th Edition of the "Encyclopedia Britannica," by Dr. Arthur
Evans. He says, "Trees and curiously shaped stones were also
worshipped, and artificial pillars of wood or stone . . . The essential
feature of this cult is the bringing down of the celestial spirit by
proper incantations and ritual into these fetish objects . . . ." This
exactly describes the attitude of the Polynesian towards their so-called
"idols," of whatever form.

Coming back to the Pacific, we find in Mangaia Island of the
Cook Group, stone axes with the most elaborately carved handles, of
such a form that they never could be used for practical purposes.
They are entirely ceremonial, and were formerly looked on as
possessing god-like powers. Some very fine illustrations of these axes
are to seen in a paper by Dr. Hjalmar Stolpe of Stockholm, entitled
"Evolution in the Ornamental Art of Savage Peoples," a translation
of which, made by the wife of our life member Dr. H. Colley March,
was published in "The Transactions of the Rochdale Library and
Scientific Society" (year not given).

Mr. Elsdon Best in Bulletin No. 4 of the Dominion Museum, in
"The Stone Implements of the Maoris," has some notes on the sacred
character of stone axes. The sacred character of certain stone axes
seems to be a wide spread belief.*

* A reference to "processional axes" in New Guinea may be quoted here:
See p. 334 of "Work and Adventure in New Guinea," by the Rev. J. Chalmers
and Rev. W. Wyatt Gill.

TRADITIONS OF AND NOTES ON THE PAUMOTU OR (TUAMOTU) ISLANDS.

Collected by the Rev. Père Hervé Audran, of Fakahina, Paumotu Islands.*

TRANSLATED FROM THE FRENCH BY B. H. ROCKEL, M. A.

PART V.

(Continued from Vol. XXVIII., page 167.)

FORMER POLITICAL CONDITIONS AT FAKAHINA.

IN the remote past the island was divided into three distinct districts peopled by three families known under the names of (1) Gati-Tane at Gake; (2) Gati-Mahinni at Raro and at Kereteki; (3) Gati-Tekopu (this family probably emigrated to Hao). These three tribes were almost always at enmity and often at war amongst themselves. If by any mischance a member of the Gati-Tane living at Te Matahoa ventured to enter the territory of another tribe, he would certainly be seized and immediately sent to the ovens; such, too, would be the fate of any member of another tribe venturing to enter his district. A trespasser was a prisoner of war. On principle these unfortunates were never spared. The Polynesians knew no mercy so far as the fate of these victims was concerned. According to the testimony of early navigators and of the natives to-day the population of the group was numerous, more vigorous, more industrious, less prone to error and more moral than it is to-day. These facts contradict the law of continuous progress invoked by those scientists who claim for themselves the honour of descent from a simian ancestor, but they are facts all the same. That the race which now inhabits our islands has degenerated more or less under the influence of isolation and of the errors of unbelief, everything, including the beauty and richness of its language, goes to prove. But the most powerful proof lies in the thousand legends which we are gradually discovering, and which are revealing to us the ancient traditions. The investigator is surprised and delighted to find in the midst of a mass of incoherent stories the idea of the immortality of the soul, of judgment after death, of hell,

* We deeply regret to say that the author of these papers fell a victim to the influenza epidemic of late last year. We have reduced this paper considerably as it contained matter outside that ordinarily published by the Society.—EDITOR.

the idea of sacrifice and of prayer, and the memory of a beneficent
superior being who has created men and who, curiously enough considering the prevalence of polygamy, gave the first man one wife, and
one only.[1]

ROYAL DESCENT IN NIUHI.

The ancient history of the Paumotu Islands is in utter confusion,
and the most experienced annalist would find himself helpless and at
a loss in dealing with the subject. The elders have disappeared,
taking into the grave with them the traditions and the greater part of
the ancient songs, which are the sole source for a written history in
these distant isles where writing was unknown. To attempt, then, to
reduce the history of those times of change to the systematic regularity
of present times would be to attempt the impossible. It is useless to
think of establishing a genealogy of kings of these different districts in
the male line of descent, a line of kings who ruled over the whole
island. This idea of a united monarchy would clearly be far from the
reality, while to prove hereditary occupation of the throne would be
an insuperable difficulty. There seem to have been at Fakahina of old
three separate tribes, each with its own king : The Gati-Tane at Te
Matahoa or Gake, the Gati-Mahinui and the Gati-Tekopu in the west
at Raro, and in the south at Kereteki. But these two latter tribes
intermingled and lost their identity, so that while nominally there were
three tibes in the island, there were in reality only two. The Gati-
Mahinui and the Gati-Tekopu joined forces and formed in reality one
tribe, although the Gati-Tekopu supplied several distinguished kings,
amongst these being Maitupoa, Tagihia, Tu-Garue and Maruake. The
latter was chief or king when the Paiore incident took place. The
following is a list of kings who have reigned in Fakahina :—

I.—In the tribe of Gati-Tane.	II.—In the tribe of Gati-Mahinui.
1. Tane-tupu-hoe	1. Mahinui Te Tauira
2. Te-tohu	2. Marere-nui
3. Toa-rere	3. Te-fakahira
4. Te-mapu	4. Rogo-te-kapu
5. Rua-kai-atua	5. Tai-te-ariki
6. Te-ata	6. Tehu
7. Tane	7. Mahinui
Etc.	Etc.

If an average of twenty-two years be allowed for each reign,
Fakahina has had kings only for a period of 154 years.

---

1. I intend shortly to undertake a study of the numerous points of contact
between Polynesian traditions and our knowledge of revealed religion.

RELIGION IN FAKAHINA: MARAES, TAHUAS, OFFICIATING PRIESTS AND THEIR JURISDICTION.

In pagan times Fakahina contained many *marae*, the six chief being:—1 Aehau; 2 Oromea; 3 Ragi-te-tau-noa; 4 Pekai; 5 Vai-tomoana; 6 Tugata.

In the Tuamotu Group the chief officiating priest, who conducted, so to speak, divine worship, and represented the archpriest in our cathedrals, was known as the *kaunuku*. He was a great personage and very holy. Further, he enjoyed the highest privileges. He was exempt from ordinary work and from that forced labour at times so troublesome, such as cooking and the preparation of the turtle, for which the common people were liable. The smoke from the ovens was not to come near him or to touch him. Throughout the whole island there was but one authority (that of the king) superior to his, while at times his influence was as powerful as even that of the king. He alone was responsible for the ordering and carrying out of everything that concerned the celebration of the annual festivals and the performance of the religious ceremonies on the *marae*. All these were under his sole jurisdiction. It was the *kaunuku* whose duty it was to regulate them as he thought fit, provided that he preserved the ancient usages. To the high-priest belonged by right the privilege of taking from the *fare-tini-atua*, corresponding to our tabernacle, the sacred stone, and laying it on the turtle for some minutes before cutting its throat. A few paces distant from the *kaunuku* stood two other officiating priests called *huhuki*, who were his assistants and, so to speak, the deacon and sub-deacon, and consequently of subordinate rank. These latter were not the ordinary priests, but were of royal blood. When the turtle was divided up, the head, *pepenu*, the fat part that surrounds the neck, *genegene*, and the heart, *mafatu*, were always set apart and reserved for the *kaunuku*. The children, young people, old men and the women were rigorously excluded from the *marae*. It was only those of maturer age, say, thirty years or so, who could cross the sacred enclosure, take part in the ceremonies of the cult, and have the right and permission to eat of the turtle.

FAMOUS NIUHIAN VOYAGES.

The islanders still retain the memory of several famous voyages.

1. MARERE:—The undoubted cause of many Polynesian voyages and migrations was the quarrels stirred up on account of women. This was the case with Marere as with many others. He had relations here with Te-kopu-hei-ariki, a woman of royal blood, and from these relations were born two children, Te-fakahira and Tu-te-ragi-nui. On the birth of her son Te-kopu-hei-ariki raised him aloft, according to an ancient custom among the nobility, at the same time singing a new song, of which the following words are still preserved; "Nafea

vau o Te-kopu-hei-ariki toku ariki." Shocked at hearing these words from his wife, and in anger at being deceived in her character, he went on board his canoe and fled to Takume. There he formed a connection with another woman named Te-pogi. By her he had also three children, Puraga, Te-taukupu and Te-fau. But a matrimonial experience similar to his former one caused him to leave Takume. He made for Fagatau, where he made a third alliance, this time with a woman named Mahuru, by whom he had a child named Varoa. The name of Marere's canoe is unknown to-day.

2. TEHU :—This man has remained famous in Fakahina not only because of his numerous long voyages of exploration, but chiefly because he presented his country with fruit-trees and food-plants. As a matter of fact it was he who, on his return from one of his voyages on board of his "Katau," introduced the coconut, the *taro*, the *ape*, etc., into the island. Thus he has become the great benefactor of his countrymen, in whose memories his name is deeply engraved.

3. TE-FAKAHIRA :—Doubtless inheriting the qualities of his father Marere, and especially his love for long and perilous voyages, Te-fakahira too traversed all the seas of the archipelago, and visited Takoto, Re-ao and Hao without reckoning the thousand other islands unknown to us. At Hao he became the father of a son named Te-mauri, whom, on his return, he brought back home with him.

4. TE-MAURI :—After having grown up at Fakahina, and, like his father, smitten with a love for travel and adventure, he set out. He went first to Marekau, where, according to the story, he had three wives, Takua, Vero-matau-toru and Te-rapure-ariki. He then went on to Hao, where he became acquainted with Gahina.

5. FARUIA :—According to tradition this man went as far as Vairatea. He was a colossus and an athlete. He lifted his canoe on to the land, and, with the assistance of his crew, he killed all the inhabitants of the island. It was, no doubt, to avenge this massacre that the inhabitants of all the adjoining islands formed an alliance and, on board of seven canoes, came and made war on him. But he defeated them and killed most of them. He had with him his old father, whom he carefully hid in the tap-roots of a pandanus, strictly charging him not to come out of this hiding-place. But the unfortunate old man hearing that his son was scattering the ranks of his enemies, and that he had killed most of them, moved by compassion or some other feeling, came out of his hole. Misfortune soon overtook him, for some of the enemy in their flight chanced to meet him. He was instantly seized and put to death without mercy. As soon as Faruia heard of this he hastened to the bleeding and still warm body of his father. Stricken with grief he threw himself on the body and gave vent to his sorrow. His enemies taking advantage of the

attitude into which his infatuation had thrown him, killed him in his turn.

6. MARUAKE:—This navigator belongs to more modern times. He went to Takoto and seized the wife of Porutu. Because of his desire to take her off with him to Fakahina, or elsewhere, Porutu in anger struck him a severe blow on the head. The would-be ravisher returned to Fakahina in his wounded condition. There by means of cures and frequent washings he succeeded in healing his broken head. Three wells or water-holes, Te-vai-marigi, Te-vai-totomea and Tamunu, where he performed his frequent ablutions, are still pointed out. Naturally he now had but one idea, to take vengeance on his enemy for the wound he had inflicted, by killing him. To accomplish his aim he went to Takume and to Rairoa to obtain help, and then stood in for Takoto. He killed many of the islanders and among them Porutu. He seized the woman once and for all, and returned to Fakahina with her.

The following are the most famous canoes of the Niuhians:— 1 Pua-te-nukuroa; 2 Te-vai-tau; 3 Houpo; 4 Marama; 5 Tupou; 6 Takau, whose privateer-captain was the celebrated Tehu; 7 Tekoro, which had as its coxswain Te-ata; 8 Torona, Heko, Te-rate-maro, Te-piri.

THE FIRST VISITORS TO FAKAHINA.

1. The first *pahi* (or ocean going canoe) seen at Niuhi, and one of which there still exists a dim recollection, came from the Marquesas. This was a Nuku-Hiva *pahi*, according to the natives. The tradition relates that only one person leaped into the water and came ashore by swimming. This was a woman named Mahuru. Some of the islanders wished to kill her, while others wished to spare her. The latter proposition prevailed, and thus she was saved. Some days later her relatives came to seek her, and she was able to be placed once more on board her own canoe.

2. Such, unfortunately, was not the fate of the Paumotu *pahi* commanded by Manava-rere. This canoe came from the west. The whole numerous crew of fifty were, it seems, massacred and decapitated. The bodies were buried in the *marae* of Katipa, situated beside the open sea, while the heads were hidden in the *marae* of Oromea, close to the lagoon. *Ua taparuhia ratou e to uta.* "They were allured by the dwellers of the island."

This slaughter was carried out by the orders of Te-ragi-heikapu, the ruling chief, who directed the operation in person. Manava-rere besides being an experienced mariner was a man of great physical strength. In this respect he was a worthy match for Te-ragi-heikapu. It seems that when he was about to be captured beside the open sea, he gave a tremendous leap and found himself on the edge of the

lagoon, and then from there on to the offing. However, he was
finally seized by his *maro* and bound. He was securely tied to a large
stone lying in a small lake, *nakana*, where his enemies tried in vain to
kill him. Every morning they went to see if he were not dead.
Now, on each occasion they found him still breathing. One fine day
he said to them : *"Aita vau i higa ia koutou ; te tagata ra i higa vau i
ana o te tagata i tapu i toku gogo pito naku i tapu."* " You cannot kill
me, except by cutting my umbilical-cord ; " an expression, which in
their language, is equivalent to saying that he himself belonged to
Fakahina. Therefore he was spared, and, in due course, became the
father of a numerous line, which reckons no fewer than ten
generations to the present day.

3. The Takahi, a canoe from Fagatau, had a similar experience.
As the inhabitants of Fakahina and of Fagatau are related, the latter
were not molested, but, on the contrary, met with a friendly reception.

4. First visit of Paiore to convert the Tuamotu peoples to civilisation.
On his first visit Paiore was well received at Fakahina. He gathered
the whole population together, and remained with them two or three
days. He was entertained in native fashion, and went away delighted
with his visit.

5. Second visit of Paiore in 1860. Paiore's second visit ended in a
tragedy. His crew was composed of ten or eleven men collected from
various places, for he had with him a representative from nearly all
the other islands.   On this occasion, contrary to his behaviour on his
first expedition, Paiore did not go on shore, but allowed or even ordered
seven of his men to land. This was indiscreet, and at the same time
a grave blunder. He must have seen this afterwards, but then
it was too late. Six of the seven men sent on shore were killed.
Their names and birth-places are as follows :— 1 Tapahiha of
Fakarava ; 2 Mahiri of Makemo ; 3 Taumata of Taenga ; 4 Tu-
ata of Nihiru ; 5 Te-hei of Takoto ; 6 Tahoro of Reao. The
seventh was Turia of Makemo, who owed his escape to his fleet-
footedness. Throwing off to his pursuing foe also his vest and hat,
he managed in his mad flight to Gake, to outdistance his pursuer,
throw himself into the sea, and reach Paiore's cutter by swimming.
He, as an eye-witness and a participant in the bloody affair, related
the whole story with all its horrible details to Paiore. Under his
very eyes Paiore's sailors were pursued, captured and killed, one after
the other, on the reef.

ANCIENT NIUHIAN SONGS.

FAATARA NO TE ARIKI RA MAHINUI TE-TAUIRA E TIA I FAKAHINA.

Fanau a raro, ko Mahinui Te-Tauira: ko Niuhi kiukiu, nauuau, ragitaka mahiti ake i raro te aka o te henua, ka tagi te pahu ko te rutu ko Mapuna iavaku ki mua i o Rogo. Hopukia te moana, kauria i te moana, te moana uriuri, te moana kerekere, ka higa ki uta i te henua, heuea, te papa ka gatata, Porutu tautua, Porutu tauaro.

Kopekahaga ia o Te-Kura ma te moho ki mua i o Rogo, topa te piri o Manogi, tiraga ruperupe, ki reira, vaitorotoro knriri tagihoro e tagi te avaroa, e tagi te taha o Vavau.

Kapu ko teie Ariki. Taku tahua Kupakupa, ko te tahua ko te vai marigi Maregai ko keha. Tika i a mari Tagaroa ki te tua o te ragi, kapu ko teia Ariki.

Ara mapuhia, Taketake mai Hiva, kapu ko teia Ariki. Mau atu to maro ki mua i a Hau, koutu e tere, kapu to teia Ariki ko Mahinui Te-Tauira, turuturu ki mua i o Rogo ka haruru tana kopu, mitikia tana ta haohoa, ka ririu, tua ka ririu aro. Maeva, ko te pu ko te pahu, ko te raukava ka pupuha nukunuku ma te fakiteragi matereua. Maeva te Ariki. Maeva Te-uho te Ariki ko Mahinui Te-Tauira.

FAATARA NO MARUAKE.

Karihi e karihi nui a kae koi te matau o Rogo fatia fatia e, tara e tara, tahuri mai kona tena te potiki, toa e toa e, toa e. Te hetu ma te marama tena potiki, toa e, toa e kapu korero kapu vanaga tena potiki, toa e toa e, toa e. Kapu iti kapu ai, tena te potiki toa e ko Havaiki, ko Havaiki.

Havaiki tinihi koi ruga, Havaiki tinihi koi raro, piri mataitai ma te nariki, te huru o Te-kura ma te nariki, te mata o Te-kura ma te nariki, te hope o Te-kura ma te nariki, piri mataitai ma te nariki, maro kapu koi ruga, maro kapu koi raro, maro e kapu e Ariki.

FAATARA NO HOGA TATAOA.

Fanaua i raro ko Hoga Tataoa, ko Niuhi paka koru, takurua ki te hekeheke ko purepure, i hiti kapu ko te ie Ariki. Ko te iho, tena kahapu, mai kona, ka turaha mai kona, ka purero mai kona, ka haere mai kona, ka haere mai kona, ko purepure i hiti, ka fanau ai te Ariki Tataoa.

The following list of the all too scanty flora of Fakahina may be
of interest both to the philologist and to the botanist:—

TREES AND PLANTS.

Ancient Paumotu Language.	Modern Names.	Scientific Names.
Niu	Hakari	Palma nucifera
Mahame	Gatae	Pisonnia ombellifera
Piupiu	Geogeo	Tournefortia argentea L.
Kokuru	Uu	Suriana Maritima L.
Tou	Tou	
Gagie	Mikimiki	Pemphis acidula Forster
Viri	Tima (fara)	
Nono	Hora	
Putamagomago	Putarau	Sesbania grandiflora, Pers.
Gohegohe	Kikipa	
Koporoporo		
Gapata		Scevola konigi
Rama		
Kahia		Guettaada speciaso

HERBS.

Mauku		Lepturus respens R.B. (Graminée)
Nanamu		
Mahihi		
Runa		
Parahirahi		Heliotropium anomalum H. et A.
Toroariki	Gaio	
Nau	Horahora	Lepidium piscidum
Vaianu	Ogaoga	
Kainoka		
Maukutoga		

THE FAUNA.

THE TURTLES :

Common Turtles.		Rare Species.
Kurahiva	Topitopi	
Marega	Tumimi	Mokamoka
Kea	Kogaga	Paku
Gaki	Purekau	Totoro tika
Igoa-kore	Ragihau	
Maunu	Tokau	
Tauhetika		
Heka		

A MAORI STONE AXE.

By H. D. SKINNER.

THE stone cutting tool figured in the plate, now in the collection of the British Museum, still has attached the printed label of the New Zealand Geological Survey, on which the locality is stated as "near Wellington." It was presented to the British Museum, together with a number of other stone implements bearing the same label, by the late Sir James Hector, F.R.S., then Director of the Survey.

Its special interest lies in the fact that it can have been used in no other way than as an axe, whereas there is nothing in the shape of the only other type of Maori stone axe thus far described[*] to prevent its former owner from hafting and using it as an adze, if no true adze were available. The distribution of this new type of axe is interesting. A good unfinished example from the Lukin's collection is in the Nelson Museum, and was found, I believe, at D'Urville Island. The material and technique of the British Museum specimen render it likely that it was made in the same district. Mr. Elsdon Best tells me that he has seen a greenstone example found in the neighbourhood of Wellington. An example in the Canterbury Museum is, as Mr. Speight informs me, almost certainly from the Canterbury district, while an unfinished tool of the same type, found near Cape Saunders, Otago, is in the collection of Miss B. Howes. Thus three known examples come from the South Island, and the remaining two from the extreme south of the North Island. The type does not seem to have been recorded in any other part of the Pacific.

Maori stone axes previously described appear to belong to an entirely different type, being designed, so far as can be judged, for insertion either in the slot in the cleft foot of a wooden haft (Fig. 3 , or against the side of the foot, which was specially flattened for the purpose.[†]

Figure 2 indicates the relation of stone implements to wooden haft in the case of such tools as Figure 1. Figure 3 indicates the same

---

[*] Elsdon Best : "Dominion Bulletin," No. 4. pp., 136-152.

[†] Best. loc. cit., p. 137, and Plate XLII.

NOTES AND QUERIES.

[291] The Three Fingers in Maori Carvings.

We notice in Mr. H. B. Cotterill's "Ancient Greece," 1913, a picture of what one might call a "plaque," found in the excavations at Knossus, Island of Crete, depicting, according to the title of the picture, "Genii (Priests?) watering a sacred tree." What will interest Maori scholars are the two figures of the ? priests, who have each three fingers to their hands and three toes on each foot. We need hardly call attention to the fact that on Ancient Maori Carvings the human figures, in nearly all cases, have only three fingers. The same three fingers have been traced on carvings in India. What is the original meaning of this peculiarity ?

The Minoan civilization of Crete also, apparently, recognised the supernatural powers of certain axes—double-headed in those cases, and called Labrys—as did the Maoris. Both the Minoan and Polynesian peoples belong to the Caucasian race.

Editor.

[292] Polynesian Voyages.

In that excellent publication "The Museum Journal" for March-June, 1919, issued by the Museum of Philadelphia, we notice a paper, with an illustration, on a South Sea Native Chart, derived from the Marshall Group of islands. The chart does not differ much from one described and pictured in "Hawaiki," p. 187 (third edition). But the author of this paper makes one statement which it is necessary to correct. He says the Marshall Islanders made the most extensive voyages of any of the South Sea peoples—and some of their voyages extended to 600 miles. A reference to the first paper in this number of our "Journal" will show that the distance of 600 miles has been exceeded by the Polynesians over and over again. One voyage is thus mentioned, that of Tangiia from the Fiji Group to Easter Island, is 4,200 miles in a straight line. Many voyages have been made by the Polynesians from Tahiti to New Zealand and back, in the tenth to the fourteenth century, and the distance that separates these two places is about 2,400 miles. The Marshall Islanders are Micronesians not pure Polynesians.

Editor.

PROCEEDINGS.

POLYNESIAN SOCIETY.

———

THE Council met at the Library, Hempton Rooms, on the 3rd December, 1919, when there were present : The President, and Messrs. Bullard, Newman and W. W. Smith.

After the minutes of the preceding meeting a letter from Mr. J. B. Roy was read resigning his seat on the Council. It was resolved that the Council receives with regret Mr. Roy's resignation, and tenders its warm thanks to him for his services for the last six years.

It was resolved that Mr. W. H. Skinner be appointed as a member of the Council.

Letters were read from Mr. Redcliffe Brown, of Tonga, resigning his membership on account of ill-health. Also one from Dr. Gregory, of Havard, announcing the news of an expedition to study Polynesian and other matters in the Pacific under his direction, and at the cost of the Pauahi Bishop Museum of Honolulu. From Mr. Thos. G. Thrum, of Honolulu, with thanks for his appointment as a Corresponding Member.

The following new members were elected :—

> Mrs. Ann Elmsley, Hill Side, Waverley.
> J. Corlett, P.O. Box 38, Taumaru-nui.
> P. Alfred Grace, Tokaanu, Taupo.
> William Cooper, Gisborne.
> The Turnbull Library, Bowen Street, Wellington.
> Ian Roy, c/o J. B. Roy, New Plymouth.

Papers received :—

> Niuē Folk-lore. By G. N. Morris.
> Notes on the Paumotu Heavens. By J. L. Young.

It was reported that the " Bulletin of the Société d'Etudes Oceanienne " of Tahiti, announces the death of two of our Corresponding members, the Rev. Pére Audran, and M. Tati Salmon, through influenza.

We notice by the " New Zealand Gazette," of 20th November, that the following members of this Society have been honoured by the inclusion of their names in the list of the first twenty Fellows elected by the New Zealand Institute.

> Mr. Elsdon Best, Hector Medallist.
> Dr. Patrick Marshall, M.A., Dr.Sc., F.G.S.
> Mr. Stephenson Percy Smith, F.R.G.S., President Polynesian Society.
> Dr. James Allan Thompson, M.A., Dr. Sc., A.D.S.M., F.G.S.

The Society offers these gentlemen its congratulations on the honour conferred.

INDEX TO VOL. XXVIII.

Compiled by W. H. Skinner.

REGISTERED FOR TRANSMISSION AS A MAGAZINE.

Vol. XXVIII.   [PUBLISHED QUARTERLY.]   No. 1.

THE JOURNAL

OF THE

POLYNESIAN SOCIETY

CONTAINING THE TRANSACTIONS AND
PROCEEDINGS OF THE SOCIETY.

Published under the Authority of the Council, and Edited
by the President.

No. 109.   MARCH, 1919.

CONTENTS.

(Authors are alone responsible for their respective statements.)

New Plymouth, N.Z.

PRINTED FOR THE SOCIETY BY THOMAS AVERY.
AGENT FOR AUSTRALIA: ANGUS AND ROBERTSON, 89 CASTLEREAGH STREET, SYDNEY.
1919.

POLYNESIAN SOCIETY.

OFFICERS FOR 1919.

Patrons:

THE RIGHT HON. LORD PLUNKET, Late Governor of New Zealand.
THE RIGHT HON. LORD ISLINGTON, P.C., K.C.M.G.,
Late Governor of New Zealand.
THE RIGHT HON. THE EARL OF LIVERPOOL, M.V.O., G.C.M.G.,
Governor-General of New Zealand.

President:

S. PERCY SMITH, F.R.G.S.
(Also Editor of Journal.)

Council:

M. FRASER.	P. J. H. WHITE.
W. L. NEWMAN.	W. W. SMITH.
J. B. ROY.	G. H. BULLARD.

Joint Hon. Secretaries and Treasurers:

W. W. SMITH and W. L. NEWMAN.

THE Society is formed to promote the study of the Anthropology, Ethnology, Philology, History, and Antiquities of the Polynesian races by the publication of an official journal to be called "THE JOURNAL OF THE POLYNESIAN SOCIETY," and by the collection of books, manuscripts, photographs, relics, and other illustrations of the history of the Polynesian race.

The term "Polynesia" is intended to include Australasia, New Zealand, Melanesia, Micronesia, and Malaysia, as well as Polynesia proper.

Candidates for admission to the Society shall be admitted on the joint recommendation of a member of the Society and a member of the Council, and on the approval of the Council. Forms of Application can be obtained from the Hon. Secretary.

Every person elected to membership shall receive immediate notice of the same from the Secretaries, together with a copy of the Rules, and on payment of his subscription of one pound shall be entitled to all the benefits of membership. Subscriptions are payable in advance, on the 1st of January of each year, or on election.

Papers will be received on any of the above subjects if sent through a member. Authors are requested to write only on one side of the paper, to use quarto paper and to leave one inch margin on the left-hand side, to allow of binding. Proper names should be written in ROMAN TYPE.

The price of back numbers of the Journal, to members, is 1s. 3d.

Members and exchanges are requested to note that the Society's Office is at New Plymouth, to which all communications, both exchanges, etc., should be sent, addressed to Hon. Secretaries.

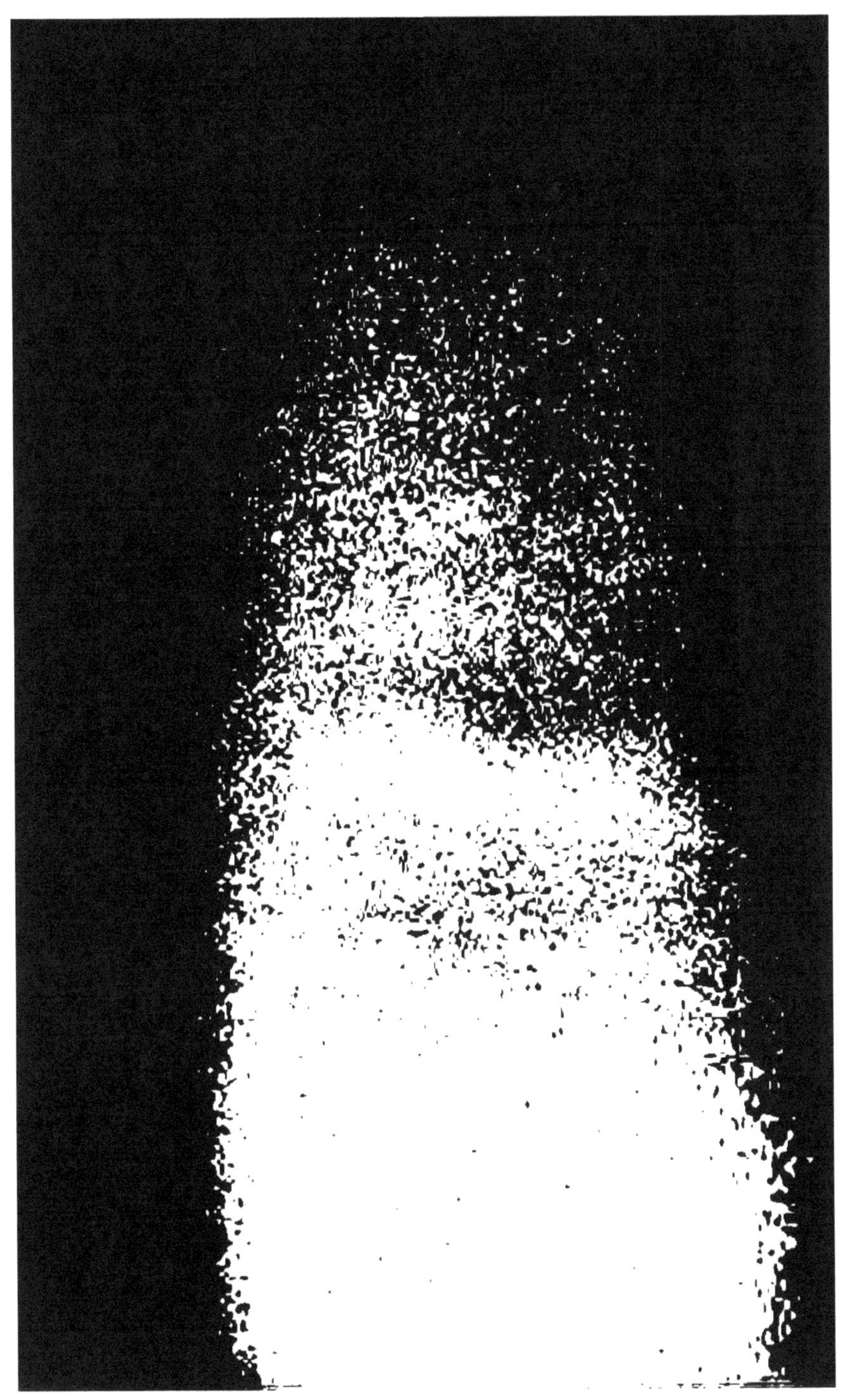

Publications of Polynesian Society.

The Journal is published in the first week of January, April, July, and October, and contains about 60 pages each issue, with occasional illustrations.

A few copies of the second edition of Volumes III. and IV. (1894-5), and first edition Vol. V., price ten shillings a volume, are now available. Vols. I. and II. are out of print.

Volumes VI. to XXVI. are all available at five shillings a volume. Authors' copies of most of the papers that have appeared in the 'Journal' are on sale at 1d. a page.

Memoirs of the Polynesian Society.

Vol. I.—"History and Traditions of the Taranaki Coast," 8vo., cloth, 561 pages, with a number of illustrations and maps. Price,   10s. 6d.

Vol. II.—"The Moriori People of the Chatham Islands: Their History and Traditions." 8vo., paper, about 220 pages, illustrated.   Price,   5s.

Vol. III.—"The Lore of the Whare-wananga."—Part I.: 'Things Celestial.' About 200 pages. Cloth bound.

Vol. IV.—Part II.: 'Te Kauwae-raro, or Things Terrestrial,' 279 pages. Cloth bound.

      Price (each Part) to Members,   8s.
                To others   10s.

"Rarotonga Records," being extracts from the papers of the late W. Wyatt Gill, LL.D., 125 pages, map, paper cover   3s

WANTED.—A copy of Tregear's Comparative Mā Dictionary.—Apply to Hon. Secretary.

REGISTERED FOR TRANSMISSION AS A MAGAZINE.

Vol. XXVIII. [PUBLISHED QUARTERLY.] No. 2.

THE JOURNAL

OF THE

POLYNESIAN SOCIETY

CONTAINING THE TRANSACTIONS AND
PROCEEDINGS OF THE SOCIETY.

Published under the Authority of the Council, and Edited
by the President.

No. 110. JUNE, 1919.

CONTENTS.

(Authors are alone responsible for their respective statements.)

New Plymouth, N.Z.

PRINTED FOR THE SOCIETY BY THOMAS AVERY.
AGENT FOR AUSTRALIA: ANGUS and ROBERTSON, 89 CASTLEREAGH STREET, SYDNEY.
1919.

POLYNESIAN SOCIETY.

OFFICERS FOR 1919.

Patrons:

The Right Hon. Lord Plunket, Late Governor of New Zealand.
The Right Hon. Lord Islington, P.C., K.C.M.G.,
Late Governor of New Zealand.
The Right Hon. The Earl of Liverpool, M.V.O., G.C.M.G.,
Governor-General of New Zealand.

President:

S. Percy Smith, F.R.G.S.
(Also Editor of Journal.)

Council:

M. Fraser.	P. J. H. White.
W. L. Newman.	W. W. Smith.
J. B. Roy.	G. H. Bullard.

Joint Hon. Secretaries and Treasurers:

W. W. Smith and W. L. Newman.

THE Society is formed to promote the study of the Anthropology, Ethnology, Philology, History, and Antiquities of the Polynesian races by the publication of an official journal to be called "The Journal of the Polynesian Society," and by the collection of books, manuscripts, photographs, relics, and other illustrations of the history of the Polynesian race.

The term "Polynesia" is intended to include Australasia, New Zealand, Melanesia, Micronesia, and Malaysia, as well as Polynesia proper.

Candidates for admission to the Society shall be admitted on the joint recommendation of a member of the Society and a member of the Council, and on the approval of the Council. Forms of Application can be obtained from the Hon. Secretary.

Every person elected to membership shall receive immediate notice of the same from the Secretaries, together with a copy of the Rules, and on payment of his subscription of one pound shall be entitled to all the benefits of membership. Subscriptions are payable in advance, on the 1st of January of each year, or on election.

Papers will be received on any of the above subjects if sent through a member. Authors are requested to write only on one side of the paper, to use quarto paper and to leave one inch margin on the left-hand side, to allow of binding. Proper names should be written in ROMAN TYPE.

The price of back numbers of the Journal, to members, is 1s. 3d.

Members and exchanges are requested to note that the Society Office is at New Plymouth, to which all communications, books, exchanges, etc., should be sent, addressed to Hon. Secretaries.

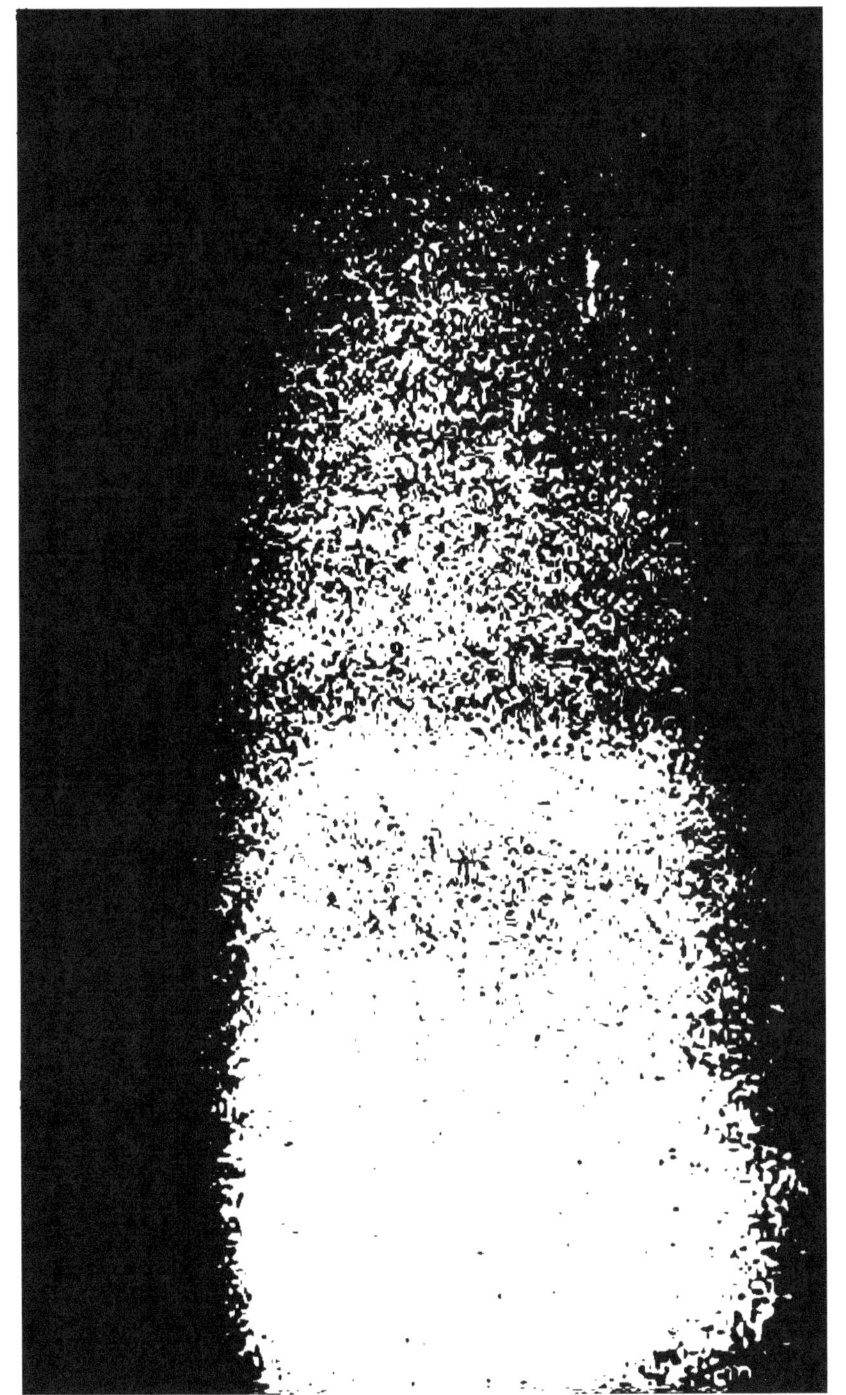

Publications of Polynesian Society.

THE JOURNAL is published in the first week of January, April, July, and October, and contains about 60 pages each issue, with occasional illustrations.

A few copies of the second edition of Volumes III. and IV. (1894-5), and first edition Vol. V., price ten shillings a volume, are now available. Vols. I. and II. are out of print.

Volumes VI. to XXVII. are all available at five shillings a volume. Authors' copies of most of the papers that have appeared in the 'Journal' are on sale at 1d. a page.

Memoirs of the Polynesian Society.

Vol. I.—"HISTORY AND TRADITIONS OF THE TARANAKI COAST," 8vo., cloth, 561 pages, with a number of illustrations and maps. Price,   10s. 6d.

Vol. II.—"THE MORIORI PEOPLE OF THE CHATHAM ISLANDS: THEIR HISTORY AND TRADITIONS." 8vo., paper, about 220 pages, illustrated.   Price,   5s.

Vol. III.—"THE LORE OF THE WHARE-WANANGA."—Part I.: 'Things Celestial.' About 200 pages. Cloth bound.

Vol. IV.—Part II.: 'Te Kauwae-raro,' or 'Things Terrestrial,' 279 pages. Cloth bound.

Price (each Part) to Members,   8s.
To others   ... 10s.

"RAROTONGA RECORDS," being extracts from the papers of the late W. Wyatt Gill, LL.D., 125 pages, map, paper cover ....   3s.

WANTED.—A copy of Tregear's Comparative Maori Dictionary.—Apply to Hon. Secretary.

REGISTERED FOR TRANSMISSION AS A MAGAZINE.

Vol. XXVIII. [PUBLISHED QUARTERLY.] No. 3.

THE JOURNAL

OF THE

POLYNESIAN SOCIETY

CONTAINING THE TRANSACTIONS AND
PROCEEDINGS OF THE SOCIETY.

Published under the Authority of the Council, and Edited
by the President.

No. 111.   SEPTEMBER, 1919.

CONTENTS.

(Authors are alone responsible for their respective statements.)

New Plymouth, N.Z.

PRINTED FOR THE SOCIETY BY THOMAS AVERY.
FOR AUSTRALIA: ANGUS AND ROBERTSON, 89 CASTLEREAGH STREET, SYDNEY.
1919.

———o———

THE Society is formed to promote the study of the Anthropology, Philology, History, and Antiquities of the Polynesian ... tion of an official journal to be called "The Journal of ... Society," ... by the publication of books, manuscripts, ... other illustrations of the History of the Polynesian race.

The term "Polynesia" is intended to include Australasia, Melanesia, Micronesia, and Malaysia, as well as Polynesia proper.

Candidates for admission to the Society shall be admitted ... recommendation of a member of the Society and a member of the ... the approval of the Council. Forms of Application can be obtained ... Hon. Secretary.

Every person elected to membership shall receive immediately ... same from the Secretaries, together with a copy of the Rules, and ... of his subscription of one pound shall be entitled to all the benefits of ... Subscriptions are payable in advance, on the 1st of January of each ... election.

Papers will be received on any of the above subjects if sent through ... Authors are requested to write only on one side of the paper, to use ... and to leave one inch margin on the left-hand side, to allow of ... names should be written in ROMAN TYPE.

The price of back numbers of the Journal, to members, is 1s. 3d.

Members and exchanges are requested to note that the ... Office is at New Plymouth, to which all communications, ... exchanges, etc., should be sent, addressed to Hon. Secretary.

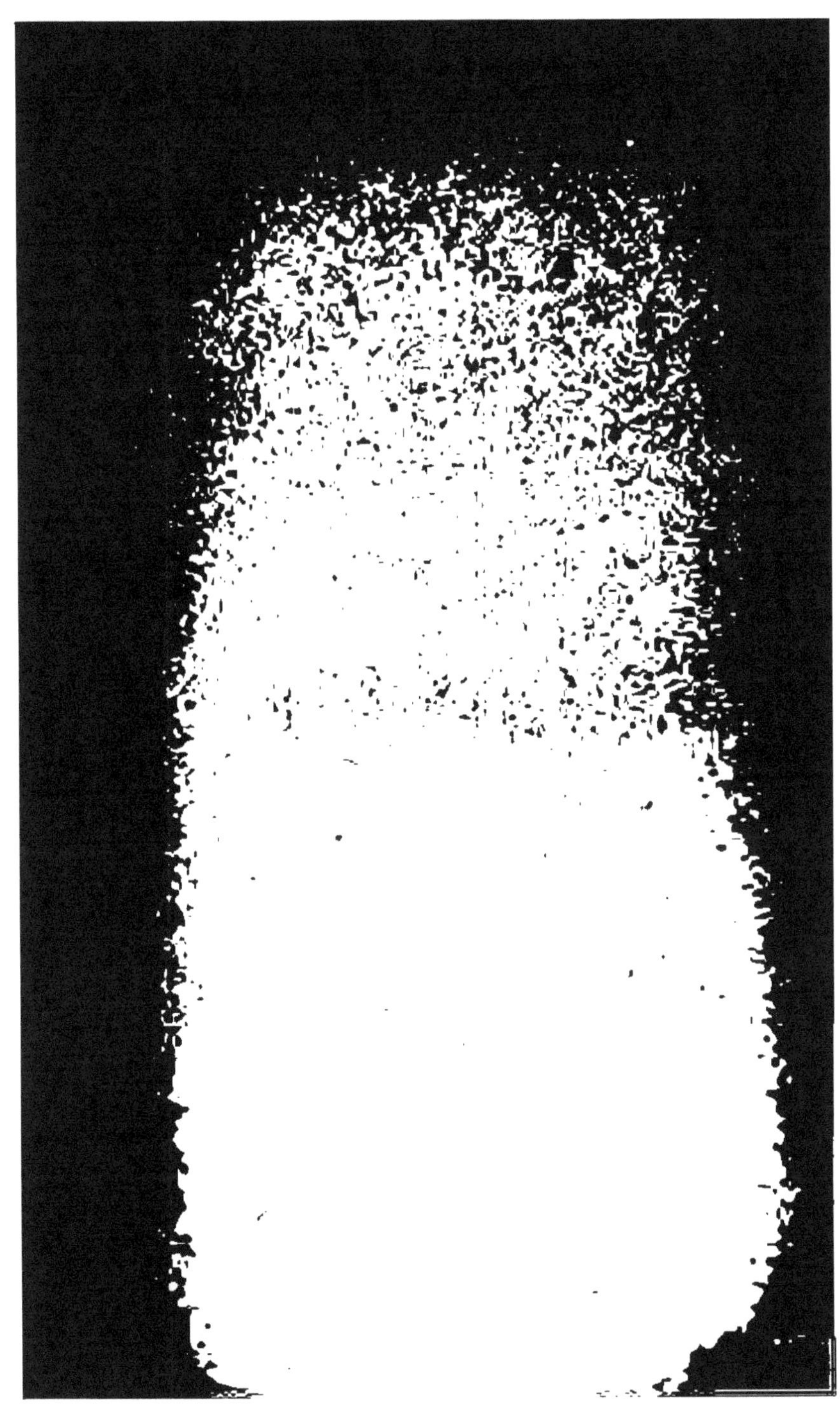

Publications of Polynesian Society.

THE JOURNAL is published in the first week of January, April, July, and October, and contains about 60 pages each issue, with occasional illustrations.

A few copies of the second edition of Volumes IV., and V. (1892-6), price ten shillings a volume, are now available, the others are out of print.

Volumes VII. to XXVII. are all available at five shillings a volume. Sold only to members of the Society. The volumes are unbound, and in numbers as published quarterly. Postage additional, fourpence a volume.

Memoirs and Reprints of the Polynesian Society.

Vol. I.—"HISTORY AND TRADITIONS OF THE TARANAKI COAST," 8vo., cloth, 561 pages, with a number of illustrations and maps. Price, **10s. 6d.**

Vol. II.—"THE MORIORI PEOPLE OF THE CHATHAM ISLANDS: THEIR HISTORY AND TRADITIONS." 8vo., paper, about 220 pages, illustrated. Price, **5s.**

Vol. III.—"THE LORE OF THE WHARE-WANANGA."—Part I.: 'Things Celestial.' About 200 pages. Cloth bound.

Vol. IV.—Part II.: 'Te Kauwae-raro,' or 'Things Terrestrial,' 279 pages. Cloth bound.

Price (each Part) to Members, **8s.**

To others ... **10s.**

"RAROTONGA RECORDS," being extracts from the papers of the late W. Wyatt Gill, LL.D., 125 pages, map, paper cover ... **3/**

"THE LAND OF TARA," 123 pages, with map, paper cover ... ... **3s.**